Social Network Analytics for Contemporary Business Organizations

Himani Bansal
Jaypee Institute of Information Technology, India

Gulshan Shrivastava
National Institute of Technology Patna, India

Gia Nhu Nguyen
Duy Tan University, Vietnam

Loredana-Mihaela Stanciu
University Timisoara, Romania

A volume in the Advances in Business Information Systems and Analytics (ABISA) Book Series

IGI Global
DISSEMINATOR OF KNOWLEDGE

Published in the United States of America by
IGI Global
Business Science Reference (an imprint of IGI Global)
701 E. Chocolate Avenue
Hershey PA, USA 17033
Tel: 717-533-8845
Fax: 717-533-8661
E-mail: cust@igi-global.com
Web site: http://www.igi-global.com

Library of Congress Cataloging-in-Publication Data

Names: Bansal, Himani, 1985- editor.
Title: Social network analytics for contemporary business organizations / Himani Bansal [and three others], editors.
Description: Hershey, PA : Business Science Reference, [2018]
Identifiers: LCCN 2017035066| ISBN 9781522550976 (hardcover) | ISBN 9781522550983 (ebook)
Subjects: LCSH: Online social networks. | Social sciences--Network analysis. | Data mining. | Computational linguistics.
Classification: LCC HM742 .S62867 2018 | DDC 302.30285--dc23 LC record available at https://lccn.loc.gov/2017035066

This book is published in the IGI Global book series Advances in Business Information Systems and Analytics (ABISA) (ISSN: 2327-3275; eISSN: 2327-3283)

British Cataloguing in Publication Data
A Cataloguing in Publication record for this book is available from the British Library.

For electronic access to this publication, please contact: eresources@igi-global.com.

Advances in Business Information Systems and Analytics (ABISA) Book Series

Madjid Tavana
La Salle University, USA

ISSN:2327-3275
EISSN:2327-3283

Mission

The successful development and management of information systems and business analytics is crucial to the success of an organization. New technological developments and methods for data analysis have allowed organizations to not only improve their processes and allow for greater productivity, but have also provided businesses with a venue through which to cut costs, plan for the future, and maintain competitive advantage in the information age.

The **Advances in Business Information Systems and Analytics (ABISA) Book Series** aims to present diverse and timely research in the development, deployment, and management of business information systems and business analytics for continued organizational development and improved business value.

Coverage

- Data Governance
- Business Intelligence
- Management Information Systems
- Big Data
- Forecasting
- Decision Support Systems
- Data Strategy
- Business Systems Engineering
- Business Information Security
- Legal information systems

IGI Global is currently accepting manuscripts for publication within this series. To submit a proposal for a volume in this series, please contact our Acquisition Editors at Acquisitions@igi-global.com or visit: http://www.igi-global.com/publish/.

The Advances in Business Information Systems and Analytics (ABISA) Book Series (ISSN 2327-3275) is published by IGI Global, 701 E. Chocolate Avenue, Hershey, PA 17033-1240, USA, www.igi-global.com. This series is composed of titles available for purchase individually; each title is edited to be contextually exclusive from any other title within the series. For pricing and ordering information please visit http://www.igi-global.com/book-series/advances-business-information-systems-analytics/37155. Postmaster: Send all address changes to above address.

Titles in this Series

For a list of additional titles in this series, please visit: www.igi-global.com/book-series

Business Architectures for Risk Assessment and Strategic Planning Emerging Research and Opportunities
James McKee (Wollongong University, Australia)
Business Science Reference • ©2018 • 118pp • H/C (ISBN: 9781522533924) • US $155.00 (our price)

Handbook of Research on Emergent Applications of Optimization Algorithms
Pandian Vasant (Universiti Teknologi Petronas, Malaysia) Sirma Zeynep Alparslan-Gok (Suleyman Demirel University, Turkey) and Gerhard-Wilhelm Weber (Middle East Technical University, Turkey)
Business Science Reference • ©2018 • 812pp • H/C (ISBN: 9781522529903) • US $445.00 (our price)

Cloud Computing Technologies for Green Enterprises
Kashif Munir (University of Hafr Al-Batin, Saudi Arabia)
Business Science Reference • ©2018 • 424pp • H/C (ISBN: 9781522530381) • US $215.00 (our price)

Smart Technology Applications in Business Environments
Tomayess Issa (Curtin University, Australia) Piet Kommers (University of Twente, The Netherlands) Theodora Issa (Curtin University, Australia) Pedro Isaías (Portuguese Open University, Portugal) and Touma B. Issa (Murdoch University, Australia)
Business Science Reference • ©2017 • 429pp • H/C (ISBN: 9781522524922) • US $210.00 (our price)

Advanced Fashion Technology and Operations Management
Alessandra Vecchi (London College of Fashion, University of London Arts, UK)
Business Science Reference • ©2017 • 443pp • H/C (ISBN: 9781522518655) • US $200.00 (our price)

Maximizing Business Performance and Efficiency Through Intelligent Systems
Om Prakash Rishi (University of Kota, India) and Anukrati Sharma (University of Kota, India)
Business Science Reference • ©2017 • 269pp • H/C (ISBN: 9781522522348) • US $175.00 (our price)

Maximizing Information System Availability Through Bayesian Belief Network Approaches Emerging Research and Opportunities
Semir Ibrahimović (Bosna Bank International, Bosnia and Herzegovina) Lejla Turulja (University of Sarajevo, Bosnia and Herzegovina) and Nijaz Bajgorić (University of Sarajevo, Bosnia and Herzegovina)
Information Science Reference • ©2017 • 180pp • H/C (ISBN: 9781522522683) • US $140.00 (our price)

IGI Global
DISSEMINATOR OF KNOWLEDGE

701 East Chocolate Avenue, Hershey, PA 17033, USA
Tel: 717-533-8845 x100 • Fax: 717-533-8661
E-Mail: cust@igi-global.com • www.igi-global.com

I dedicate this book to my daughter, Jiya
- Himani Bansal
I dedicate this book to my son, Keyur
- Gulshan Shrivastava
I dedicate this book to my daughter, Minh Thu Vu Nguyen, and son, Bao Gia Nguyen
- Gia Nhu Nguyen
I dedicate this book to my daughter, Maria
- Loredana-Mihaela Stanciu

Table of Contents

Detailed Table of Contents

Over the last decade, technology has thrived to provide better, quicker, and more effective platforms to help individuals connect and disseminate information to other individuals. The increasing popularity of these networks and its huge content in the form of text, images, and videos provides new opportunities for data analytics in the context of social networks. This motivates data mining experts and researchers to deploy various mining apparatus and application-specific tools for analysing the massive, intricate, and dynamic social media knowledge. The research detailed in this chapter would entail major social network concepts with data analysis techniques. Moreover, it gives insight to representation and modelling of social networks with research datasets and tools.

Social networks have drawn remarkable attention from IT professionals and researchers in data sciences. They are the most popular medium for social interaction. Online social networking (OSN) can be defined as involving networking for fun, business, and communication. Social networks have emerged as universally accepted communication means and boomed in turning this world into a global town. OSN media are generally known for broadcasting information, activities posting, contents sharing, product reviews, online pictures sharing, professional profiling, advertisements and ideas/opinion/sentiment expression, or some other stuff based on business interests. For the analysis of the huge amount of data, data mining techniques are used for identifying the relevant knowledge from the huge amount of data that includes detecting trends, patterns, and rules. Data mining techniques, machine learning, and statistical modeling are used to retrieve the information. For the analysis of the data, three methods are used: data pre-processing, data analysis, and data interpretation.

With increased ICT (Information and Communication Technology), the day-to-day life is shifting online. E-government is one of the crucial parts of the developing world. This chapter contains a detailed introduction of e-government, which includes a broad definition, pillars, goals, stages, delivery models of e-government, advantages, and disadvantages. The difference between e-governance and e-government is also clarified. This chapter clears up the concept of e-government and how e-government can have impact on society. Next is the background section, which covers the research and surveys done by UN (United Nations) and other researchers in order to monitor and analyze the developments of e-government across different countries, social implications of e-government, requirements to develop a robust e-government, future scope of the e-government, etc. Finally, the direct and indirect implications of e-government are stated along with a short review of the status of e-government across a few countries.

Spam on the online social networks (OSNs) is evolving as a prominent problem for the users of these networks. Spammers often use certain techniques to deceive the OSN users for their own benefit. Facebook, one of the leading OSNs, is experiencing such crucial problems at an alarming rate. This chapter presents a methodology to segregate spam from legitimate posts using machine learning techniques: naïve Bayes (NB), support vector machine (SVM), and random forest (RF). The textual, image, and video features are used together, which wasn't considered by the earlier researchers. Then, 1.5 million posts and comments are extracted from archival and real-time Facebook data, which is then pre-processed using RStudio. A total of 30 features are identified, out of which 10 are the best informative for identification of spam vs. ham posts. The entire dataset is shuffled and divided into three ratios, out of which 80:20 ratio of training and testing dataset provides the best result. Also, RF classifier outperforms NB and SVM by achieving overall F-measure 89.4% on the combined feature set.

Sentiment of analysis is a study area applied to numerous environments (financial, political, academic, business, and communication) whose purpose is to search for messages posted on social media, and through

space access, in cooperative spectrum sensing, and in enhancing device-to-device communications. Socially aware mobile networks do have enough potential to amass sufficient returns in the efficacy of the spectrum and also to march and gain a considerable amount of increase in the capacity of the network. Even though there are lot of gains in its potency to be reaped yet, still there seems to be enough challenges that are both business- and technical-related that have to be taken care of. This chapter delves into the cognitive radio (CR) and its social relations and also makes sufficient exploits in establishing a scheme that will be based on social-based cooperative sensing scheme (SBC).

The enormous growth and dynamic nature of online social networks have emerged to new research directions that examine the social network analysis mechanisms. In this chapter, the authors have explored a novel technique of recommendation for social media and used well known social network analysis (SNA) mechanisms-link prediction. The initial impetus of this chapter is to provide general description, formal definition of the problem, its applications, state-of-art of various link prediction approaches in social media networks. Further, an experimental evaluation has been made to inspect the role of link prediction in real environment by employing basic common neighbor link prediction approach on IMDb data. To improve performance, weighted common neighbor link prediction (WCNLP) approach has been proposed. This exploits the prediction features to predict new links among users of IMDb. The evaluation shows how the inclusion of weight among the nodes offers high link prediction performance and opens further research directions.

In recent years, advancement in technologies has made it possible for most of the present-day organizations to store and record large streams of data. Such data sets, which continuously and rapidly grow over time, are referred to as data streams. Mining of such data streams is a unique opportunity and also a challenging task. Data stream mining is a process of gaining knowledge from continuous and rapid records of data. Due to increased streaming information, data stream mining has attracted the research community in the recent past. There is voluminous literature that has been published in this domain over the past few years. Due to this, isolating the correct study would be grueling task for researchers and practitioners. While addressing a real-world problem, it would be difficult to find relevant information as it would be hidden in data streams. This chapter tries to provide solution as it is an amalgamation of all techniques used for data stream mining.

Preface

With the more penetration of the internet into our daily life, humongous amount of data is generated every second. Whether it is the Facebook, Twitter, YouTube, or emails, we are being flooded with the data. Given this deluge of data from the current-day technologies, the idea of analytics is catching the all necessary interest of corporations and governments worldwide. This increased interest is also bringing with it a certain level of hype as well as scepticism about the promises of analytics. Not only this, abetted by the latest information and communication system technologies, many organizations has been transformed. Major leaders like Google, Amazon are becoming more location independent and making themselves strategically powerful compared to other organizations.

Analytics is not only a buzzword anymore, rather a catalyst to up scale the business for various organizations and industries. Going by literal meaning of word analytics, it's a branch that analyzes the principles of computer science coupled with mathematics and statistics. The goal of analytics is not only to find patterns in existing data but also to predict and forecast, thus, accelerating the business driven speed. Advances in information and communication systems along with more reliability of companies on data driven approaches indeed poses threat to the failure of the system. Various challenges are posed when we do the data analytics but the most important concerns are:

- The challenge to find the authenticity of the data to be used for the analytical purposes.
- The challenge to find out correct and reliable source from where the data is being generated.
- The challenge to find out the patterns and even the context of the readings measured for the analytical activity.

Numerous studies have been proposed and performed to answer the above-mentioned challenges. Without any question, it has been observed and experimentally proven that the field of data analytics has huge potential and unlimited possibilities. Further, data analytics can be divided into two broad categories: qualitative and quantitative data analysis. The former deals with qualitative approach to interpret and understand the content of non-numerical data types like images, audio, video and include common themes, point of views as well as phrases. The quantitative analysis focuses on the numerical data, which can be quantified and can easily be measured or compared by statistical methods.

At application level, Business Intelligence (BI) provides business executives and corporate workers with actionable information about key indicators, operators and customers. More advanced analytics include data mining, predictive analytics, machine learning and more, which provide us the inside of the large-scale data sets to identify trends and patterns. These automated algorithms have been evolved and are used to churn through the data sets more quickly than conventional analytical modelling.

Social Network Analysis for Contemporary Business Optimization lists a total of 13 chapters. A brief description of each chapter is as follows:

Chapter 1 discusses about the more effective platforms that help individuals to connect and disseminate information to other individuals. It also discusses about the various models and propagation of information for evolving structure of networks. This chapter also gives an insight to the representation and modelling of social networks with research datasets and the tools used for analytics.

Chapter 2 discusses about various methods and techniques used for the purpose of analysis in any social network. By saying that, OSN's have been accepted as global medium of communication. Authors tried to put focus on the various areas where social networks are used for broadcasting the information and posting various updates.

Chapter 3 throws light on the various ICT technologies for the purpose of e-governance. It provides the introduction of e-government leading to its pillars, goals and delivery models. The chapter answers the question *about* how e-governance helps society and what are its impacts. Finally it discusses about the various implications of the e-government with short review across various countries around the globe.

Chapter 4's authors are trying to perform the spam classification on the online social network, Facebook. They took a dataset of around 1.5 million posts and comments from archival and real-time Facebook data and performed the processing using RStudio. A total of 30 features were identified and further 10 were selected as best informative for the identification of spam verses non-spam posts.

Chapter 5 talks about the impact of sarcasm on the actual sentiment analysis. It also discusses about the major problem faced during the analysis if the messages are with sarcastic or ironic content.

Chapter 6 discusses about the detection of the sarcasm and history of the sentiment analysis. It throws light on the various aspects of the identification and techniques used for detection and classification of the sarcasm in text.

Chapter 7 proposes a novel approach to perform classification of the sentiments in movie review databases. The results of the algorithms are validated using k-Nearest Neighbour and Naive Bayes machine learning approaches. The empirical results show that proposed method outperforms the techniques that left the challenges unaddressed.

Chapter 8 talks about the authorship attribution on short messaging services like Twitter. Authors have provided comprehensive knowledge review of the various techniques used till date to address the problem. Features like N-grams are the area to focus. This chapter also demonstrates that attribution is possible via selection of good features and methods in small texts.

Chapter 9 explains about the Internet of Things (IoT) and Social Network of Things (SNoT) which has gained vitality in past few years. Authors talk about the context-aware social networking and network diffusion is elaborated with the aim to develop effective solutions for issues in this domain.

Chapter 10 discuss about the cognitive radio and its social relations and also make sufficient exploits in establishing a scheme that will be based on social cooperative sensing scheme.

Chapter 11 throws light on the prediction of the next link for suggesting a movie using social media content. The evaluation shows how the inclusion of the weight among the nodes offers high link prediction performance and open further research directions.

Chapter 12 discusses about the discovery of the knowledge from data stream mining. Out there, we have voluminous amount of literature, which has been published in this domain over the past few years. Thus, isolation of a correct literature can be a gruelling task for researchers. Hence, this chapter tries to provide solution as it would be an amalgamation of all techniques used for data stream mining.

Chapter 13 provide the insights of a study that is an effort to resolve the problem of how to measure the content provided by any website in terms of its credibility. Various models have been proposed in this paper to identify several factors pertaining to the credibility of the content and user's trust on any website and accordingly analyse the identified factors to access the websites.

Himani Bansal
Jaypee Institute of Information Technology, India

Gulshan Shrivastava
National Institute of Technology Patna, India

Gia Nhu Nguyen
Duy Tan University, Vietnam

Loredana-Mihaela Stanciu
Politehnica University Timisoara, Romania

Chapter 1
Social Network Analysis:
Tools, Techniques, and Technologies

Somya Jain
Jaypee Institute of Information Technology, India

Adwitiya Sinha
Jaypee Institute of Information Technology, India

ABSTRACT

Over the last decade, technology has thrived to provide better, quicker, and more effective platforms to help individuals connect and disseminate information to other individuals. The increasing popularity of these networks and its huge content in the form of text, images, and videos provides new opportunities for data analytics in the context of social networks. This motivates data mining experts and researchers to deploy various mining apparatus and application-specific tools for analysing the massive, intricate, and dynamic social media knowledge. The research detailed in this chapter would entail major social network concepts with data analysis techniques. Moreover, it gives insight to representation and modelling of social networks with research datasets and tools.

1. OVERVIEW OF SOCIAL NETWORKING

Starting from Internet Messengers, websites, emails and blogs; Online Social Networks (OSNs) have emerged as a popular media. According to Boyd et al., a social network is defined as "a platform to create social relations among those who share similar interests, activities, backgrounds or real-life connections. Social networks are web-based services that enable people to make public profile, produce a listing of users with who to share connections view and cross the connections within the system". In general, a social network is formed by the nodes and edges where nodes represent the individual identity and edges between the nodes signify interactions or relationship between them. Picture of how social network is represented using nodes and edges is presented in Figure 1. Here, rectangular nodes A to E are the individuals and their social ties are represented by undirected edges. For example A has social relations with B, E, and C.

DOI: 10.4018/978-1-5225-5097-6.ch001

Figure 1. Social Network

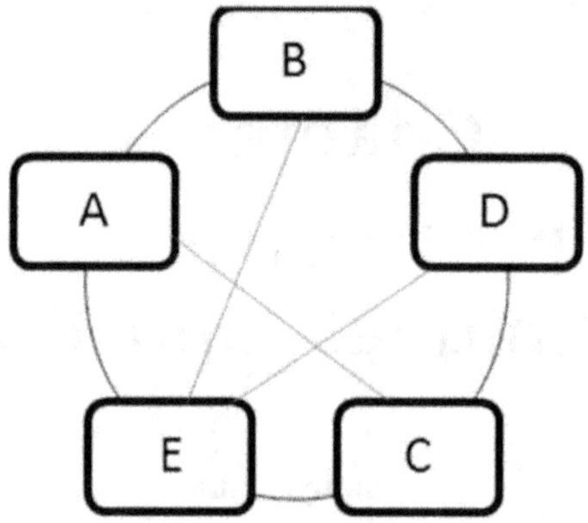

The emergence of online social networks is the golden milestone achieved in the history. There are many well-liked online social networks namely Facebook, Twitter and MySpace which seems to be popular now days. Additionally, variety of multimedia networks like Flickr and YouTube has conjointly seen an increasing level of recognition in recent years. Many other professional and educational social networks have also become popular like LinkedIn and other forums. Moreover, with the escalation of online social media, voluminous amount of social data gets generated (Kaytoue et al, 2015). As the information available online is evolving day by day, it becomes very difficult to manage and process without any help of information processing tools and management. This creates urge for applying suitable metrics for investigating the performance of network in terms of robustness, efficiency etc. and to compare different network statistics accordingly. One of the most critical tasks is to model the social network graph mathematically for further analysis over it (Newman, 2003; Jansen et al, 2015). Modelling is the initial phase to proceed further towards rigorous analysis in social networks. Therefore, there exists the need for experimenting with models for directed and un-directed graphs with high precision.

With the widespread of social networking platforms, the demand for developing models to propagate information among the networked societies is also on the rise. In the recent years information propagation in social network plays a vital role in advertising new products or services, including viral marketing and brand promotion (Kimura et al, 2010). For maximizing the spread of advertisement and promotions, many organizations use social network mining to identify the target audience. The materials in this context will be of great assistance to social network analysts, technical experts and researchers. Readers from generic computer science background without explicit pre-requisites would also find it interesting. Moreover, scholars belonging to social sciences or marketing domain, may find familiarity to learn representations of social network elaborative over datasets, tips, tools, techniques and technologies.

This chapter would be an insight to introduction of social network analysis and its emergence. In the first section, an exhaustive survey of available analytical tools is included with a particular emphasis on datasets, visualization platforms and programming interfaces (Correa, 2011). In the subsequent section, social networking techniques are surveyed that covers survey related to modelling of social network, methods for mining the colossal social data followed by process of diffusion process in networks. The chapter also presents the several key identified challenges in context of selected domains, latest applications and services which have been considered to be of greater eminence for further research.

2. NEED FOR ANALYSIS IN SOCIAL NETWORK

Small scale as well as large scale social networks exhibit many hidden properties and structure which needs different social network analysis task to perform such as centrality calculation, community detection, homophily investigation, and other similarity measures. These tasks are needed to represent the network information in a compact form and finding the sub graphs which are having strongly connected component to reduce the effort and complexity of work to perform. Analysis of social network and media for gathering the communication information between people regarding any service or products will be more cost effective in real time. It will add many helpful benefits and advantages in market designing and in advertisement sector by analysing communities. Today, dynamic network analysis is becoming the new area of interest in research where time is the key feature to work upon.

In the last years, prosperity of graph mining brings about many diverse social networks analysis techniques to be applicable on wide range of different networks. All the real-world phenomena in social networks are rendered using graphs for representing users as per their interactions and behaviour. Prior to begin, analytical exploration with different real-world testing model with synthetic datasets is also necessary for establishing verification and validation of proposed research work. However, real world datasets supplement the significance to the model of research.

3. SOCIAL NETWORK ANALYTICAL TOOLS

There are incredible tools and platforms available and by using them social data can be dig out for analysis. Before analysis of social networks, gathering of data is mandatory. Analysis techniques provide better insight in to social network data. Tools can leverage the large data set which helps the researchers to save their time in pre-processing; analysis task to visualization of networks. Many of the online social networks release the data in the form of large graphs which needs to be processed as the graphs encapsulates the information in it.

Therefore, there is a need of powerful tools to process the graph structure and present it in a compact form for further input to mining techniques. Random graph is presented in figure 2 with 150 vertices and 0.03 edge creation probability which is generated with the help of Erdos-Renyi random graph generator. Moreover, efficiently extracting and understanding the information from graphs is another area of research.

Tools have been extensively used for crawling the dataset. There are different categories of tools available in the market each corresponds to their advantages and limitations. Apart from tools, many programming interfaces and APIs (application programming interfaces) are available which assist in better interoperability and automating task. Using of standard APIs aids in reducing the development and troubleshooting time.

Some of the available analytical tools are described below:

- **NetLogo (Wilensky, 1999):** It is free and open source software tool. It works as a simulator for modelling the social network or any other network dynamics. It provides a great programming environment to the users. It is well known among researchers.
- **Netlytic (Gruzd, 2016):** It is a cloud based social network analyser tool. The utility of this stool enables to analyse the communication network and captures the messages, tweets or any other

Figure 2. Random Graph Structure

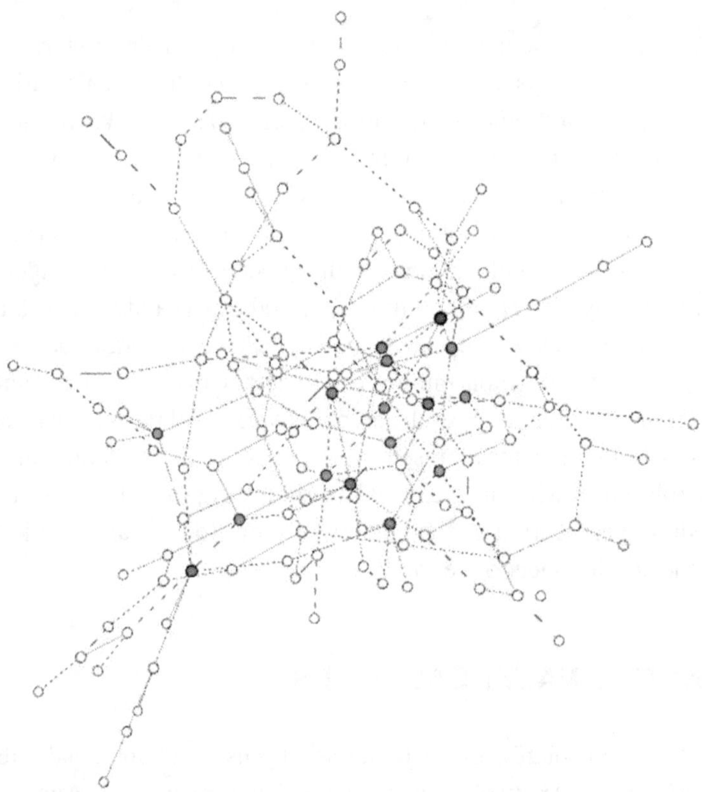

posts and helps in summarization of the large amount of text captured. Visualization is also its side feature added in it.

- **Pajek (Batagelj et al, nd):** This tool is especially for windows only. It is used for analysing the large networks. It has menu-driven functionality with visualization capabilities.

3.1. Social Data

As the use of online social sites and services increasing day by day they release tremendous amount of social data. Social data is defined as the data about socially active individuals which represents nodes in the social network. Data of social individuals can be personal details, geographical details; content they post on social networks in the form of tweets or posts, profile image, video or links shared by them, interests, likes and check-ins. For example, figure 3 represents possible social data emerged in social networks.

Users can make this data publically available or hide this by using security features offered by online social networks. Researchers, scientific organisations can obtain or access the data by using specific APIs provided by the service vendors or can request the data needed for research by proper permissions. Some of the benchmark datasets are available and provided for research by some universities. Social data seems to be used by different business organizations for marketing their product or service by using advertisements and locating their target customers. Many problems are also associated with social data

Figure 3. Sources for Social Data

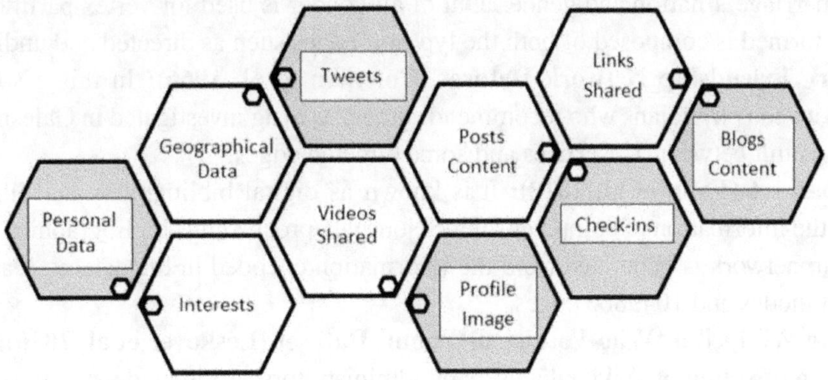

such as its limited availability or sometimes unavailability, fake data entered by fake users and missing data. By considering all such limitations aggregating qualitative social data is a big challenge. Analysing the complex social data enables personalization of products and business sector to take strategic decisions. It will further help to develop new business models for overall international development.

3.2. Datasets

Data analyst of social data first needs to collect and understand the properties of dataset. They also need to reduce the size of dataset if it was so large to work upon it. Earlier, researchers do a very tedious job for collecting the network data. They do so by the process of questionnaire survey which was filled by different people but in recent time it is no longer in use. In general, there are two categories of datasets namely empirical dataset and synthetic dataset. Empirical datasets are widely used due to its true relevance whereas the use of synthetic datasets is also coming to existence for online social network graphs. Synthetic datasets are nowadays used by the researchers due to privacy concerns of online users. There are three kinds of empirical datasets which are used by the social analyst and in each category there are number of datasets available. First and foremost type of dataset is in which social network is represented in the form of graph and where online social networks release the data in terms of nodes and edges. Therefore small and large graphs generated from it can be analysed by using some algorithms. Second category of dataset is in the form of log file generated by the communication between different users in email system, smart phone record logs or any other device which store the records over time. These are not direct online social network data. Third category is actual data logs of any online social network server such as shopping behaviour of user or tweets posted by user or any metadata shared by online user (Nettleton, 2013). All the types of datasets exhibits common structure i.e. graph structure. So, summarization of the graphs using any tools or computer programs is critical. In the sub sequent section various benchmark datasets, its types and their sources are presented for the purpose of research. Below there is a list of some available datasets presented for research and academics purpose:

- **Zachary's Karate Club Dataset (Zachary, 1977):** It contains the information of social network formed between 34 karate club members. Network formed is undirected with 34 nodes and 3 edges only.

- **White's Kinship Dataset (Freeman 1987b):** Kinship network is represented by three properties i.e. marriage, filiation and gender. Out of all gender is used for vertex partition in the graph. Network formed is composed of both the types of edges such as directed and undirected.
- **Galesburg Friendship Network Dataset (Coleman et al, 1966):** In this a social network is formed between physicians who recommend some new drug investigated in Galesburg. Friendship graph was built between 17 vertices and some directed edges.
- **DBLP Dataset (Yang et al, 2012):** It is known as digital bibliography and library project. It contains the information of computer science journals/proceedings bibliographies. Undirected co-authorship network is generated from the information encoded in the dataset. Dataset comprises of 317080 nodes and 1049866 edges.
- **Wiki-Vote Wikipedia 'Who-Votes-On-Whom' Dataset (Leskovec et al, 2010):** It contains the information of voting of Wikipedia users or administrators. A directed network is formed consist of 7115 nodes and 103689 edges where nodes represents users and edges denotes vote between them.
- **Live Journal Online Social Network Dataset (Yang et al, 2012):** It allows online users to form a social network by the means of blogs. Friendship network formed consist of 3997962 nodes and 34681189 edges.
- **Epinions 'Who-Trust-Whom' Network Dataset (Richardson et al, 2003):** In this trust network is formed between the customers who give review about product. Graph generated comprises of 75879 nodes and 508837 directed edges.
- **Enron Dataset (Klimmt et al, 2004):** In this network is formed between the employees of Enron who sent emails to each other for communication. The communication network formed is undirected comprises of 36692 nodes and 183831 edges, where nodes represent individuals and edges denotes emails.
- **Cit-HepTh Dataset (Leskovec et al, 2005):** It is known as high energy physics theory citation network which comprises of 27770 nodes and 352807 connecting edges. It contains all the citations and forms a labelled directed graph.
- **College Football Dataset (Girvan et al, 2002):** It is a network formed between different football teams who played with other. Graph generated between teams consist of 115 vertices and 616 edges.
- **Dolphin's Dataset (Lusseau et al, 2003):** It is a social network formed between the communities of dolphins in doubtful sound. The network formed consists of 62 vertices which are dolphins and 159 undirected edges.
- **Classroom Networks Dataset ("Educational Research Institute", 2012):** There are two varieties of this dataset one is classroom network with two groups and other one is classroom network with 3 groups. In this social interactions of classrooms are represented using vertices and directed edges.
- **LastFM Dataset ("Last.fm Dataset", nd):** It's a music site and dataset contains the information about tags of songs and similar songs. In total it contains 108493 nodes and 5115300 connecting edges.

3.2.1. Sources

Many large and small graph datasets explained above can be available from different dataset repositories of social networks. Surveys and questionnaire were also one of the sources of data. Researchers can avail the datasets from SNAP (Stanford large dataset collection), World bank data repository, Koblenz network collection, Barabasi's network lab at north eastern university, M.E.J Newman datasets repository, UC Irvine network data repository, Pajek datasets and soon (Leskovec and Krevl 2014). Also datasets can be obtained directly from blogs and by mining the social network sites such as Yelp.com, Facebook and Twitter by using application programming interfaces (APIs).

3.2.2 Application Programming Interfaces (APIs)

APIs provides the excellent source for social data. There are some of the online social services which provide their APIs for the purpose of scrapping the social data from their sites with some restrictions. For example Facebook, Twitter, Yelp, FourSquare and many more social networks offers their APIs for research purpose. Also in government organisations and non-government organisations (NGOs) the use of APIs are increasing. Researcher, academicians, and programmers can use APIs by keeping in mind the ethics of using public data for research. Earlier, programming APIs were used but now in addition to them Web APIs are recent adoption for accessing the data in the era of social science.

Here are some of the online social networks with their APIs:

- **Open Congress API:** This API is used to get the information about congressional delegates and their casting votes.
- **USA Spending API:** This API let the developers get the data of government federal contracts and subcontracts.
- **Facebook Social Graph API:** This API is used to gather the social data of Facebook graph. It enables the programmers to get ins and outs from the social graph of nodes and edges.
- **Twitter Search API:** This API allows fetching the friendship network i.e. a list of friends and followers on twitter.
- **YouTube API**: This API gives accessibility to the statistics of YouTube Videos.
- **Zomato API:** This API is used to get the wealth of information from the Zomato site such as details of restaurants, their timings, ratings and soon.
- **Restful API:** It is very powerful API widely used for doing different functions such as creating, updating, reading, deleting and searching over social data collected from social networks.

3.3. Platforms

Platform plays an important role in social networking which enables developers to develop new social networks and social ties so that people can interact with each other and indulge in social relations. Platform is any piece of software or hardware on which any application or any social network service will run. Moreover, social networking platforms have been actively used for knowledge sharing and management where a tremendous amount of knowledge is dumped and propagated via different social services. Organisations can develop their own customised social network which offers variety of services to users. Also each and every social network is different in terms of their purpose, function and services they provide. So, business organisations needs to figure out on which social media platform they need to spent time for promoting their business. Today, there is a long list of platforms are available for networking out of which some of them are as follows: Facebook, Twitter, Instagram, Facebook Live, LinkedIn, SnapChat, XING and hi5. Also there are many platforms available for blogging and email marketing such as Constant Contact, Marketing cloud, Xanga and Tumblr.

3.3.1. Visualization

Visualization plays a critical role in depicting the complex structure of online social networks. It works as a tool for showing the entire actor and their relationships in a more detailed way. As network is evolving it is difficult to represent it by using mere statistics so there is fundamental need of visualization tools for depicting the clear picture of social networks. (Correa, 2011) According to literature visualization of social networks can be represented in four ways. In the first form of visualization, social networks can represent in the form of node and edges layout which is known as structural visualization. Second form is known as semantic visualization in which extended form of node and edges layout is used where node and edge are some other aspects of social networks. Third form is known as statistical visualization in which social networks distributions such as their degree, node centrality and clustering coefficient is rendered. Last form of visualization is temporal form in which temporal (time) attribute is used to represent the dynamics of social networks. Visualization helps the analyst for broader view of the network structure. Here is some visualization tools listed:

- **Gephi (Bastian et al, 2009):** It is free and open source tool. This tool is well known and widely used for visualization of large networks. It offers data exploratory and link analysis as the main applications.
- **NetDraw (Borgatti et al, 2002):** This tool is used for visualization of graphs for windows platform only. It is associated with UCInet which is used for analysis purpose. It is free for use but UCInet is paid.
- **GraphViz (Ganser, 2000):** It is known as graph visualization software. It can be used as standalone or library. This tool is used for drawing graphs which takes input in the form of text in DOT language.
- **Prefuse (Heer et al, 2005):** This tool is free to be used for interactive information visualization. Requirement of JAVA programming knowledge is mandatory for using the tool. It also encompasses a rich feature set from modelling to interaction.
- **Manyeyes (Viegas et al, 2007):** This tool is solely for visualization of networks and other data types.
- **SoNIA (Moody et al, 2005):** It is known as social network image animator. It is also JAVA based which can be used for both dynamic and longitudinal visualization of networks. It has rich feature set from development to testing of both static and dynamic layout techniques.

3.3.2 Programming Interfaces

Apart from analytical and visualization tools there are some libraries which can be used by the researchers for analysis and experimentation. Some of the actively used libraries by the developers are as follows: Python NetworkX graph library contains the python packages which enables the users to study the dynamics of the network structure; their creation and updation, igraph library for C language mainly used for the purpose of graphs, matplotlib is a powerful python library for the purpose of drawing graphs, scrapy pyhon library used for the purpose of extracting the information from API such as url or any other information from a profile, Stanford network analysis platform (SNAP) library for C++ programming language is used for representing and analysing the large graphs. JAVA universal network/graph (JUNG) framework can be used for modelling, analysing and visualizing the graph and many more.

4. SURVEY OF TECHNIQUES IN SOCIAL NETWORK

This section produces a picture of literature and theory to describe the features and components of social networks. The overall survey is done and organized in to six major sections such as network modelling, random graphs, graph mining, identity resolution, social mining and centrality, and approaches for information diffusion behaviour in social networks. In figure 4 scope of the survey shows the major themes of the survey done.

4.1. Network Modelling

Mathematical Modelling helps in better apprehension of structure of network, network properties, and behaviour of network agents. This section gives introduction of models related to expansion of network. Modelling of real world networks is still in its infancy. No theoretical framework is designed for cross

Figure 4. Scope of Survey

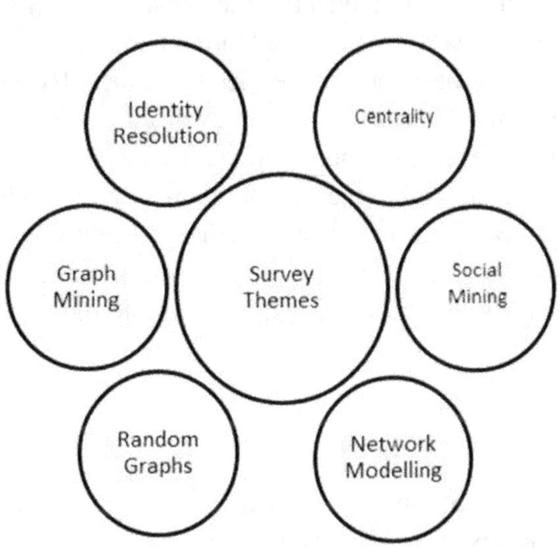

checking the doings. Development of more sophisticated models for better understanding and knowledge of the Network topography, and to go about as a substrate for the investigation of processes occurring on systems is the need of an hour. Mathematical modelling of different networks can be done through different models developed by the researchers such as random graph models, exponential random graphs, p* models, Markov model, small-world model, geometric models and models of growing graphs (Newman, 2003; Bonato et al, 2010). Expansion of network growth in terms of increasing nodes and edges in real world can be demonstrated using Price's model and Barabasi and Albert model (Newman, 2003). According to study, among two different network growth models one can be applied for directed graph i.e. Price's model and other i.e. Barabasi and Albert model for un-directed graph. Price's model is considered as simple model so far. Edges and nodes both are nominated for information carrying resource in network which can be mined for various applications. Pros and Cons are associated with each model. Properties of different networks which are considered in the literature to describe the network are degree distribution and its measure with some other properties namely transitivity or clustering, community structure, giant component, centrality, correlation and network resilience. Apart from degree distribution other network properties can also be well structured with respect to their cause and effect for good apprehension. Now, among all the available models to choose appropriate one to apply can be done through unsupervised learning where sub graphs generated from each model can be used to select model (Janssen et al, 2015).

4.2. Random Graphs

One of the models which can apply on real world networks is random graph model and its extensions by incorporating several fundamental properties of network. Application of Random model ranges from strengthening the problems of networks to the process of information diffusion in the network. The random graph model with its principal features can be generalized and produce different versions of it. Earlier model which was constructed was "random net" which lacks the property of non-Poisson degree distribution which gives birth to configuration model. Other extensions such as bipartite and community structured models encapsulated the property of transitivity in random graphs.

Researchers had used random graph to model the Facebook social network group which is dynamic in nature and also the closeness of users is represented through it (Pallegedara et al, 2014). The research can be extended for modelling heterogeneous online social networks. Exponential random graph model (ERGM) can also be used to form collaborative network among diabetic patients (Song et al, 2014). The work was motivated for helping patients by improving online social network in which patients interact with each other on the basis of their similar medical problem. The research done by researchers can be carried forward to broader scope by focusing on chronic diseases rather than only diabetes data. Modelling of real-world networks such as Facebook, Twitter or any desired network with the help of random graphs serves as an incentive phase for the solution in evolving structure of network that aids in finding centrality and other interesting facts.

4.3. Graph Mining

In the last years, graph mining has become an active area of research which can be used as an apparatus for finding the hidden concepts in social networks. Understanding of network data by representing online social network as a graph will be helpful in analysis purpose in social networks (Kimura et al,

2010). Main features of online social network graph are power laws with small diameter and community structure for the purpose of typify. Robins et al. (2005) work demonstrated the purpose of graph mining in which researchers have explained forecasting, communities' structure and how to model online social network graph plus evolution and its structure. Emerging graph topological characteristics, recommendation, and graph analysis with geographic and geometric information were considered as hot topics in the year 2012. Today graph mining and sequence mining are the main supporting theories used to develop algorithms for mining the triggering patterns. The heart of the research in social networks lies in analysis of dynamic graphs for capturing the structural changes with time in the graph. Recently, triggering pattern mining problem is mainly addressed by the authors and was mathematically formulated and explained using small dynamic attributed graphs (Kaytoue et al, 2015). Quantitative and qualitative experiments are done in the study by taking number of parameters for showing scalability and efficiency of algorithms developed. Understanding the concept and properties of dynamic graphs, how they evolve and can analyse for different applications will be a major breakthrough. Due to Online Social Network dynamics, survey for external demographic and dynamic geo location data need to be explored for better view of user behaviour and interaction which aids in predicting future online activities. Propagation of information to the legitimate audience or particular individual and the representation of graph in the expanding phase of online social networks is the open challenge to be focused by researchers.

4.4. Identity Resolution

Identity resolution is prediction of two or more entity refers to same real world entity. In online social networks identity resolution problem is defined in terms of identity reference which is a set of attributes, where each reference corresponds to a set of unknown individuals. Each incident is a hyper-edge that connects multiple references. To solve this problem, a framework of identity resolution is delineated by considering 2 aspects: identity attributes and matching algorithms. Identity attributes are features that can be used to describe certain distinctive characteristics of identity references. A matching algorithm defines the computational procedure of recovering the matching entities from the given set of references. Author describes three identity attributes namely personal, social behaviour, and social relationship attributes, along with them three matching algorithms (supervised): pair wise comparison approach, transitive closure, and collective clustering (Li et al, 2015). Researchers developed a model to addresses the problem of identity resolution across two online social networks namely Facebook and Twitter by exploiting only publically accessible data by not violating any authorization issue (Jain et al, 2013). Solution strategy for cross platform matching consists of 2 phases namely identity search and identity matching algorithm based upon similarity measures. Identity search method takes 3 parameters into an account: search by profile, search by content and search by network attributes and then gives result by finding similar attribute if any and generating the candidate set which are the nominees of the identity to be matched. Entity or identity resolution will facilitate in building friend recommendation feature by finding a user's friend's identities on multiple social networks with their information on one social network and may recommend her to attach to the prompt friend's identities. Mutual friend graph and friendship graph can be built from a given social graph which serves as the foundation for finding out the network similarity among users (Akcora et al, 2011; Akcora et al, 2013). Surmising the missing attribute values of any user profile using the notion of homophily can further help in finding out the profile similarity.

4.5. Social Mining and Centrality

Measuring homophily or segregation and centrality in social networks are considered as the main components for social mining. Segregation tells about the degree to which the individuals in a close group are different from other group i.e. there is a big gap between intra groups (Bojanowskia et al, 2014; Rossetti et al, 2016). By incorporating social phenomena among individual analysis through homophily saves time and space for predicting usage for any service or product. Graph centrality is focused more to be applied on online social networks for finding out the most central node. In literature, study related to centrality starting from its origin till late 70's are highlighted by researchers in which focus is on explaining the existing centrality measures theory in a more formalized way along with the concepts of basic graph theory for better understanding. There are total nine measures out of them three were based on distance between points or nodes, other three were based on betweenness and rest of all based on closeness property. Also, graph which is of star or wheel topology-alike gains maximum centrality score whereas graphs which are replica of ring or mesh topology gains minimum score (Freemann, 1979). Recently, path flows and random walk flows is taken as the main ingredient for entropy centrality calculation and a model based upon it is developed by the researchers and concludes that walk based is more helpful for influential community identification (Nikolaev et al, 2015). Traditionally centrality can be measured for the directed or undirected graphs but now the author has shown the idea of measuring centrality among unrelated users with the help of hyper graphs (Bonacich et al, 2004; Zudilova et al, 2017). Similarity measures also play a vital role in various applications such as profile matching, vertex similarity, content matching in social networks (Mogo et al, 2017; Zhang et al, 2015). By reviewing the concepts of graph theory, community detection and homophily for gaining the new knowledge can be used in different phases: inception, pre-processing, transition between two stages and pre-processing in social networks.

4.6. Diffusion in Social Network

As social network analysis is becoming interesting, one of the major works of research is also going towards in developing models for propagation of useful information in a network of people. In the recent years main target of researchers is to find out the most convincing nodes or vertices in social network graph which enables to spread the information to a major chunk with maximum speed. According to the literature there are two levels of information diffusion such as micro-level and macro-level (Fu et al, 2016). Modelling the process of information diffusion can be done through explanatory and predictive models (Guille et al, 2013). Predictive models are further classified as graph based and non-graph based models. Two algorithms namely independent cascade and linear threshold are graph based which are used by the researchers actively and also work is constantly being done to improve the models. Models need to be optimized for the purpose of finding influential nodes in the large-scale network and must be readily applicable for real world problems. Optimization problems can be further optimized using nature inspired algorithms or other optimization technique which may result in better form. Recently, authors had tried to extract influential nodes using graph based models by incorporating with the bond percolation and the concepts of graph theory under the same greedy algorithm for better efficiency (Kimura et al, 2010)

5. RECENT TECHNOLOGICAL TRENDS

The analysis of online social networks provides unprecedented challenges, applications and opportunities from the perspective of online business, knowledge discovery and social mining. List of recent trends in terms of services, applications and open challenges is presented in figure 5.

5.1. Services

- **Friendship Networks:** Building friendship networks for example Facebook, Google+ and MySpace for social connections.
- **Information Sharing:** This service enables to share the information in the form of content, photos, videos and other multimedia data in social group. YouTube and Flickr online social platform are becoming well-liked in the zone.
- **Educational and Professional Social Network Groups**: Forming such kind of networks for example LinkedIn, and other educational forums helps individual in their professional and educational matters according to their interest.
- **Bookmarking Sites:** This online social service allows one to organize their bookmarks with the help of tags. It will indirectly help in improving the web search. Reddit, Delicious, Pinterest and many more the examples of popular social bookmarking sites.

Figure 5. Recent Technological Trends

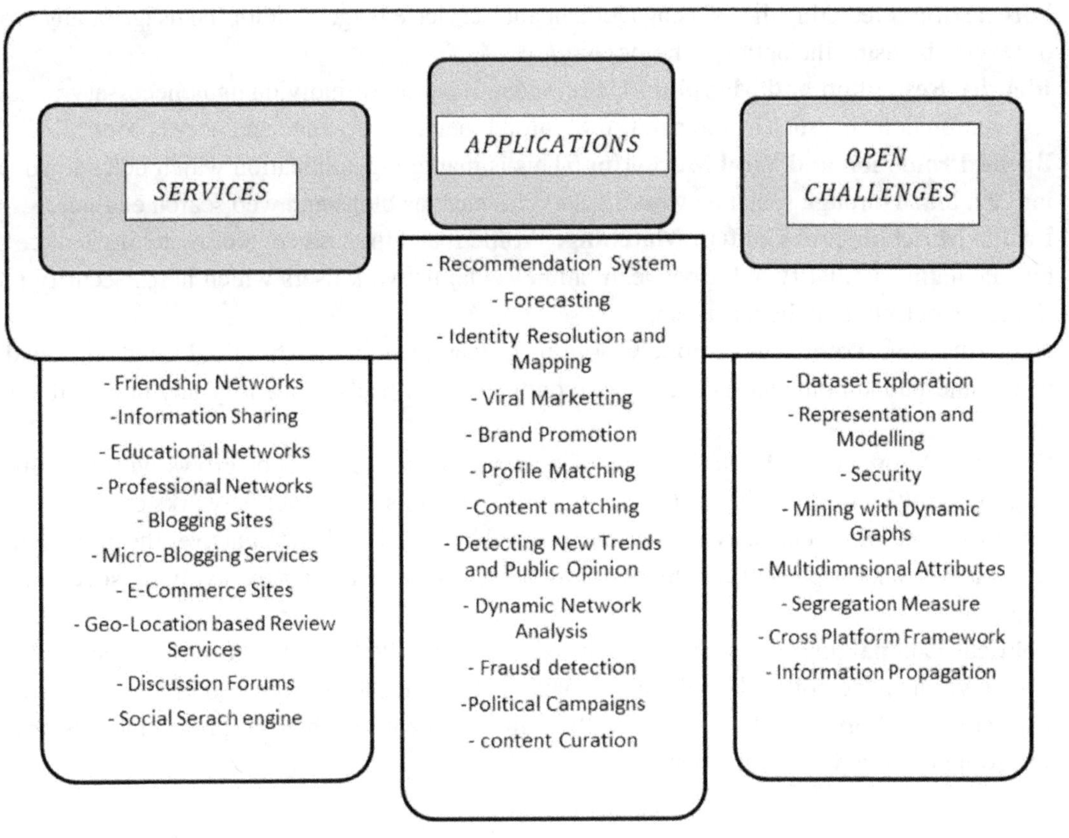

- **Micro-Blogging Services:** Twitter, FriendFeed and Tumblr are the famous micro-blogging sites available. This service enables the users to share micro posts which can be small sentence, image or and web link. Today, Micro-blogging services are used in the field of marketing and news diffusion process.
- **E-Commerce Sites:** There is endless number of sites available today for business and trading. Some of the sites are as follows Ebay, FlipKart, Snapdeal, Myntra, Amazon and many more. It helps in spreading business in online market place by launching and promoting new products.
- **Geo-Location Based Review Services and Discussion Forums:** Geo-location based review services have become prime concern for the businesses and organizations. Users of it recommend others about any social event or reviews regarding any product or service availed whereas discussion forums are open for everyone to participate in it, to discuss or give their views on any educational, political and other topic.
- **Social Search Engines:** This service makes use of online communities and works as a meta-search engine. Some of the social search engines are Anoox, Google Coop and Yahoo's MyWeb 2.0.

5.2. Applications

- **Recommendation System:** Network similarity measure can be used to recommend the user for profile update on the basis of it. It can lead to new recommendation system in online social network.
- **Forecasting:** Predicting the user engagement and service engagement for the usage of any product or service by using the notion of homophily.
- **Identity Resolution and Mapping:** Unique identification of individuals is necessary in several application domains such as forensics, law enforcement, governance and access control.
- **Brand Promotion and Viral Marketing:** This is marketing application which helps in advertising of a brand through social networking services such as blogs and web search engines.
- **Profile Matching and Content Matching:** Profile matching and content matching can be done by calculating similarity index between online social network users which helps security practitioners in detecting malicious users.
- **Detecting New Trends and Public Opinion:** Detecting evolving structural trends in social networks and public opinions such as buzz monitoring will leads to identify any new outbreaks in market.
- **Dynamic Network Analysis:** Analysis of networks which changes or grows with real time for example analysis of biological networks, terrorist networks, computer networks etc.
- **Fraud Detection:** Social network data can be used by social analyst to uncover the hidden fraudulent patterns and to prevent the upcoming new frauds by analysing the evolving social network with time.
- **Political Campaigns:** This can be organised in a controlled manner on online social platform which will help the political candidate in making strategic decisions in good or worse condition.
- **Content Curation:** Timely curation of the online content will help in promoting business and spreading newsfeeds on social platforms.

5.3. Open Challenges

- **Dataset Exploration:** A wide study across variety of datasets to choose appropriate ones for conducting analysis and experimentation.
- **Representation and Modelling:** The inherent structure of online social network needs to be demonstrated in form of graphs. This helps to portray large-scale real-world social networks in graphs for performing analytical studies. It serves as an inceptive phase for the solution in evolving structure of network that aids in finding centrality and other interesting facts.
- **Security in Social Networks:** To detect and link malicious user accounts which helps the security practitioner for identification purpose.
- **Mining with Dynamic Graphs:** To find out appropriate and optimized algorithm to mine the triggering patterns in dynamic graphs and also to design a generalized method for capturing the structural changes in the graph with advancement in timeline.
- **Multidimensional Attributes of Social Entities:** The concept of multidimensionality centrality measures need to be canvassed which can be applied to online social networks for testing its strength, which is still in its infancy.
- **Segregation Measure:** It is still a big challenge for the unpredictable changes in network topology for example at one time some nodes related to other node and on some another moment it leaves the network.
- **Cross-Platform Social Frameworks:** Building of generic framework which serves as only one model applicable across multiple online social networking platforms is still behind the closed doors. Efforts can be done to bring it to grounds of realism.
- **Information Propagation:** This entails in-depth study of pattern of information spread across social networks, often triggered by certain events. For instance- viral marketing, product promotion, etc.

6. CONCLUSION

This chapter is focussed by providing the readers with the concrete concepts of social network analysis with the list of tools, datasets available for research and the most trending topics going now days. As online social network are getting engrossed in everybody's life, it is becoming reflector of the real life so it's the need of an hour for the research of optimized social network analysis which gives utilitarianism benefit. Study of different centrality measures, homophily measures, and graph mining techniques were canvassed as a solution for selecting suitable measure for any application and assisting for analysis task in social networks. Due to online social network dynamics, changing community structure survey for dynamic dataset can be explored for strengthening the overall predicting capability for future online activities. Generic framework serves one model which can be applied on inter online social platform. Assortative matching or homophily in social networks analysis were considered as a noticeable concept in research as per literature studies. Moreover, many cases of deception around the world have also been registered and the research can expand for detecting fake profiles in online social networks by taking identity resolution method as a base theory. For advertisements and promotions also many organizations use online social networking sites to identify the target audience and the count of actual audience. Therefore resolution can help in finding unique number of users.

REFERENCES

Akcora, C., Carminati, B., & Ferrari, E. (2011). Network and profile based measures for user similarities on social networks. *IEEE International Conference on Information Reuse and Integration (IRI)*, 292–298.

Akcora, C. G., Carminati, B., & Ferrari, E. (2013). User Similarities on Social Networks. *Social Network Analysis and Mining Journal Springer*, *3*(3), 475–495. doi:10.1007/s13278-012-0090-8

Bastian, M., Heymann, S., & Jacomy, M. (2009). Gephi: An open source software for exploring and manipulating networks. *International AAAI Conference on Weblogs and Social Media*.

Batagelj, V., & Pajek. (n.d.). *Program for Large Network Analysis*. Retrieved from http://vlado.fmf.uni-lj.si/pub/networks/pajek

Bojanowskia, M., & Corten, R. (2014). Measuring segregation in social networks. *Social Networks Journal Elsevier*, *39*, 14–32. doi:10.1016/j.socnet.2014.04.001

Bonacich, P., Holdren, A. C., & Johnston, M. (2004). Hyper-edges and multidimensional centrality. *Social Networks Journal Elsevier*, *26*(3), 189–203. doi:10.1016/j.socnet.2004.01.001

Bonato, A., Janssen, J., & Prałat, P. (2010). A Geometric Model for On-line Social Networks. *Proceedings of the International Workshop on Modeling Social Media ACM*. doi:10.1145/1835980.1835984

Borgatti, S. P., Everett, M. G., & Freeman, L. C. (2002). *Ucinet for Windows: Software for Social Network Analysis*. Analytic Technologies.

Coleman, J. S., Katz, E., & Menzel, H. (1966). Medical Innovation: A Diffusion Study. Bobbs-Merrill.

Correa, C. D., & Ma, K. L. (2011). Visualizing social networks. In Social Network Data Analytics. Springer Science+ Business Media. doi:10.1007/978-1-4419-8462-3_11

Educational Research Institute, School Effectiveness Study. (2012). Retrieved from http://eduentuzjasci.pl/en/oprojekcie-2/502-the-project.htmlEgan

Freeman, L. C. (1978b). Segregation in social networks. *Sociological Methods & Research*, *6*(4), 411–429. doi:10.1177/004912417800600401

Freeman, L. C. (1979). Centrality in Social Networks Conceptual Clarification. Social networks Journal. *Elsevier Sequoia S.A.*, *1*(3), 215–239.

Fu, S., Hu, C., Hu, Y., Sun, B., Ying, W., & Shi, P. (2016). Information Diffusion Mechanisms in Online Social Networks. *IEEE First International Conference on Data Science in Cyberspace (DSC)*, 312-317. doi:10.1109/DSC.2016.46

Gansner, E. R., & North, S. C. (2000). An open graph visualization system and its applications to software engineering. *Software, Practice & Experience*, *30*(11), 1203–1233. doi:10.1002/1097-024X(200009)30:11<1203::AID-SPE338>3.0.CO;2-N

Girvan, M., & Newman, M. E. J. (2002). Community structure in social and biological networks. *Proceedings of the National Academy of Sciences of the United States of America*, *99*(12), 7821–7826. doi:10.1073/pnas.122653799 PMID:12060727

Gruzd, A. (2016). *Netlytic: Software for Automated Text and Social Network Analysis*. Retrieved from http://Netlytic.org

Guille, A., Hacid, H., Favre, C., & Zighed, D. A. (2013). Information Diffusion in Online Social Networks: A Survey. *ACM SIGMOD*, *42*(2), 17–28. doi:10.1145/2503792.2503797

Jain, P., Kumaraguru, P., & Joshi, A. (2013). @I Seek 'fb.me': Identifying Users across Multiple Online Social Networks. *Proceedings of the 22nd International Conference on World Wide Web (WWW) 13 Companion*, 1259-1268.

Janssen, J., Hurshman, M., & Kalyaniwalla, N. (2015). Model Selection for Social Networks Using Graphlets. *Internet Mathematics. Taylor & Francis*, *8*(4), 338–363. doi:10.1080/15427951.2012.671149

Kaytoue, M., Pitarch, Y., Plantevit, M., & Robardet, C. (2015). What effects topological changes in dynamic graphs? Elucidating relationships between vertex attributes and the graph structure. *Social network Analysis and Mining Journal Springer, 5*(1), 1-17.

Kimura, M., Saito, K., Nakano, R., & Motoda, H. (2010). Extracting influential nodes on a social network for information diffusion. Data mining Knowledge discovery. *Journal of the Association for Computing Machinery*, *20*(1), 70–97.

Klimmt, B., & Yang, Y. (2004). *Introducing the Enron Corpus*. CEAS Conference.

Last.fm dataset. (n.d.). *The official song tags and song similarity collection for the Million Song Dataset*. Retrieved from http://labrosa.ee.columbia.edu/millionsong/lastfm

Leskovec, J., Huttenlocher, D., & Kleinberg, J. (2010). *Signed Networks in Social Media*. CHI. doi:10.1145/1753326.1753532

Leskovec, J., Kleinberg, J., & Faloutsos, C. (2005). Graphs over Time: Densification Laws, *Shrinking Diameters and Possible Explanations. ACM SIGKDD International Conference on Knowledge Discovery and Data Mining (KDD).*

Leskovec, J., & Krevl, A. (2014). *SNAP Datasets: Stanford Large Network Dataset Collection*. Retrieved from http://snap.stanford.edu/data

Li, J., & Wang, A.G. (2015). A framework of identity resolution: evaluating identity attributes and matching algorithms. *Security Informatics Journal, 4*(6).

Lusseau, K., Schneider, O. J., Boisseau, P., Haase, E., Slooten, E., & Dawson, S. M. (2003). The bottlenose dolphin community of Doubtful Sound features a large proportion of long-lasting associations. *Behavioral Ecology and Sociobiology*, *54*(4), 396–405. doi:10.1007/s00265-003-0651-y

Mbogo, G. K., & Visheratin, A. A. (2017). Build hybrid scientific similarity networks using research papers and social networks. Procedia Computer Science, 2507, 211.

Moody, J., Daniel, A., Farland, M., & Moll, S.B. (2005). Visualizing Network Dynamics. *American Journal of Sociology*. doi:10.1086/421509

Nettleton, D. F. (2013). Data mining of social networks represented as graphs. *Computer Science Review Elsevier Journal*, *7*, 1–34. doi:10.1016/j.cosrev.2012.12.001

Newman, M. E. J. (2003). The structure and function of complex networks. *SIAM Review*, *45*(2), 167–256. doi:10.1137/S003614450342480

Nikolaev, A. G., Razib, R., & Kucheriya, A. (2015). On efficient use of entropy centrality for social network analysis and community detection. *Social Networks Journal Elsevier*, *40*, 154–162. doi:10.1016/j.socnet.2014.10.002

Pallegedara, D., & Pan, L. (2014). Investigating Facebook Groups through a Random Graph Model. *Journal of Multimedia. Finland*, *9*(1), 25–35.

Richardson, M., Agrawal, R., & Domingos, P. (2003). *Trust Management for the Semantic Web*. ISWC.

Robins, G., Pattison, P., & Woolcock, J. (2005). Small and other worlds: Global network structures from local processes. *American Journal of Sociology*, *110*(4), 894–936. doi:10.1086/427322

Rossetti, G., Pappalardo, L., Kikas, R., Pedreschi, D., Giannotti, F., & Dumas, M. (2016). Homophilic network decomposition: A community-centric analysis of online social services. Social Network Analysis and Mining (SNAM). *Journal Springer*, *6*(103), 1–18.

Song, X., Jiang, S., Yan, X., & Chen, H. (2014). Collaborative Friendship Networks in Online Healthcare Communities: *An Exponential Random Graph Model Analysis. In International Conference on Smart Health. Springer.*

Viegas, F. B., Wattenberg, M., Ham, F. V., Kriss, J., & McKeon, M. (2007). ManyEyes: A Site for Visualization at Internet Scale. *IEEE Transactions on Visualization and Computer Graphics*, *13*(6), 1121–1128. doi:10.1109/TVCG.2007.70577 PMID:17968055

Wilensky, U. (1999). *NetLogo: Center for Connected Learning and Computer-Based Modelling*. North Western University. Retrieved from http://ccl.northwestern.edu/netlogo

Yang, J., & Leskovec, J. (2012). *Defining and Evaluating Network Communities based on Ground-truth*. ICDM.

Yang, J., & Leskovec, J. (2012). *Defining and Evaluating Network Communities based on Ground-truth*. ICDM.

Zachary, W. W. (1977). An information flow model for conflict and fission in small groups. *Journal of Anthropological Research*, *33*(4), 452–473. doi:10.1086/jar.33.4.3629752

Zhang, S., Zheng, X., & Hu, C. (2015). A Survey of Semantic Similarity and its Application to Social Network Analysis. *Proceedings of IEEE International Conference on Big Data (Big Data)*, 2362-2367.

Zudilova, T. V., & Ivanov, S. E. (2017). The clustering methods in graph models of social networks. *Applied Mathematical Sciences*, *11*(21), 1007–1017. doi:10.12988/ams.2017.7389

Chapter 2
Social Networking Data Analysis Tools and Services

Gopal Krishna
Aryabhatt Knowledge University, India

ABSTRACT

Social networks have drawn remarkable attention from IT professionals and researchers in data sciences. They are the most popular medium for social interaction. Online social networking (OSN) can be defined as involving networking for fun, business, and communication. Social networks have emerged as universally accepted communication means and boomed in turning this world into a global town. OSN media are generally known for broadcasting information, activities posting, contents sharing, product reviews, online pictures sharing, professional profiling, advertisements and ideas/opinion/sentiment expression, or some other stuff based on business interests. For the analysis of the huge amount of data, data mining techniques are used for identifying the relevant knowledge from the huge amount of data that includes detecting trends, patterns, and rules. Data mining techniques, machine learning, and statistical modeling are used to retrieve the information. For the analysis of the data, three methods are used: data pre-processing, data analysis, and data interpretation.

INTRODUCTION

This Chapter on Social Networking Data Analysis Tools and Services introduces the various perspectives of the online social networking sites(OSNs), its various aspects such as its applications, types of data available on OSN, different types of analysis for these huge amount of data, the tools used to analysis these data, the platform components, system architecture and research issues on OSN. It will help the academician, researchers and practitioners to improve their capacity to gain an accurate and deep understanding of about OSN. The term social network or online social network or social media is referred to depict web-based services that permit persons to make a profile inside a certain domain so that they may interact with other users in the specified network. Graph theory is applied in the social network that consist of *vertices* and *edges* employed to symbolize social relations on OSN sites. A huge number of domains and sectors, ranging from business analysis and economic to public administration,

DOI: 10.4018/978-1-5225-5097-6.ch002

from governance to scientific researches in many fields, involve with social networking data analysis tools and techniques. On the one hand, social networking data is enormously important to increase the productivity in businesses and progressive discovery in research disciplines, that provide a lot of opportunities for the enormous development in many areas. OSN data are very complex because of its three features named as size, noise and dynamism. For the analysis of these data, data mining techniques are used for identifying the relevant knowledge from the huge amount of data that includes detecting trends, patterns and rules. Data, information and knowledge are three important data mining paradigms. The huge amount data in social networks datasets are needed for automated processing and analyzing of information within a realistic time.

Fascinatingly, huge data sets are required to mine significant model from data in data mining techniques. OSN sites emerged as an ideal platform to mine with data mining techniques and tools. Data mining tools may have varieties from unsupervised or semi supervised machine learning techniques to supervised machine learning techniques. Sometimes users make decisions based on contents shared by unknown person on OSN sites. These escalating the level of dependence on the trustworthiness of these sites. OSN has also provided users the freedom to give opinions and reviews in real time with very little or no restriction.

BACKGROUND

Social networking provides facilities to the users to share their views, photos, posts, videos and others contents such as their events and activities to connect with people in their network. It is similar to the inter personal social gathering in villages, markets, towns to discuss on the various issues and events.

But the main difference is that OSN enables users to connect with other users at difference locations, across the globe. Generally social networking can be noticed in different views first as which main purpose is to socializing with friends like facebook and instagram other can be networking for non-social interpersonal communication such as LinkedIn for a career and employment oriented site. So, there are many OSN sites through which people can be interlinked via cross-posting without invading the personal privacy.

The history and background of social networking is very interesting since the evolution of human civilization. It refers to the evolution of personal communication among the people. The medium of personal communication has changed a lot from the evolution of human civilization. The hand written letter was the oldest practice of communication across long distance from one person to another. It was started in 500 B.C., and became popular and broad medium in future centuries. In the year 1792, the telegraph was invented through which messages was delivered for the far distance than previous methods. Since through telegraph messages were short, it was a tremendous change in the communication in the society for the long period of time to convey news and information. Another way of communication started in the year 1865 was postal services for the personal, professional, and other communication. After that telephone and radio was another revolutionary invention in 1890 and 1891 respectively that are still in use today and developing day by day. Both has changed the lifestyle of people in the communication across the long distances immediately that was a new and amazing experience for mankind. In the 20th century, technology started to change immediately after the development of computers. Scientists and engineers started to develop the techniques to connect the computers that later lead to the birth of Internet. CompuServe was the earliest form of Internet in 1960s. Fundamental form of emails were developed during this period. After the evolution of internet networking technology has upgraded by 1970s, through UseNet allowed users communicate in the form of virtual newsletter. By 1980s, personal computers were becoming more popular and social media were being used on large scale. In 1988, Inter relay chats or IRCs were used firstly and continued to be used widely into 1900s. Six Degrees was the first online social networking site that was created in 1997. Using this user enabled to create a profile and making other user friends. In the year 1999, blogging sites evolved and made online social media became sensational and popular. In 2000s sites like Orkut, LinkedIn, MySpace achieved tremendous attention and response from users. Photobucket and Flickr promoted online photo sharing. In 2005, YouTube came into existence which became the excellent medium for online video sharing and becoming popular day by day. Facebook and Twitter came out in 2006 and became most popular and successful across the globe on internet in the present era. There are many more online social media sites Spotify, Tumblr, Foursquare and Pinterest are also giving remarkable presence in the social networking world. In this age there are large variety of online social networking sites that are linked to each other to allow cross-posting through which users can reach the maximum numbers of people according to their choice and requirements without disturbing the personal confidentiality.

ISSUES, CONTROVERSIES, AND PROBLEMS

How Online Social Networking Sites (OSNs) Work

Social networking sites has millions of users and their millions of updates per second. So the question arises that how these data managed by the social networking sites? What software and servers are there to manage all these? What are the tools and services to maintain and manage all these? The answers behind these questions are open-source software and thousands of servers. The operating system behind the most of the social networking sites such as MySpace, Twitter and LinkedIn are all Linux. F5 Big-IP is used by Facebook, which is a member of Linux appliances used for the network management. The web servers used is Apache and ONE Web Servers is used by LinkedIn in along with Apache. Sun's MySQL is used by most of the Social networking sites for database management system to manage the user's messages and status updates. So, the most part of the social networking sites consist of the Linux, Apache, MySQL, PHP/Python/Perl. The APIs (Application Programming Interface) are there for the developers to develop the applications that will run on their network and to add the new features to the sites. OSN Sites has maintain the secrecy on their overall functionality suc as Twitter uses Ruby on Rails an open source web framework. Jabber/XMPP (Extensible Messaging and Presence Protocol) is used by Twitter for the routing of millions of the instant messages. Facebook handle 260 billion-page views per month according to the Royal Pingdom, a Swedish site that track Internet sites uptime. For this at present it runs 30K servers. From the hardware point of view, expensive and high-tech equipment (servers) is required for the better management of the social network. Each server acts as high-speed memory ranges from 256 GBs to 512GBs of RAM. All these servers are linked together into clusters. Servers are placed in data centers with major Internet's Network Points(NAPs). NAPs are at the major Internet Service Providers(ISPs) are connected to each other and direct access are provided for the Internet's fastest connections. After all these next step is to work out exactly how to change all these technologies into money.

Social Network Analysis

The analysis of social network can be viewed from individualism in the sociology to the structural analysis that defines the primary unit of analysis of new analytical methods development such as friendship relationship among persons, communication links among employees in an organization etc. The interesting features of a relation is patterns and structures. There are attributes of the users among whom the relationship exits. A structure list is the degree of friendship is transitive. Relations(*strands*) are defined by the strength, direction and content. The information exchanged among the user in a relation referred as resources.

A relation can be categorized as directed or undirected such as one person may connected with a second person can be termed as support. Support cab be of two type, one can take or give support or both. Alternately, users can maintain an undirected relationship or friendship in which they both maintain the friendship or relationship without following any particular direction. In course of maintaining the relationship or friendship, there may be chance of unbalanced relationship. Unbalance in the relationship refers that one user may claim a close friendship but in return other a weaker friendship or one is more active and other is less or there may be difference in the communication frequency. It can termed as asymmetrical relation.

Relation can also be defined in terms of strength. It can be defined i terms of the frequency of the communication among the user's weather on once in a day, work days, weekends, weekly, monthly, yearly or rarely. The strength of relationships can be measured in various aspects. These measurement criteria may be social capital shared among the users such as services, money or goods for the exchange of trivial or vital information.

It is required to connect users to be in relationship through a tie. A tie based relationship can be maintained by the pair on the basis of one to one relationship that may of similar background, or in same firm. A multiplex tie is maintained based on the relationship that may share on the basis of the other criteria such as information being shared, attending events together, visiting the places together etc. Ties can be differing in strength content and direction. It may be weaker or stronger in terms of context. Weak ties refer to the infrequent communication, less intimacy such as for those users who are connected with each other but their interest is not similar. In the strong ties the frequency of communication is higher, there is fine scope of content and idea sharing such as among college friends or batch mates. Since, both category of ties is important for the exchange of resources in the networks. More resources are shared in the network where strong ties are there whatever users want. In contrast in the weakly tied networks, users have less scope for the frequent content and resource sharing. They provide more access to the different resources of the social network. The users who never communicated with each other within a circle or organization, there is provision of electronic tie for the efficient flow of resources, data, content and information. There may be activity sharing to maintain the proper connectivity among them.

Multiplexity

The multiplex or multi-stranded is a tie that may be defined as multiple relations among the users in the network. It is found by the social network analysts that there is more scope for the connectivity, intimacy, support, and durability if multiplexity is used in network. But there are still some issues among the social network analysts that the internet, emails, personal messaging etc do not fulfill the criteria of multiplexity. This issue is more extended by the boutique approach. This approach is applied to online that encourages the specifications in ties. This trend demonstrates the multiple communication among the various user groups in the online social networking. It results in the broad sustainability, multiplexity and supportive among the internet participants. However, there is little scope for the research in terms of multiplexity ties over specialization, online, social network relations grow during time.

Functionalities and Features of Online Social Networking

There are large variety of online social networking sites for the different purposes. But there are some core features of every OSNs. The features of OSNs are mentioned as follows:

As OSN can be represented digitally for its users(nodes) and relationships or connections among them in real world along with networking services for conversations/chatting. It provides the medium to:

1. Allow individual to create a digital representation of themselves (generally called profiles or account) and establish their online social relation with other users (i.e., contact list or friend list).
2. To update and enhance the previous and pre-existing relation among users also provide support and maintenance of real world relations in the digital world.
3. Based on common activities, common interest, locations new online relationships can be established just like real world relationships. Following functionalities are provided by the online social networking sites to their users for the online social interactions and self-representation:

Personal Space Management

An online social networking sites should support a user to:

1. Create or delete a profile or an account.
2. Edit or update personal and general information in the account or profile.
3. Upload or edit user generated contents or posts like blog- postings, status update, photos, locations, interests etc.

Note that, generally in most of the online social networking sites, a user's activities in his personal space will be displayed to his friend list automatically. Therefore, any activity like uploading and editing user post or information are the important communication primitive between a user's and their friend list or contact list.

Social Connection Management

Online Social Networking sites connect individuals or users to through the formal means to establish their relationship (e.g.- friend lists) with each other represented by the social ties. New social ties or links can be established for those who share common interests and hobbies. These can have maintained or invoked through a social connection for which online social graph or simple labeled graph is used to create all data stored in the OSN sites. In the social graph the nodes or vertices denote the user and the edges represent the relationship between users. The user's profile is maintained by nodes and each link is tagged with a social link *label*. A few OSN sites provide not only a simple relationship but also establishes the trust relationships, categorize the relationships, and also make the various access without compromising the privacy and security of the users. The space in which the user's profile and social edges or connections are refer as digital personal space and collection of registered user's personal spaces are referred as the digital social space.

Means of Communication

There are various means of communications for users, since communication is the main theme or idea of any OSN sites. Public messages that is blogging and private messages in the various modes such as photos, audio, texts, video, and so on using personal spaces. Another mode may be the asynchronous communication and asynchronous communication. Many other OSNs also provide facilities to play real time online games in pair or group wise.

Exploring Digital Social Space

There is restriction for the existing users to interact with another users that encourages users to build new social relations can be termed as socialization. Searching the new or unknown users in the OSNs is also the main feature that can be authenticated and authorized in the two steps. The two-important means through which the personal space of an unknown users can be reached as:

1. **Global Keyword Search (or Social Search):** The Global keyword search is the first mean of search. For the successful search accessing the search list is the main task. Search policy can be specified by the users to be access through a global name search.
2. **Social Graph Traversal (or Social Traversal):** The Social Graph traversal is the second mean to access the search listing through traversing online social graph. Users can search the new users by traversing or accessing the contact list or friend list of new users or person. An user can restrict other user to view his account by the traversal policy that specifies the set rules. Usability and sociability is the main traditional goal of OSNs that can be achieved by supporting all the functionalities in the design of new secured and privacy preserving OSNs.

System Architectures of Online Social Networking

There are two standard for the implementation of an OSN are Peer-to-Peer Architecture Client Server Architecture that provide distribute system and Centralized system respectively.

1. **Peer-to-Peer Architecture:** This is based on the decentralized architecture for the design of next-generation OSNs carry on the cooperation among the user also called independent parties. The database of in the personal space of the users are stored and maintained in the distribute form. It may take support of real social networks and geographical proximity to support local services in the unavailability of Internet. Global search is the example of the P2P architecture in a distributed manner is an challenging task.
2. **Client Server Architecture:** This is based on the centralized system and web-server. This is followed by the commercial social media such as LinkedIn Corp., Facebook Inc, XING AG etc. in

which all functionalities are there like storage, maintenance, and access. It's a basic and conventional architecture. It is easier to implement and has an benefit of being genuine and while it also suffers from some defect like any single entity can cause an issue for the failure.

Trust, Privacy, and Security Concerns in Online Social Networking

Privacy and security issues with the trust impact is the main concern in the online social networking sites. To maintain the balance between the privacy and security in the OSNs for the better implementation of usability and sociability, various standard principles of network security are there such as confidentiality, integrity and availability. After the joining OSNs, users create their profiles to connect with their existing friends as well as new people. In the profile they include their general information such as name(real name or pseudonym), age, profession, personal interest, hometown etc. There are facilities to post their status, activities, photos, videos, chatting, personal messaging, public testimonials etc in order to stay connected with each other and make them updated Users send friend request or follow request through messages and other ways to connect with their friends and to add them to the social network. The main purpose of joining the social network is the communication and establish the relationships. Trust can be defined as "the willingness of a person to be accessible to the activities of the other person based on the expectation that the other will perform the specific activity to the user.

Trust is the major and critical determinant of sharing information and establishing new relationships. Trust is main component that is to be believed in the perception of social and interpersonal exchange

Figure 1. A three-tiered OSN Architecture: Client server architecture and Peer-to-peer architecture

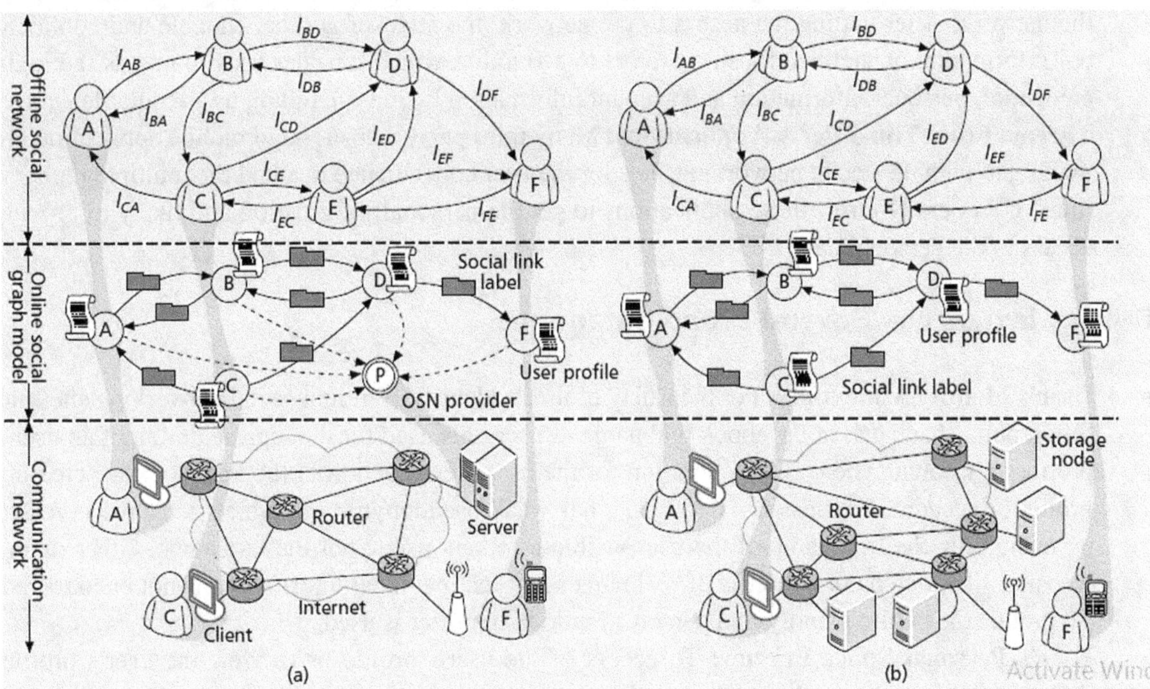

that confirm the precondition for self disclosure. Electronic commerce research has found trust to be strongly related to information disclosure. Privacy issue in the OSNs sites is generally is undefined since it maintains all records of interactions, posts, updates and preserve them for potential use in data mining and data analysis. The unwanted, illegal disclosure and improper use personal data of someone can cause hazard or damaging their lives. To the security of these data and information these OSNs sites require explicit policies and data safety techniques in order to achieve social network privacy and security goal that ensures a higher level of cyber security.

Security Issues Can Identified As

- **Identity Theft:** The identity misuse or identity theft happens when someone uses personal information of other persons without his or her knowledge for some intentional harm. It is one of the most committed cybercrime. For example a cybercriminal can access online banking of any customer through social media or application and perform the online transaction that leads to loss. Another example is that an attacker or cybercriminal who create a fake profile of HR of any organization on a social networking site and post an attractive job opening. The users may become the victims by posting their personal information and resumes. The attacker or cybercriminal can share the personal information with the third party advertising or job consultancy companies. The uncontrolled features of social networking platform provides the attackers, fraudsters, cybercriminals a factual opportunities of criminal activities.
- **Malwares, Viruses and Phishing Attacks:** These kinds of attacks can occur through the email communication, user posts, link sharing, direct messages and harmful tweets on social media. There are various methods used by the cyber-attackers to spread the malicious software on social media. The purpose of this attack is to obtain the personal information of users and get access to the network. After getting the access to the network, the attacker get the valuable and confidential information of victims. Phishing refers to a fraud in which intruder tries to access the login credential, personal information and account information by masquerading as a reputable entity.
- **Threats From Third Party Applications:** Many third party websites and mobile application are integrated with the social networking sites for the user convenience to avoid the multiple registrations. Users easily allow these applications to get the personal information and likely to provide access to the personal data.

Privacy Issues has Several Broad Categories

- **User's Identity Anonymity:** For the safety of user's identity, different social networking sites has different mechanisms. In Facebook real name or user id is used for the representation of an user's profile or account. There is no validation for the user identification in the Facebook for creating profile or account. Friendster, a dating site has weak pseudonymity in which account is created by using only the first name of the user visible to others users, not the last name. Other dating websites like Match.com, the use of real names and real personal information is not encouraged. To protect the public identity of a person a random identifier is used.
- **User's Personal Space Privacy:** To access of the user's profile or to view the user's profile, different mechanisms are there for the different online social networking sites. The OSNs like Friendster and Tribe.net have feature in which profile can be viewed publically. In Facebook, there

is customization for the view of profiles, where user can restrict other users to view his profile based on the category or group. In MySpace also users have their choice or option either they want to show their profile or not to public or friends. Except few OSN sites most of them have feature for the customization of viewing of profile or general information. LinkedIn allows users to select hiding their friend lists.

- **User's Communication Privacy**: There are various information other than personal information such as length and time of the established connection, IP address of the network, no. of profiles visited, sent and received messages and so on may also be disclosed by the OSNs in the digital space of the users. So, there is need for the privacy in these areas. To achieve this, unauthorized entities should not be granted directly by the users. This leads to the access control in terms of data privacy. Also unauthorized and unauthenticated entities should not be linked up with the multiple private information databases.
- **Authentication and Data Integrity:** Authentication and Data Integrity is the main aspect of any digital communication. Since social networking reestablishes the preexisting social relationship. So, formally OSN can be said as a digital representation of an Real Life Social(RSN) Network or Offline Social Network. There is one to one mapping in social graph to represent the RSN. Data integrity in the context of OSNs means that this consistency should be kept; that is, any attempt of deviating an online social graph model from its corresponding RSN is a kind of attack, and should be detected and corrected with appropriate mechanisms.

Generally, there are two categories of attacks on social graph:

1. Forging nodes/identities and
2. Forging social links/connections

Forging is one of the main mechanism through which many security issues can be solved. It is primary issue in the most of the OSN sites. Forging a node refers to identifying the theft or intrusion in the network. The most common example of forging is that an intruder or attacker may create a fake profile or account of any famous or important personality or celebrity or brand for their own sake or benefits or distract the attentions. Also to disturb the digital image of any OSN sites, an attacker can create multiple fake identities. Thus, legitimacy is very important to prevent all these activities. It refers to the key used between the trusted parties who are authorized and authenticate their identities. Authentication can be achieved by using an entity through which the real identity of the party can be claimed. In OSN sites availability and accountability must be satisfied to fulfill the security requirements. Availability refers to the published data that should be continuously available. Accountability refers to the misbehavior of the data should be detectable.

Classes of Adversaries

It is incomplete discussion of security if, the adversary model is not discussed. There are many categories of adversaries but in Social network context it can be of two types:

- **Inside Attackers or Intruder:** Inside attackers are those adversaries whose primarily role is to be seems as legitimate player in the OSN but in some cases malicious acts are done by them; for example, a malicious OSN provider, a malicious third-party application provider, a malicious user of the OSN, or a malicious party that has access to the network infrastructure (e.g., an eavesdropper of a wireless link or a malicious ISP).

- **External Attackers or Intruders:** An eternal intruder or attacker is not a legitimate player in the OSN, but can carry out attacks on the OSN system or on the network infrastructures used by the OSN.

Measurements and Structure of Online Social Network

In online social network, the density of the network measures the amount of interconnections between the users that is unexpectedly pursued in the all categories of network classified as: rapid growth, decline and the slow but steady growth. The members in these networks can be categorized into three groups: the singletons, the giant component and the middle region.

- **Singletons:** The users in this group who have joined the social network but never established the connectivity with other users. The degree of these users is zero. Their participation is negligible and viewed as loners.
- **Giant Component:** This group represents the users on the large scale whose connectivity is through the paths in the social network. The users in this network find themselves as strongly connected with each other either directly or indirectly. Users are very active in this group.
- **Middle Region:** This group consists of different small and isolated subgroups in which users interact with each other but not within network on the large scale. It may represents the both active and inactive users of the total fraction of users.

Data Mining vs. Privacy

For the social and marketing analysis of data collected or aggregated in the social media is a major source that provide the useful and important information regarding the evolution of a social group in the collaborative solution of problems. Data mining is also used for the optimized use of OSN services based on the specification of user's group such as interests and preferences. There may be possibilities of conflicts between Privacy requirements in OSN and the social data mining. The adversaries can attack on the personal information of the users declared on the OSN and some background knowledge that can be prevented by node anonymization. It refers to the replacement corresponding users name with meaningless random identities. On the basis of graph topology, adversaries still can discover user's identities. So to overcome this problem age perturbation is introduced in the graph for anonymization procedure.

Social Network Analytics Tools

- **Scientific Programming Tools:** Provides platform for searching, sourcing and examining text. Tools include: R(statistical programming), MATLAB(used for numeric scientific programming) and Mathematica(used for symbolic scientific programming). Python is used for the natural language detection. Apache UIMA (Unstructured Information Management Applications) is an another open-source tool through which big data analysis and data mining is done.

- **Business Toolkits:** It is the collection of tools and services used for sourcing, searching and analyzing the text for a variety of commercial uses. SAS (Sentiment Analysis Manager), a sub-domain of the SAS Text Analytics program, are used for scraping content sources, including conventional websites and social media channels, as well as internal organizational text sources, and creates reports that describe the expressed feelings of consumers, customers and competitors in real time. RapidMiner is a well-known toolkit provides an open-source community that provides data mining and machine learning tasks. Lexalytics is also a tool used for the commercial sentiment analysis engine and IBM SPSS Statistics is one of the most used programs for statistical analysis in social science.
- **Social Media Monitoring Toolkits:** These tools include sentiment analysis tools for tracking and measuring the customers review about company or its products and services. The examples of social media monitoring include: Social Mention, Amplified Analytics, Lithium Social Media Monitoring and Trackur
- **Text Analysis Toolkit:** These tools used for text analysis and NLP. Vendors in the text analysis area are: OpenAmplify and Jodange whose tools are used in sentiment analysis. . Lexalytics Sentiment Toolkits is also a powerful toolkit that performs the automatic sentiment analysis on input documents. Especially efficient when the input document is too large, but data scraping is not performed. Python NLKT(Natural Language Toolkit) is an open-source python analysis tool based Python module. Another examples of commercial software for text mining are AeroText, Attensity, Clarabridge, IBM LanguageWare, SPSS Text Analytics for Surveys, Language Computer Corporation, STATISTICA Text Miner and WordStat.
- **Social Media Analytics Platforms:** This include social media archive, data feeds, data mining and data analysis tools. They can be categorized into two categories:
    - **Social Network Media Platform:** Provides data mining and analytics on Twitter, Facebook, and other social network media.
    - **News Platforms:** Platforms such as Thomson Reuters providing news archives/feeds and associated analytics and targeting companies such as financial institutions seeking to monitor market sentiment in news.
- **Data Visualization Tools:** These tools offer business intelligence(BI) capabilities and allow users of different field to expand the approaches in Big Data. SAS Sentiment Analysis and SAS Social Media Analytics have a user-friendly interface for developing models; users can upload sentiment analysis models directly to the server in order to minimize the manual model deployment. More advanced users can use the interactive workbench to refine their models.

FUTURE RESEARCH DIRECTIONS

Research Issues on Social Network Analysis

- **Linkage-Based and Structural Analysis:** Refers to the linkage manners of the ONS so as to establish appropriate edges, links, groups and relevant fields.
- **Dynamic Analysis and Static Analysis:** Static analysis is supposed to be used in streaming networks. It changes gradually over time and batch mode analysis is done. Conversely, it is very dif-

ficult to carry out dynamic analysis for streaming networks like YouTube and Facebook due to the high speed data and large capacity.

- **Recommender System in Social Network Community**: In social network recommendations for a user are based on the ranking of her/his mutual connections among nodes in social network groups.
- **Semantic Web of Social Network:** It is the domain for information sharing and its feasible reuse over different tools and groups. Semantic web improves the facts of the fame of Semantic Web Community.
- **Aspect-Based/Feature-Based Opinion Mining:** It is the process of mining the customers review field. It is important to sum up the opinion as the review to determine the divergence of the overall reviews either positive or negative or ambiguous.
- **Topic Detection and Tracking on Social Network(TDT):** *TDT* utilizes diverse methods for determining the evolution of new topics (or events) and for tracking their successive evolvements over a period of time.
- **Natural Language Processing(NLP):** It is a field of linguistics, computer science and artificial intelligence that is related with the communication between computers and human(natural) languages. Specially, it is the method of mining significant.
- **News Analytics of Social Network:** Refers to the different quantitative and qualitative measurement of unstructured data whose attributes are novelty, sentiments and relevance.
- **Scraping:** Online data(unstructured text) collection from OSNs and other websites and also known as site scraping, web data extraction and web harvesting.
- **Sentiment Analysis on Social Network:** Refers to the application of NLP, text analytics and computational linguistics to recognize and mine biased information. It consists of following analysis:
    - Sentiment Orientation (SO)
    - Product Ratings and Reviews
    - Reviews and Ratings (RnR) Architecture
    - Aspect Rating Analysis
- **Text Analytic on Social Network:** It deals with information retrieval (IR), lexical analysis for the study of word frequency distributions, data mining techniques including link and association analysis, pattern recognition, information extraction, visualization, tagging/annotation, and predictive analytics.
- **Opinion Mining / Opinion Mining Analysis on Social Network:** Refers t, opinion/sentiment mining. It is the field of research that endeavor to build automated model to find out human sentiments and ideas from the text written in natural language.

Major Components in the Experimental Computational Environment in Social Networks

1. **Data:**
    a. **Data Storage:** For the data aggregation and data mining it provide facilities of principle data storage in specified area.
    b. **Data Protection/Security:** It can be achieved through applying certain mechanism to stop the user to access particular information.
    c. **Data Streaming:** Refers to access and combine real-time feeds and archived data for analytics.

d. **Programmable Interfaces:** APIs(application Programming Interfaces) are used for scrapping and storing certain data available that cannot be collected automatically.
e. **Data Scraping:** Method of scraping any new type of social media such as news, blogs, RSS feeds, wikis, etc.

2. **Analysis:**
a. **Analytics Dashboards:** For the deep access to the raw data non-programming interfaces are required.
b. **Programmable Analytics:** To deploy advanced data mining and other simulation using simulator tools and languages like MATLAB, Java and Python, programming interfaces are required.
c. **Stream Processing:** For the stream processing of real-time data feeds in OSNs facilities are required.
d. **High-Performance Computing:** At last the platform required to support non-programming interfaces to NoSQL databases, MapReduce/Hadoop and Grids of processors.
e. **Decentralized Analytics:** Decentralized analytics is needed to if more valuable/sensitive data owned by financial institutions, governments, retailers and other commercial organization in a highly secure way.

3. **Platform Component:** The platform comprises the following modules, which are
a. **Back-End Services:** Back-end services consists of various services which allow connections to data providers, helps in managing, executing and maintaining the data in models. Hence we can say it is the core of platform functionalities.
b. **Front-end Client APIs:** Front-end client APIs is a set of graphical and programmatic interfaces which can be used to communicate, execute and test analytical models. For the simplification of the functionalities and to define the same structure of the analytical method the programmatic interface is required. Enabling the users to visualizing the data in different format, users should be allowed to detect the concerned events and information.
c. **Connectivity Engine:** Connectivity engine is a means through which we can communicate throughout the world like data providers, financial brokers etc. The control of communication of the outside venues is controlled by a dedicated connector utilized by the platform. This is possible because the outside institutions provide either a dedicated API or uses a communication protocol such as the FIX protocol and the JSON/XML-based protocol). The platform provides a generalized interface to allow standardization of a variety of connectors.
d. **Internal Communication Layer:** Internal messaging system is used obtained from the idea of event driven programming. It is allowed in the internal layer in which analytical platform utilizes variety of events as a major medium of interaction among the various entities either for producer or consumer of events.
e. **Aggregation Database:** In the aggregation database there is fast and vigorous aggregation of data at the entry level. Different mechanisms in the aggregation of data are filtrations, reconstruction and storage of data in big data style. The analytical platforms is facilitated by the aggregation database for the storage, extraction and management of large amount of data. Along with the replay of historical data, complex functionalities are allowed to perform various analysis and evolution.

f. **Client SDK:** It is the collection of Application Programming Interfaces(APIs) through which various operations can be performed such as designing, development, implementation, testing and maintenance of the analytical model by using the Integrated Development Environment(IDEs). IDEs are used for the connection establishment at the server side also to develop and execute models for the platform required by the users.
g. **Shared Memory:** Memory usage requirement is reduced by the buffer type functionality that speeds up the delivery of temporal/ historical data to models and the analytics-related elements of the platform. The aim is to have a central point in the memory (RAM) which will manage and provide a temporal/historical data from the current point of time up to a specified number of time stamps back in history). Since the memory is shared, and kept in RAM rather than in the files or the DBMS, Therefore the access to it is instant and bounded only by the performance of hardware and no model will have to keep and manage history by itself.
h. **Model Templates:** Two generic types of models are supported by model templates: push and pull. Push specifies set of data stream which are registered during initialization, and each time a new data feed arrives to the platform execution of the model logic is triggered. This is quick, have low latency, high frequency models and the feed is achieved at the cost of small shared memory buffers. In pull it is based on a schedule templates and are executed and requested.. It has a direct connection to the big data facilities and hence can request as much historical data as necessary, at the expense of speed.

4. **System Architecture:** The following section outlines the key components of the overall system. The basic idea is that each external feed has a dedicated connectivity engine (API) and this streams data to the message bus, which handles internal communication, analytics and storage.
   a. **Connectivity Engines:** The main functionality of connectivity engines is to establish the connection between external data sources and the APIs, blogs, news feeds of OSN sites. as per the requirements of social media the APIs platform are expanding constantly and data is also increasing day by day as the number of users and their posts are increasing continuously.
   b. **Messaging Bus:** The incoming messages or data streams from various sources and connectivity engines for the representation of internal data and information across the different modules at the platform are served by the message bus as the internal communication layer. To maintain all these information and data an efficient database is maintained.
   c. **Data Warehouse:** The data warehouse refers to the collection of historical data in which terabytes of text based entries are supported. There is large variety of metadata are there which is increasing the scope in the field of research and development. Entries are organized by source and accurately time-stamped with the time of publication, as well as being tagged with topics for easy retrieval by simulation models. HBase is currently used as the platform, but Apache Cassandra or Hive may be used in future.
   d. **Simulation Manager:** Simulator manager is a web based GUI through which users can select various filters to apply the different data sets for uploading them in an external API for clients to interact with data is provided by simulation manager. All client-access to the data warehouse and the data sets uploaded by the user for aggregation with UCL's social data for particular simulation are facilitated. We can also switch between historical mode and live mode.

CONCLUSION

The social networking is of one of the important theme of many popular websites after the evolution of data science. There are many applications of online social networking that can be seen in our daily life. In the near future the online social networking will play a vital role in the online commercial and personal transactions and communication. Online social networks are consist of huge number of nodes or clusters connected to each other with a high-degree of nodes. Many research issues such as sentiment analysis, data scraping, semantic web, opinion mining etc led to the data explosion and data services for which different variety of software tools are required. Social media analytics platforms are used in sentimental analysis. Many Data mining tools and technique are also required in the social networking data analysis tools and services. Privacy and security is also important concern. Various aspects and strategies for maintaining the security and privacy are user's identity anonymity, user's personal space privacy, user's communication privacy. and authentication and data integrity. The impact of social networking in everyday life can be easily noticed for the people of every age group and almost every sectors and domains ranging from scientific research to administration, education to corporate sector, governance to entertainment, business analysis and economic to public administration etc. Graph theory is the main technique applied in the social network for the representation of social relations in online social networking that involve with social networking data analysis tools and techniques. But still there is scope in future for research and development for many domains of social networking that will provide good and bright opportunities business, research, academics and many other areas. title should be "Conclusion", not "Conclusions". Provide discussion of the overall coverage of the chapter and concluding remarks.

ACKNOWLEDGMENT

This work is supported by many intellectual persons. I would like to express my deep gratitude towards the Mr. Krishna Murari, Registrar of Netaji Subhas Institute of Technology, Patna, Bihar, India for providing good academic environment. Dr. Prabhat Kumar, HoD, Department of Computer Science & Engineering, National Institute of Technology Patna, India, Dr. J. P. Singh, Assistant Professor, Department of Computer Science & Engineering, National Institute of Technology Patna, India for his motivation and inspiration. I would also take this opportunity to express my deep sense of thankfulness to Dr. S. B. Singh, Principle, of Netaji Subhas Institute of Technology, Patna, Bihar, India and Mrs. Soni Sweta, HoD and all Teaching Faculties of Department of Computer Science & Engineering, Netaji Subhas Institute of Technology, Patna, Bihar, India. In addition, I would also like to thank my parents and friends for their support and motivation. throughout the entire course of time. At last but not least I am grateful to IGI Global publication for giving this opportunity to explore my knowledge and ideas in Social Networking.

REFERENCES

Batrinca, B., & Treleaven, P. C. (2015). Social media analytics: A survey of techniques, tools and platforms, *Open access at springer. AI & Society*, *30*(1), 89–116. doi:10.1007/s00146-014-0549-4

Dwyer, C., Hiltz, S. R., & Passerini, K. (2007). Trust and Privacy Concern Within Social Networking Sites: A Comparison of Facebook and MySpace. *Proceedings: Americas Conference on Information System.*

Handrick, D. (n.d.). *Complete History of Social Media: Then and Now.* Retrieved from https://smallbiztrends.com/2013/05/the-complete-history-of-social-media-infographic.html

Miles, , Huberman, & Lotto. (1986). Qualitative Data Analysis: A Sourcebook of New Methods. *Educational Evaluation and Policy Analysis*, *8* (3), 329-331.

Mislove, A., Macron, M., Gummadi, K. P., & Druschel, P. (n.d.). Measurement and Analysis of Online Social Networks. *Proceedings of the 7th ACM SIGCOMM conference on Internet measurement.* DOI: doi:10.1145/1298306.1298311

Zhang, Sun, Zhu, & Fang. (2010). Privacy and Security for Online Social Networks: Challenges and Opportunities. *IEEE Network*, *24*(4). DOI: 10.1109/MNET.2010.5510913

Chapter 3
Social Implications of E-Government

Rimjhim
Indian Institute of Technology Patna, India

Vijay Kumar
Steel Authority of India Limited, India

ABSTRACT

With increased ICT (Information and Communication Technology), the day-to-day life is shifting online. E-government is one of the crucial parts of the developing world. This chapter contains a detailed introduction of e-government, which includes a broad definition, pillars, goals, stages, delivery models of e-government, advantages, and disadvantages. The difference between e-governance and e-government is also clarified. This chapter clears up the concept of e-government and how e-government can have impact on society. Next is the background section, which covers the research and surveys done by UN (United Nations) and other researchers in order to monitor and analyze the developments of e-government across different countries, social implications of e-government, requirements to develop a robust e-government, future scope of the e-government, etc. Finally, the direct and indirect implications of e-government are stated along with a short review of the status of e-government across a few countries.

INTRODUCTION

Recent advancements have yielded many technologies, equipments, instruments, etc. and the same have evolved advanced skills, techniques, short-cuts, etc. And these all together have directly optimized the way of performing an action (job, service, task, etc.). One live example of such optimized action is E-government. E-government is one of the crucial parts of E-services. Services which use ICT (Information and Communication Technology) is termed as E-services. ICT is being vigorously used in various applications and services. All the E-services have not only improved the quality of services provided to the consumers but has also eased the task of providing services and getting services.

The world has witnessed many changes and advancements with much faster pace in the last few decades. All these have been possible due to improvement in ICT (Information and Communication

DOI: 10.4018/978-1-5225-5097-6.ch003

Technology). Use of mobile phones, internet, clouds, computers and other digital media are encapsulated in Information and Communication Technology. Today's life rotates around ICT at every level, be it micro or macro. At macro level, it is used around the globe by many MNCs, large industries and firms, governments, etc. of which we are a part either as a consumer or employee. At individual level, ICTs are used in most of our day-to-day activities, be it in contacting people, in cash transactions, in booking tickets, getting governmental subsidies, etc. The ICTs have diminished the distances between various parts of the world which subsequently, has made the whole world appear in one screen. The use of ICT by government to deliver various governmental services to people at their fingertip is called e-government. Government services includes almost all the services being provided directly or indirectly by the government. Online applications for getting government identification cards, passports, visas, online release of government data and even online railway ticketing system are a part of e-government. Nowadays, there are online portals for direct interaction between government and public. These all are included in services provided by E-Government.

E-government is no less than a revolution which has led to more transparency, less corruption, faster delivery of services, faster dissemination of information, etc. This is done by minimum middlemen involvement and maximum use of information and communication technologies such as internet, mobile, clouds, etc. E-government is like having a virtual government office which will provide all the services in an easy way. Government office with lots and lots of papers and piles of files are made available on palmtops and laptops (ICT devices). It was a time that for getting a government identification card, it was required to visit the government office with all the documents for number of times. Now, due to e-government the services are made available on our computer or mobile screen. Time and cost of commuting are relaxed along with many other implicit easiness. A very cliché example can be of a man from a village who needs a service from the government. Since, the government headquarters are in main town, the man takes a bus and reaches the office. After reaching the office, he has to look for the exact room of his concern. In the concerned room, as usual there is a long queue, he waits for his turn and finally when his turn is about to come he notices that other people have brought their photos also. He doubts whether he has brought it or not and after verifying, comes the worst part of his day. He has forgotten to bring his photograph. And for now, there are only two options with him either he can go back to home and bring a photograph, or he can go to a photo studio for a photograph. If he goes home, he cannot come back today as home is too far and if goes to a photo studio, they will give the photographs after two days. This is an example of redial one can have, and this can take place many number of times till the delivery of the service. This scenario is from perspective of common people. For government, it becomes really very difficult to manage all the documents and formalities. The huge repository of files, documents, letters, etc. are hectic to handle and no one can be made accountable for the faults. There can be many human errors, discrepancies, delay, misplacements, etc. Additionally, manual verification, manual signature on each document, manual creation of each and every document can be extremely cumbersome. Many fraudulent, brokers, miscreants are there who always misconduct and adds to already existing anxiety. Government is a very large body and handling such a large system manually can be erroneous. This example clearly manifests the hardships both government and citizen can probably face for getting and providing a government service. Now, with advent of e-government, any individual who wants a service, can directly visit the concerned website, check for the required documents, upload these documents online, few of them can be verified instantly and rest takes a bit time. The service is delivered within specified time, if not, there are provisions to make online complains. Apart from this, there are online help centers which provide 24x7 assistance. In this system, record keeping is much easier. No manual intervention is required, records are safe, no queues, no waiting, no need to travel, no missing documents and no overhead of carrying along your documents. Thus, e-government no doubt substantially eases the process of both giving service and taking service.

Government has tried empowering people with the help of ICT. Best example is JAM trinity in India where J stands for Jan Dhan account, A stands for Aadhar card and M stands for Mobile. Social inclusion was achieved via Jan Dhan account, where every household was to have one bank account linked with Aadhaar number. With this government tried to transfer subsidies directly to the household which has resulted in minimal leakage of subsidies. This has resulted in targeted delivery of services within specified time limit. Aadhaar card has helped in overcoming duplication of identities by miscreants, instant verification of authenticity, etc. There are many more benefits of e-government that we will see as we move forth in this chapter.

E-Government and E-Governance

The stimulating factor for evolution of e-government is e-commerce. The success of e-commerce in USA, UK, canada has encouraged the inclusion of the letter "e" in government. The inclusion of "e" in any term stands for "electronics". E-Government is often confused with E-Governance but there is difference between these two. Sheridan & Riley (2006) have highlighted the major differences between the two. They state that e-government is a part of e-governance. E-Government is using ICT for various governmental services. E-government is a system while e-governance is a functionality. E-Governance is the act of governing and being governed by use of ICT. Thus, e-government is a one-way communication while e-governance is two way communication. The use of ICT in governance has made the task of governing more efficient and effective. There are several enhancements which has sprouted with e-governance which are stated further in this chapter. Governance actually stands as a connecting bridge between government and people.

Pillars of E-Government

The e-government implementation in different countries act as a symptom of development and progress. For a successful implementation of e-government there are a few aims and requirements which can be combinedly coined as Pillars of e-government. According to Bataineh & Shanab (2016) and Kolachalam (2012) there are four pillars of e-government.

1. **Leadership and Vision:** E-government is all about transforming the relationship between government and the governed in gradual way. Government should develop citizen-centric e-government models, benefiting citizens and businesses most, while cost saving is concomitant. But when e-government models are implemented in any established setup, enterprises face following problems:
    a. Staffs in department are reluctant to accept the change as they have to learn about the process afresh and also they are not benefited from it in any way. So, staff needs to be motivated for the same.
    b. They also fear loss of jobs because machines will take their place, which is only partially true. This myth should be removed from their minds.
    c. They are also worried about the additional income that they were accruing due to bribes being paid by individuals for getting jobs done.

For resolving these issues, dedicated and committed leadership is required. So that leaders can foresee the upcoming scenarios, motivate other employees and bring innovations are required.

2. Governance Perspective
3. **Integration and Collaboration:** E-government is not just about providing computers in offices and automating manual records and existing system. Rather, it is about re-engineering the relationship between government and citizens in a completely new realm. New set of work culture, rules and regulations, procedure, etc. needs to be defined. This re-engineering of process is done at two levels:
    a. Front-end
    b. Back-end

    At the front end, the number of offices one needs to visit is reduced, there is more transparency, timely services, etc. While at the back-end, more and more departments are interconnected due to simplified and more connected organizational structure, adding more flexibility to the process of delivery of services to the end users.
4. **Technology and Infrastructure:** Technology and infrastructure are the backbone for any e-government model. For establishing an e-government, a country must have strong stand on technology and infrastructure. The investments, benefits and implementation level of e-government are completely dependent on the available technology and infrastructure. There is a minimum required amount of technology which need to be insured before implementing an e-government. At the same time the reachability of the technology and infrastructure to common man should also be ensured.

Goal of E-Government

The basic aim of e-government is to provide faster and hassle-free services to citizens which would reduce government expenditure. These are inbuilt with few more aims such as narrowing the gap between government and citizens, eliminate corruption, increase transparency and to eradicate several other bottlenecks hindering development of a country. Few goals are described as following:

1. **To Develop an Informed Society:** Information is power and giving this power to the common people is one of the aims of e-government. For every government schemes, services, policies, etc. common people have the right to know even the minute details. This results in a well informed and empowered citizen. As a result of e-government, preliminary information is always available with the person beforehand of getting any service. All the requirements, including service delivery time, service cost are open to all. There is no third person in middle. This openness not only ensures ease but also helps in empowering people at every level. Services are meant for the people, they need to know every details of the services including which department of government is responsible of providing which services and whether the charges for services are appropriate or not.
2. **To Increase Citizen Participation and Interaction:** The government functionalities and decisions must be equally decided by citizen and government both. This reflects actual democracy where for each event, citizen and government participation both co-exists. With e-government, the system becomes informed and encourages equal participation by both government and citizen. The level of participation increases with e-government, as for participation there is no need of physical availability or any hardships. The participation can be done by a single click on computers or mobiles.

3. **Transparency in Governing Process:** Transparency means that the governing process, their aim, need, expenditure, procedure, etc. should be open to all. Anyone can have access to all such information. The transparency is promoted so as to make the government corruption free. People have right to know about the actions taken for them or actions related to them. This also helps in pre-measurement of pros and cons of all the policies, schemes, etc. This not only help in making better plan but also exposes government to citizen and vice-versa. The idea of transparent and open government policies is not new but due to e-government it has become easy to ensure transparency. The documents and files are available online, all the policies, fund flow, schemes, etc. are centralized and synchronized. The schemes, reforms started by local government are also centralized and synchronized at country and world level. This is not confined within a country but the same is happening round the globe. This helps in corruption free and smooth running of government.
4. **To Reduce Reaction Time of Government:** The common problem of government being indifferent to their public can be resolved by e-government. For the schemes and services of government a format and rules are made which are same globally and this helps avoiding delays in services delivery. For example, the time limit to issue some license is fixed and government has to abide by the limits. Moreover, the service providing and processing all the formalities for providing services has become very fast and easy due to e-government. Thus, the overall outcome is fast delivery of services. There are many more addition technologies like Twitter and facebook which compels government to be effective and on time. The aim of e-government is like "being online and not in line"
5. **To Make Government Accountable:** It is the responsibility of government to justify their every action and take responsibility in time of need. since, rules, schemes, laws, costs, etc. are predefined, open and same for all. For any discrepancies, government can be made accountable. For any unpredictable situation or for any emergency, government has some responsibility. E-government aids in making government more responsible and making people more concerned of their rights and .

Stages of E-Government

There are different number and types of stages for e-government. A five stage model is quite famous for a complete cycle of an e-services by e-government. They are as follows:

1. **Publication of Information:** This refers to the publication of important information online. A preliminary publication consists of information for rules and regulation, schemes, forms etc. This stage varies for different countries. Basically for a developing country it consists of only preliminary publication and for a developed country this stage come up with launch of a well-developed and informative and interactive website. Information being published on the websites should be of daily use to common people and it should be in local language, so that information being published is easily conceived by people. Various government agencies should publish their basic information on websites.
2. **Interactivity:** This is an intermediate stage for connecting users and service providers. Government should consider public opinion for policy making and for establishing a direct interaction session this stage helps. Reviews of all stakeholders should be considered while designing and improving the efficiency of the system. Interaction can be in the form of complaints, suggestions, public

forum meetings, etc. This is the stage where service providers and service seekers interact with each other.

3. **Electronic Delivery of Documents:** This is an additional facility provided by e-government. There is no need to go to post office and collect the documents. Digital documents are delivered which guarantees deliveries on holidays also. The digital deliveries are fast and reliable. Digital receipt can also be generated with proper digital authentication. The digital document includes intermediate documents as well as final documents also. Intermediate document can be payment receipt, application receipt, etc. and final document can be the services which are served in form of document like issuing a government card.
4. **Processing Services:** Processing services has many parts such as verification of documents, payments, and offline processing, etc. There are many documents which are created and verified online. While a few requires an offline verification or processing. It depends on the type of service whether the processing will be online, offline or both. For payments there are online payments system which are very secure and fast. Payments are also verified and for this also similar processing scenario exists as document verification. Apart from this the system aids with proper tracking system which contain all the information about the status of processing.
5. **Electronic Delivery of Services:** The online outlet for delivery of services is available to the remotest place. This is the final stage where services are delivered online. This includes only soft- services like documents, id-cards, notices, warrants etc. For the hard services which cannot be delivered like construction of any hospital or imprisonment of criminals, etc. notices, decisions, updates are issued online.

Delivery Models of E-Government

The e-government has many goals and inclusion of ICT takes place at various levels and between various entities. E-government provides service to many entities and even to their own employees also. Sometimes, the government also receives services. With focus on the entities taking services from e-government, delivery models are there which represents the variance of the service providers and service seekers. There are basically five delivery models of e-government, G2B(Government to Business) & B2G(Business to Government), C2G(Citizen to Government) & G2C(Government to Citizen), G2E(Government to Employees), G2G(Government to Government) and Non-Profit to Government(N2G) & Government to Non-profit(G2N) .

G2B and B2G

This model includes all kind of information and services exchange between government and businesses. This kind of information flow is bidirectional i.e. government are sometimes clients of businesses and vice-versa. Government also seeks many type of services from businesses and vice-versa The development of electronic marketplace, e-transactions and e-procurements are covered in this model. This also includes tender procurements, business of electronic goods and services. Often these are supported by online meetings, video conferencing, etc. and all the information are made available online. Electronic auctions and e-learning are few examples which are run under this model.

G2C and C2G

The G2C model is for providing various services to the public. The administration has a role in G2C model. The various kind of services refers to issue of various documents by government, online release of various information regarding schemes and bills of government. In C2G, people can give their feedbacks, suggestions and views online. Apart from this electronic voting, electronic complains, tax payments, etc. are also a part of this model. This model is the base for creating an interacting, impartial, convenient platform for bringing government close to the citizens.

G2E

This model refers to the internal communication and exchange of information between employees of the government. This facilitate fast and easy processing and management within the organization. All the internal information, tenders, notices, letters, bills, tenders, etc. are made available online for the internal access. There are two kinds of information with the government, one which is open to all and one which is specific. Everyone doesn't need or have right to access all the information. The appropriate specified information is made available according to the requirement and accessibility. For internal management of finance, employees, services, etc. this model plays a vital role. This also include several kind of employee specific managements tasks such as leave management, service allocation management, knowledge management, training management, salary management, etc. This model refers to an e-office which is a fast, easy and online miniature of a real government office.

G2G

This model refers to the dissipation of information between agencies, organization, and various department of the government. Usually, for any government there exist a hierarchy of governance level. For example, there are different government bodies at district level, state level and country level. Within a government there exist various departments also like department of railways, department of education, etc. There are a lot of services which passes various levels and various departments. Additionally, there are information accessibility constraints also. For managing and processing such affairs within government comes under this model. This is the model which supports in making a corruption free government. The schemes, funds, status information are easily available. An example can be court system. There are cases which are transferred to from high court to supreme court, for such cases both the courts must have proper and detailed information about each and every processing, documentations and records. This model aids in proper flow for the same.

N2G and G2N

This model is for nonprofit organizations, political and social organizations, etc. This model can be confused with G2B and B2G but the latter is mainly with the purpose of profit and the former is for the purpose of welfare. This can include social reforming organizations, charitable organization, cultural organizations. The main purpose of non-profitable organizations is welfare it may be civic, social, cultural, etc. There is no intention of selling and purchase of service. Ethics are more important than assets. The type of information which such organizations need and the documents are different from the business organizations.

BACKGROUND

In the digital era, no doubt e-government is sprouting very fast and countries across the world are motivated to follow this. In fact, the count of countries following e-government has increased substantially. Moreover, e-governance and its implications has directly or indirectly become a major research area. Since, e-government is different for different countries, so, there are different researches in terms of different countries. The requirement, bottlenecks, aspects, etc. are different for different countries. Chen et. al (2017) has done a detailed research on administrative aspect of e-government in China. The e-government as has actually helped a lot in improving administration in China. The paper details how technology is reforming the government and what challenges have aroused out of technology. Hackney & Tassabehji (2016) has done a detailed analysis on efficiency of e-government from citizen perspective in developing countries, special focus in on Africa. They concluded that time and cost are the major factors which attract citizens to use e-government. For measuring the factors they have done empirical analysis. Norris & Reddick has done analysis on behaviour of local e-government in USA. They have found that the growth of local e-government was not as predicted by other researchers. They presented the factors which has lead to such a difference.

UN E-Government Surveys

The United Nations(UN) surveys at regular intervals on the trends of e-government all over the world. There are 9 state-of-art surveys on e-government conducted by UN. In all the surveys, UN publish a list of top 10 countries with EGDI (e-government development index), which is shown in Table.1. They publish a development report which highlights the major advances and requirements for future. The summary of all the surveys are stated as follow:

2001

This was the first survey on e-government. According to this survey of (United Nations [UN], 2001), the idea of e-government originated in USA. This was just a beginning and it was the time when idea of using vast ICT in governance was proposed. A research was done to learn the aspects of ICT in governance. Several analyses were done to check if inclusion of ICT can improve or aid in governance.

2003

This survey was a bit advanced than that done in 2001. According to (United Nations [UN] 2003), it was already known that e-governance will certainly help in numerous ways. The focus was on requirements for implementation of e-government. No doubt a very strong infrastructure of ICT is required to make it successful. For countries not having developed ICT, the implementation was almost impossible. Even if for a country, having developed ICT, it was not in reach of every common people. For underdeveloped and developing country establishment of e-government was out of scope. Additionally, they also surveyed on how willingly people across the world are going to accept this e-government. The motivation of e-governance was increasing people participation in governance.

2004

As stated by (United Nations [UN], 2004), there was a wide variance between countries according to status and standard of ICT. The reasons for these variance were analyzed. Every country has different access opportunities and digital divide. A taxonomy of countries according to access opportunities was released. The future focus was to remove the bottlenecks in access opportunities and digital equivalence. Efforts were made to track progress of ICT across different countries of the world.

2005

In survey done by (United Nations [UN], 2005), the links between e-government and development were explored. Emphasis was given on citizen-government partnership in order to establish *social inclusive government*. The e-government in developing countries was analyzed. It was found that few developing countries having developed ICT would obviously benefit from e-government but most of the developing countries were still striving for basic societal needs. These countries needs a technological revolution along with few societal reforms to benefit from e-government.

2008

According to the (United Nations [UN], 2008) survey of e-governance status of different countries across the world, it was observed that success or failure of e-government was more a technology issue than a societal issue. It somehow proved that e-government in a country will always will successful if the technology of the country is developed.

For establishing a successful e-government it is required to develop ICT of the country rather than motivating people and society. Additionally, the world was looking forward to a more integrated and automated e-government. Efforts were taken to integrate e-government to back-office.

2010

By this time, e-governance was working well in many countries. The (United Nations [UN], 2010) survey emphasized the role of e-government during financial crisis. The transparency and more integrated government-citizen relationship was key to gain people's trust during financial crisis. This was the sixth survey and by this time there was a significant and markable development of online services. The same was observed in many developing countries also. It was found that cost of technological infrastructure development was a hindrance in development of e-governance.

2012

Institutional framework for e-government was examined in (United Nations [UN], 2012) survey, and was found that for overcoming internal barriers, a national coordinating authority should be there. The countries should promote more online users to make e-government more effective. More participation from the people should be encouraged. In fact, e-government was viewed as a powerful tool to combat the issue of digital inequality and digital divide.

2014

The (United Nations [UN], 2014) survey, included survey of maximum number of countries regarding e-government. This was themed with multi-faceted challenges of the society. It was pre-decided that there should be sustainable development and here aspects of e-government for the same was addressed. Inclusion of mobile and other media was also addressed to assist multichannel delivery and tracking of services. Focus was given to open e-government data to induce transparency. The challenges faced by different countries and efforts taken by them to establish a sound e-government was also emphasized.

2016

The (United Nations [UN], 2016) survey report, is the latest survey report, the world has today. An increase was observed in number of countries using e-government. One-stop platform to provide and access public services was now available with many countries. In 2003, only 45 countries were having facility of one-stop platform but for now the count has increased to 90. Along with count the qualities (effectiveness, user-friendliness) of one-stop platform has also increased. In 2003, only 33 countries provided facility of online transactions but now the count is 148. Many countries make their government data open to all in order to make system more informative. The count of countries making data open is 128. The developed countries were making advances in ICT and same was observed with few developing countries also.

E-Government Development Index

E-government Development Index(EGDI) was developed by UN to measure the national e-government capabilities and readiness to adopt e-government. This index is used by government, researchers, policy makers, national and international authorities to get a deeper understanding of benchmarks and growth. The index is based on expert analysis of national websites and strategies used by e-government to deliver services. EGDI is a combined index for three other indices named as online service index(OSI), telecommunication infrastructure index(TI) and human capital index(HCI). These three indices are explained as following:

Online service Index: This is a measure of quality of online services. The quality can be measured in various terms like in formativeness of a site, types of provided services, feedback given by the people, etc.

Telecommunication Infrastructure Index: This index mainly deals with the number of people involved with ICT. This includes count of mobile users, count of internet users, count of telephone line subscribers, etc. per hundred citizens. OSI measures the capability of government to provide e-governance and TI measures the capability of citizens to avail the e-government services.

Human Capital index: This index measures a compound of literacy rate, number of enrollment in primary, secondary and tertiary education.

SOCIAL IMPLICATIONS

E-government bridges the gap between society and government. This makes the communication between government and citizens easier, more regular and more authenticated. Since e-government is a part crucial part of social it has direct social implications. It can have many other implications also like on economy, government. etc. Society is epitome of all other factors like economy, government, etc. So, social implications can be broadly termed as a integration of all other implications. In this section, social implications are explained which includes all other implications.

- **Democratization:** Democracy is a form of government, which is elected by the people and for the people. The e-government ensures that government and people are more close and interact more to each other. Since for providing public services the platform is same for every citizen, the equality to all is ensured. Many time for getting services the remote places lag but the e-government overcomes this limitation. This also support Rural Communities Empowerment as ruler society sometimes are isolated from the government policies and schemes. But e-government reduces the chance of isolation.
- **Transparency:** Due to availability of online information and online services. The government schemes are more visible and transparent. People know the details of every scheme and government knows the conduct of people. The transparency helps in combating corruption. The fund flow is clear, schemes are transparent, records are well maintained. These all aid in combating corruption.
- **Effectiveness and Efficiency of Service Delivery:** Services are electronically delivered and thus they are fast and effective. Record keeping and tracking are much easier. The services availing is convenient.
- **Modernization**: Development of ICT is a symptom of modernization. People using more electronics and getting globally closer is a sign of modernization. For establishing an e-government a strong ICT need to be developed. Government is paying heed to improve the existing ICT in a country. Public services are basic requirements and availability of these services online gives a exposure to the people about ICT.
- **Cheaper Delivery of Services:** This is more an economic implication. The cost are fixed, same for all and also have reduced. There can be initial hike in the costs due to electronic implementation but the cost reduces with time. There are cases where despite getting low cost for online services people prefer offline service. This can outcome of either low penetration of ICT in a county or fear of privacy and security issues.
- **Control Over Government Expenditure:** The open to all paperless offices and centrally authenticated budgets, cost and payment systems has empowered common man to have a control over the expenditures of the government. A proper tracking system exists which provides necessary information to the citizen.
- **Growth of Tax Revenue:** Insufficient tax collection is very common problem in many countries. E-government has somehow improved the number of tax payees. The *e-SAT,* system of Mexico helps in collection of around 80% of the tax.

All the social implications are no doubt positive but these implications face lots of challenges. The challenges are elaborated later in this chapter.

Advantages of E-Government

The fundamental insight of e-government for citizens is availability of government and its services on any electronic device such as mobile, laptop, etc. and similarly for government its availability of citizens on any electronic media. There are countless advantages that e-government can deliver, some of them

Table 1. A table showing E-development index from UN Survey from year 2003 to 2016

2016		2014		2012		2010		2008		2005	
United Kingdom	0.9193	Republic of Korea	0.9462	Republic of Korea	0.9283	Republic of Korea	0.8785	Sweden	0.9157	United States	0.9062
Australia	0.9143	Australia	0.9103	Netherlands	0.9125	United States of America	0.851	Denmark	0.9134	Denmark	0.9058
Republic of Korea	0.8915	Singapore	0.9076	UK and Northern Ireland	0.8960	Canada	0.8448	Norway	0.8921	Sweden	0.8983
Singapore	0.8828	France	0.8938	Denmark	0.8889	UK and Northern Ireland	0.8147	United States	0.8644	United Kingdom	0.8777
Finland	0.8817	Netherlands	0.8897	United States	0.8687	Netherlands	0.8097	Netherlands	0.8631	Republic of Korea	0.8727
Sweden	0.8704	Japan	0.8874	France	0.8635	Norway	0.802	Republic of Korea	0.8317	Australia	0.8679
Netherlands	0.8659	United States of America	0.8748	Sweden	0.8599	Denmark	0.7872	Canada	0.8172	Singapore	0.8503
New Zealand	0.8653	United Kingdom of Great Britain and Northern Ireland	0.8695	Norway	0.8593	Australia	0.7863	Australia	0.8108	Canada	0.8425
Denmark	0.851	New Zealand	0.8644	Finland	0.8505	Spain	0.7516	France	0.8038	Finland	0.8231
France	0.8456	Finland	0.8449	Singapore	0.8474	France	0.751	United Kingdom	0.7872	Norway	0.8228

are already highlighted above. The e-government, is not a reform made by government to improve the society, but it is a revolution, in which both government and people are actor and audience both. Both of them get numerous advantages and numerous challenges. This is a mutually cooperative revolution which runs on a balanced wheels of government and citizen. The advantages of e-government also has two aspects, one from aspect of government and one from aspect of people.

- **Aspect of People:** It is more convenient to get services from the government. Convenience can be measured in terms of time required, cost, speed, overheads, etc. All the functionalities of government has become very transparent, which ensures a corruption free environment. In a nutshell, it is easier to receive satisfactory service from government.
- **Aspect of Government:** It helps in direct and easy interaction with the common people, ensuring a more democratic environment. Its very easy and less time taking to provide services to the citizens. It s easy to handle functionalities of different government employees also. In a nutshell, it is easier to provide satisfactory service to the people.

Disadvantages and Challenges of E-Government

The disadvantages and challenges differs across different countries. For example, there are many developing countries where Internet and electronics are not easily accessible by common people. But for developed countries accessibility is not an issue. There are many more disadvantages like this e-government creates huge amount of unemployment, the services can suffer from privacy breach etc.

According to infoDev (2002), Challenges and Opportunities of E-Government Implementation can be enumerated as following:

- **Infrastructure Development:** For implementation of e-government, basic infrastructure is required at the initial stage which advances with passage of time. Countries has worked hard to get this basic infrastructure immediately, in particular, developing countries. These new basic infrastructure projects have to be compatible with already existing infrastructure with which it will work in tandem. States have developed various models for developing these infrastructure projects like outsourcing, PPP model, BOT model, etc. Where infrastructure cannot be developed due to feasibility constraints, local communities are involved for faster delivery of services.
- **Law and Public Policy:** For smooth implementation of ICT in various government agencies, new laws have to be enacted and existing laws have to be amended. This should be done only after consulting all stakeholders such that conflict doesn't arise at later stage. Roles and responsibilities of various authorities have to be delineated.
- **Digital Divide:** The gap between people and regions that have access to ICT and those that don't or have little access is termed as digital divide. The benchmark for deciding this digital divide has changed with time, for example earlier it used to be landline and then mobile and now internet. This digital divide is mainly due to poor penetration of ICT amongst regions like rural and urban, class like educated and uneducated, poor and rich to name a few. This digital divide can be addressed by digital literacy campaigns such that even the remotest area is not left behind. For e-Literacy, governments have to make holistic plan to reach out to people and make them e-literate. This e-literacy campaigns have to be in vernacular language and it should be lucid one. Pictorial representations and videos should be used wherever possible for teaching. Special target groups like women, old age people, etc. should be targeted in particular, so that no one is left behind in this effort to bridge the digital divide gap.
- **Trust:** In day to day e-government application, there is exchange of personal information of an individual between different agencies. When it comes to sharing of information to government agencies, a person is concerned about the confidentiality of the shared information and about its misuse. For trust building, government must provide suitable safeguards to prevent data misuse. These safeguards can be in the form of laws and rules. Standard operating procedure should be followed while accessing personal information of any individual. Limiting the access of information by an authority can help in preventing misuse of any information. This privacy issue should be tackled by embedding a privacy system in the design of e-government system.

In this connected age of technology, there are possibilities wherein individual data may be hacked by miscreants for personal gain. So, to protect it, there should be a strong framework for protecting this data from being misused illegally. Data collection should be minimum to ensure that not much data is divulged in case of hacking.

- **Transparency:** Transparency is the sign of a robust system. Transparency makes the system stronger by making people aware about the working structure of the system. Wherever transparency is greater, the system self-evolve through feedback mechanism and results in robust and more trustworthy system. Transparency can be brought about by dissemination of information related to the service.
- **Interoperability:** An e-government system should have an interoperability feature so that same set of data can be used by various departments. Data storage should be centralised so that individual does not have to approach concerned authority for providing data for availing services each time. This would prevent repetition of efforts by government agencies to collect information.
- **Records Management:** Digitizing records reduces the space required to maintain them. These digitized records can be accessed easily any time. Dissemination of information is also fast. The data should be organised so as to be useful, so that searches across set of datas can be made easily and efficiently without wastage of time.
- **Education and Marketing:** E-government services are designed to help people in getting better and timely services. But providing services is not enough, they should be aware of how to get access to the service online. For this basic reason, authorities first need to educate people and market their product. They should teach people about the benefits they would accrue by using the e-government services.
- **Cost Structure:** E-government models should be designed within the available fund and should not be budget deficit. As e-government models replaces the existing system, they should help government in saving penny. This would encourage government to switch to ICT. Savings accrued due to implementation of e-government models can be used to make people e-literate, hold awareness campaigns, etc.
- **Benchmarking:** Benchmarking helps to improve the e-government efficiency as a whole because there are predetermined targets which are to be achieved within stipulated time. There should be a feedback mechanism which would help the e-government service to self improve and lead to more efficiency . This benchmarking could also help government to work more like e-commerce which are more dedicated to timely and speedy availability of services.

E-Government in Different Countries

In spite of the fact that for developing countries there are many challenges to implement e-government but for developing countries these services are more beneficial. Many research have been done to analyse the scope of e-government in different countries and it has been proved that for developing countries e-government will be more beneficial. In many countries of Africa, government has already started its implementation.

E-Government in India

India is poised to become a global leader, and for achieving this goal it is taking every possible step to lead. Global integration of Indian economy in the year 1991 is its biggest example. And now with the integration of ICT in every facade of the government be it administration, police, judiciary, legislation, etc. Indian government is trying to integrate its various departments under one roof with the help of ICT, so as to monitor day to day governmental activities in real time. This has lead to better and timely delivery of services where officials are made accountable for missing target. With ICT, things have become much easier where paper work involved has reduced drastically leading to lesser time for processing any service request. It has also reduced corruption due to least number of intermediaries involved.

E-Government in USA

USA is already a developed country, time for worrying about the availability of ICT has gone. The e-government is already working and people participation is also not an issue. What is going on these days in USA is management of technology and development of more advanced secure technology. It has been observed in USA, that investment done on technology of e-government was underutilized, so, they are focusing on proper management of investment in technology. Moreover, there can be lots of security and privacy issues, the USA government is trying to develop more secure and safe e-government system.

E-Government in China

The main focus of chinese e-government is to reduce the gap between rural and urban areas. Other than this they are trying to improve their transparency level to empower citizen and administrative process. Being a developing country, it is still struggling for many basic necessities of e-government like infrastructure development, reachability to common man, etc.

FUTURE RESEARCH DIRECTIONS

The world is developing day by day and so is the e-government. With the development in technologies, living standard, economic standard, etc the research area in terms of e-government is also changing. Earlier, the researchers focused on need of technology, easiness in governing, readiness of the people to accept e-government, etc. Now there is a shift of research, researchers are analyzing e-government from people perspective, implementation of e-government with minimum cost, proper management of e-government. The data generated by e-government can create security and privacy issues, the focus is on creating a robust security system. The e-government and inclusion of new and sophisticated technology has attracted researchers from computer science, information technology and electronics also. They focus on technology part of the e-government. The e-government generates a huge data and this data has attracted data scientists for their research as these data can be useful in analyzing the trends and predicting the future trends. And lastly, due its vast and overwhelming impact on social and economics of a country department of sociology, humanities, economics are also attracted a lot. They focus on e-government in terms of societal and economic impacts.

REFERENCES

Bataineh, L., Bataineh, L., Abu-Shanab, E., & Abu-Shanab, E. (2016). How perceptions of E-participation levels influence the intention to use E-government websites. *Transforming Government: People. Process and Policy*, *10*(2), 315–334.

Bhatnagar, S. (2003). *The economic and social impact of e-government.* A background paper for UN-DESA publication: E-government the citizens and the state: Debating governance in the information age. World Public Sector Report.

Chen, Y., Dawes, S. S., & Chen, S. (2017, June). E-government Support for Administrative Reform in China. In *Proceedings of the 18th Annual International Conference on Digital Government Research* (pp. 329-335). ACM. doi:10.1145/3085228.3085269

Fang, Z. (2002). E-government in digital era: concept, practice, and development. *International Journal of the Computer, the Internet and Management, 10*(2), 1-22.

Hackney, R. A., & Tassabehji, R. (2016). *Advancing e-Government in Developing Countries: a quantitative analysis towards citizen-cenric public services within sub-Saharan Africa.* Academic Press.

infoDev. (2002). *The E-government Handbook for developing countries.* A Project of Infodev and The Center for Democracy and Technology.

Kolachalam, S. (2012). An Overview of E-government. *Economia Aziendale Online*, (1), 1-12.

Norris, D. F., & Reddick, C. G. (2013). Local e-government in the United States: Transformation or incremental change? *Public Administration Review, 73*(1), 165–175. doi:10.1111/j.1540-6210.2012.02647.x

Sheridan, W., & Riley, T. B. (2006). Comparing e-government vs. e-governance. *Commonwealth Center for e-Governance*, 1-5.

Stefanie, A., & Claudio, C. (2011). *The Economic and Social Impacts of E-government.* Freiburg University.

United Nations (UN). (2002). *Benchmarking E-government: A Global Perspective.* New York: Stephen A. Ronaghan.

United Nations (UN). (2004). *UN Global E-government Survey.* New York.

United Nations (UN). (2006). *Global E-government Readiness Report 2005.* New York: From E-government to E-inclusion.

United Nations (UN). (2008). UN E-Government Survey 2008, From E-government to connected government. New York: UN.

United Nations (UN). (2010). United Nations E-government Survey 2010, Leveraging e-government at a time of financial and economic crisis. New York: UN.

United Nations (UN). (2012). *United Nations E-government Survey 2012, E-government for people.* UN.

United Nations (UN). (2014). United Nations E-government Survey 2014, E-government for the future we want. New York: UN.

United Nations (UN). (2016). United Nations E-government Survey 2016, E-government in support of sustainable development. New York: UN.

Wahid, F. (2011). Explaining history of egovernment implementation in developing countries: an analytical framework. Electronic Government, 38-49.

Chapter 4
Thwarting Spam on Facebook:
Identifying Spam Posts Using Machine Learning Techniques

Arti Jain
Jaypee Institute of Information Technology, India

Reetika Gairola
Jaypee Institute of Information Technology, India

Shikha Jain
Jaypee Institute of Information Technology, India

Anuja Arora
Jaypee Institute of Information Technology, India

ABSTRACT

Spam on the online social networks (OSNs) is evolving as a prominent problem for the users of these networks. Spammers often use certain techniques to deceive the OSN users for their own benefit. Facebook, one of the leading OSNs, is experiencing such crucial problems at an alarming rate. This chapter presents a methodology to segregate spam from legitimate posts using machine learning techniques: naïve Bayes (NB), support vector machine (SVM), and random forest (RF). The textual, image, and video features are used together, which wasn't considered by the earlier researchers. Then, 1.5 million posts and comments are extracted from archival and real-time Facebook data, which is then pre-processed using RStudio. A total of 30 features are identified, out of which 10 are the best informative for identification of spam vs. ham posts. The entire dataset is shuffled and divided into three ratios, out of which 80:20 ratio of training and testing dataset provides the best result. Also, RF classifier outperforms NB and SVM by achieving overall F-measure 89.4% on the combined feature set.

INTRODUCTION

In the today's world the change in the Internet technology has led us to the usage of different Online Social Networks (OSNs)[1] (Andreassen et al., 2016; Brown et al., 2008; Egele et al., 2017; Panicker & Devadas, 2015), also known as the changing web. The out bursting popularity of these OSNs have at-

DOI: 10.4018/978-1-5225-5097-6.ch004

tracted huge number of users to use their platform which results into the sharing and storing of users' personal information on these networking sites. These networks help the users to interact, exchange and collaborate with their social-circle. These OSNs are also helping its users to communicate with their social community and keep their users updated with different domains such as news, active learning, job searching and web application development etc. Such vital information has aroused the interest of spammers[2] to take the advantage of the trust among users to deceive them for spammers (Adewole et al., 2017) own benefits. Facebook OSN is currently among one of the leading OSN present across the world and having over 2.05 billion[3] monthly active users. Facebook is around five times greater than its next greatest partner Twitter. A survey report[4] shows that out of 5,173 adults suggested that 30% of people get their news from Facebook, while only 8% receive news from Twitter and 4% from Google Plus. The users of Facebook not only uses Facebook for communicating with their friends but also for keeping regular updates about what is happening around the globe.

Spammers at present are discovering different ways to reach out to the users of the OSNs for spreading spam messages (Bhat & Abulaish, 2013; Prieto et al., 2013) and thereby, making the OSNs as vulnerable and exposed targets. Mostly, these spam messages are sent in high volume so that they can influence large amount of users in a short span of time. Moreover, these messages reduce the memory of the inboxes. These messages are targeted to specific audience or can be used to perform tricks such as phishing, identity theft (Gao et al., 2012). Apparently, spam which was earlier in the form of text containing irrelevant information for the users is now currently it is being noticed as it being spread using images and videos too. To do so, spammer evades the programmed filters using different techniques such as obfuscating keywords, wrapping long urls, and using image or video instead of textual content.

In this chapter, a methodology to segregate spam vs. ham post[5] from Facebook OSN is provided by combining the textual, image and video features using three supervised Machine Learning (Shalev-Shwartz & Ben-David, 2014) techniques, namely- Naïve Bayes (NB) (Lee et al., 2010), Support Vector Machine (SVM) (Shalev-Shwartz & Ben-David, 2014) and Random Forest (RF) (Breiman, 2001) using RStudio®[6]. Our methodology comprises of various stages. Firstly, data extraction is done from the Facebook posts which contain text, image and video posts followed by the data pre-processing (DP) stage. DP stage consists of stop words removal, stemming, lemmatization, photo pre-processing and url link blacklisting. The next stage consists of relevant features extraction for the identification of whether a post is spam or not. In this stage, a total of 30 features mare extracted from Facebook which includes *"status type"*, *"created time"*, *"updated time"*, *"name of the photo"* etc. Then the data is shuffled and split into different training and test data ratios i.e. 60:40, 70:30 and 80:20 respectively. Then ML techniques are applied to train the three classifiers (NB, SVM and RF). Further, using RStudio these classifiers are used in the testing phase to predict whether a given post is spam or ham. Finally, the classifiers are evaluated on the basis of standard metrics- precision, recall and F-measure.

BACKGROUND

Spam and ham posts classification of Facebook users' posts is a noticeable and prominent research issue which has been addressed by various researchers in their work. It is observed that these researchers have spam campaigns using individual features- textual features (Meligy et al., 2015), image features (Gao et al., 2012) and video features (Benevenuto et al., 2009). On one end, researchers primarily have worked on the textual posts. On the other end, few researchers have tried to classify based on image or video features. Rarely, video features have been used. Still an integrated research work is needed based on the combination of the three media types- Image, Text and Video features altogether. Research efforts in this work have been made to improve the accuracy and efficiency of the spam detection on Facebook OSN for all the three kinds of posts (text, image and video). Our proposed methodology shows the combination of these three features together to identify spam posts on Facebook, and separate those from the legitimate ham posts using the three classifiers (NB, SVM and RF).

Further, this section discusses about literature survey relevant to spammers identification on varying OSNs and Machine Learning techniques that have been used to classify spam posts. In comparison, our focus in on detection of spam messages, so that OSNs can be secured from spams that are generated by spamming bots or legitimate accounts or any other such phenomenon.

OSNs Spammer Identification

Research in spam message detection in OSNs has received growing interests in the past few years. So far, researchers' prime focus is on spam message detection using the textual information as posted by spammer using ML techniques (Chan et al., 2015; Martinez-Romo & Araujo, 2013). Spam detection is considered as a continuous fight among spammers and spam filters. Certain existing studies for spam detection in OSNs focus on identifying spam message as quite challenging. Spammer at present are finding different ways such wrapping long URLs, shuffling keywords etc. to propagate spam rigorously (DeBarr & Wechsler, 2010; Panicker & Devadas, 2015; Prieto et al., 2013; Rajalaxmi & Ramesh, 2014; Swami & Khade, 2014). These spammers may change the syntax (Gao et al., 2012) and use the techniques (Meligy et al., 2015) that can deceive the OSN users to wide extent. Hence, a lot of work needs to be done in this area to wipe out these scrap messages from the internet. Regardless of Facebook having an immune system of its own, users still experience a huge number of spam and noxious substance on general premises. Many existing ways to deal with the identification of spam in other OSN like Twitter can't be used on Facebook because of various issues (Chu et al., 2012) such as missing data e.g. account holder age, limit on post length, network details etc. Certain studies in this field looks into content based analysis and then researchers treat textual contents as collection of documents where individual messages are pre-processed and are represented using Vector Space Model (VSM) (Zhang & Wang, 2009) for text representation. Each document can also be represented using boolean occurrence of words in the document or by counting the frequency of occurrence of each word. Authors (Zhang & Wang, 2009) have proposed Bayesian model for SMS spam classification using content analysis techniques. Authors (Jin et al., 2011) introduce both image, text content features and social network features to indicate spam activities. Authors (Jeong et al., 2016) have dealt with spam in Twitter using three schemes- TSP-Filtering, SS-Filtering and Cascaded-Filtering (combine TSP and SS). These schemes are scalable and inspect user-centered two hop social networks and have better performance in terms of true positives and false positives. Authors (Gao et al., 2012) drop spam messages before they reach the intended recipients, and protect users from various kinds of fraud. They evaluate the system using 187 million wall posts from Facebook, and 17 million tweets from Twitter and observed that the true positive rate reaches 80.9% while the false positive rate reaches 0.19% in the best case. They also reveal large-scale spam campaigns in OSNs through offline studies. Although offline analysis tools are designed but none of them are usable for online spam detection. Authors (Stein et al., 2011) present framework of adversarial learning system which performs real-time read and action in Facebook. However, they lack consideration of valuable features and their performance prevents us from any further comparison. Authors (Thomas et al., 2011) filter malicious urls in real-time OSNs to identify malicious messages. Although their approach performs deep analysis of urls but our approach uses alternative information i.e. message content for the investigation. Authors (Song et al., 2011) propose sender-receiver relationship for Twitter messages. Authors (Adewole et al., 2017) consider datasets from SMS spam detection domain and Twitter microblog; and have used 18 features from content, behavioural or graph based features for spammer detection in Twitter. It is noted that the mention behaviour of spammers based on such features differs from that of the legitimate users. Authors (Yoon et al., 2010) have provided hybrid model which combines content analysis and challenge-response for mobile spam detection. Content based spam filter classifies messages as spam, legitimate or unknown. Unknown message is further authenticated using challenge-response protocol which determines whether the message is sent by human or automated program. Authors (El-Alfy & Al-Hasan, 2016) have introduced DCA algorithm for improving the performance of anti-spam filters within email and SMS data. Authors (He et al., 2014) have discussed Self-Monitoring (SM) skills for textual posts on Facebook. Popularity of the Social Networking Site- Facebook has grown unprecedented during the past few years. They have investigated the research question- whether posts on FB can also be applicable for the prediction of user psychological traits such as self-monitoring skill which are linked with the user expression behaviour within the online scenario. They also present a model to evaluate the relationship between the SM skills and the posts; evaluate the quality of responses to the Snyder Self-Monitoring Questionnaire via Internet; and explore the textual features of the posts in different SM-level groups.

ML Techniques

Researchers in the past have used various machine learning models (Cresci et al., 2017; Soman & Murugappan, 2014; Stringhini et al., 2010; Swami & Khade, 2014; Xu et al., 2016; Zhu et al., 2016) to detect spam on the social networking sites as they give promising results. Authors (Lee et al., 2010; (Stringhini et al., 2010; Yang et al., 2011) have used ML techniques to detect spamming bots in OSNs. These are the accounts that are created by spammers and are used exclusively for spamming purposes. Authors (Yardi et al., 2009) have made use of ad-hoc criteria for Twitter to identify spamming bots. Additionally, (Benevenuto et al., 2009; Chu et al., 2012) have applied supervised ML techniques to detect spammers in Youtube, Social bookmarking sites. Such websites don't focus on communication among users but their functionality is video and bookmark sharing respectively. Hence, they ignore textual and image features sets. Authors (Chan et al., 2015) have investigated the capabilities of existing spam filters for defending against certain adversarial attacks. They have proposed reweight method with rescaling function to prevent an adversarial attack using SVM based ML classifier. Although security level of spam filter in this model is increased, however, its classification accuracy over untainted samples is dropped significantly. Authors (Ezpeleta et al., 2016) have discussed a new perspective of the spam detection by focusing on spam similarities in different OSNs but dataset was not real-time extraction of data at all. They have worked on various features of spam messages using linear regression and SVM classifiers. Authors (Gao et al., 2012) have described spam campaigns, instead of individual spam messages, for spam classification. Their system can be deployed at the OSN server side to provide online spam filtering but their system is restricted to only the textual content. Although SVM provides them 98.4% accuracy on the text message features but no image and video features are considered. Authors (McCord & Chuah, 2011) have compared the performance of RF, SVM, NB and K-Nearest Neighbor classifiers. Another, authors (Tayal et al., 2015) had discussed about relevant ML algorithms such as K-means, KNN but they focus only on crime related activities in India which are not related to spam detection. Authors (Ahmed

& Abulaish, 2013) have identified features that are common to both Facebook and Twitter OSNs. They have used three different classification algorithms- NB, Jrip and J48, and observed false positive value of 0.089 and 0.075 on Facebook and Twitter dataset respectively.

SUPERVISED CLASSIFIERS

Machine learning (Breiman, 2001; Shalev-Shwartz & Ben-David, 2014) is a field of artificial intelligence which gives the computer an ability to learn itself without human intervention. The process involves searching and analyzing the data to identify a common pattern and design the possible set of actions. Machine learning algorithms are broadly categorized as supervised and unsupervised. Supervised learning (Galán-García et al., 2016) require a dataset containing both input and desired output, in addition to furnishing feedback about the accuracy of predictions during training. First step is to train the machine using the given dataset. Once training is over, the algorithm is used to predict the output for the new data. Formally, it can be defined as an input factor *(x),* yield variable *(y)* and some calculations done in order to take the mapping capacity from the contribution to the yield as $y = f(x)$.The objective of the algorithm is to approximate the input to the output mapping function so adequately that the output variable *(y)* can be predicted correctly given the new input data *(x).* Supervised algorithms are further grouped into two types of problems: regression and classification. A classification problem means when the input variable maps to a target category as output, such as "happy" or "notHappy" or "spam" and "notSpam". Regression problem basically estimates the relationship between variables and generates a continuous value as output. For example: predict the house price when size of the house is given. Unsupervised algorithms do not require any training using dataset with desired outcome data. Instead, they use an iterative approach to identify the common features of the data and then group the similar data together. Whenever new data arrives, it extracts the features and establishes the similarity with the existing data and concludes the output. In other words, unsupervised learning algorithm takes only the input data *(x).* The objective of this kind of learning algorithms is to model the underlying structure or distribution in the data in order to learn more about the data. Unsupervised learning problems can be further grouped into two types of problems: clustering and association. Clustering problem means the distribution od data is analyzed to form the cluster of similar data. For example, cluster of people who like coffee. An association rule learning problem is when the relation between the data is identified. For example: people who buy bread also tend to buy milk. Since the problem of identifying the spam post is a classification problem, three supervised classifiers namely: Naïve Bayes (NB), Support Vector Machine (SVM) and Random Forest (RF) are applied. These classifiers are explained in detail in the following sub-sections.

Naïve Bayes

Naive Bayes Classifier (McCord & Chuah, 2011) technique is based on the so-called Bayesian theorem and is particularly suited when the dimensionality of the inputs is high. It is a classification algorithm for binary (two-class) and multi-class classification problems. Despite its simplicity, Naive Bayes can often outperform more sophisticated classification methods. They are probabilistic, which means that they calculate the probability of each category for a given sample, and then output the category with the highest one. The way they get these probabilities is by using Bayes' Theorem, which describes the probability of a feature, based on prior knowledge of conditions that might be related to that feature. NB

(McCord & Chuah, 2011) acknowledges that the effect of the estimation of an indicator *(x)* on a given class *(c)* is free of the estimations of the different indicators. Hence NB classification can be given as in equation *(1)*:

$$P(c|x) = (P(x|c).P(c)) / P(x) \quad (1)$$

Here, *P(c|x)* is the back likelihood of target class given indicator. This is called the posterior probability, *P(c)* is the probability of target class *c* being true (regardless of data). This is called the prior probability of class, *P(x|c)* is the probability which is the likelihood of indicator *x* given class *c*, *P(x)* is the earlier likelihood of indicator *x* (regardless of the class).

After calculating the posterior probability *P(c|x)* for a number of different classes, the class with the highest probability is selected. This is the maximum probable class and can formally be called the Maximum a Posteriori (MAP) class.

Support Vector Machines

Support Vector Machines (Shalev-Shwartz & Ben-David, 2014) are perhaps one of the most popular and talked about machine learning algorithms. It is one of the high-performing algorithm with little tuning. Support Vector Machines are based on the concept of decision planes that define decision boundaries. A decision plane is one that separates between a set of objects having different class memberships. SVM (Shalev-Shwartz & Ben-David, 2014) is an arrangement of regulated learning strategies utilized for characterization, relapse and exceptions recognition. Binary classification is performed by using a real-valued function $f: x \subseteq N$ in the following way:

Input $x = (x_1,...,x_n)$, assign to the positive class, if $f(x) \geq 0$, and otherwise to the negative class.

The case where $f(x)$ is a linear function of $x \in X$ with *a* and *b* as linear variables is considered, so that it can be written as in equation *(2)*:

$$f(x) = (w.x) + b \quad (2)$$

Here, $w = \sum_{i=1}^{N} a_i y_i x_i$

Now, substitute for *w* in equation *(2)* which results in equation *(3)*, and on rearranging the variables equation *(4)* is generated:

$$f(x) = (\sum_{i=1}^{N} a_i y_i x_i)x + b \quad (3)$$

$$f(x) = (\sum_{i=1}^{N} a_i y_i)x_i x + b \quad (4)$$

Figure 1 shows the SVM linear classification of two different classes *A* and *B*. The distance between the line and the closest data points is referred to as the margin. The best or optimal line that can separate the two classes is the line that as the largest margin. The margin is calculated as the perpendicular distance from the line to only the closest points. Only these points are relevant in defining the line and in the construction of the classifier. The margin points are the supporting data points, also known as the supporting vectors which help in segregating the two different classes *A* and *B*. They support or define the hyperplane. The hyperplane is learned from training data using an optimization procedure (like gradient descent) that maximizes the margin.

Random Forest

Random Forest (Breiman, 2001) is one most powerful machine learning algorithms. It is a type of ensemble machine learning algorithm called Bootstrap Aggregation or bagging. It can be used for the problems of classification and regression both. RF is a sort of group learning process where a group of prescient models intercept the given expectation undertaking. RF utilizes both the bagging and the random subspace methodology for including randomization within group. It is important to know that every prescient model for utilizing a group is simply being squandering the calculation time. Then choice trees make a decent decision for the group learning, as a result different outfit with changing speculations with regards to the hidden relationships is needed. Figure 2 shows how a feature *f* can be used for obtaining an output *Y*. In this process, firstly different choice trees are created named as *T1, T2* upto *Tn*. Further, these sub trees are exploited and then decision is made by the information present in the nodes. Now this different sub trees information are sacked and are presented in the form of the output *Y*. Bagging choice trees admirably and get strong prescient power. It takes the differing qualities, one additional level by fusing the arbitrary subspace technique. RF utilizes sacking and random subspaces to make group with solid assorted qualities, diminish inclination, and prescient power tends to increment definitely.

Figure 1. SVM Classification

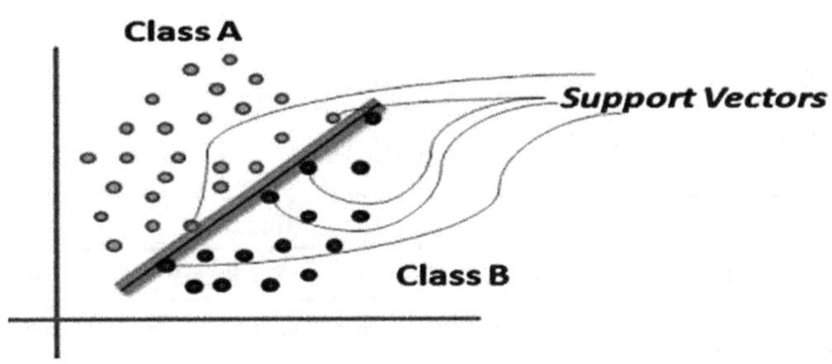

Figure 2. Random Forest Bagging Strategy

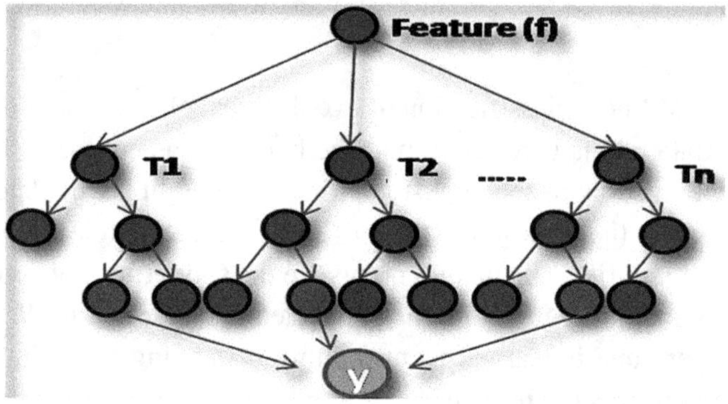

OSN DATASET COLLECTION

In this research work, Facebook dataset is used that is extracted from both the archival and the real-time extraction of posts during October 2016 to April 2017 from the Facebook Graph API[7]. Graph API Explorer is used for testing purposes, authentication of API calls, and to extract data out of Facebook platform. Facebook Graph API explorer and Facepager tool are used to extract the different kinds of posts and finally posts are organized on row per record basis. These tools are low-level HTTP-based API that can be used to file query, post new stories, manage advertisements, uploading photos and a variety of other tasks that an application is programmed for. The main components on this Facebook social graph are composed of the following three components:-

- **Node:** Node represents distinct users, photos, Facebook pages, or comments on particular posts.
- **Edge:** Edge represents connections between Facebook pages, photos, or comments on photos.
- **Field:** Field represents different sets of information that can be gathered about users e.g. birthday, current location, gender and many more.

Table 1 shows the topics that are covered from the various fields for which the posts and comments are extracted using the Graph API Explorer. The dataset contains 1.5 million posts and comments in total.

Table 1. Topics Coverage of Various Fields

Fields	Topics
Entertainment	Coldplay, Bahubali2, Dangal, Logan, Oscar, Lion, Thor:Ragnarok, Grammy Awards
Life Style	International Women's Day, End of Season Sale, Christmas, Iphone7, Galaxy 8
Politics	Narendra Modi, UP Elections, Yogi Adityanath, Nitesh Kumar, Jaya Lalita, Barack Obama, Hilary Clinton
Sports	India Vs. Australia, ODI, UEFA Championship league, Messi, Virat Kohli, Ms Dhoni, WWE, Ronaldo
News	Jammu & Kashmir, Syria, Russia, H1V1 Visa
# of posts and Comments	1,500,000

PROPOSED METHODOLOGY

The proposed methodology describes various stages that are considered for the separation of spam vs. ham post from Facebook OSN using combined features, namely- textual, image and video features and applying three ML techniques (NB, SVM and RF) as shown in Figure 3.

Once raw data is collected from the Facebook posts (both archival and real-time), Data Preprocessing (DP) stage comes into picture using RStudio®. DP consists of stop-words removal, stemming, lemmatization, photo pre-processing and url link blacklisting. Next stage consists of relevant features extraction, total of 30 features are extracted from Facebook. The entire data is then shuffled and split in varying training and test data to predict spam vs. ham posts using three supervised classifiers.

Data Preprocessing

The input for this section is raw extracted as well as repository provided dataset, which is pre-processed to make use of it while classifying to ham and spam post. Various pre-processing steps are involved during this process as detailed below-

- **Removing Stop-Words:** Stop-words (Lo et al., 2005) are the words that are commonly used but have no relevance in a language. English has some words for example: *"a"*, *"the"*, *"is"*, *"was"*, *"be"*, *"in"*, *"to"*. Removal of these words is necessary because by removing such words important words can be focused that are present within the sentences and which are critical for the spam detection.
- **Stemming:** Stemming is a heuristic process which groups different words with the same root together. On applying stemming derivate affixes are being chopped off from the word. For example: *"working"*, *"worked"*, *"works"* can be grouped to root word as *"work"*.

Figure 3. Proposed Architecture

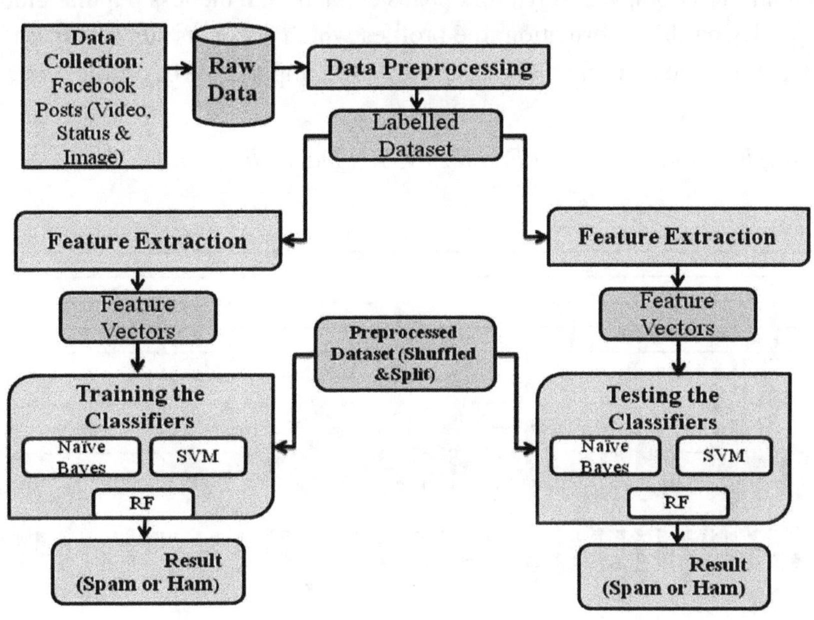

- **Lemmatization:** Lemmatization is the process to return the base of the word by applying morphological analysis and vocabulary search. Therefore it is termed as the lemma. For example: when on word *"toughest"* lemmatization is applied it returns *"tough"* or *"tougher"* on the basis that the used token is grammatically occurring or morphologically fit to our requirement.
- **Photo Pre-Processing:** The photo is compared by using the color value of every single expected pixel and actual pixel present in that image. If certain expected pixels differ from the actual pixels then the check fails and hence is considered as a spam.
- **URL Links Blacklisting:** Black list is the list of URL links who are promoting spam on daily basis. Such urls are being analyzed by maintaining a database build from the famous antivirus websites and comparing the results. If the url is present in this database it is considered to be a spam url.

Feature Extraction

Feature extraction stage comprises of informative features (Bhat & Abulaish, 2013; Lin & Huang, 2013) that are essential for a higher prediction rate. Features play an important role in the identification of spam and some of the relevant selected features are discussed below.

- **Keyword Related Feature:** Keywords refer to those words that lie within the posts/reviews such as *"buy", "vote", "free", "iphone"* etc. But there exist few regularly used words as a part of spam/ abusive/ pornographic messages. The presence of these words in a post shows that there is a high probability of that post is a spam/ abusive/ pornographic post. Figure 4 depicts frequency count of pornographic keywords from a scale of 0-1000 of different keywords encountered after cleaning the data. Here, x-axis contains words, and y-axis points to count hits.
- **Profile Related Feature:** Profile demographic related feature is important information that can be used for detecting spam posts which includes the *"name of account", "length of the username", "average time between posts"*. For example, Facebook page with popular football club name *"FC Barcelona"* has comparatively more pages created than the less popular club name *"Dempo Sports Club"*. Using this information, the profiles which accounts support spam content on their Facebook pages can be identified. Figure 5 shows the importance of profile related features (such

Figure 4. Pornographic/ Spam Keyword Frequency Hits Depending on the Most Occurring Keywords in a Post

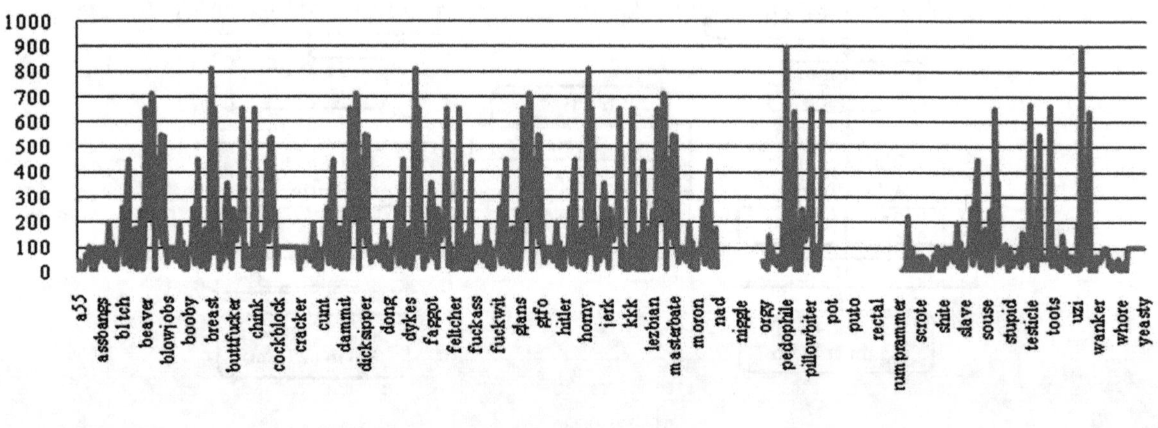

as “username”, “age”, “birthday”, “gender”, “length of username”) with respect to the individual percentage of information (such as “username” occurs with 60%, “gender” occurs with 75%) in overall Facebook posts.

- **Content Related Feature:** Content related features includes text attributes (*“text post length”* etc.), photo attributes (*“name of photo”*, *“caption attached” etc.*), videos attributes (*“video length”*, *“source” etc.*). For example, consider post- *Buy new iphone 7 exclusively for 50k*, click on- “https://fastfilez.com/9L4U” which is analyzed to know whether post is spam or not.
- **URL Related Feature:** URL mentioned in the posts contains many number of characters, length of the link, number of links. For example, if a user mentions http://www.freecharge.com in his post the number url components are analysed in this process. Some of the links are already marked as bad or malicious urls in many antivirus databases and are used to find spam posts. Figure 6 shows occurrence of urls in a spam post. The x-axis represents bad urls and y-axis represents the times the url is present in spam post from a scale of 1 to 10. URLs with high peaks reflect more usage in a spam posts frequently as compared to others.
- **Trending Topics Related Feature:** Trending topics are the most recent mentioned terms on Facebook at a given time instance. Such instance can be moment, week, or month etc. The users can use the hashtag, if there are many posts containing the same term that helps the term to become a trending topic. The endpoint search is done in the Graph API Explorer e.g. *“query = mannkibaat”* and “*related type = pages*” or *“type = groups”*, then concurrent pages and groups are displayed with their respective ids. Figure 7 shows some of the trending topics on which different users are posting their opinions.

Figure 5. Percentage of Information Extracted Using Profile Related Features

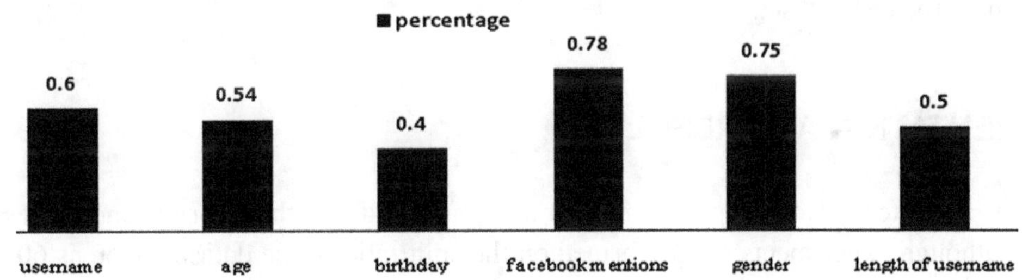

Figure 6. Bad Urls vs. Occurrence in Spam Posts

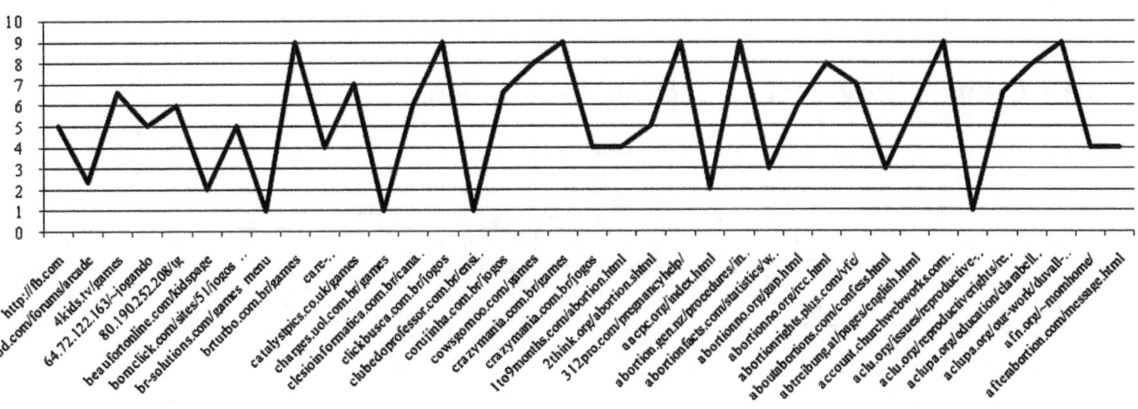

Figure 7. Trending Topics on Facebook

Training and Testing Using Supervised Classifiers

The entire Facebook OSN dataset is shuffled and split in varying training and test data to predict spam vs. ham posts using three supervised classifiers (NB, SVM and RF). The training and test ratio is considered as 60:40, 70:30 and 80:20 respectively. Among all, 80:20 training and test ratio gives the best result on collaborated textual, image and video features, as seen in the next section. Figure 8 shows that ML techniques are applied to train the dataset and then three classifiers predict whether a given post is spam or ham on the test dataset.

EXPERIMENTATION AND RESULTS

This section illustrates various experiments that are conducted and their corresponding results using RStudio®. Although experiments are performed on the split ratio of the dataset taken as 60:40, 70:30, 80:20 for training and test data respectively. But here the results are drawn from the 80:20 ratios as it gives the best outcomes. The following are the findings of our experimentation.

Figure 8. Classifiers Applied to Classify Post as Spam vs. Ham

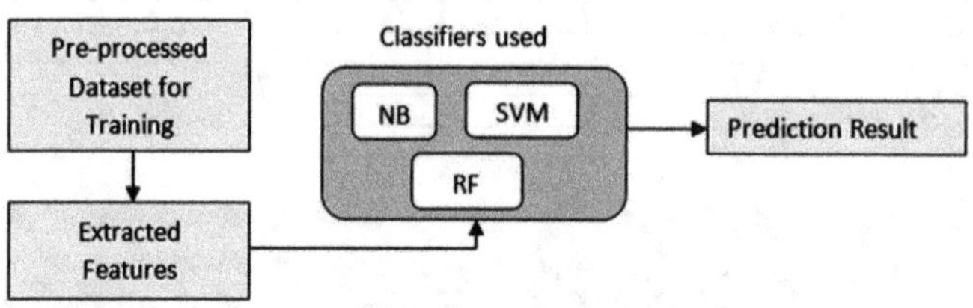

Top Frequent Keywords in Spam Posts

During the extraction of keywords as features it is observed that most spammers use common words to draw the attention of the users of the platform. It is being experimented that some words such as *"click-here"*, *"free"*, *"hurry"* are usually found in a spam post to trick the users of Facebook. Table 2 shows the top 20 most occurring keywords that are found in spam posts.

Top Trending Topics in Spam Posts

The most recent topics which are gathering big attention of the users of the Facebook are termed in the trending topics. These topics may usually last for a day, week or a month. The users can use the hashtag symbol *"#"*, to address a trending topic. These topics are used to extract similar posts on the Facebook and are used as raw data. It is being noted that with the release of iphone7 there is a tremendous growth in the page creation, posts about the release, it features and specifications. Many such topics are centre of attraction and a way to propagate more spam posts on the network. Table 3 shows some of these trending topics that are found in spam posts.

Percentage of URL Links for Spam Content

Post containing url links have high possibility of containing spam content than a normal post with no url. According to the 17,112 urls that are found in the total data, 11,652 are supporting spam content and 5,460 are the ones with the non-spam content. Figure 9 shows percentage of URL links supporting spam content.

Table 2. Top 20 Most Occurring Keywords in Spam Posts

Top 20 Most Occurring Keywords in a Spam Post			
Guarantee	Free	Offer	Save
Winner	Sex	Call	Unlimited
Hurry	Gift	Apply	Viagra
Clickhere	Try	invest	Doorstep
Congratulation	Porn	Alert	iphone7

Table 3. Top 10 Trending Topics in Spam Posts

Top 10 Trending Topics Found in Spam Post	
#stocknews	#mannkibaat
#upelections	#iphone7
#uefachampionsleague	#donaldtrump
#narendramodi	#jammuandkashmir
#coldplay	#bahubali2

Figure 9. Percentage of URL Links Supporting Spam Content

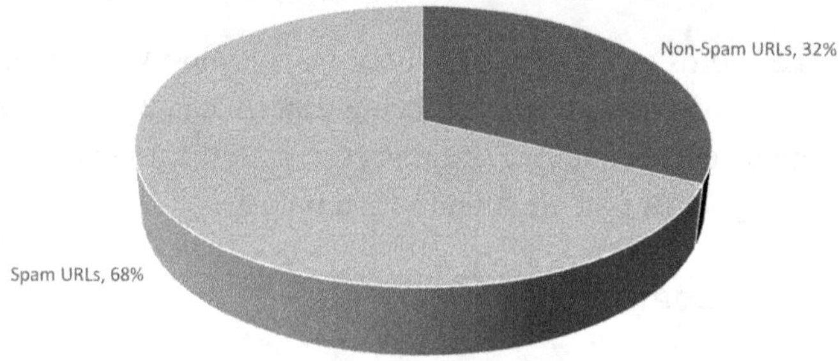

Overall Features for Spam Posts

The feature extraction phase contains total of 30 features to determine whether a post is spam or not. Table 4 lists all of these 30 features.

Top Informative Features for Spam Posts

Among all the 30 features, top 10 features are listed that are extracted as most informative features for spam detection. Table 5 lists these top 10 most informative features for spam content.

Table 4. Overall 30 Features Extracted

	List of Features Used
Textual	text length, tag person name, time, location, comments, via field, post length, links mentioned, facebook mentions, shared_stories
Image	name of the photo, caption attached, tagged person name, links references, location date, time posted, comments on the photos, URL link, length of link
Video	name of the video, video length, caption, location, date mentioned, source, live (real-time streaming videos), characters in URL, URL link, length of link, tags, time posted,

Table 5. TOP 10 Most Informative Features

Most Informative 10 Features
Shared_stories
name of the account
number of urls
Comments
length of url name of photo
video length
status tag
Caption
Real-time streaming video

Combination of all three features (Text, Image and Video)

Standard metrics (Precision, Recall and F-measure) are used for measuring the usefulness of our detection scheme on the combined features- textual, image and video features. Table 6 shows the confusion matrix for our spam detection system.

Here,

- **TP:** TP represents true positive i.e. number of spam messages that are correctly classified as spam messages
- **TN:** TN represents true negative i.e. number of spam messages that are falsely classified as non-spam messages
- **FP:** FP represents false positive i.e. number of non-spam messages that are falsely classified as spam messages
- **FN:** FN represents false negative i.e. number of non-spam messages that are correctly classified as non-spam.

Hence, standard metrics are defined as:

- **Precision:** Model precision is defined as number of successful classification divided by number of classification, as seen in equation *(5)*

$$\text{Precision} = \text{TP} / (\text{TP} + \text{FP}) \tag{5}$$

- **Recall:** Model recall is defined as number of positive predictions that are successfully retrieved, as seen in equation *(6)*

$$\text{Recall} = \text{TP} / (\text{TP} + \text{FN}) \tag{6}$$

- **F-Measure:** Model F-measure is defined as weighted average of precision and recall, as seen in equation *(7)*

$$F\text{-}measure = 2.\frac{\Pr ecision.\operatorname{Re} call}{\Pr ecision + \operatorname{Re} call} \tag{7}$$

Table 6. Confusion Matrix Table

	Prediction	
	Spam	***Non Spam***
Spam	*TP*	*TN*
Non spam	*FP*	*FN*

Table 7 shows the overall precision, recall and F-score values that are obtained for classifiers (NB, SVM and RF) while considering combined features- textual, image and video features.

In addition, classification results using F-score are also achieved for individual and combined features on all three classifiers. Figure 10 shows RF has outperformed SVM and NB when applied on the different features set. Image feature and video feature clearly shows that NB is not so effective in finding the spam posts. Although using textual features, SVM shows good results, but when combined features are considered then RF is the best classifier among all with F-score of 89.4%.

CONCLUSION

With the wide-spread popularity of Online Social Network (OSN), huge interest among spammers within OSN is also raising at an alarming rate. Particularly, Facebook has been experiencing wide spam threats from the past decade. This research work shows how spam posts on Facebook OSN can be detected using supervised machine learning techniques- (NB, SVM and RF) while combining textual, image and video features altogether using RStudio®. For this purpose, raw data of 1.5 million posts & comments is collected (both archival and real-time) from the Facebook Graph API. The Data Pre-processing stage comprises of stop-words removal, stemming, lemmatization, photo pre-processing and url link blacklisting. Feature extraction includes- keywords feature, profile related feature, content related feature, URL related feature and trending topics related feature. The entire data is then shuffled and split in varying training and test data. Among all, 80:20 training and test ratio gives the best result on collaborated textual, image and video features. Out of total 30 features, 10 features are considered as the best informative features for identification of spam vs. legitimate posts. The top 20 most occurring keywords and top 10 trending

Table 7. Classification Results using Combined Features

Classifier Used	Precision	Recall	F-Measure
NB	0.69	0.56	0.64
SVM	0.78	0.76	0.81
RF	0.88	0.86	**0.89**

Figure 10. F-score vs. Features Category Graph on Three Classifiers

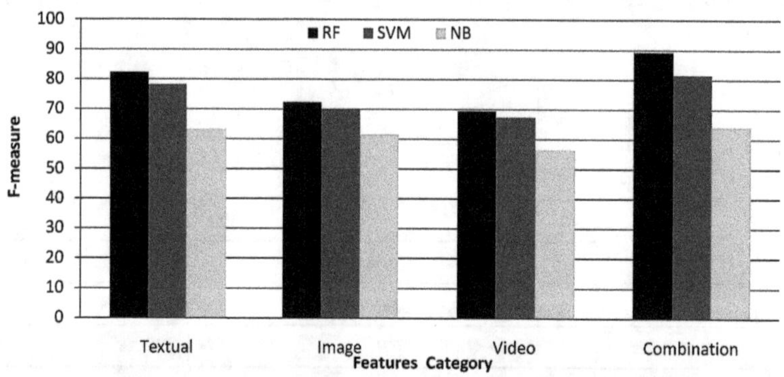

topics that are found in spam posts are also filtered out. F-score on individual and combined features are computed for all the three classifiers. RF has outperformed SVM and NB when applied on the different features set. Image feature and video feature clearly shows that NB is not so effective in finding the spam posts. Although using textual features, SVM shows good results, but when combined features are considered then RF is the best classifier among all with F-score of 89.4%. In future, researchers may explore with the combined (textual, image and video) features for spam detection over Facebook, Twitter or any other OSN using semi-supervised and unsupervised techniques.

FUTURE DIRECTIONS

In future, researchers may explore with the combined (textual, image and video) features for spam detection not only on Facebook OSN but also on other OSNs. These OSNs include Twitter, Google Plus, Linkedln, YouTube, Instagram, Tumblr, Pinterest. Researchers may apply certain other supervised techniques (such as discriminant analysis, nearest neighbours), semi-supervised techniques (such as bootstrapping), and/or unsupervised techniques (such as clustering, mixture models, generative adversarial networks, expectation maximization algorithm).

REFERENCES

Adewole, K. S., Anuar, N. B., Kamsin, A., & Sangaiah, A. K. (2017). SMSAD: A framework for spam message and spam account detection. *Multimedia Tools and Applications*, 1–36. doi:10.1007/s11042-017-5018-x

Ahmed, F., & Abulaish, M. (2013). A generic statistical approach for spam detection in online social networks. *Computer Communications*, *36*(10), 1120–1129. doi:10.1016/j.comcom.2013.04.004

Andreassen, C. S., Billieux, J., Griffiths, M. D., Kuss, D. J., Demetrovics, Z., Mazzoni, E., & Pallesen, S. (2016). The relationship between addictive use of social media and video games and symptoms of psychiatric disorders: A large-scale cross-sectional study. *Psychology of Addictive Behaviors*, *30*(2), 252–262. doi:10.1037/adb0000160 PMID:26999354

Benevenuto, F., Rodrigues, T., Almeida, V., Almeida, J., & Gonçalves, M. (2009). Detecting spammers and content promoters in online video social networks. In *Proceedings of the 32nd International ACM SIGIR Conference on Research and Development in Information Retrieval*. New York: ACM.

Bhat, S. Y., & Abulaish, M. (2013). Community-based features for identifying spammers in online social networks. In *Proceedings of the International Conference on Advances in Social Networks Analysis and Mining*. IEEE. doi:10.1145/2492517.2492567

Breiman, L. (2001). Random forests. *Machine Learning*, *45*(1), 5–32. doi:10.1023/A:1010933404324

Brown, G., Howe, T., Ihbe, M., Prakash, A., & Borders, K. (2008). Social networks and context-aware spam. In *Proceedings of the ACM conference on Computer Supported Cooperative Work*. ACM.

Chan, P. P., Yang, C., Yeung, D. S., & Ng, W. W. (2015). Spam filtering for short messages in adversarial environment. *Neurocomputing*, *155*, 167–176. doi:10.1016/j.neucom.2014.12.034

Chu, Z., Widjaja, I., & Wang, H. (2012). Detecting social spam campaigns on twitter. In *Proceedings of International Conference on Applied Cryptography and Network Security*. Singapore: Springer. doi:10.1007/978-3-642-31284-7_27

Cresci, S., Di Pietro, R., Petrocchi, M., Spognardi, A., & Tesconi, M. (2017). The paradigm-shift of social spambots: Evidence, theories, and tools for the arms race. In *Proceedings of the 26th International Conference on World Wide Web Companion*. ACM.

DeBarr, D., & Wechsler, H. (2010). Using social network analysis for spam detection. *Advances in Social Computing*, 62–69.

Egele, M., Stringhini, G., Kruegel, C., & Vigna, G. (2017). Towards detecting compromised accounts on social networks. *IEEE Transactions on Dependable and Secure Computing*, *14*(4), 447–460. doi:10.1109/TDSC.2015.2479616

El-Alfy, E. S. M., & Al-Hasan, A. A. (2016). Spam filtering framework for multimodal mobile communication based on dendritic cell algorithm. *Future Generation Computer Systems*, *64*, 98–107. doi:10.1016/j.future.2016.02.018

Ezpeleta, E., Zurutuza, U., & Hidalg, J. M. G. (2016). A study of the personalization of spam content using facebook public information. *Logic Journal of the IGPL*, *25*(1), 30–41. doi:10.1093/jigpal/jzw040

Galán-García, P., Puerta, J. G. D. L., Gómez, C. L., Santos, I., & Bringas, P. G. (2016). Supervised machine learning for the detection of troll profiles in twitter social network: Application to a real case of cyberbullying. *Logic Journal of the IGPL*, *24*(1), 42–53.

Gao, H., Chen, Y., Lee, K., Palsetia, D., & Choudhary, A. (2012). Towards online spam filtering in social networks. In *Proceedings of the Network & Distributed System Security Symposium (NDSS)*. ACM.

He, Q., Glas, C. A., Kosinski, M., Stillwell, D. J., & Veldkamp, B. P. (2014). Predicting self-monitoring skills using textual posts on Facebook. *Computers in Human Behavior*, *33*, 69–78. doi:10.1016/j.chb.2013.12.026

Jeong, S., Noh, G., Oh, H., & Kim, C. K. (2016). Follow spam detection based on cascaded social information. *Information Sciences*, *369*, 481–499. doi:10.1016/j.ins.2016.07.033

Jin, X., Lin, C., Luo, J., & Han, J. (2011). A data mining-based spam detection system for social media networks. In *Proceedings of the VLDB Endowment*. ACM.

Lee, K., Caverlee, J., & Webb, S. (2010). Uncovering social spammers: social honeypots+ machine learning. In *Proceedings of the 33rd International ACM SIGIR Conference on Research and Development in Information Retrieval*. ACM. doi:10.1145/1835449.1835522

Lin, P. C., & Huang, P. M. (2013). A study of effective features for detecting long-surviving twitter spam accounts. In *Proceedings of the 15thInternational Conference on Advanced Communication Technology (ICACT)*. IEEE.

Lo, R. T. W., He, B., & Ounis, L. (2005). Automatically building a stopword list for an information retrieval system. *Journal on Digital Information Management*, *5*, 17-24.

Martinez-Romo, J., & Araujo, L. (2013). Detecting malicious tweets in trending topics using a statistical analysis of language. *Expert Systems with Applications*, *40*(8), 2992–3000. doi:10.1016/j.eswa.2012.12.015

McCord, M., & Chuah, M. (2011). Spam detection on twitter using traditional classifiers. In *Proceedings of the International Conference on Autonomic and Trusted Computing*. Springer. doi:10.1007/978-3-642-23496-5_13

Meligy, A. M., Ibrahim, H. M., & Torky, M. F. (2015). A framework for detecting cloning attacks in OSN based on a novel social graph topology. *International Journal of Intelligent Systems and Applications*, *7*(3), 13–20. doi:10.5815/ijisa.2015.03.02

Panicker, N. J., & Devadas, L. (2015). Filtering the walls in online social networks. *International Journal of Advanced Research in Computer Science and Software Engineering*, *5*(5), 45–52.

Prieto, M. V., Alvarez, M., & Cacheda, F. (2013). Detecting linkedin spammers and its spam nets. *International Journal of Advanced Computer Science and Applications*, *4*(9), 189–199.

Rajalaxmi, R. R., & Ramesh, A. (2014). Binary bat approach for effective spam classification in online social networks. *Australian Journal of Basic and Applied Sciences*, *8*(18), 383–388.

Shalev-Shwartz, S., & Ben-David, S. (2014). *Understanding machine learning: From theory to algorithms*. New York: Cambridge University Press. doi:10.1017/CBO9781107298019

Soman, S. J., & Murugappan, S. (2014). A study of spam detection algorithm on social media networks. *Journal of Computational Science*, *10*(10), 2135–2140. doi:10.3844/jcssp.2014.2135.2140

Song, J., Lee, S., & Kim, J. (2011). Spam filtering in twitter using sender-receiver relationship. In Recent advances in intrusion detection (pp. 301-317). Springer Berlin/Heidelberg. doi:10.1007/978-3-642-23644-0_16

Stein, T., Chen, E., & Mangla, K. (2011). Facebook immune system. In *Proceedings of the 4th Workshop on Social Network Systems* (pp. 8). ACM.

Stringhini, G., Kruegel, C., & Vigna, G. (2010). Detecting spammers on social networks. In *Proceedings of the 26th Annual Computer Security Applications Conference (ACSAC)*. Austin, TX: ACM.

Swami, A. D., & Khade, B. S. (2014). A text based filtering system for OSN user walls. *International Journal of Advanced Research in Computer Science and Software Engineering*, *4*(2).

Tayal, D. K., Jain, A., Arora, S., Agarwal, S., Gupta, T., & Tyagi, N. (2015). Crime detection and criminal identification in India using data mining techniques. *AI & Society*, *30*(1), 117–127. doi:10.1007/s00146-014-0539-6

Thomas, K., Grier, C., Ma, J., Paxson, V., & Song, D. (2011). Design and evaluation of a real-time url spam filtering service. In *Security and Privacy (SP), 2011 IEEE Symposium on*. IEEE. doi:10.1109/SP.2011.25

Xu, H., Sun, W., & Javaid, A. (2016). Efficient spam detection across online social networks. In *Proceedings of the International Conference on Big Data Analysis (ICBDA)*. IEEE. doi:10.1109/ICBDA.2016.7509829

Yang, C., Harkreader, R., & Gu, G. (2011). Die free or live hard? empirical evaluation and new design for fighting evolving twitter spammers. In Recent Advances in Intrusion Detection (pp. 318-337). Springer Berlin/Heidelberg.

Yardi, S., Romero, D., Schoenebeck, G., & Boyd, D. (2009). Detecting spam in a twitter network. *First Monday*, *15*(1). doi:10.5210/fm.v15i1.2793

Yoon, J. W., Kim, H., & Huh, J. H. (2010). Hybrid spam filtering for mobile communication. *Computers & Security, 29*(4), 446-459.

Zhang, H. Y., & Wang, W. (2009). Application of Bayesian method to spam SMS filtering. In *Information Engineering and Computer Science, 2009. ICIECS 2009. International Conference on*. IEEE. doi:10.1109/ICIECS.2009.5365176

Zhu, T., Gao, H., Yang, Y., Bu, K., Chen, Y., Downey, D., & Choudhary, A. N. et al. (2016). Beating the artificial chaos: Fighting OSN spam using its own templates. *IEEE/ACM Transactions on Networking*, *24*(6), 3856–3869. doi:10.1109/TNET.2016.2557849

ADDITIONAL READING

Chapelle, O., Schölkopf, B., & Zien, A. (2006). Semi-supervised learning. *Adaptive Computation and Machine Learning series.*

Hinton, G. E., & Sejnowski, T. J. (Eds.). (1999). *Unsupervised learning: foundations of neural computation.* MIT Press.

ENDNOTES

1. http://socialnetworking.lovetoknow.com/about-social-networking/definition-online-social-networking
2. https://www.technologyreview.com/s/403272/who-are-the-spammers/
3. https://www.statista.com/statistics/272014/global-social-networks-ranked-by-number-of-users/
4. http://www.journalism.org/2013/10/24/the-role-of-news-on-facebook/
5. ham- legitimate message which doesn't contain malicious text, image or video content
6. https://www.rstudio.com/
7. https://developers.facebook.com/tools-and-support/

Chapter 5
Impact of Sarcasm in Sentiment Analysis Methodology

Priscilla Souza Silva
Federal University of South and Southeast of Pará, Brazil

Haroldo Barroso
Federal University of Sul and Sudeste of Pará, Brazil

Leila Weitzel
Fluminense Federal University, Brazil

Dilcielly Almeida Ribeiro
Universidade Federal do Sul e Sudeste do Pará, Brazil

José Santos
Federal University of Sul and Sudeste of Pará, Brazil

ABSTRACT

Sentiment of analysis is a study area applied to numerous environments (financial, political, academic, business, and communication) whose purpose is to search for messages posted on social media, and through these to identify and classify people's opinions about particular item as positive or negative. Rating the sentiment expressed in opinionated messages is such an important task that currently companies invest a lot of money in collecting this type of information and the development of methods and techniques to classify the sentiment that they express, so that they can use the results as useful information in preparing marketing and sales strategies efficiently. However, one of the major problems facing the feelings of analysis is the difficulty of methods to properly analyze messages with sarcastic and/or ironic content, as these linguistic phenomena have the characteristic of transforming the polarity or meaning of a positive or negative statement into its opposite.

INTRODUCTION

With the advent of the Web, and increased use of online channels (such as social networks, blogs, social networking sites, online newspapers, forums, recommendations websites and online business tools that allow users to register their opinions on goods and services) in which users exchange information and share their knowledge, criticism, opinions and feelings about a topic of interest, made in the last decade

DOI: 10.4018/978-1-5225-5097-6.ch005

the amount of textual information written in natural language reached gigantic proportions. As Cambria et al. (2013), extract and process properly all this mountain of information has become something extremely interesting to the business world, because through this data companies can get a continuous and faster feedback on the opinion of the public about their products and brand. The academic world in turn is largely responsible for the development of tools and methods to treat such data.

However, despite the relevance of such information, collect and analyze resulting web opinions became an impractical task for the human being in time due to the large amount of textual data published. So to treat and automatically analyze the opinions and sentiments expressed in this type of data has emerged an area called Sentiments Analysis (AS) also called Opinion Mining (LIU, 2010a).

The sentiment analysis according to Benvenuto, Ribeiro and Araújo (2015), is a field of study that uses computer processing to define automated techniques to extract subjective information from texts in natural language, such as opinions and feelings in order to create knowledge structured that can be used by a support system or decision maker. Basically these techniques identify the sentimentthat users have regarding any interest entity (a specific product, a company, a place, a person, among others) based on the Web shared texts, allowing a user to get a report containing what people comment on any item, without having to seek and read all the reviews and news about manually.

Currently companies like Walmart, MCDonalds and IBM, are investing in research groups in sentiment analysis, it realized the value of the opinions expressed in social media and how these views may affect them positively or negatively (CHEN, Zimbra, 2010). Other emerging sectors interested in these data are: a policy to keep its members informed about public opinion regarding their actions; famous accompanying its level of popularity among Internet users; producers interested in knowing about the acceptance of the films produced, among other sectors.

Among the different data sources used by the AS, social networks represent the most conducive environment to identify opinions and feelings about different entities, since they are places where people argue about everything expressing political opinions, religious or even about brands, products and services. In addition to these opinions when properly collected and analyzed, allow not only to understand and explain many complex social phenomena, but also provides them.

However, despite the Web and especially social networks facilitating access and distribution of opinionated information, the task of identifying, classifying, and summarizing data views in text format, it is not trivial and has many challenges, which induce inconsistencies the results generated by sentiment analysis applications. Generally, these challenges are related to the difficulty that computers have to automatically process natural language (human). The automation of processing of human language has its principles in the study area called Natura Language Processing (NLP). This area relates directly with AS, they share the study of unstructured data (LIU; HOGAN; CROWLEY, 2011).

Natural language in turn is somewhat complex mainly when it comes to social networking as there are many nuances in a text message. This complexity is a challenge that are factors of human language, such as words and / or phrases with ambiguous meanings, sarcasm and irony, slang, spelling mistakes, regionalism, dialects, among others.

Given these challenges, it is important to consider that studies on automatic detection and classification of sarcasm and / or irony are still at the beginning. However, a difficulty of analysis is one that has an ability to transform a polarity of a positive or negative statement into its opposite or change its meaning (GONZÁLEZ-IBANEZ, MURESAN, WACHOLDER, 2011). For this, the elements that characterize the language figures, use simple language techniques such as word games, which have a capacity for analyzing applications of analysis of feelings (LUNANDO, PURWARINTI, 2013).

Thus, the recognition and treatment of sarcasm and / or irony are of utmost importance for better performance of methods, algorithms and techniques that make up the systems used for the determination of polarity in messages with opinion, available in great quantity on the Web (KALAMKAR, PHAKATKAR, 2013).

Currently, several scientific studies in computing and other areas of knowledge, such as linguistics (Cheang, PELL, 2011), is turning its efforts to the characterization, detection and sarcasm rating and irony in informal dialogues shared on the Web. The authors (BUSCHMEIER; CIMIANO; KLINGER, 2014), for example, presented an analysis of the funds invested in irony detection in a set of data from this product on the reviews on the Amazon.com site. Veale and Hao (2010), pointed out a linguistic approach to separate ironic expressions not ironic figurative expressions, comparing more than one smiles corpus collected on the Web.

In Reyes, Rosso and Veale (2013), the problem of irony detection is addressed only to you share posts on Twitter, where a set of textual features is used to recognize the irony linguistic level. Already in Riloff et al. (2013), the focus is on identifying the sarcastic tweets that express a positive sentimenttoward a negative situation. A model for classifying sarcastic tweets using a set of lexical features is shown in (Barbieri; SAGGION; RONZANO, 2014).

A recent episode that illustrates the importance of studying the sarcasm in social media occurred in 2014, when the agency Secret Service of the United States announced the hiring developers for the construction of a sarcasm detector system in online social networks, the objective was automate real-time analysis of what is published on social networks especially on Twitter (BBC, 2014).

According Benevenuto, Ribeiro and Araújo (2015), the broad applicability of sentiment analysis in various segments has led many companies and researchers from different areas to employ time and money on solutions that perform the extraction of affective factors (thoughts and feelings) in messages shared by the public in social networks, focusing primarily on the identification and orientation of a text classification as positive, negative or neutral.

However, as Maynard and Greenwood (2014) and Gonçalves et al. (2013th), many existing methods in the literature, has been employed in the development of applications without a concrete understanding of its applicability in different contexts, its advantages, limitations and compared efficiency to other methods, and that several of them have never been evaluated in a context involving sarcasm and / or irony. And most importantly, after a thorough analysis of the work in which they are presented methods in such a context, it is clear that there are few efforts to evaluate and quantitatively compare the performance of these methods in a context involving messages with sarcastic content or ironic.

In this context, taking into account the possible impact that the sarcasm presence / irony may have on the performance of sentiment analysis methods, the objective of this study was to evaluate and compare in quantitative terms the performance of different analysis methods feelings sort polarity messages with sarcastic content removed from Twitter, and identify the impact of sarcasm presence on the performance of these methods.

Sentiment Analysis

For Liu (2010a) sentiment analysis a way to automate the analysis of opinions, feelings, evaluations, attitudes, affections, visions, emotions, and subjectivities expressed in the web in text format, for someone about something. Several approaches can be related to AS as Web of opinion extraction mainly from social networks; classification of the extracted opinion as to its polarity (positive, negative or neutral); comparison messages as the opinions they express, etc.

Some scholars such as Liu (2010a) identify the sentiment analysis task as what you might call classification feelings or classification polarity of feelings. However researchers from AS not only restrict the sentiments of classification. Examples of studies linked the area, but they are not facing the sort of feelings or polarity is the research on subjectivity detection (identify if a particular piece of text or posting on Web channels, has opinionated content) as shown at work Pang and Lee (2004), and others such as improving summarization stage, or applying aS the answers and questions systems (SOUZA, 2012).

To perform the classification task usually feelings analysis uses techniques based on areas of Natural Language Processing (NLP) and text mining, for determining whether a given text is expressing a positive, negative or neutral. This is because these areas are pioneers in the treatment of natural language through machines in specific information in text format. PLN is a set of computational techniques for analyzing and representing natural occurrences of text in one or more levels of linguistic analysis. Your goal is to achieve a processing similar to human language, so that computer systems are able to perform different kinds of tasks that involve communication between man and machine or simply by processing useful way of texts and creating value for the user (LIDDY, 2003). In short, it is an area that deals with diverse linguistic elements and grammatical structures, such as morphology, syntax, semantics, among others. Some of his techniques can be used to assist in the pre-processing of textual data step (extremely important step for sentiment analysis task), such as stopwords removal technique, segmentation of words stemming, among others (CARVALHO FILHO, 2014). These techniques are applied in order to improve the structure and organization of data to be analyzed.

The text mining, also known as mining text data is the pattern extraction area, trends or interesting knowledge and non-trivial unstructured data through a set of methods used to browse, organize and find information large textual databases (BERRY, Kogan, 2010). Performs tasks such as sorting, grouping, information extraction, categorization and summarization. When coupled with sentiment analysis it has currently been used for monitoring social media in order to identify what is said about brands on enterprises, mainly (PANG; Lee, 2008). It is in the NLP techniques and text mining that sentiment analysis is based to accomplish their tasks.

Basically, the architecture of a complete system of sentiment analysis is complex, so it is usually divided into large steps. For Angulakshmi and Chezian (2014), these steps include: data recovery, classification and summarization (presentation of results). Figure 1 illustrates the relationship between the steps.

Understanding Sarcasm and Irony

Typically, but not exclusively, sarcasm and irony are figures of speech that occur frequently in content generated by Internet users on blogs, forums, social networks and online microposts like Twitter, Facebook, Myspace and Youtube, especially in English. In this environment, automatically identify when someone is being sarcastic or ironic is a challenge, since human language writing involves complex elements and difficult to understand by machines because as mentioned in the previous section computers do not process accurately messages and words according to the context in which they were written (RILOFF et al., 2013).

According to the English dictionary NTC's American Inglês (SPEARS, GROUP 1998, our translation), Sarcasm is the "activity of saying or writing the opposite of what you mean, or speak in a way in order to make someone feel stupid or show you that you are angry. " Generally, the sarcasm there is

Figure 1. Steps of sentiment analysis

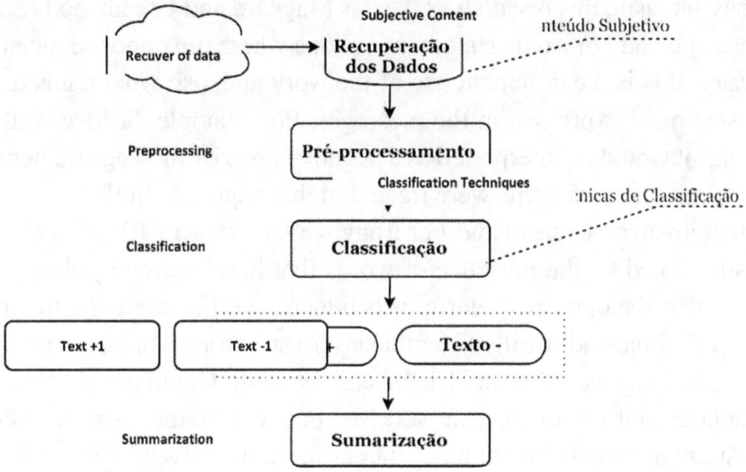

the use of indirect language tools for ridicule or mockery, often considered rude and offensive, being used for destructive purposes and of hypocritically manipulated and false politeness. Sarcasm example can be seen in the tweet "This is my brilliant son, who failed out of college #sarcasm" (the Portuguese translation would be "This is my brilliant son, who could not get out of #sarcasmo college"), in which it is found a sense of thanks to the emergence of a negative setback in a disapproving dialogue.

The irony in turn is "a form of humor that you use words to express the opposite of what the words really mean" (SPEARS, GROUP 1998, our translation). It can be regarded as a discrepancy between what you say and what you feel, or what is expected and what actually occurs (Singh, 2012). This kind of message is usually accompanied by a playful tone and has less offensive weight than sarcasm. For example, "I loved my iPhone 6s! #irony" ("I love my iPhone 6s! #irony"), In this post funny tone the user shows his disapproval towards the mobile device, taking into account problems the model presented during its launch.

In the view of Conz (2010), the sarcasm and irony have a close connection, as both tend to be used to make a statement that has an emotional sense. Often people say that something is ironic when in reality it is sarcastic and vice versa. However, in reality sarcasm is a concept that makes use of irony. In most cases, the subtle difference between the two is that sarcasm is almost cruel scathing order, often hurting the sensitivity of the person who receives it, while the irony is more polite and subtle. Traditionally the distinction between the two is that sarcasm is an irony more explicitly.

Today, especially in social networks, sarcasm and irony are generally used in statements in which people "say the opposite of the truth, or the opposite of their true feelings in order to be funny, to emphasize a point or mock something or someone "(MAYNARD, GREENWOOD, 2014).

To Gonçalves et al. (2015), one of the main difficulties for the identification task or sarcastic or ironic messages Web classification is the lack of agreement among most researchers (sociologists, psychologists, computer scientists, etc.) on how to define or differentiate ironic sarcasm. While several studies suggest that sarcasm and irony are terms associated with the same linguistic phenomenon (Conz, 2010; INGLE et al., 2014; MAYNARD, GREENWOOD, 2014), other researchers and Singh (2012) argue that these phenomena differ.

Therefore, considering that the database used in this study has messages (tweets) of users who do not differentiate irony sarcasm, this research as well as Maynard and Greenwood (2014) and Ingle et al. (2014) defines a sarcastic and / or ironic statement as "one where the opposite meaning of the sentence is intentional," because this is the dominant use of the work and also what tends to influence / impact the polarity of the sentiment expressed in the messages. For example, "I love walking to work in the rain # #irony sarcasm," it would be interpreted as a negative polarity message on her sarcastic and ironic sense. Thus the irony and sarcasm terms were treated in this paper as similar.

In this context that involves sarcasm and / or irony web, in view of Riloff et al., (2013), feelings of analysis can be easily fooled by the presence of words that have a strong polarity, which are used as sarcasm, the it means that the opposite polarity was intentional. For example, the following tweet that includes the words "yay" (oba) and "thrilled" (enthusiastic) are strong words, but actually express a negative feeling: "yay it's a holiday weekend and I'm on call for work! Could not be more thrilled! #sarcasm. " ("Wow! A long holiday and I'm on duty at work! It could not be more excited! #sarcasmo"). In this case, the #sarcasm hashtag reveals the intended sarcasm, but not always the methods used to classify feelings have the benefit of explicit nature sarcasm tags in a message.

Hashtags are usually used as metadata in tweets, is to express a pragmatic information in textual form, as irony, or evaluation (eg the #not hastags, #win, #fail), or to classify them on the topic (eg #google, #android, etc.). Research in the area AS exploit the use of hashtags as feelings of labels, i.e., the methods classify the orientation of the polarity of messages according to keywords within hashtags having.

For automatic identification of these linguistic phenomena, some studies suggest the creation of methods to seek for common grammatical factors in sarcastic / ironic phrases (eg, interjections and adverbs). In Kreuz and Caucci (2007), were created patterns and grammatical formulas for sarcasm identification and irony. Another strategy for identification of sarcasm / irony in messages posted on social networks, is the filtering technique for hashtags that denote sarcasm. For example, Gonzalez-Ibañes et al. (2011), created a textual database only sarcasm satisfaction messages, each message was kneecap with #sarcasm and #sarcastic hashtags.

Correlated Works

In the research of Gupta and Yang (2017), a system was developed that performs an analysis of shared sentiment through SemEval-2017. This system has the main characteristic of the ability to detect sarcasm in order to improve performance when classifying sentiment in text. For this was constructed an affect-cognition-sociolinguistic characteristics of sarcasm and, this model was trained with the SVM algorithm to detect sarcastic expressions in various tweets. As a result, the authors identified in the features derived from the detection of sarcasm have consistently benefited as key evaluation analysis metrics to varying degrees in four A-D subtasks.

In Poria, Cambria, Hazarika and Vij (2016), a structure was proposed that learned sarcasm automatically from a corpus of sarcamo, using a convolutive neural network called CNN, pre-trained to extract characteristics of sentiment, emotion and personality for a detection of sarcasm. Such features, along with network baseline capabilities, are proposed models that outperform the state of the art in reference datasets.

METHODS APPLIED IN THE SEARCH SCOPE

In the literature there are several methods of analysis of feelings, which are differentiated by the classification techniques they use to determine the sense or polarity expressed in a message. Among these techniques there may be mentioned approaches based on lexical dictionaries, machine learning, natural language processing, psychometric scales that hybrid methods (combination of different methods) and advanced linguistic and statistical techniques.

In Pang vision and Lee (2008), current detection methods and / or feelings or polarity Web posted messages classification, can be divided basically into two groups based on techniques lexical dictionaries and machine learning. The methods based on machine learning commonly rely on manually labeled databases to train (teach) algorithms called classifiers. On the other hand, methods using lexical dictionaries and lists of words associated with specific feelings (Benevenuto; RIBEIRO; Araujo, 2015).

Dictionary lexicon of feelings, is a kind of dictionary words or terms that instead of having as content the meaning of each word, has in place a quantitative meaning (ie, can be a number between -1 to 1, where - 1 is the most negative sentimental value and 1 the most positive value) or qualitative value (ie positive / negative, happy / sad, love / hate). approaches assume that lexical individual words have what is called prior polarity, which is an independent semantic context and guidance that can be expressed with a numerical value or polarity of class (TABOADA et al., 2011).

In addition to the lexical dictionaries another technique used for sorting or messages polarity analysis, is the Machine Learning. It consists of a subfield of artificial intelligence (AI) applied to development of algorithms and techniques that allow computers to be able to learn and evolve their performance on certain tasks, through experience gained in the repetition of such tasks (MITCHEL, 2006). Simon (1983) also defines learning machine (AM) as any change and a system to improve its performance in an automatic way at a later repetition of the same task or another task using the same database. According to Becker and Tumitan (2013), the main purpose of machine learning techniques is automatically find general rules (ie, standards) in large databases that allow find information implicitly represented. In general, the techniques and AM algorithms can be divided into two types: supervised learning and unsupervised learning.

The following are the twelve methods of AS that were evaluated in this study, as well as the polarity classification techniques or sense in which they are based.

- **SentiWordNet:** It consists of a lexical base in text file format used for feelings of classification. It was developed by the Bank of English language words WordNetnota (Miller, 1995), which consists of nouns, verbs, adjectives and adverbs cognitive synonyms grouped in sets (synsets), each expressing a different concept. The synsets are interconnected by means of conceptual-semantic and lexical relations. The SentiWordNet is the result of automatic annotation of each synsets of WordNet, which was assigned to each word three numerical values indicating which P (Positive), N (negative) O (neutral) the terms contained in each sysnet are. Currently SentiWordNet is in version 3.0, available at <http://sentiwordnet.isti.cnr.it/>.
- **PANA-t:** A lexicon method is adapted from an expanded version of a scale well known in psychology called the Positive and Negative Affect Schedule (Watson, CLARK; Tellegen, 1985). It aims to detect the users mood fluctuations on Twitter through the posts. It consists of a psychometric scale based on a broad lexicon of words associated with 11 categories of humor: cheerfulness, confidence, serenity, surprise, fear, sadness, guilt, hostility, shyness, fatigue and attention. It is

designed to detect any increase or decrease of feelings of levels over a period. The table in Figure 7 summarizes the items that make up the PANAS-t range (GONÇALVES; PAINS; Benevenuto, 2012).

- **Emolex:** The EmoLex Mohammad and Turney (2013th), is a lexicon created from the Amazon Mechanical Turk Servicenota in which people were paid to sort the terms. Each entry is associated with 8 basic feelings in English: joy, sadness, anger, etc. The base was built using EmoLex terms of Macquarie Thesaurusnota and words of General Inquirernota and Wordnet. The words that compose it include some nouns, verbs, adjectives and adverbs most common of the English language. The method also includes not only the presence but also of unigrams various bigramasnota, which are commonly used in texts.
- **NRC Hashtag:** Developed by Mohammad Kiritchenko and Zhu (2012), consists of a dictionary of words with associations for positive and negative feelings, linked to eight emotion categories: happiness, sadness, anger, fear, trust, disgust, anticipation and surprise . The lexicon is distributed in three files: unigrams-pmilexicon.txt (54.129 terms), bigrams-pmilexicon.txt (316.531 terms) and peer-pmilexicon.txt (480.010 terms). To create this lexicon thousands of tweets were automatically labeled based on the occurrence of hashtags linked to positive and negative words. From the auto-labeling found with relatively simple scores, which words occur more frequently in positive or negative tweets.
- **Opinion Lexicon:** Also known as Sentiment Lexicon (HU; LIU, 2004), is a lexical database publicly available, it contains approximately 6,800 words, and in 2006 with positive semantic orientation and 4783 negatively. It was initially built from Wordnet, a word database in English grouped into sets of synonyms (synsets).
- **VADER:** Proposed by (HUTTO; GILBERT, 2014) VADER (Valence Aware Dictionary for Sentiment Reasoning) is a method for sentiment analysis developed for the context of social media. In its construction the authors created a list of words based on dictionaries already well established as LIWC, ANEWnota and GInota. Then they were added numerous lexical present buildings in microblogs such as emoticons, acronyms and slang to express feelings, resulting in 9000 new candidates to be included in the dictionary. Then, it was found through the "knowledge of crowds" (AMT) which of these actually had applicability through score by Turkers ranging from -4 (extremely negative) to 4 (extremely positive). Finally, remaining 7000 lexical constructions in the dictionary that is to include the average between the evaluations obtained from the AMT should be different from 0 (neutral) and standard deviation of the scores below a threshold established by the authors. The word "okay" for example has a score of 0.9, while "great" has the value 3.1 and "horrible" is -2.5 (Benvenuto; RIBEIRO, ARAUJO, 2015).
- **Sentiment140:** Sentiment140-Lexicon or simply Sentiment140 (MOHAMMAD; KIRITCHENKO; ZHU, 2013b), is a lexicon of words associated with positive and negative feelings. The method was created with a database consisting of about 1.6 million tweets labeled as positive or negative. The corpus used to create this method can be found in http://saifmohammad.com/Lexicons/Sentiment140-Lexicon-v0.1.zip
- **SentiStrength:**It is a tool to estimate the polarity of short texts in informal language, for it uses a lexicon labeled by humans and is automatically enhanced by machine learning. Your main language is English, but also has implementations that allow the classification in other languages. It also uses classification techniques based on machine learning that enable its improvement automatically. It also has a dictionary of terms based on an optimized version for social networks

LIWC dictionary. This form is characterized as a hybrid method (Thelwall, 2013). Given a message, said tool classifies its polarity within a range of [-5, 5] -5 which represent the most negative scores and 5 the most positive. It is available for download at <http://sentistrength.wlv.ac.uk/>.

- **Combined Method:** Developed by (Goncalves et al, 2013th.) Combined Methos (in Portuguese, Method Combined) is a method which is the combination of 7 methods used in the literature for the task of analyzing feelings, being: PANAS-t, emoticons, SentiStrength, SentiWordNet, SenticNet, SASA and Happiness Index. It analyzes the harmonic mean (F-measure) the precision and recall of each method and distributes different weights for each. To evaluate the performance of the method, the developers tested on SentiStrength database consisting of labeled messages by human, then they calculated the F-measure, and the average coverage on such data.
- **AFINN:** AFINN (Nielsen, 2011), is a lexicon that provides a list of English words associated with an affective valence or score, is list includes words with feelings, internet slang and obscenities. The scores (scores) of the words vary on a scale of -5 indicating a very negative feeling, 5 indicating a very positive feeling. Currently there are two versions: AFINN-111 latest version with 2477 words and phrases, and AFINN-96 with 1468 words and original sentences in 1480 lines.
- **Pattern.en:** It is a package of python programming language to deal with natural language processing. One of its modules is responsible for inferring the sentimentin the text. Designed to be fast it is based on polarities associated with WordNet. This module is called "text" and contains: a quick labeler part-of-speech into English (which identifies nouns, adjectives, verbs, etc. in a sentence), tools for verb conjugation and noun, individualization and pluralization in English, a WordNet interface; a lexicon with 8,500 common English verbs and their conjugated forms, and analyze feelings (Smedt; NIJS; Daelemans, 2014). The Pattern.en packs a lexicon of adjectives (eg, good, bad, amazing, annoying, ...) which often occur in product reviews, annotated with the scores for a sense of polarity (positive negative ↔) and subjectivity (↔ goal subjective).

Support Vector Machine. Support Vector Machine (SVM) consists of a machine learning method for supervised binary classification based on the theoretical foundations of statistical learning developed by Vapnik (1995). A method is implemented by algorithms which visualize the data as input two sets of vectors in an N-dimensional much space (N is the number of vector attributes), and attempt to classify correctly new data (Goncalves, 2010).

The idea behind the SVM is to find optimal separation hyperplane, that is, debt and better differentiates two classes (categories) of data. To do this, first the algorithm must manually receive labeled data for training (if the message classification these data are the vectors of words or terms), and after performing various intelligent training tests with labeled data is the same as points in the feature space, and then build hyperplanes capable of separating the different classes identified in the labeled data, so that new input data which are not part of the test set are sorted correctly (HASTIE; TIBSHIRANI; FRIEDMAN, 2008).

COLLECTION AND HANDLING OF DATA

To validate the proposed approach was counted using a database of short messages (tweets) labeled (classified) manually as positive, negative or neutral, comprised of several subjects. To collect the data necessary to carry out the experiments with the methods, the microblogging service launched was used in 2006, Twitter, one of the reasons for choosing this social network was to be a dissemination tool of information responsible for a lot real-time available opinionated content, in addition to its wide use for academic work with the same line of research of this work. One of its main features is the maximum size prefixed in 140 characters to post tweets. Thus, we have a positive point, posting short messages that emit sentimentabout only one object.

The collection resulted in a total of more than 3,000 tweets. This complete a manual filtration was performed with the purpose to separate and select messages that compose the database being used in experiments. After this initial screening process performed manually, the database is initially collected summed to a total of 1137 tweets.

The data collected initially passed through a treatment (pre-processing) in order to remove the inconsistencies that could disrupt the classification process performed by methods and algorithm. In addition to that second (SANTOS, 2010; Benevenuto; RIBEIRO, ARAUJO, 2015) preprocessing is an integrated and essential step of the AS task. Thus, 1137 tweets resulting from the previous step undergone a treatment where considered structures were discarded irrelevant to the process of classification of the polarity of data, called tokens. These structures included: irrelevant words stopwords calls, present terms specifically Twitter, punctuation and special characters.

Messages that made each tweet were also classified (labeled or tagged) manually by creating so labels to identify the sentiment expressed by each message as positive, negative or neutral. The labeled data took two tasks: comparison basis for the results generated by the methods (ie a point of comparison between the actual polarity of the messages and trial methods), and as a basis for experiments with SVM algorithm, since this uses data labeled to train the algorithm. Possible labels were:

- **Positive:** Messages that do not express any opinion or feeling;
- **Negative:** Messages that express a negative feeling, but are written with the structure of positive texts;
- **Neutral:** Messages that do not express any opinion or feeling.

Experiments Done

After preparation of the data were performed experiments with the methods provided by iFeel Web tool and Support Vector Machine algorithm. These experiments were performed in two ways: the first messages were submitted to the algorithm and methods in the presence of hashtags (markers) that indicate sarcasm, in the second test were removed from these hashtags messages and the base resubmitted for classification.

The first experiment consisted in sentiment analysis performed by the 11 methods provided by the Web iFeel system, on the set of 1137 tweets collected and properly treated in the previous steps. The methods used were SentiWordNet, PANAS-t, Sentistrength, EmoLex, NRC Hashtag, Opinion Lexicon, Pattern.en, AFINN, VADER, Sentiment140 and Combined Method. We are chosen specifically for these methods use different polarity classification techniques allowing diversity in the results generated. The objective of this experiment was basically to test the performance of the methods mentioned above, to correctly classify the polarity (feeling) messages (tweets) positive, neutral and mostly negative. For the messages labeled as negative (representing the sarcastic nature of messages), they are in fact sentences written with words and key terms that have a positive character, but express a negative sentimentwhen analyzed according to the context in which they were written ie are the messages that suffered from the reverse polarity caused by the presence of sarcasm.

The second experiment in turn, was the classification of the set of tweets with and without the presence of sarcastic nature of hashtags, the algorithm based on learning SVM machines, whose goal was was also to test the performance of classifying the polarity sarcastic nature messages. This experiment was divided into two tasks: classification of tweets with the presence of sarcastic nature of hashtags and without the presence of these.

An important note is the fact that the experiments with the SVM algorithm neutral tweets had to be discarded, since the aforementioned standard for algorithm disregards goals texts (neutral polarity) as the default output generated by it is binary, which means that text is likely to belong to only one of two classes - negative (0) or positive (1). Then, after the disregard of neutral tweets set 1137 tweets, the database resulted in a total of 906 tweets for experiments with the algorithm.

Finally the results of the classifications made by the methods and algorithm, and with the correct labeling of messages in the test base, it was estimated then performance evaluation metrics: recall, precision, F-measure and accuracy. The values were used to compare the performance of the methods and organize the results in the shape of tables and graphs. These metrics are best addressed in the next section.

Metrics for Performance Comparison

A key aspect in the evaluation of methods for analyzing feelings regards used metrics. In this context, four key metrics are commonly used to validate the efficiency of a method, they are: precision, recall, F-measure and accuracy. Specifically in sentiment analysis area these metrics are used in the literature for methods of assessment and detection algorithms or polarity classification of feelings (Sokolova, Lapalme, 2009; Gonçalves et al, 2015;. RIBEIRO, 2015). These metrics were used for performance evaluation of the methods tested in this research.

- **Precision (P):** Measures portion of samples of a class that were classified correctly, ie, evidence the percentage of messages belonging to a class of polarity that were correctly classified by taking into consideration the method of trial and error method for this class. To find the precision of a class X must divide the number of messages classified correctly by the total of classified messages as belonging to class X. As shown by the following equation (Sokolova, Lapalme, 2009).

$$Precision = \frac{\text{TP}}{\left(\text{TP} + \text{FP}\right)}$$

TP is the total of true positive of the class is calculated and FP total false positives class in question.

- **Recall (R):** The recall measure (R) measures the proportion of classified samples as a class in relation to all kind of samples, that is, the percentage of messages of a certain polarity class that were correctly classified by the method from total messages comprising the particular class. Their percentage evidence adjustment capability of the method to the total of messages belonging to certain polarity class. This percentage is calculated according to the following equation (Sokolova, Lapalme, 2009).

$$Recall = \frac{\mathrm{TP}}{\left(\mathrm{TP} + \mathrm{FN}\right)}$$

TP is the total of true positive of the class which is the total FN calculating and false negative of the class in question.

- **F-Measure:** It is the harmonic mean or balance between precision and recall. Feelings commonly used in analysis area to assess the classification ability of a method to determined polarity class. Its result provides one measure of comparison that allows comparison of the classification capacity between different methods. Thus, the better the method evaluated closer to 1 is the metric value, and if the method has a low rating capacity it will have a value of F-measure closer to 0 (Sokolova, Lapalme, 2009).

$$F - measure = \frac{2 \cdot \left(Precision \cdot Recall\right)}{\left(Precision + Recall\right)}$$

Applied to the scope of this work, this metric was used to directly compare the overall performance classification of the different methods and tested algorithm.

- **Accuracy:** The measurement accuracy (A) the accuracy English, denotes the proportion (percentage) Total method hit regardless of the polarity class, that is, the sum of the hits of all the polarity classes divided by the total number classified messages (Sokolova ; Lapalme, 2009). In this research the accuracy was used in comparing the performance of the methods globally on all the problem of sentimentclasses. It is calculated according to the following equation.

$$Accuracy = \frac{\mathrm{TP}}{\left(\mathrm{TP} + \mathrm{FP} + \mathrm{FN}\right)}$$

It is noteworthy that the F-measure is a weighted measure of precision and recall and was used to measure the overall ability of the method of classification for a particular class, that is, the most important measure to evaluate the performance of the methods and algorithm studied

COMPARISON RESULTS

This section presents the quantitative results as a percentage of polarity classification performed by the 11 methods and algorithm. These results are: the recall, precision and F-measure, obtained by each method for each class polarity (positive, negative, and neutral) exists in the test data base.

Each following diagram, shows the values of precicion, recall and F-measure er achieved by each of the 11 methods implemented on the Web iFeel tool, according to two tests carried out on the satisfaction test based on the 1137 tweets: the first test was the classification of tweets with the presence of sarcastic nature of hashtags and the second test was the classification without the presence of sarcastic nature of hashtags. For each table there is a chart corresponds, allowing for better visualization and comparison of results. The y-axis (represented by a scale of 0 to 100) equals the percentage achieved by any method each evaluation metric (i.e., the method of classification performance), while the x-axis represents the sentimentanalysis method tested

The following charts bring the results of the classifications made by the methods of the Test Base with and without the presence of sarcasm die hashtags.

For the classification of tweets with positive polarity, the methods with greater precision, recall and F-measure, respectively:

- Sentistrength, more precisely at a rate 46.30%, in the experiment with the presence of sarcastic nature of hashtags;
- Increased recall was the PANAS-t (17.50%) in both tests;;
- Emolex (20.97%), had a higher F-measure, the test without hashtags.

In the ranking of 786 negative tweets that had sarcastic content from the first test (negative tweets with the presence of sarcastic nature of hashtags) and the second test (negative tweets without hashtags), the results were as follows:

- **Precision:** The first test Sentistrength method (85.64%) had the highest accuracy rate. As for the second test the best was the Pattern.en with 76.19%. The method Vader got the worst rate in both tests - 59.81% (with hashtags) and 60.19% (no hashtags);
- **Recall:** For the first test the Combined Method (71.12%) reached better recall, in the second test NRChashtag (66.03%) was the best. The method as poor recall in both tests was PANAS-T at the rate of 2.04%;

Figure 2. Comparison of test results hashtags (tweets positives)

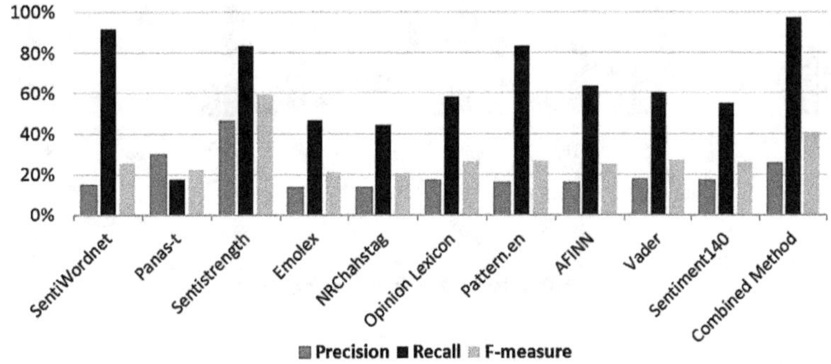

Figure 3. Comparison of test results without hashtags (Neutral tweets)

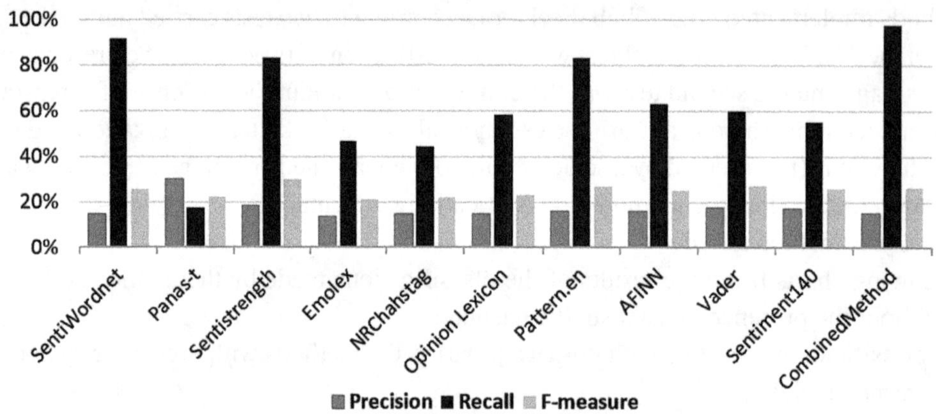

Figure 4. Comparison of test results with hashtags (negative tweets)

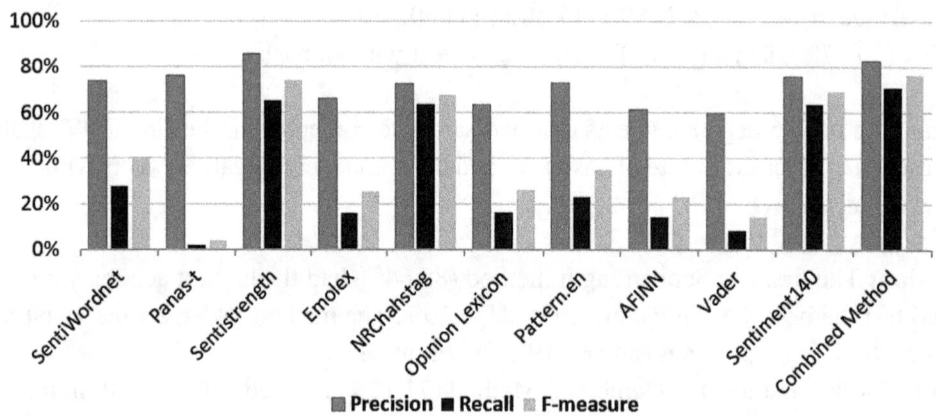

Figure 5. Comparison of the test results without hashtags (negative tweets)

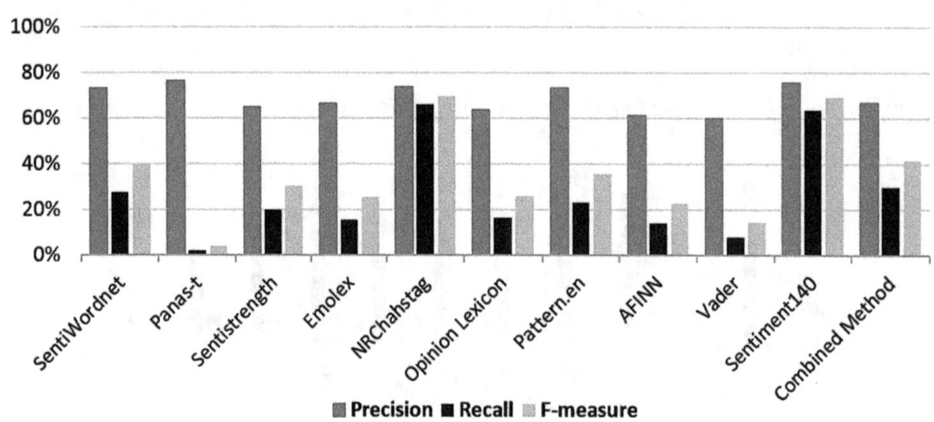

- **F-Measure:** With a percentage of 76.47% the Combined Method was the best performing method to classify the class of negative tweets, however for the second test was the best NRChashtag with 69.52%. The worst performance was in the NAPA-T (3.97%) in both tests.

Taking into consideration the total of 231 neutral tweets labeled in accordance with the tables and graphs presented above:

- The method with higher accuracy in the test was hashtags NRChashtag the rate of 35.09%, since the test without hashtags the highest rate was achieved by Pattern.en (35.20%);
- The PANAS-T had the highest recall in both tests (96.10%), and Combined Method worse in both tests (0.43%);
- The highest percentage of F-measure to the test with hashtags was hit by Sentistrength (39.42%), as the test without hashtags Vader fared better with 37.97%. The worst result of F-measure was the Combined Method method (0.85% and 0.84%).

Figure 6. Comparison of the test results with hashtags (neutral tweets)

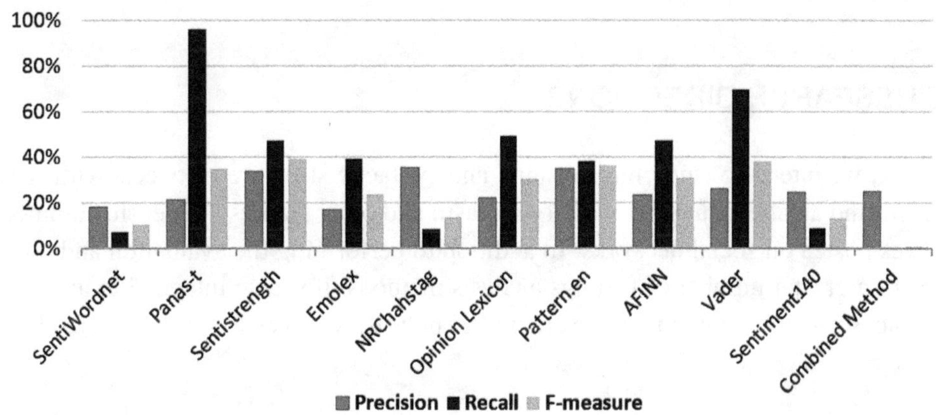

Figure 7. Comparison of the test results without hashtags (neutral tweets)

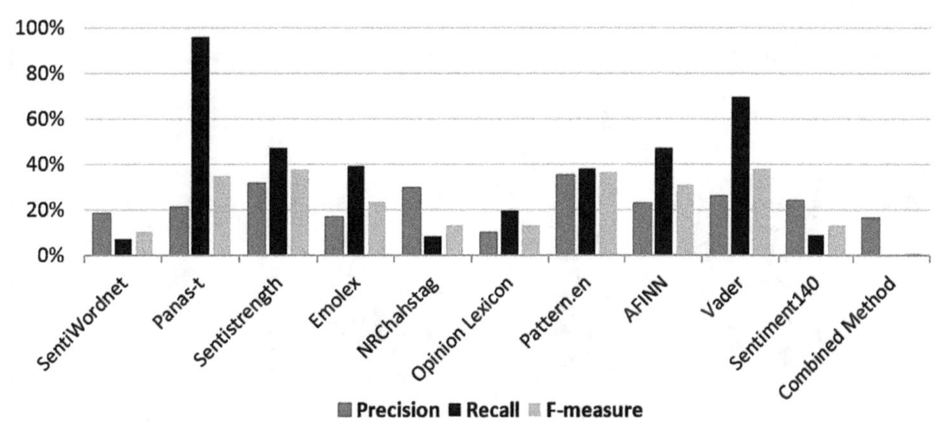

The graph in Figure 8 shows the results of the classifications carried out by the SVM algorithm for the experiments with and without the presence of sarcasm die hashtags.

In tests with the Support Vector Machine algorithm (SVM), and with the methods implemented in the Web iFeel tool, the algorithm performed better to sort the tweets in the presence of sarcastic nature of hashtags. As the graph in Figure 8.

For further enrichment of this work was also carried out to compare the performance of methods in terms of accuracy, which is to hit rate on the three polarity classes, to experiment with hashtags (Figure 8) and without hashtags (Figure 9) .

As the chart 9, among the methods implemented in iFeel system to the test with presence of hashtags, the method with the highest percentage of correct answers was the Sentistrength (63,50%). Have the lowest percentage of correct answers was with the PANAS-T method (22.78% performance). As for the test on the tweets hashtags after removal of the NRChashtags method was better with a percentage of 52.07%, while Opinion Lexicon (21.55%) achieved the worst percentage. However when comparing the SVM algorithm with other methods implemented in iFeel, it is observed that the SVM had a higher rating performance, with a lead of 34.08% over the NRChashtags method, the classification without hashtags.

Analyzing the results also realize is that the most accurate rate achieved was when the methods classified the tweets even with the hashtags.

FUTURE RESEARCH DIRECTIONS

As future work, we intend to study the semantic and syntactic structure of tweets with sarcastic content in order to find a pattern that can identify sarcasm and other figures of speech, commonly used in short messages posted on social networks. In addition to performing the evaluation and comparison of performance of a greater number of feelings analysis methods. It is also intended to test this more and equalized database, ie, a base in which the amount of polarity samples for each class are equal.

Figure 8. Results obtained by the SVM algorithm

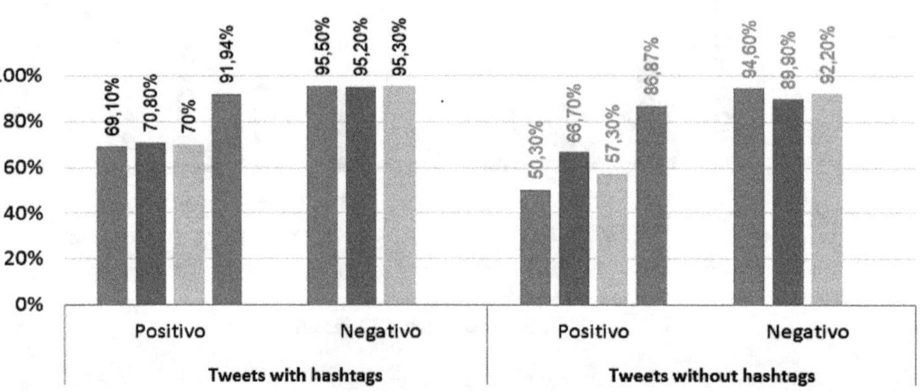

Figure 9. Accuracy experiment with sarcastic nature of hashtags

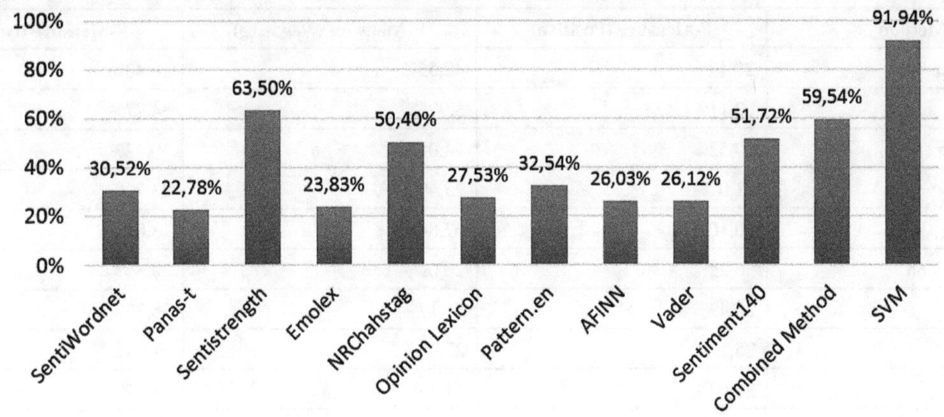

Figure 10. Accuracy of experiment without sarcastic nature of hashtags

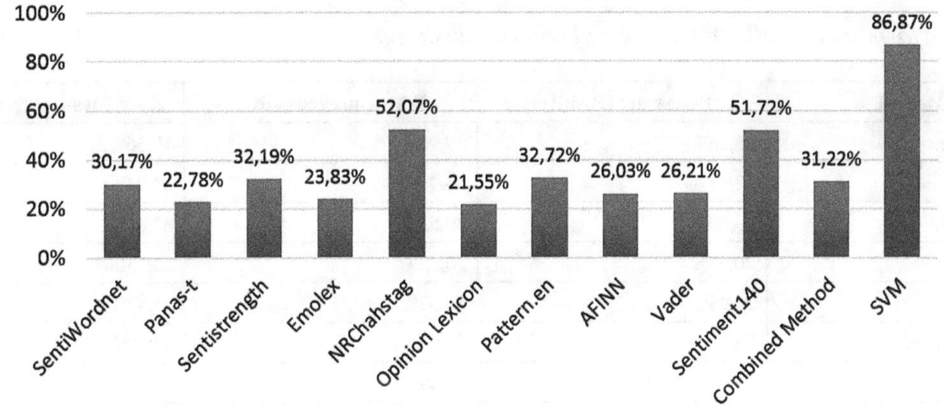

CONCLUSION

In this work we tried to evaluate 12 different methods of analysis of feelings existing in the literature, and how different performances they present to classify a polarity of messages with sarcastic content, taken from Twitter. The approach adopted was to quantitatively identify the performance of these methods in the context of sarcasm.

Following are two tables. Table 1 with the result of the classification performed by the methods with the presence of sarcasm and, table 2 without the presence of hashtags.

Through the results obtained for an F-measure metric, it was possible to verify that among 12 methods of analysis of quality feelings, which obtained a higher capacity of classification of the messages (tweets) with sarcastic content, in the presence or not of sarcastic hashtags (SVM) with the confidence values of 95.35% and 92.94% (Figure 8). What characterizes what is best classified as messages even without the help of hashtags, which help you in identifying sarcasm. While that obtained the classification performance for the PANAS-method with a percentage of 3.97% performance (Figures 4 and 5).

Table 1. Performance of all methods tested with hashtags

Method	F-Measure (Positive)	F-Measure (Negative)	F-Measure (Neutral)
SentWordNet	25,49%	40,55%	10,43%
Panas-t	22,11%	3,97%	34,77%
Sentistrength	59,52%	74,08%	39,42%
Emolex	21,01%	25,49%	23,70%
NRChashtag	20,10%	67,84%	13,89%
Opinion Lexicon	26,22%	26,09%	30,36%
Pattern.en	26,49%	35,17%	36,36%
AFINN	25,17%	22,96%	31,01%
Vader	27,02%	14,33%	37,97%
Sentiment140	25,93%	69,20%	13,25%
Combined Method	40,55%	76,47%	0,85%

Table 2. Performance of all methods tested without hashtags

Method	F-Measure (Positive)	F-Measure (Negative)	F-Measure (Neutral)
SentWordNet	25,26%	39,96%	10,56%
Panas-t	22,11%	3,97%	34,77%
Sentistrength	29,90%	30,52%	37,85%
Emolex	20,97%	25,49%	23,73%
NRChashtag	21,95%	69,52%	13,42%
Opinion Lexicon	23,22%	26,09%	13,49%
Pattern.en	26,46%	35,49%	36,59%
AFINN	25,17%	22,96%	31,01%
Vader	27,07%	14,54%	37,97%
Sentiment140	25,98%	69,20%	13,21%
Combined Method	26,09%	41,58%	0,84%

Another important point observed from the results found, which strengthened an idea of the impact caused by the sarcasm, was the fact that the methods Sentistrength, combined method and SVM had in their results a considerable reduction of performance, when classifying the tweets with meaning sarcastic (tweets negatives) Without the presence of sarcastic hashtags. As shown in the graphs of Figures 4 and 8, the three methods cited obtained the following performance when classifying negative tweets with the presence of hashtags: 74.08%, 76.47% and 95.35% respectively, but after performing the (Tables 5 and 8), respectively. The results obtained in this study were similar to those of the F-measure. According to these results it is possible to conclude that the Sentistrength suffered a performance decrease of 43.56% in its performance performance, the Combined Method a reduction 34.89% and the SVM a decrease of 3.11%.

These phenomena observed within the scope of this research reveal that some of the tested methods presented inconsistent classification results when compared to the manually classified database (labeled) by humans. Thus, it is possible that different methods of feeling analysis found in the literature may present inconsistent results due to the inversion of polarity caused by the presence of sarcasm in shared messages in social media. This performance drop occurred mainly when the methods classified the messages without the presence of sarcastic hashtags, which are labels with words that aid some methods in identifying the polarity inversion present in the messages. Thus, the complexity of identifying and classifying polarity in sarcastic messages is shown.

Finally, it is emphasized that the identification of these changes in the performance of the methods are of high importance when it comes to organizations that use the results generated by methods of analysis of feelings to guide their decision making.

REFERENCES

Angulakshmi, G., & Chezian, R. (2014). Article. *International Journal of Advanced Research in Computer and Communication Engineering*, *3*(7), 5.

Barbieri, F., Saggion, H., & Ronzano, F. (2014). Modelling sarcasm in twitter, a novel approach. *WASSA, ACL, 2014*, 50.

BBC. (2014). *US Secret Service seeks Twitter sarcasm detector*. Retrieved from http://www.bbc.com/news/technology-27711109

Becker, K., & Tumitan, D. (2013). Introdução à mineração de opiniões: Conceitos, aplicações e desafios. *Lectures of the 28th Brazilian Symposium on Databases*.

Benevenuto, F. Ribeiro, F., & Araújo, M. (2015). Métodos Para Análise de Sentimentos em Mídias Sociais. *Brazilian Symposium on Multimedia and the Web (Webmedia)*.

Berry, M., & Kogan, J. (2010). Text Mining: Applications and Theory. Wiley. doi:10.1002/9780470689646

Buschmeier, K., Cimiano, P., & Klinger, R. (2014). An impact analysis of features in a classification approach to irony detection in product reviews. *Proceedings of the 5th Workshop on Computational Approaches to Subjectivity, Sentiment and Social Media Analysis*, 42–49. doi:10.3115/v1/W14-2608

Cambria, E. (n.d.). New avenues in Opinion mining and sentiment analysis. *IEEE Intelligent Systems, 28*(2), 15–21.

Carvalho Filho, J. A. (2014). *Mineração de Textos: Análise de Sentimentos Utilizando o Tweets Referentes a Copa do Mundo* (Dissertação de Mestrado). Universidade Nova de Lisboa, Quixadá.

Cheang, H. S., & Pell, M. D. (2011). Recognizing sarcasm without language: A cross-linguistic study of English and Cantonese. *Pragmatics & Cognition, 19*(2), 203–223. doi:10.1075/pc.19.2.02che

Chen, H., & Zimbra, D. (2010). AI and Opinion Mining. *IEEE Intelligent Systems, 25*(3), 74–80.

Conz, J. (2010). IRONIA VERBAL: Teorias e Considerações (Graduação em Letras). Universidade Federal do Rio Grande do Sul, Porto Alegre.

Gonçalves, M. A. (2010). *Abordagens para Avaliação Automática da Qualidade de Conferências científicas: um estudo de caso em ciência da computação* (Dissertação de Mestrado). Universidade Federal de Minas Gerais, Belo Horizonte.

Gonçalves, P. (2013a). Comparing and combining sentiment analysis methods. In *Proceedings of the First ACM Conference on Online Social Networks (COSN '13)*. New York, NY: ACM. doi:10.1145/2512938.2512951

Gonçalves, P., Dores, W., & Benevenuto, F. (2012). Panas-t: Uma escala psicométrica para medição de sentimentos no twitter. *Proceedings of the Brazilian Workshop on Social Network Analysis and Mining (BraSNAM)*.

Hastie, T., Tibshirani, R., & Friedman, J. (2008). The elements of statistical learning: data mining, inference and prediction (2nd ed.). Springer.

Hu, M., & Liu, B. (2004). Mining opinion features in customer reviews. In *Proceedings of the 19th National Conference on Artifical Intelligence*. AAAI Press.

Hutto, C. J., & Vader. (2014). A parsimonious rule-based model for sentiment analysis of social media text. *Eighth International AAAI Conference on Weblogs and Social Media*.

Ingle, A. (2014). Sentiment analysis: Sarcasm detection of tweets. Nagpur.

Kalamkar, P. N., & Phakatkar, A. G. (2013). Opinion mining in figures of speech in text. *International Journal of Scientific Engineering Research*, *4*(10), 1132–1134.

Kreuz, R. J., & Caucci, G. M. (2007). Lexical influences on the perception of sarcasm. In *Proceedings of the Workshop on Computational Approaches to Figurative Language*. Stroudsburg, PA: Association for Computational Linguistics. doi:10.3115/1611528.1611529

Liu, B. (2010b). Sentiment analysis: Amultifaceted Problem. *IEEE Intelligent Systems*, *25*(3), 76–80.

Liu, K., Hogan, W. R., & Crowleya, R. S. (2011). Natural language processing methods and systems for biomedical ontology learning. *Journal of Biomedical Informatics*, *44*(1), 163–179. Retrieved from http://migre.me/thZEQ

Lunando, E., & Purwarianti, A. (2013). Indonesian social media sentiment analysis with sarcasm detection. *Advanced Computer Science and Information Systems (ICACSIS), 2013 International Conference*, 195–198. doi:10.1109/ICACSIS.2013.6761575

Maynard, D., & Greenwood, M. A. (2014). *Who cares about sarcastic tweets? Investigating the impact of sarcasm on sentiment analysis*. LREC.

Miller, G. A. (1995). Wordnet: A lexical database for English. *Commun. ACM, 38*(11), 39–41.

Mitchell, T. (2006). *The discipline of machine learning*. Academic Press.

Mohammad, S. (2012). #emotional tweets. In **SEM 2012: The First Joint Conference on Lexical and Computational Semantics – Volume 1: Proceedings of the main conference and the shared task, and Volume 2: Proceedings of the Sixth International Workshop on Semantic Evaluation (SemEval 2012)*. Montréal, Canada: Association for Computational Linguistics.

Mohammad, S. M., Kiritchenko, S., & Zhu, X. (2013b). *Nrc-canada: Building the state-of-the-art in sentiment analysis of tweets*. Academic Press.

Mohammad, S. M., & Turney, P. D. (2013a). Crowdsourcing a word-emotion association lexicon. Academic Press.

Pang, B., & Lee, L. (2004). A sentimental education: Sentiment analysis using subjectivity summarization based on minimum cuts. *Proceedings of the ACL*, 271–278. doi:10.3115/1218955.1218990

Poria, S. (2016). *A Deeper Look into Sarcastic Tweets Using Deep Convolutional Neural Networks*. Nanyang Technological University.

Raj, K. G., & Yinping, Y. (2017). CrystalNest at SemEval-2017 Task 4: Using sarcasm detection for enhancing sentiment classification and quantification. In *Proceedings of the 11th International Workshop on Semantic Evaluation*. Vancouver, Canada: SemEval '17.

Reyes, A., Rosso, P., & Veale, T. (2013). *A multidimensional approach for detecting irony in twitter. In Language Resources and Evaluation* (pp. 1–30). Springer Netherlands.

Riloff, E. (2013). *Sarcasm as contrast between a positive sentiment and negative situation*. EMNLP.

Santos, F. (2013). *Mineracão de Opinião em Textos Opinativos Utilizando Algoritmos de Classificação* (Graduação). Universidade de Brasilia, Brasilia.

Simon, H. A. (1983). Machine learning: An artificial intelligence approach. Springer Berlin Heidelberg.

Smed, T. D., Nijs, L., & Daelemans, W. (2014). Creative Web Service with Pattern. Academic Press.

Sokolova, M., & Lapalme, G. (2009). A systematic analysis of performance measures for classification tasks. *Inf. Process. Manage., 45*(4), 427–437.

Souza, M. V. S. (2012). *Mineração de Opiniões Aplicada a Mídias Sociais* (Dissertação de Mestrado). Universidade Católica do Rio Grande do Sul, Porto Alegre. Retrieved from http://migre.me/thZxK

Spears, R. (1998). *NTC's American English learner's dictionary: The essential vocabulary of American language and culture*. NTC Pub. Group.

Taboada, M. (2011). Lexicon-based methods for sentiment analysis. Computational Linguistics, 37(34), 267–307.

Thelwall, M. (2013). *Heart and Soul: Sentiment Strength Detection in the Social Web With SentiStrength*. Academic Press.

Vapnik, V. N. (1995). *The nature of statistical learning theory*. New York, NY: Springer-Verlag New York, Inc. doi:10.1007/978-1-4757-2440-0

Veale, T., & Hao, Y. (2010). Detecting ironic intent in creative comparisons. *ECAI, 215*, 765–770.

Watson, D., Clark, L. A., & Tellegen, A. (1988). Development and validation of brief measures of positive and negative affect: The panas scales. *Journal of Personality and Social Psychology, 54*(6), 1063–1070. doi:10.1037/0022-3514.54.6.1063 PMID:3397865

Chapter 6
Analysis of Online Social Networks for the Identification of Sarcasm

Pulkit Mehndiratta
Jaypee Institute of Information Technology, India
Shelly Sachdeva
Jaypee Institute of Information Technology, India

ABSTRACT

With the ever-increasing acceptance of online social networks (OSNs), a new dimension has evolved for communication amongst humans. OSNs have given us the opportunity to monitor and mine the opinions of a large number of online active populations in real time. Many diverse approaches have been proposed, various datasets have been generated, but there is a need of collective understanding of this area. Researchers are working around the globe to find a pattern to judge the mood of the user; the still serious problem of detection of irony and sarcasm in textual data poses a threat to the accuracy of the techniques evolved till date. This chapter aims to help the reader to think and learn more clearly about the aspects of sentiment analysis, social network analysis, and detection of irony or sarcasm in textual data generated via online social networks. It argues and discusses various techniques and solutions available in literature currently. In the end, the chapter provides some answers to the open-ended question and future research directions related to the analysis of textual data.

1. INTRODUCTION

It is always fascinating to know "What going on the other person's mind", and it has been an important part of the information for most of us while taking any decision or collaborating. Before the internet revolution, we used to ask our friends about their take on any topic, thing, or person. They were the people whose opinions and experience helped us taking our decision wisely and make maximum out of it. With the internet penetrating into our lives along with many applications and technologies, we are now connected with a vast pool of people who are not our friends or acquaintances neither they are known to us; also they are not the experts or professional of that particular field. Still, the opinion and

DOI: 10.4018/978-1-5225-5097-6.ch006

sentiment they have are important to us and helps us to take the decision. It is also true the other way around, that more and more people are making their opinions available to strangers with the help of the internet. Thus, evolves a field of science known as sentiment analysis, also known as *opinion mining*.

1.1. Sentiment Analysis and Opinion Mining

Sentiment analysis is a field of study where we analyze people's opinions, sentiments, attitudes and emotions towards various topics and entities like products, services, events, issues, related attributes and much more. While academicians use sentiment analysis and opinion mining often, in the industry its only sentiment analysis. The word sentiment analysis was first used by Nasakawa in the year 2003, on the other hand, Dave et. al. (2003) used opinion mining for the very first time in the same year. Hence in broad terms, sentiment analysis and opinion mining focus on the views which eventually imply negative or positive polarity of sentence.

Although we have a very long history related to natural language processing and linguistics but very little has been explored and researched in the field before the arrival of the 21st century, after this the area has seen active research by academicians and industrialists. The major reason of this thrust is because of the applications it has in the various domains. Many commercial applications like Amazon, eBay are largely dependent on these applications that predict or judge the mood of the consumer and present it to the other user to follow. Also, this field offers many challenging problems which had never been addressed or evaluated before. But, the most important factor that propels the research in this field is a huge volume of opinionated data which is available for the very first time on the world wide web (WWW), on various social networks and many commercial sites. Without this, it would not have been possible to conduct research in the field. It can be said that sentiment analysis and opinion mining has a major impact on natural language processing apart from that, it plays important role in managerial science, economics, as all these are affected by opinions of other people.

1.2. Technology Background of Sentiment Analysis

Sentiments are central to almost every human being; activities related to them and have a large impact on the behavior of ours. With the rapid growth of online social media, we have ample of data in form of reviews, blogs, micro-blogging sites, comments, Twitter, Facebook and various other posting on OSNs that can be and should be used for the decision-making process. They have real-life applications and implications that help us in one way or the another. Apart from these applications, many researchers have published various application-oriented articles in the literature. Starting with McGlohon et. al. (2010) analyzed reviews that helped to rank the products and merchants selling them. Similarly, Liu in 2007 published a model to predict the sales performance. Twitter sentiment has been linked with multiple studies some tried to rate the movies so as to predict the box-office collection, others tried to predict the result of ongoing elections (O'Connor et al, 2010; Tumasjan et al, 2010; Yano et al, 2010; Asur et al, 2010; Joshi et al, 2010). Many studies also tried to find out the pattern in the stock market one such study is explained in (Bollen, 2011). While there are approaches proposed to calculate the trading strategies of any brokerage firm (Zhang, 2010). We are not only limited to this, people have tried to find out the social relation graph for various users in (Groh et al, 2011). Thus, we have many studies in the literature that prove to be useful and provide us multiple types of solutions and algorithms to work with.

1.3. Algorithms to Perform Sentiment Analysis

Various approaches and techniques are present and evaluated till date majorly grouped into four categories: knowledge-based techniques, semantics techniques, language models and statistical methods. Knowledge-based methods are basically focused on the methods where we try to classify the sentiment based on the presence of the various unambiguous effect words of positive or negative categories respectively. Some techniques also add arbitrary knowledge or affinity to a particular sentiment. On the other hand. The statistical methods use various machine learning methods support vector machines (Pang et al, 2004), bag-of-word techniques (Maas et la, 2011), probabilistic models to find out the sentiments in the textual data. Many such techniques have been proposed in the past to classify/identify the sentiment in the data.

In one technique, authors (Turney, 2003) try to characterize the words and phrases according to emotive tone. In another study, authors (Hatzivassiloglou, et al, 1997) have tried to get the automatic acquisition of the sentiment expressed, but the study was limited to adjectives and only one sentiment could be assigned to one word. The semantic techniques use a very discourse relation between the various components of text and that of the classification method used. Most of the time the overall sentiment of the text is revealed at the end. Similarly, various language model techniques like n-grams are used to check the frequency of the words in documents. Further, they can be used for checking the importance of the word in the text document with the help of techniques like TF-IDF method (O'Keefe et al, 2009).

1.4. Applications of Sentiment Analysis and Opinion Mining

As the acceptance of the opinion mining and sentiment analysis is increasing day by day, natural language processing community is showing a lot of interest in this field and its applications. The integration of the internet also has changed our lifestyles to a much greater extent altogether and this has helped researchers to gather the user-generated content easy and fast. Some the major application areas where sentiment analysis and opinion mining is playing a vital role are as follows:

- **Purchasing Services and Products:** Nowadays if one has to buy or lease anything, then taking a right decision does not take much effort as opinions and experiences of the others are available in abundance for any service or product. Companies like Amazon, Flipkart and more are analyzing, structuring and helping the customer to understand the pros and cons of every product and thus making shopping experience better online.
- **Quality Improvement:** For manufacturing industry it is important to indulge with the user to get the feedback of the products they design and develop and to come up with the better or improved version next time. The review of the critics is as important for any product or service as favorable opinions. Major technology giants like Amazon, Google, Apple and Microsoft have a crucial role to play to improve the quality of the products.
- **Market Research:** With the help of sentiment analysis and opinion mining, companies can judge the mood of the user about the particular product or the services they provide. Similarly, the trends of the market for any field whether it's the policies, new box office release, new song album of an artist; market analysis and research help the companies accomplish wonder by finding out what customers want and how they want it.

- **Decision and Policymaking:** It is always important to think twice and take the viewpoint of another person before taking any important decision, deciding policies or deciding the course of action. By using sentiment analysis, policymakers can accommodate user's point of view, his/her state of the mind towards a policy and utilize that particular information to improve the quality of the decision before its actual implementation and acceptability.

There are various other areas applications like recommendation systems, spam detection, and classification, monitoring of various blogs and news forums; all these domains are linked to sentiment analysis and opinion mining in one way or the other.

1.5. Challenges of Opinion Mining and Sentiment Analysis

The field of sentiment analysis has gained much attention over the past two decades, still there are many areas and topics where sentiment analysis needs to get evolved. Some of the key areas are:

- **Detection of Sarcasm:** Textual data contains sarcastic words and ironic phrases in them all the time. In most scenarios, a positive word can have a negative sense of meaning, The usage of these words lead to poor results and can deteriorate the perform of opinion mining and sentiment analysis algorithm. Many techniques have already been proposed in the literature to perform the detection of sarcasm in the text but still, a lot is to be done.
- **Spam and Fake Review:** The world wide web contains both authentic and fake content. It is of utmost importance that for effective and accurate sentiment analysis the data should be cleaned and processed thus, any fake or unwanted content is eliminated from the dataset. This process can be done by identification of the fake and spam content from the authentic data set and also detecting the outliers in the dataset. This can also be done by considering the content reputation.
- **Availability of the Software:** Mining of opinion is an expensive process and at present only big organizations and government can afford to handle such kind of data and perform the analysis on it. It is almost beyond par of what common user can handle. It is important that everyone should be benefited from this technology. Hence, technology is required to make these software available to the common man.
- **Independence of Domain:** Most of the words used for sentiment analysis and opinion mining are domain dependent. Thus, it may happen that one feature yield very good results for one domain and not at all suitable for the other leading to very poor performance. It is to be considered to have some generic words and phrases that enable the user to correctly find the sentiment in the sentence or paragraph.
- **Natural Language Processing Overheads:** The NLP does provide some overheads like implicitness, inference, ambiguity, and co-references. All of the mentioned features put a negative impact on the overall sentiment of the sentence thus, leading to the poor classification of the sentiment in the sentence or phrase.

2. SARCASM AND IRONY

In the past few years, it has been observed that usage of the online social network has increased due high penetration of the internet in the developing countries. With this increase, there is an amplification in the volume of data generated in the form of text, images, videos and much more. Nowadays, with online social media forming part of our daily routine, people can share a large amount of information without being personal to one entity. Even for large enterprises, it is important to have social media presence thus, teams are working day and night to mark an overall presence in each and every domain.

Given the high volume and velocity of the data generated, companies use various online tools available in the market for the sentiment analysis and mining opinion of the real-time product user. Some of the tools available in the market are HootSuite[1], Spredfast[2], Sprout Social[3] etc. While these external tools perform well for the basic tasks like to analyze the data, to provide customer service and much more. Still, these tools lack the necessary sophistication in detection of sarcasm for the text. This is quite a task for the team managing the social media front. They are the one who has to put extra effort and man hours to complete the task of the detection of sarcasm in text.

Sarcasm is an act of saying or writing something which has opposite meaning with respect to the context. It is an indirect language tool used majorly to ridicule and present mockery, which is often considered rude and offensive along with a way showing false politeness. An example of being sarcastic is as:

"Thanks #uber for charging $102 for 3 miles ride #sarcasm #:-("

The above-mentioned example has a negative setback in a disapproving dialogue.

On similar grounds, irony can be defined as a feeling which shows a disagreement in what you feel and what you say, what you expected and what is the resultant outcome. It is less offensive and ridicule as compared to sarcasm but still sometimes used interchangeably. The only major difference between the two is that the usage of sarcasm is bit brutal and rude to the person who receives it as compared to irony which is more subtle and polite in nature. Also, the major problem of discovering the sarcasm and irony in the text is lack of agreement among the various research communities. People from sociology, psychology, and computer science are trying day and night that how the sarcasm can be detected and differentiated from the normal polite text and ironic statements.

Not only this, as the tools available in the market fail to detect the usage of sarcasm in the text, this further encourages people to post rude, and sarcastic messages. There are cases in the past where company representative was not able to detect the sarcasm in a text message and this not only hamper their performance but the also ruins the public image of the companies. A few years back, US Secret Services publicly issued a notice for seeking help to detect sarcasm from online social media explicitly stating that the currently no tool or software can do this dubious task. Thus, this chapter shows a brief outline of the various techniques used till date from the past in various domains.

Our focus is more towards online social network mainly Twitter[4]. The main reason for considering Twitter over other online social networks is that it's more informal in nature. Also, the usage of slang and abbreviations along with the limitation of 140 characters, makes deciphering of sarcasm and irony in the text more complex and ambiguous task to perform.

2.1. Various Approachs to Detect Sarcasm in Textual Data

For many years the sarcasm has been widely studied topics among the psychologists, linguistic and behavioral experts. Theories have been proposed in the past like echoic reminder theory (Kreuz et al, 1989), implicit display theory (Utsumi, 2000) and many more have been studied and researched. According to echoic reminder theory, the user is able to detect sarcasm based on his previous experiences and affairs. Positive statements can be viewed and considered as sarcastic without any external/explicit allusion based on the past experience. The original article also identifies and discusses the need for usage of sarcasm in positive situations when those can easily be understood by not using any sarcastic utterance. One interesting motivation discussed in the article is that the usage of sarcasm in a particular situation not only provide the insight of the objective evaluation but also reflects the user's attitude and perception towards the situation.

Another theory is commonly known as implicit display theory, claims that utterance of ironic words and phrases implicitly display an ironic situation having three properties: expectation, emotional attitude, and incongruity. The theory states that the speaker has an expectation in mind which fails. This results into incongruity between expected and actual observed result which further results into negative emotion, leading to the utterance of ironic/sarcastic words or phrases. Further, the model proposed to detect sarcasm based on degrees of allusion, indirect expression of negative attitude, pragmatics insincerity, context-independent polarity, and manifestness of the expectations.

Automatic sarcasm detection is relatively new compared to other fields in linguistics and deemed to be a difficult problem (Pang et al, 2008). According to early work by Tepperman et al (2006), sarcasm has been detected based on spectral and contextual features. Not only this Davidov et al. (2010) devised a semi-supervised algorithm to detect sarcasm in product reviews from Amazon and tweets. The algorithm is based on the usage of high frequency and content words.

Also, some punctuation based features have also been considered to design the classifier using a weighted k-nearest neighbor algorithm. On similar grounds, Gonzalez et al. (2011) devised an algorithm based on the numerous lexical features along with many pragmatic features like emoticons and replies. Reyes et al. (2012) focused on developing a model to train the classifier for detection of irony based on ambiguity, polarity, unexpectedness and emotional cues. A very accurate approach to detect the sarcasm in text based on the feature like unigrams, bigrams, trigrams has been developed by Liebrecht (2013) using Balanced Window Classifier. In the year 2013, Riloff et al. (2013) stated that there is a contrast between positive sentiment and a negative situation thus, can be used to detect the sarcasm in the textual data. Wang et al. (2015) use a dataset of tweets marked as happy, sarcastic and sad, The tweets are labeled using a classifier, as the main task of the algorithm is to detect a sequence of labels. Bamman and Smith (2015) used hashtags as a feature of the dataset. They stated that the positive tweets are the once having the #sarcasm associated with them and negative tweets have no such labels in them. Recently, in the study by Rajadesigan (2015), a dataset of tweets labeled by hashtags along with the historical context of 80 tweets per user is used to construct an approach named SCUBA. Brief of various techniques used in the past have shown in chronological order in Figure 1.

If we broadly categorize the various approaches of sarcasm detection then they will be majorly distributed among three categories: Rule-based Methods, Statistical Methods, Deep Learning Solutions [Figure 2].

Figure 1. Approaches of Sarcasm Detection in Textual Data

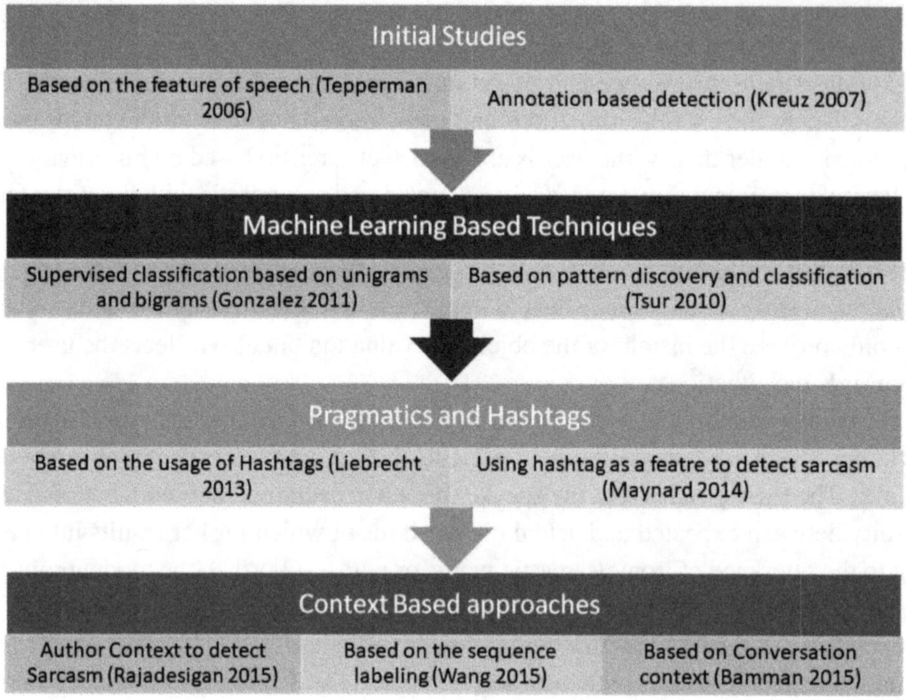

Figure 2. Various Approaches of Sarcasm Detection

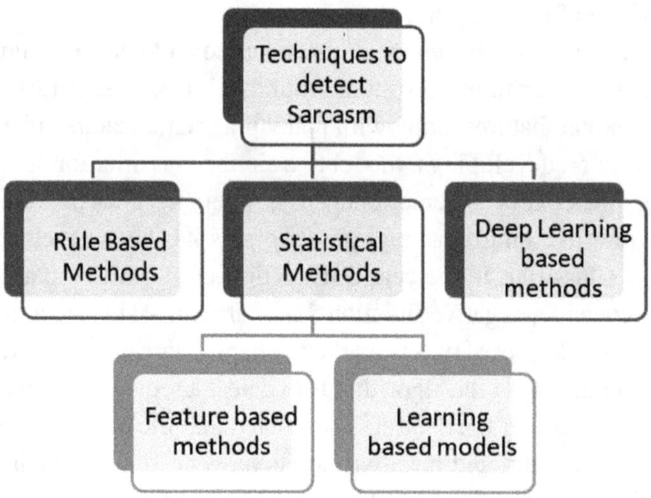

2.1.1. Rule-Based Methods

These are the techniques which identify the utterance of sarcasm based on some evidence in the text or phrase. The evidence is captured in terms of the rules defined and are the indicators of the sarcasm. Most techniques use patterns like hashtags(#) as they highlight the sarcasm and helps in prediction. Maynard et al. (2014) used a hashtag tokenizer to split the hashtag made of concatenated words. Similarly in (2013), Riloff et al. present a classifier that looks for a positive verb and negative situation phrase in the sentence. All these methods are experimental studies and can easily be tweaked according to the need.

2.1.2. Statistical Methods

These are the machine learning based methods majorly focusing on the statistical parameters which can be learned through features. Most of the research done in the detection of sarcasm is this domain. Researchers find patterns in the datasets that actually indicates its presence as extracted from a large sarcasm labeled corpus. Features like pragmatics such as emoticons and user mentions are also considered. Many other features like human annotators can also be used, one such study has been proposed by Mishra et al. (2014) where the human has to look at the sarcastic sentence and the feature set for classification is based on the gaze. Liu et al. (2016) introduced the concept of POS (Part-Of-Speech) sequences and imbalances in the semantics as an active feature to detect sarcasm. Some models of learning are based on the machine learning methods like SVM (Support Vector Machines), Naïve Bayes or even advanced learning method like SVM-HMM (Hidden Markov Model). Recently Joshi et al. (2015) experimented this technique for the conventional dataset and it performed better than classification algorithms.

2.1.3. Deep Learning Approaches

In past few years, a new dimension to analyze and detect sarcasm has evolved the architecture of the approach is based on the deep learning. Once again Joshi et al. (2016) used similarity between word embeddings as a feature for detection of the sarcasm. Another approach has been proposed by Ghosh and Veale (2016) where they are using convolutional neural networks for the identification of sarcasm in a deep learning architecture.

2.2. Various Trends in Sarcasm Detection Approaches

As discussed in Figure 1, it shows us the trend how the techniques of sarcasm detection have evolved over the years. Started with basic fundamental techniques towards supervised/machine learning based approaches further extending to feature based learning and context. The field of sarcasm has seen it all but still, a lot of stones are to be unturned. Majorly the trends are divided into 2 major categories: pattern discovery for sarcasm and importance of the context with respect to sarcasm detection.

2.2.1. Discovery of Pattern

In the beginning, the trend to detect sarcasm was shifting towards discovering the pattern that can support and help to detect it in the textual data and thus its implied sentiment. Researchers used to seed the dataset with the labeling of the few sentences. A similar technique was implemented by Riloff et al. (2013) where they proposed the hypothesis that sarcasm occurs more frequent when we have positive verbs but the negative situation. Various other studies have been proposed on similar grounds based on Amazon's Mechanical Turk (2017).

2.2.2. Role of Context in Sarcasm Detection

Recently the trend to discover sarcasm has been shifted more towards the context. It refers to any information beyond the common knowledge as its situational/time-series dependent. Wallace et al. (2014) were the first to introduce the need for the context in the detection of sarcasm in the text data. Further, the technique was enhanced by incorporating new ways to detect sarcasm based on the type of context. The various types of context are as follows:

- **Author Specific Context:** It is the textual footprint of the author of the target text. The approach is now more intuitively and interesting. The method states that if a tweet has sarcasm then it is because of the words having contrast sentiment in it or maybe due to contrast in the author's human experience. Many other approaches based on author specific context are also using the past tweets of the author.
- **Conversation Context:** The context refers to the conversation of which target text is a part. The techniques in this method use features of the authors who respond to a targeted tweet.
- **Tropical Context:** This shows that some techniques can evoke sarcasm more frequently, compared to others. Techniques belong to this category are like timestamp based methods, they usually create the sequence of tweets and this can further be used to detect sarcasm in textual data.

3. CHALLENGES IN SARCASM DETECTION

Over the years, researchers have worked in the field of natural language processing, linguistics, pattern discovery and machine learning to detect sarcasm in textual data. People have tackled various issues in many different ways and found answers to these frequent issues. Some of the key challenges people face are related to the dataset, the feature set, labelling the dataset and the classification method to be used for managing the task.

3.1. Challenges Related to Dataset

The quality of the dataset used for the analysis always poses a challenge for the researchers; not having a good dataset cannot result into groundbreaking results. Most of the research in the past done on online social networks like Twitter uses hashtag(#) as a most important factor that helps to detect sarcasm but many times these hashtags are removed as part of data pre-processing task. Thus, it becomes difficult to identify the sarcasm if the context is incorporated. Various studies have been proposed in (Ghosh et al, 2016; Lukin and walker, 2016) where human annotation has been taken into consideration for some portion of the dataset and rest is used for the automatic classification. Also, it's important to consider annotation across various communities across the globe because sometimes a sentence annotated to be sarcastic for one community may not be sarcastic for the other one.

3.2. Challenges Related to Features

The main reason to identify sarcasm is that it misleads the already existing sentiment classifiers and decrease their accuracy. But, there are methods that use sentiment as the main feature for identification of sarcasm in the text. Various studies have been developed (Reyes et al, 2012; Bamman et al, 2015; Rajadesingan et al, 2015; Joshi et al, 2015) that try to find the polarity of the words and sentences in two dimensions and further enhance the method for detection of the sarcasm. Some rule-based techniques have also been developed and implemented for the same. But, the question still holds that if we can use sentiment as a feature for the classification of sarcastic sentences.

3.3. Challenges Related to Distorted Data

The detection of sarcasm is not only difficult task to perform because of its implicit nature of intent but, also due to the fact that it is a very infrequent phenomenon to occur. Most of the techniques proposed in the past had this issue of having too little data to identify the pattern in it and then learn a machine for the same. Still, the problem holds true to this day and need to be addressed. Also, the feature set used for the identification of the sarcasm is very sparse and limited in nature, hence, better feature set and dataset (without skews) is required.

4. DISCUSSION

The detection of sarcasm as an automated process is still a thing of the future and numerous extensions and modifications to the present state of the art are required. Various methods whether it's the rule-based or the statistical approach altogether, more work is to be done to improve the accuracy of the methods. A rich feature set is to be developed which is constantly updated to handle the fancy ways of usage of sarcasm. Datasets used for this purpose, need to be more straightened compared to currently existing skewed and distorted datasets. Based on the various components of the sarcasm detection, following is a small but comprehensive list of various future directions in the field where one can work and enhance the existing techniques.

1. Exposure to the various types of sarcasm in the text, one can easily work in the field to detect various aspects and nature of the sarcasm.
2. The detection of sentiment and sarcasm are always linked together, thus further work to enhance the detection using the sentiment of the sentence is one area to work and enhance the current state-of-the-art.
3. Deep learning and the neural networks have given an all-new dimension to sentiment analysis and sarcasm detection. But still, the techniques are in their infantry. Major contribution can be done to the field by improving the models based on neural networks thus, to imitate the human brain and sarcasm.
4. Sarcasm is always a cultural specific phenomenon, a sentence which is sarcastic for one community might not be sarcastic for the other one. Thus, it's important to understand the language and learn. This will not only benefit the already existing methods but also new algorithms to be developed in future.

REFERENCES

Asur, S., & Huberman, B. A. (2010, August). Predicting the future with social media. In *Web Intelligence and Intelligent Agent Technology (WI-IAT), 2010 IEEE/WIC/ACM International Conference on* (Vol. 1, pp. 492-499). IEEE. doi:10.1109/WI-IAT.2010.63

Bamman, D., & Smith, N. A. (2015, May). *Contextualized Sarcasm Detection on Twitter*. ICWSM.

Bollen, J., Mao, H., & Zeng, X. (2011). Twitter mood predicts the stock market. *Journal of Computational Science*, *2*(1), 1–8. doi:10.1016/j.jocs.2010.12.007

Chen, T., Xu, R., Lu, Q., Liu, B., Xu, J., Yao, L., & He, Z. (2014, April). A sentence vector based oversampling method for imbalanced emotion classification. In *International Conference on Intelligent Text Processing and Computational Linguistics* (pp. 62-72). Springer. doi:10.1007/978-3-642-54903-8_6

Dave, K., Lawrence, S., & Pennock, D. M. (2003, May). Mining the peanut gallery: Opinion extraction and semantic classification of product reviews. In *Proceedings of the 12th international conference on World Wide Web* (pp. 519-528). ACM. doi:10.1145/775152.775226

Davidov, D., Tsur, O., & Rappoport, A. (2010, July). Semi-supervised recognition of sarcastic sentences in twitter and Amazon. In *Proceedings of the fourteenth conference on computational natural language learning* (pp. 107-116). Association for Computational Linguistics.

Ghosh, A., & Veale, T. (2016). Fracking Sarcasm using Neural Network. In WASSA@ NAACL-HLT (pp. 161-169). Academic Press. doi:10.18653/v1/W16-0425

González-Ibánez, R., Muresan, S., & Wacholder, N. (2011, June). Identifying sarcasm in Twitter: a closer look. In *Proceedings of the 49th Annual Meeting of the Association for Computational Linguistics: Human Language Technologies: Short Papers-Volume 2* (pp. 581-586). Association for Computational Linguistics.

Groh, G., & Hauffa, J. (2011, July). *Characterizing Social Relations Via NLP-Based Sentiment Analysis*. ICWSM.

Hatzivassiloglou, V., & McKeown, K. R. (1997, July). Predicting the semantic orientation of adjectives. In *Proceedings of the eighth conference on European chapter of the Association for Computational Linguistics* (pp. 174-181). Association for Computational Linguistics. doi:10.3115/979617.979640

Joshi, A., Sharma, V., & Bhattacharyya, P. (2015, July). Harnessing Context Incongruity for Sarcasm Detection. ACL, (2), 757-762. doi:10.3115/v1/P15-2124

Joshi, A., Tripathi, V., Patel, K., Bhattacharyya, P., & Carman, M. (2016). *Are Word Embedding-based Features Useful for Sarcasm Detection?* arXiv preprint arXiv:1610.00883

Joshi, M., Das, D., Gimpel, K., & Smith, N. A. (2010, June). Movie reviews and revenues: An experiment in text regression. In *Human Language Technologies: The 2010 Annual Conference of the North American Chapter of the Association for Computational Linguistics* (pp. 293-296). Association for Computational Linguistics.

Kreuz, R. J., & Glucksberg, S. (1989). How to be sarcastic: The echoic reminder theory of verbal irony. *Journal of Experimental Psychology. General, 118*(4), 374–386. doi:10.1037/0096-3445.118.4.374

Liebrecht, C. C., Kunneman, F. A., & Van Den Bosch, A. P. J. (2013). *The perfect solution for detecting sarcasm in tweets# not*. Academic Press.

Liu, Y., Huang, X., An, A., & Yu, X. (2007, July). ARSA: a sentiment-aware model for predicting sales performance using blogs. In *Proceedings of the 30th annual international ACM SIGIR conference on Research and development in information retrieval* (pp. 607-614). ACM. doi:10.1145/1277741.1277845

Lukin, S., & Walker, M. (2017). *Really? well. apparently bootstrapping improves the performance of sarcasm and nastiness classifiers for online dialogue*. arXiv preprint arXiv:1708.08572

Maas, A. L., Daly, R. E., Pham, P. T., Huang, D., Ng, A. Y., & Potts, C. (2011, June). Learning word vectors for sentiment analysis. In *Proceedings of the 49th Annual Meeting of the Association for Computational Linguistics: Human Language Technologies-Volume 1* (pp. 142-150). Association for Computational Linguistics.

Maynard, D., & Greenwood, M. A. (2014, May). *Who cares about Sarcastic Tweets? Investigating the Impact of Sarcasm on Sentiment Analysis*. LREC.

McGlohon, M., Glance, N. S., & Reiter, Z. (2010, May). Star Quality: Aggregating Reviews to Rank Products and Merchants. ICWSM.

Mishra, A., Kanojia, D., & Bhattacharyya, P. (2016, February). *Predicting Readers' Sarcasm Understandability by Modeling Gaze Behavior*. AAAI.

Nasukawa, T., & Yi, J. (2003, October). Sentiment analysis: Capturing favorability using natural language processing. In *Proceedings of the 2nd international conference on Knowledge Capture* (pp. 70-77). ACM. doi:10.1145/945645.945658

O'Connor, B., Balasubramanyan, R., Routledge, B. R., & Smith, N. A. (2010). From tweets to polls: Linking text sentiment to public opinion time series. *ICWSM, 11*(122-129), 1-2.

O'Keefe, T., & Koprinska, I. (2009, December). Feature selection and weighting methods in sentiment analysis. *Proceedings of the 14th Australasian document computing symposium*, 67-74.

Pang, B., & Lee, L. (2004, July). A sentimental education: Sentiment analysis using subjectivity summarization based on minimum cuts. In *Proceedings of the 42nd annual meeting of Association for Computational Linguistics* (p. 271). Association for Computational Linguistics. doi:10.3115/1218955.1218990

Pang, B., & Lee, L. (2008). Opinion mining and sentiment analysis. *Foundations and Trends® in Information Retrieval, 2*(1–2), 1-135.

Rajadesingan, A., Zafarani, R., & Liu, H. (2015, February). Sarcasm detection on Twitter: A behavioral modeling approach. In *Proceedings of the Eighth ACM International Conference on Web Search and Data Mining* (pp. 97-106). ACM. doi:10.1145/2684822.2685316

Reyes, A., & Rosso, P. (2012). Making objective decisions from subjective data: Detecting irony in customer reviews. *Decision Support Systems, 53*(4), 754–760. doi:10.1016/j.dss.2012.05.027

Riloff, E., Qadir, A., Surve, P., De Silva, L., Gilbert, N., & Huang, R. (2013, October). *Sarcasm as Contrast between a Positive Sentiment and Negative Situation* (Vol. 13). EMNLP.

Tepperman, J., Traum, D., & Narayanan, S. (2006). " Yeah Right": Sarcasm Recognition for Spoken Dialogue Systems. *Ninth International Conference on Spoken Language Processing*.

Tumasjan, A., Sprenger, T. O., Sandner, P. G., & Welpe, I. M. (2010). Predicting elections with Twitter: What 140 characters reveal about political sentiment. *ICWSM*, *10*(1), 178–185.

Turney, P. D., & Littman, M. L. (2003). Measuring praise and criticism: Inference of semantic orientation from association. *ACM Transactions on Information Systems*, *21*(4), 315–346. doi:10.1145/944012.944013

Utsumi, A. (2000). Verbal irony as implicit display of ironic environment: Distinguishing ironic utterances from nonirony. *Journal of Pragmatics*, *32*(12), 1777–1806. doi:10.1016/S0378-2166(99)00116-2

Wallace, B. C., Kertz, L., & Charniak, E. (2014). Humans require context to infer ironic intent (so computers probably do, too). *Proceedings of the 52nd Annual Meeting of the Association for Computational Linguistics*, 2, 512-516. doi:10.3115/v1/P14-2084

Wang, Z., Wu, Z., Wang, R., & Ren, Y. (2015, November). Twitter sarcasm detection exploiting a context-based model. In *International Conference on Web Information Systems Engineering* (pp. 77-91). Springer. doi:10.1007/978-3-319-26190-4_6

Yano, T., & Smith, N. A. (2010, May). What's Worthy of Comment? Content and Comment Volume in Political Blogs. ICWSM.

Zhang, L., Liu, B., Lim, S. H., & O'Brien-Strain, E. (2010, August). Extracting and ranking product features in opinion documents. In *Proceedings of the 23rd international conference on computational linguistics: Posters* (pp. 1462-1470). Association for Computational Linguistics.

KEY TERMS AND DEFINITIONS

Online Social Networks: These are some computer-mediated applications that allow people, communities, or companies to create, share, or exchange information, career interests, ideas, pictures, videos, and networks. They are built on the ideology and technological foundation of Web 2.0, which allows the exchange of user-generated content.

Opinion Mining: Opinion mining is referred to the use of natural language processing, text analysis, and computer linguistics to extract subjective information in the textual materials. In other words, it is extracting and analyzing judgments on various aspects of given items.

Sarcasm: It is considered to be the use of satirical or ironic words that mean the opposite of what one really want to say, especially in order to insult someone, to mock someone, to show irritation, or just for fun and is often interchangeable with irony.

Sentiment Analysis: Sentiment analysis is considered to be the automatic extraction of the sentiment-related information from the textual data. It is mostly used for commercial purposes, but in the recent past, researchers have shown great interest in the effective dimension of the social web like Facebook and Twitter.

ENDNOTES

1. https://hootsuite.com/
2. https://www.spredfast.com/
3. https://sproutsocial.com/
4. https://www.twitter.com

Chapter 7
A Novel Algorithm for Sentiment Analysis of Online Movie Reviews

Bisma Shah
Jamia Hamdard, India

Farheen Siddiqui
Jamia Hamdard, India

ABSTRACT

Others' opinions can be decisive while choosing among various options, especially when those choices involve worthy resources like spending time and money buying products or services. Customers relying on their peers' past reviews on e-commerce websites or social media have drawn a considerable interest to sentiment analysis due to realization of its commercial and business benefits. Sentiment analysis can be exercised on movie reviews, blogs, customer feedback, etc. This chapter presents a novel approach to perform sentiment analysis of movie reviews given by users on different websites. Also, challenges like presence of thwarted words, world knowledge, and subjectivity detection in sentiments are addressed in this chapter. The results are validated by using two supervised machine learning approaches, k-nearest neighbor and naive Bayes, both on method of sentiment analysis without addressing aforementioned challenges and on proposed method of sentiment analysis with all challenges addressed. Empirical results show that proposed method outperformed the one that left challenges unaddressed.

INTRODUCTION

Sentiment Analysis (SA) is an on-going field of research in text mining field and is used for the computational treatment of opinions, sentiments and subjectivity of text. It is used to understand the mind-sets, opinions and sentiments of people in general in regards to a specific product or a movie or an occasion. It helps in identifying and extracting subjective information in source materials and categorizes them as positive, negative, or neutral. Decision making process has always been influenced by the huge data available and the human nature to always rely on opinion of other people regarding a particular product

DOI: 10.4018/978-1-5225-5097-6.ch007

or an event. This unique feature has a significant impact on deciding matters that have financial, medical, social, business or other ramifications. Keeping in view the large amount of comments or reviews for a particular product and the colossal advancement in web users, there arises a dire need to build up a framework that gathers, constructs, analyzes and characterizes the remarks or reviews present online. A review is usually written by a person who has used a particular product or a service. The nature of review is immensely affected by an individual's interests, opinions and viewpoints. People who give biased reviews consequently impact the reputation of a forum or an organization to which the review is being contributed. Increase in the number of such people has posed a huge challenge to characterize and sort out the real issues and prospects of the product by virtue of which a user questions the authenticity of the content. In view of improving the scope of a particular product, huge organizations depend on individual reviews of clients and consider it to be of incredible significance in putting content construct advertisements on websites that effectively help a forthcoming buyer. Also movie enthusiasts and voters employ the same approach for analysis of certain information as an ever increasing number of individuals are utilizing social networking sites, online shopping and trend analysts who in the wake of scrutinizing the reviews available settle on different issues. For instance putting the promotion of a Kitchen Aid Mixer on a food blog impacts purchase choices as well as goes far in altering the advertising technique. Reviewers are being enthusiastically promoted by the advertising division of an organization by sending samples of product to be assessed or supporting discounts in blogs or in social networking locales like Facebook and Twitter. This has prompted the expansion in the volume of information accessible and the need to characterize the accessible data effectively as these have a larger impact on the reputation of a particular organization.

Large amount of data generated online by reviews can be processed so as to extract useful information from them, using suitable methods and approaches of Sentiment analysis, thereby supporting operational, managerial, and strategic decision making (Liu, 2010). But it is not sufficient to consider just the subjective nature of opinion for decision making (Buche, Chandak, & Zadgaonkar, 2013). Additionally, the written work aptitudes and selection of words by benefactors to a great extent rely on upon the proficiency of language and the demeanor of the author. There exist different kinds of opinions of users like regular, implicit, direct, indirect and comparative. The flexibility of expression and anonymity also accompanies a cost. Individuals with concealed plans effortlessly game the framework to give people the impression that they are independent members from the general population and post fake sentiments to promote or defame some targeted products, services, affiliations, or individuals without revealing their actual intentions, or the individual or affiliation that they are secretly working for. People with these intentions are popularly known as *opinion spammers* and their exercises are called *opinion spamming* (Abbasi, Chen, Thoms, & Fu, 2008). Moreover, online reviews are composed by the customers from their edge of interests and inclinations, they can be a mix of a positive and negative opinion and that may not necessarily help in categorizing reviews as positive or negative. For instance, consider the sentence "The Chinese dishes of this restaurant are not as good as their Thai dishes". Relative opinions like these are different in natural language processing. When a positive word "good" is negated like "not as good as", readers find it challenging to assimilate even how good the Thai dishes were, because this decides the taste of the Chinese dishes too. So while handling negation, it must be properly figured out that the presence of negation updates which part of the meaning expressed (Liu, 2012; Abbasi, France, Zhang, & Chen, 2011).

In today's web world, textual information which is available can be basically categorized into two broad categories, facts and opinions. Facts present the objective statements about the events and objects.

The subjective statements that reflect the sentiments and perception of a person about an event or an object are called Opinions or sentiments. Extracting subjective information from text and determining the overall contextual polarity or opinion of the writer of the text is called Sentiment Analysis. According to Liu (2012), " Suppose given is an arrangement of judgemental text documents D in which sentiments or opinions related to a particular object are given, the role of sentiment analysis (also called opinion mining) is to find out those features and attributes of the object that have been commented on in each document d belonging to D and to determine the polarity of the comments (that is, whether the comments are positive, negative or neutral) ". Sentiment Analysis is technically very challenging but also practically very useful. For instance, for businesses it is always useful to know public or consumer opinions about their product and services so as to know the reasons of their profits or losses. Also, the customer who wants to buy a product would like to know the opinions about that product from the existing users.

This chapter aims to characterize the polarity of an opinion in a movie dataset comprising of movie reviews given by the users by adopting text classification approach. The MATLAB R2014a serial update 2 (version 8.3.0.532) classification tool is used to train a classifier for the purpose of data classification. In this chapter, k-Nearest neighbor (kNN) and Naive Bayes classifier is used and then comparisons have been made between the proposed method addressing the challenges faced and the method where challenges are not addressed on the basis of analysis of various evaluation measures like accuracy, precision, recall and Fscore. Besides introduction, this chapter throws light on need of Sentiment analysis, gives the statement of existing problem, lays down the criteria for categorization of various methods of Sentiment analysis, gives various applications of Sentiment analysis, surveys the previous researches done in the field of Sentiment analysis, discusses the challenges faced while analyzing sentiments, presents the proposed solutions and recommendations to the existing problems, depicts the results obtained, highlights the future scope of current research work and at last concludes the discussion.

Need of Sentiment Analysis

Social media has turned into a fundamental part of social life. It influences the convictions, values, and demeanors of individuals, and also their aims and practices. Social media, besides acting as a personal communication media, has emerged as a platform to impart feelings about items and services or even political and general occasions among its users. Moreover, it empowers governments and organizations to connect with individuals while enabling users to make informed decisions. Because of its widespread prevalence, a gigantic amount of user opinions or reviews are being produced and shared daily. Therefore, extracting information, key ideas, and thoughts from social media content is essential for generating knowledge and formulation of strategies, and hence the need for Sentiment Analysis.

Problem Statement

Methods used to analyze data in the past included surveys, interviews, questionnaires etc. But these traditional methods were time consuming, limited in scale and required more manpower. Analyzing the information manually for sentiments does not make sense, especially when the information is huge in volume and having various Internet slangs. Thus the concept of Sentiment Analysis or Opinion Mining came into being. Sentiment classification has gained a lot of attention in recent years (Pang, Lee, & Vaithyanathan, 2002). The main aim of Sentiment analysis is to identify and extract opinions and attitudes from a given piece of text towards a particular subject (Pang, & Lee, 2008).

With time, a lot of approaches for Sentiment analysis came into existence. As an example, one method of Sentiment Analysis involved finding the sentiments by first searching for opinion words in the text and then on the basis of count of positive and negative words in the text, evaluated the final sentiment of text. But still these methods including the one just mentioned lagged behind in one way or the other. Some possible reasons include inefficiency to handle the challenges like presence of thwarted words in reviews, finding sentiments in reviews having occurrence of world knowledge words in them, subjectivity detection in sentiments, etc. So the authors have proposed a solution that will serve as a method of solving these problems faced in sentiment analysis. This chapter proposes a novel algorithm to handle all the aforementioned challenges while determining the overall sentiment of reviews and then compares various performance metrics of the proposed algorithm and the already existing method of Sentiment Analysis mentioned above in which these challenges are not handled.

The objective of this chapter is to recognize and classify sentiments expressed in a piece of text in movie reviews given by users, particularly so as to decide whether the writer's attitude towards a particular topic (or theme), product, etc. is positive, negative or neutral.

The scope of this chapter is to analyse the sentiments expressed by the users or the reviews given by users on movies. A particular movie review is scanned for the presence of positive, negative or neutral sentiment using the proposed algorithm. Moreover, different challenges are addressed while analyzing the sentiments. The ability to handle these challenges enables the proposed research method to analyze sentiments more accurately.

Criterion for Categorization of Different Methods of Sentiment Analysis

Different methods of Sentiment analysis can be categorized based on certain criterion or from different points of views. These include: technique used, view of text, level of detail of text analysis, rating level, etc.

1. **Technical Point of View:** Sentiment Analysis methods fall into four categories from a technical point of view: machine learning, lexicon-based, statistical and rule-based approaches. These are discussed below:
    a. **Machine Learning Approach:** The machine learning approach involves training a known dataset by using several learning algorithms so as to determine the sentiment in a given piece of text.
    b. **Lexicon-Based Approach:** In lexicon-based approach, semantic orientation of words or sentences is used for estimating the polarity of sentiments expressed by the users in a review. The "semantic orientation" can be thought of as a measure of subjectivity and opinion in text.
    c. **Rule-Based Approach:** In rule-based approach, opinion words are searched in a text and then classification is done on the basis of the number of positive and negative words. Different **rules** are being considered here for classification such as dictionary polarity, booster words, negation words, *idioms*, mixed opinions, emoticons etc.
    d. **Statistical Approach:** In statistical models, each review is represented as a blend of latent aspects and ratings. Aspects and their ratings are assumed to be represented by multinomial distributions and attempts are made to group head terms into aspects and sentiments into ratings.
2. **Global or Specific Point of View:** Distinctions can be made between methods which rate a review keeping in view the sentiment strength for different aspects of a product and methods which

endeavor to rate a review on a global level. A large proportion of techniques that focus on global review classification consider just the polarity of reviews (positive/negative) and are dependent on machine learning techniques. But the techniques that perform a more detailed classification of reviews (e.g., three or five star ratings) utilize more linguistic features like intensification, negation, modality and discourse structure (Carrillo de Albornoz, Plaza, Gervás, & Díaz, 2011).

3. **Different Classes of Sentiment Analysis:** Sentiments of reviews can be categorized into three classes, that is, positive, negative and neutral sentiments (Bholane Savita, & Gore, 2016):
   a. **Positive Sentiments:** This alludes to positive state of mind of speaker or reviewer about the text. Happiness, joy, smile, etc. are the emotions reflected with positive sentiments. For example, in case of political reviews, presence of more positive reviews/sentiments about the politician indicate that people are happy with his work.
   b. **Negative Sentiments:** This alludes to negative state of mind of speaker or reviewer about the text. Sadness, jealousy, hate, etc. are the emotions reflected with negative sentiments. As an example, in case of political reviews, presence of more negative reviews/sentiments about the politician indicate that people are not happy with his work.
   c. **Neutral Sentiments:** Neutral sentiments reflect no emotions or opinion about the text. These are neither preferred nor neglected. In spite of the fact that this class suggests nothing, it plays a crucial role in distinguishing positive and negative classes in a better way.
4. **Levels of Sentiment Classification:** Based on levels of classification, there exist three classes of sentiments: phrase level, document level and aspect level.
   a. **Phrase Level Classification:** Two or more than two words constitute a Phrase. In Phrase level classification, sentiments are classified by taking whole phrase into consideration. Also called Sentence level or Word-level classification, it determines polarity of sentiments for each sentence of a review and even for each word of a sentence. Initially it decides if the phrase is neutral or polar; in case the phrase comes out to be polar, then it is categorized into positive and negative classes. Drawback of phrase level classification is that presence of refuted or negation words sometimes leads to inaccurate results.
   b. **Document Level Classification:** Document level classification intends to determine the polarity of sentiments for the entire review. A single theme or topic is taken into consideration to categorize the sentiments as positive, negative, or neutral. Drawback of document level classification is that it is not useful for comparison of two products having similar features.
   c. **Aspect Level Classification:** Aspect level classification deals with finding if the opinion expressed about a particular feature or aspect is positive, negative or neutral. An aspect can be thought of as some component of an entity. The opinion information obtained from this classification level is very fine grained and that can be helpful in various domains of sentiment analysis. In this classification, the overall opinion is related to the feature of the entity. An example of entity is Apple iPhone and aspect can be its battery, camera, screen etc.

Applications of Sentiment Analysis

Reputation of the product, which is derived from the opinion of others is an important information when consumers have to make a decision or a choice regarding a product or service. Sentiment analysis is a field of research that can be used to reveal this information about a product or service. Sentiment analysis finds its applications in the following:

1. Helping customers in the choice of products or services by providing recommendations based on the intelligence of the crowd. People usually get attracted to certain specific aspects while choosing a product or service. A single global rating could not help as it could be deceiving. Ratings on certain aspects of the product or a service can be estimated by reorganizing reviewer's opinions using Sentiment analysis.
2. Companies can enhance the aspects that are discovered unsuitable by the customers after knowing customer's opinion on their products or services. Also priority in importance of aspects for the customers can be determined.
3. Various other technologies incorporate Sentiment analysis as a component. One thought could be to bar the most subjective area of a document and hence enhance data mining in text analysis or proposing web advertisements for products or services according to opinion of viewers (and expelling the others).
4. Various potential outcomes are possible in the Human/Machine interface area if we can recognize what individuals think regarding a particular product or service or an event.
5. Sentiment analysis can be also used in business for competitive advantage. Analyzing how much positive or negative customer's reviews on a certain product are does not serve sufficient. Sentiment analysis can help businesses to analyse the reviews of their competitors' products or services and hence provides them the opportunity to perk up their performance.
6. Sentiment analysis can be used in politics as well. Campaign managers are able to monitor the opinion of different voters on different issues and can be used to find out how voters relate to the speeches and actions of the candidates running for various positions in elections.

Background

This section exemplifies the related works in the field of sentiment analysis done so far to determine the polarity of sentiments in texts by employing various methods of text mining like text classification, text clustering and natural language processing. Pang, Lee, & Vaithyanathan (2002) employed three machine learning techniques-Naive Bayes, Maximum entropy classification and Support vector Machine (SVM) on the data of movie reviews; and identified various factors that make sentiment classification more complex as compared to topic based categorization. Turney (2002) classified reviews of four different domains (reviews of automobiles, books, movies and travel destinations) by designing an unsupervised learning algorithm. A data-driven method for automatically learning the content selection rules from a corpus and its associated database was introduced by Barzilay and Lapata (2005) for a concept-to-text generation system in which a content selection component was utilized for deciding which information should be produced as output by a natural language generation system. Emotional estimations for natural-language texts was presented by Ma, Prendinger, & Ishizuka (2005) in a method which was based on a keyword spotting technique. By dividing a text into words, this system estimates emotions for each of these words and performs a sentence-level processing technique. A new method was proposed by Wilson, Wiebe, & Hoffmann (2005) for analyzing the sentiments of phrases that worked in two stages: firstly, it checks for the presence of facts or sentiments in an expression and then elucidates the polarity of sentiments present in that expression.

The foundation of the research area of sentiment classification was laid down by the work of Ortony, Clore, & Foss (1987). They developed a taxonomy of affective lexicon and paid special attention to isolate the terms having an emotional connotation. A keyword based approach was introduced by Rimon

(2005) for classifying sentiments. This approach used terms, mainly adjectives (e.g. awesome, awful) as sentiment indicators. Sources such as WordNet or machine learning algorithms that infer the best indicators from tagged samples in the domain of interest, can be used to manually prepare and semi automatically compose the list of indicators. To perform document wise sentiment polarity classification, Matsumoto, Takamura, & Okumura (2005) used syntactic relations between words in sentences. Frequent word sub-sequences and dependency sub-trees were extracted from sentences in a document dataset by using text mining techniques, which were then used as features of support vector machines. Dave, Lawrence, & Pennock (2003) examined several kinds of products and proposed a method that automatically distinguished positive and negative reviews on these products. Information retrieval techniques for feature extraction and scoring are drawn by the classifier used, and various metrics results and heuristics change as per the testing situation. Unlike the research of Pang, Lee, & Vaithyanathan (2002), this method achieved best accuracy rate by using word bigram-based classifier on the dataset. From the results, they concluded that the unigram-based model does not always produce best results and that data or information used determines the best settings of the classifier. Sentiment Analysis can be thought of as the process in which subjective information is identified in source materials (Pang, & Lee, 2008; Liu, 2012).

A comparative study on sentimental analysis and its application in recommendation system was provided by Chidananda, Sagnika, & Sahoo (2017). The study of various methods for predicting the stock market was given by Jadhav and Wakode (2017) by using the sentiment score of financial news on Twitter data.

Deng, Sinha, & Zhao (2017) proposed domain-dependent lexicons to deal with the fact that some words can reveal different sentiments, positive or negative, on the basis of the domain being used. Developments in the kinds and uses of online networking sites such as forums, blogs, etc. have enabled users to impart their insights on different domains (Moslmi, Albared, Al-Shabi, Omar, & Abdullah, 2017). Aydogan and Akcayol (2016), after carrying out an exhaustive study on Sentiment analysis employing different Machine learning algorithms found that SVM and Naïve Bayes have higher estimation capability and hence are most commonly used. A survey presented by Brindha, Prabha, & Sukumaran (2016) on different classification approaches (KNN, Naive Bayes, SVM, Decision Tree and Regression) revealed that almost all classification approaches were suited to the characteristics of text data. They further inferred that better quality of text results and exact information can be obtained in addition to reduced access time by further study on classification development.

The performance of Sentiment analysis is heavily dependent on how effectively a training set is defined. For accurate analysis of text, quality of dataset plays an important part. Likewise, syntax analysis of sentence helps in increasing accuracy and means of the results (Hussein, 2016). Gathering people's sentiments, opinions, emotions and attitudes, etc. regarding certain products, topics, individuals, associations and services is referred to as Sentiment Analysis (Pradhan, Vala, & Balani, 2016). Pagolu, Challa, Panda, & Majhi (2016) examined sentiments of people in tweets by employing two different textual representations, namely, Word2vec and N-gram. Moreover, relationship between stock market movement of company and sentiments in tweets was analyzed by applying Sentiment analysis and various machine learning approaches like logistic regression, SMO and Random Forest to extracted tweets. The emotions identified in the text were used by Rangel and Rosso (2016) for author profiling, especially detecting the age and gender of author. The opinions extracted from user reviews are important not only for users but also for companies in the sense that this information can help users in making decisions regarding purchasing different products and hence this forms the basis for enhancing the quality of services and products offered by various companies (Zarate, García, Martínez, & Palacios, 2016).

Positive and negative sentiments of cancer patients were detected by a tool, namely SentiHealth (SCH-pt), developed by (Rodrigues, Dores, Camilo-Junior, & Rosa, 2016) in Portuguese language. A method for detecting the sentiment of Twitter and DailyStrength post was proposed by Korkontzelos, Nikfarjam, Shardlow, Sarker, Ananiadou, & Gonzalez (2016).

Major tasks of Sentiment Analysis include:

1. Categorization of textual documents into positive and negative polarity classes, (Dave et al., 2003; Kim, & Hovy, 2004);
2. Identification of textual topics and the opinions associated with them (Wang, Lu, & Zhai, 2010; Jo, & Oh, 2011); and
3. Summarization of opinions (Hu, & Liu, 2004; Ku, Liang, & Chen, 2006).

MAIN FOCUS OF THE CHAPTER

Challenges in Sentiment Analysis

Opinion mining, unlike traditional text mining which concentrates on analysis of facts, deals with attitudes (Pang, Lee, & Vaithyanathan, 2002). Categorization of sentiments, sentiment classification based on features and summarization of opinions are the fundamental fields of research. Analysis of the opinions on a certain object comes under the process of Sentiment categorization. Feature based classification is concerned with the process of analyzing and classifying based on the features of a particular object. Opinion summarizing deals with mining only the features of the product for which customers have expressed their opinions, and this feature makes it unique from the classic text summarizing where a subset of a review is considered and some of the original statements are rewritten to catch the fundamental idea.

Some challenges in analyzing sentiments in reviews include:

1. **Implicit Sentiment and Sarcasm:** At times, an implicit sentiment may be incorporated in a sentence, that is, a sentence may not have presence of opinion deciding keywords but still an opinion may be inferred from it. Consider the following illustration.

I bought shirt a week ago, and it became fade after one wash.

The above sentence is a negative one although there is no occurrence of any negative sentiment bearing words in it. Thus what is more important in Sentiment analysis is identifying semantics than detecting syntax.

2. **Thwarted Expectations:** Sometimes the author intentionally sets up context just to invalidate it towards the end. Consider the following example:

I decided to watch movie after I heard claims that it is best film, the actors and the supporting cast is good as well. However, it can't hold up.

Despite the fact that the above sentence contains more positive words, it is considered to be a negative sentence on account of the pivotal last sentence.

3. **World Knowledge:** Sometimes the text contains another entity to refer to one entity. In that case, the knowledge of the entity which is used to refer another is required to identify the sentiment. For detecting sentiments, world knowledge needs to be included in the system. Consider the following example:

She is as beautiful as Snow White.

Here, to identify the sentiment orientation of the text, one has to know about 'Snow White'. Consider another example:

He is a Doctor Zhivago.

Although this sentence delineates a positive sentiment, but one still needs to know about Doctor Zhivago to find out the correct sentiment.

4. **Subjectivity Detection:** Subjectivity classification aims to find if a review sentence is opinionated or non-opinionated (subjective or objective), usually in the presence of an opinion expression in a sentence. A sentence is considered an objective sentence if it has some factual information and is considered subjective if it expresses personal feelings, views, emotions, or beliefs. Subjectivity detection aims at enhancing the performance of the system by filtering out the impact of subjective words on the overall sentiment. But this is not an easy task to do.

Consider the following examples:

I hate drama movies.

I hate the movie "I love stories".

In the former example, an objective fact is presented whereas in the latter example opinion about a particular movie is depicted.

5. **Grammar and Spellings:** Users tend to commit a ton of mistakes in the semantics of the language and even the spellings of words because of being too causal when posting online. This can be handled generally by checking for them in the pre-processing stage.
6. **Trustworthiness:** The perspectives of various clients on different subjects is the most imperative property of social information, yet there are many fake accounts being made that give fake perspectives and reviews to either push or draw an entity on the stage. This poses a great challenge during analyzing sentiments.
7. **Language:** Another challenge that emerges while analyzing the sentiments is the flexibility that social media sites provide its users for posting reviews in different languages. This makes the task

of sentiment analysis a lot more difficult. This problem can be handled by either using translation mechanisms or constructing different engines for dealing with different languages.

Some of these challenges like presence of thwarted words in reviews, occurrence of world knowledge words and subjectivity detection in reviews have been addressed in this chapter.

SOLUTIONS AND RECOMMENDATIONS

This section describes the approach that the authors have proposed for analyzing the sentiments of online movie reviews as well as presenting solutions to tackle the various challenges faced in Sentiment analysis.

Dataset

The dataset used in this chapter for analysing sentiments is Kaggle movie review corpora, which contains reviews given by the users about movies. The proposed sentiment analysis method is then employed for further polarizing these reviews. This dataset contains 156060 entries of users' reviews about movies and is available at https://www.kaggle.com/c/sentiment-analysis-on-movie-reviews/data ("Sentiment Analysis on Movie Reviews | Kaggle", 2015).

Pseudo-Code

8. **Input:** Movie Review dataset.
9. **Output:** Final sentiment/polarity of a normal review as well as a review having presence of thwarted words, world knowledge words and subjective words.
10. **Pre-Processing:**
    a. **Sub-Phrase Removal:** $\left[Uid, pos\right] = unique\left(Sentenceid\right);$.Where Uid .and pos .denote id and position of unique phrases found using $unique\ ()$ .respectively. Thus only unique phrases are selected, thereby eliminating sub-phrases.
    b. **Conversion to Lower-Case:** $lower\left(phrase\right);$.Here $lower\ ()$ .function is used to convert the *phrase* written in any case to lowercase.
11. **Top n Opinion Words Selection:** Opinion words are selected based on their contribution to the overall sentiment of phrases.
12. **Feature Extraction:**
    a. **Frequency (Count) of Opinion Words**:

Check for the presence of opinion words in a review phrase

Evaluate count of positive opinion words (finalcountpos)

Evaluate count of negative opinion words (finalcountneg)

if finalcountpos> finalcountneg

$$finalsentiment = \left(\frac{finalcountpos}{finalcountpos + finalcountneg}\right).else\ if\ finalcountneg > finalcountpos$$

$$finalsentiment = -\left(\frac{finalcountneg}{finalcountpos + finalcountneg}\right).else$$

$$finalsentiment = neutral.\ feature\_1 = \left[finalcountpos; finalcountneg; finalsentiment\right].$$

Thwarted Words:

Check for the presence or absence of thwarted words in a review phrase

Evaluate count of presence of thwarted words (finalcount_presence)

Evaluate count of absence of thwarted words (finalcount_absence)

if finalcount_presence > finalcount_absence

$$finalsentiment = -\left(\frac{finalcount\_presence}{finalcount\_presence + finalcount\_absence}\right).else$$

$$finalsentiment = neutral$$
$$feature\_2 = \left[finalcount\_presence; finalcount\_absence; finalsentiment\right].$$

World knowledge:

Check for the presence or absence of world knowledge words in a review phrase

Evaluate count of presence of world knowledge words (finalcount_presence)

Evaluate count of absence of world knowledge words (finalcount_absence)

if finalcount_presence > finalcount_absence

Check weight of world knowledge word (world_weight)

if world_weight == -1

$$finalsentiment = -\left(\frac{finalcount\_presence}{finalcount\_presence + finalcount\_absence}\right).\ if\ world\_weight == 1$$

$$finalsentiment = \left(\frac{finalcount\_presence}{finalcount\_presence + finalcount\_absence}\right).else$$

$$finalsentiment = neutral\ .\ feature\_3 = \left[finalcount\_presence; finalcount\_absence; finalsentiment\right].$$

Subjectivity Detection:

Check for the presence of subjective words in a review phrase

if subjective word is present

Remove subjective word from phrase

Find count of positive opinion words (finalcount_pos), count of negative opinion words (finalcount_neg) and final sentiment (finalsentiment) as found in feature_1

else

Find count of positive opinion words (finalcount_pos), count of negative opinion words (finalcount_neg) and final sentiment (finalsentiment) as found in feature_1

$feature\_4 = \left[finalcount\_pos; finalcount\_neg; finalsentiment\right]$.Thus,

$\boldsymbol{Overall\_feature} = \left[\boldsymbol{feature}\_1; \boldsymbol{feature}\_2; \boldsymbol{feature}\_3; \boldsymbol{feature}\_4\right]$.This $Overall\_feature$ .feature set is used for training the classifier.

13. **Classification:** k Nearest Neighbor (kNN) and Naive Bayes classifiers are used to classify the sentiments and to evaluate various performance metrics of classification.

Detailed Methodology

An outline of the steps and techniques followed for sentiment analysis are depicted in Figure 1.

At first movie reviews dataset files are read thoroughly, afterwards the further process begins as follows:

14. **Pre-Processing:** Pre-processing is a process where undesirable data is removed from the whole dataset, thereby preparing desired data for classification. Preprocessing is exercised to reduce noise

Figure 1. Proposed framework for sentiment analysis

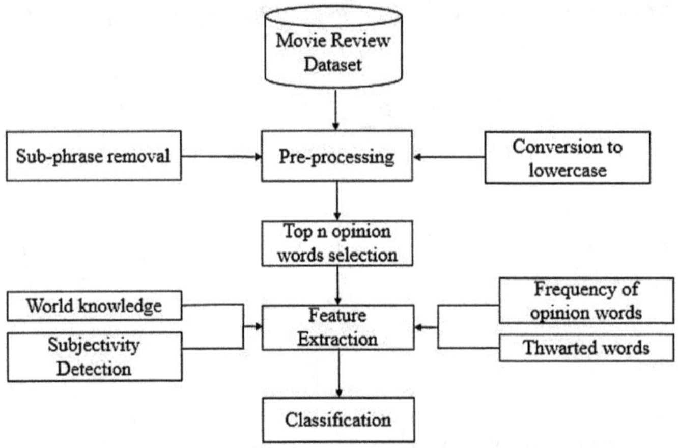

in text, which further helps the classifier to improve its performance, and accelerating classification process, thus aiding in analyzing sentiments in real time. Some pre-processing methods employed are:

a. **Sub-Phrase Removal:** The dataset from Kaggle movie review corpora being used here consists of phrases as well as the sub-phrases of movie reviews. These sub-phrases are of no use in analyzing sentiments since the polarity of opinion words that occur in sub-phrases are already considered in the original phrase. Hence removal of sub-phrases should be done to minimize the overhead for estimating the polarity of opinion words over and over again. A dataset containing only original phrases is thus obtained for analysis of sentiments.

b. **Conversion to Lowercase:** This is done to avoid distinction between words simply on case and to ensure proper matching of words. Figure 2 and 3 show respectively the movie review dataset containing sub-phrases and the dataset with sub-phrases removed.

Figure 2. Dataset containing sub-phrases

	A PhraseId Number	B SentenceId Number	C Phrase Cell	D Sentiment Number
1	PhraseId	SentenceId	Phrase	Sentiment
2	1	1	A series of escapades demonstrating the adage that what is good for the goose is also good for the gander, some of which occasionally amuses but none of which amounts to much of a story .	1
3	2	1	A series of escapades demonstrating the adage that what is good for the goose	2
4	3	1	A series	2
5	4	1	A	2
6	5	1	series	2
7	6	1	of escapades demonstrating the adage that what is good for the goose	2
8	7	1	of	2
9	8	1	escapades demonstrating the adage that what is good for the goose	2
10	9	1	escapades	2
11	10	1	demonstrating the adage that what is good for the goose	2
12	11	1	demonstrating the adage	2
13	12	1	demonstrating	2
14	13	1	the adage	2
15	14	1	the	2
16	15	1	adage	2
17	16	1	that what is good for the goose	2
18	17	1	that	2
19	18	1	what is good for the goose	2
20	19	1	what	2
21	20	1	is good for the goose	2
22	21	1	is	2
23	22	1	good for the goose	3

Sheet1 Sheet2

Figure 3. Dataset with sub-phrases removed

	1
1	"'A series of escapades demonstrating the adage that what is good for the goose is also good for the gander, some of which occ...
2	'This quiet, introspective and entertaining independent is worth seeking.'
3	'Even fans of Ismail Merchant "s work, I suspect, would have a hard time sitting through this one.'
4	"'A positively thrilling combination of ethnography and all the intrigue, betrayal, deceit and murder of a Shakespearean tragedy...
5	'Aggressive self-glorification and a manipulative whitewash.'
6	'A comedy-drama of nearly epic proportions rooted in a sincere performance by the title character undergoing midlife crisis.'
7	'Narratively, Trouble Every Day is a plodding mess.'
8	'The Importance of Being Earnest, so thick with wit it plays like a reading from Bartlett "s Familiar Quotations'
9	'But it does n"t leave you with much.'
10	'You could hate it for the same reason.'
11	'There "s little to recommend Snow Dogs, unless one considers cliched dialogue and perverse escapism a source of high hilarity.'
12	"'Kung Pow is Oedekerk "s realization of his childhood dream to be in a martial-arts flick, and proves that sometimes the dream...

15. **Top *n* Opinion Words Selection:** After pre-processing, the authors choose from the dataset opinion words, which contribute to the overall sentiment of a phrase. Weights are assigned to these selected words as per their polarity. These frequent words amount to the interesting features that need to be analysed and further leads to more accurate results while polarizing sentiments of the whole phrase.

    Figure 4 shows the selected opinion words and their corresponding weights.

16. **Feature Extraction:** Feature extraction is the process of generating set of features or appropriate characteristics of target object by transforming input data. It finds its applications in decreasing the dimensions of the feature space (Kummer, & Savoy, 2012), that is, feature extraction techniques reduce a high dimensional input to a lower dimension while preserving the desired characteristics and removing the unwanted ones. Decreased feature space imply less amount of data to be investigated, thus making the classifiers more effective as well as helping to identify relevant features to be considered in classification process. Some of the features extracted from the movie dataset are:
    a. **Frequency (Count) of Occurrence of Opinion Words:** The basic approach of statistical feature extraction is to use recurring words in the corpus as feature values. Frequency of occurrence of each of top *n* selected opinion words is counted for each review phrase of the corpora; an overall positive and negative score for the phrase text is counted and hence the overall sentiment of the phrase is calculated. If the reviews contain more positive than negative terms, it is assumed as positive review; if the reviews contain more negative than positive terms, it is assumed as negative review; otherwise it is neutral. The sentiment thus obtained is counted as first feature for the proposed algorithm. Frequency (count of occurrence) of positive opinion words, negative opinion words and hence the overall sentiment is illustrated in Figure 5.

Figure 4. Selected opinion words and their weights

	A	B	C
	SequenceNo	FeaturesWords	Weight0neutral1pos1neg
	Number	Cell	Number
1	Sequence ...	Features/Words	Weight(0-neutral,1-pos,-1-neg)
2	1	lunatic	-1
3	2	good	1
4	3	bad	-1
5	4	sanguine	1
6	5	evil	-1
7	6	not good	-1
8	7	not bad	1
9	8	ugly	-1
10	9	excellent	1
11	10	wonderful	1
12	11	furiously	-1
13	12	amuses	1
14	13	fears	-1
15	14	foibles	-1
16	15	good story	1
17	16	bad story	-1
18	17	entertaining	1
19	18	absorbing	1
20	19	melodramatic	-1
21	20	heartfelt	1
22	21	proud	1
23	22	betrayal	-1

Sheet1 | Sheet2 | Sheet3 | Sheet4 | Sheet5

Figure 5. Frequency (count) of opinion words

Fields	phrase	finalcountpos	finalcountneg	finalsentiment
1	'A series of escapades demonstrating the adage that what is good for the goose is also good for the gander , some of which ...	3	0	1
2	'This quiet , introspective and entertaining independent is worth seeking .'	2	0	1
3	'Even fans of Ismail Merchant ''s work , I suspect , would have a hard time sitting through this one .'	0	0	2
4	'A positively thrilling combination of ethnography and all the intrigue , betrayal , deceit and murder of a Shakespearean trag...	1	2	-0.6667
5	'Aggressive self-glorification and a manipulative whitewash .'	0	0	2
6	'A comedy-drama of nearly epic proportions rooted in a sincere performance by the title character undergoing midlife crisis .'	2	0	1
7	'Narratively , Trouble Every Day is a plodding mess .'	0	0	2
8	'The Importance of Being Earnest , so thick with wit it plays like a reading from Bartlett ''s Familiar Quotations'	5	0	1
9	'But it does n''t leave you with much .'	1	0	1
10	'You could hate it for the same reason .'	0	1	-1
11	'There ''s little to recommend Snow Dogs , unless one considers cliched dialogue and perverse escapism a source of high hil...	1	2	-0.6667
12	'Kung Pow is Oedekerk ''s realization of his childhood dream to be in a martial-arts flick , and proves that sometimes the dre...	0	0	2

b. **Thwarted Words:** This is one of the challenges of Sentiment Analysis that has been addressed in this chapter. Sometimes the user intentionally sets up context just to invalidate it towards the end. Consider the following example*: I decided to watch movie after I heard claims that it is best film, the actors and the supporting cast is good as well. However, it can't hold up.* Despite the fact that the above sentence contains more positive words, it is considered to be a negative sentence on account of the pivotal last sentence. Thus the impact of presence of thwarted words on overall sentiment of review phrases can be computed as:

i. **Step 1:** Create a knowledge base of thwarted words and assign weight to each thwarted word according to its polarity.
ii. **Step 2:** Check for the presence of thwarted words in reviews.
iii. **Step 3:** On the occurrence of a thwarted word, compute its corresponding weight from the knowledge base.
iv. **Step 4:** Update the polarity (sentiment) of review depending on the polarity of thwarted word to get the final sentiment of review.
v. **Step 5:** The sentiment thus obtained becomes another feature for the proposed algorithm.

Figure 6 and 7 shows the sentiments of movie review dataset without handling the presence of thwarted word challenge (already existing method) and with challenge handled (proposed method) respectively.

c. **World Knowledge:** Another challenge of Sentiment Analysis handled in this chapter is world knowledge. Sometimes the text contains another entity to refer to one entity. In that case, the knowledge of the entity which is used to refer another is required to identify the sentiment. For detecting sentiments, world knowledge needs to be included in the system. Consider the following example:

She is as beautiful as Snow White.

Here, to identify the sentiment orientation of the text, one has to know about 'Snow White'. Consider another example:

Figure 6. Sentiment of thwarted word feature before addressing challenge

Fields	phrase	finalcountpos	finalcountneg	finalsentiment
1749	'The way the roundelay of partners functions , and the interplay within partnerships and among partnerships and the general air of Gator-bashi...	1	0	1
1750	'But while the highly predictable narrative falls short , Treasure Planet is truly gorgeous to behold .'	1	0	1
1751	'Directed with purpose and finesse by England ''s Roger Mitchell , who handily makes the move from pleasing , relatively lightweight commerci...	2	0	1
1752	'I hate the movie "I love stories"'	1	1	2
1753	'I like the movie "I hate stories"'	1	1	2
1754	'I decided to watch movie after I heard claims that it is best film, the actors and the supporting cast is good as well. However, it can't hold up.'	2	0	1
1755	'He is a Doctor Zhivago. '	0	0	2
1756	'The story was monstrous. '	0	0	2

Figure 7. Sentiment of thwarted word feature after addressing challenge

Fields	phrase	finalcount_presence	finalcount_absence	finalsentiment
1748	'A muddle splashed with bloody beauty as vivid as any Scorsese has ever given us .'	0	0	2
1749	'The way the roundelay of partners functions , and the interplay within partnerships and among partnerships and the general air of Gator-bas...	0	0	2
1750	'But while the highly predictable narrative falls short , Treasure Planet is truly gorgeous to behold .'	1	0	-1
1751	'Directed with purpose and finesse by England ''s Roger Mitchell , who handily makes the move from pleasing , relatively lightweight comme...	1	0	-1
1752	'I hate the movie "I love stories"'	0	0	2
1753	'I like the movie "I hate stories"'	0	0	2
1754	'I decided to watch movie after I heard claims that it is best film, the actors and the supporting cast is good as well. However, it can't hold up.'	1	0	-1
1755	'He is a Doctor Zhivago. '	0	0	2
1756	'The story was monstrous. '	0	0	2

He is a Doctor Zhivago.

Although this sentence delineates a positive sentiment, but one still needs to know about Doctor Zhivago to find out the correct sentiment.

This challenge is handled as:

i. **Step 1:** Create a knowledge base of world knowledge words and assign weight to each world knowledge word according to its polarity.
ii. **Step 2:** Check for the presence of world knowledge words in reviews.
iii. **Step 3:** On the occurrence of a world knowledge word, check its corresponding weight from the knowledge base.
iv. **Step 4:** Update the polarity (sentiment) of the review depending on the polarity of the world knowledge word.
v. **Step 5:** The sentiment thus obtained becomes another feature for the algorithm.

Figure 8 and 9 shows the sentiments of movie review dataset without handling the World knowledge challenge (already existing method) and with challenge handled (proposed method) respectively.

d. **Subjectivity Detection:** Next challenge addressed is Subjectivity detection in sentiments. Subjectivity classification aims to find if a review sentence is opinionated or non-opinionated (subjective or objective), usually in the presence of an opinion expression in a sentence. A sentence is considered an objective sentence if it has some factual information and is considered subjective if it expresses

Figure 8. Sentiment of world knowledge feature before addressing challenge

Fields	phrase	finalcountpos	finalcountneg	finalsentiment
1749	'The way the roundelay of partners functions , and the interplay within partnerships and among partnerships and the general air of Gator-bashi...	1	0	1
1750	'But while the highly predictable narrative falls short , Treasure Planet is truly gorgeous to behold .'	1	0	1
1751	'Directed with purpose and finesse by England ''s Roger Mitchell , who handily makes the move from pleasing , relatively lightweight commerci...	2	0	1
1752	'I hate the movie "I love stories"'	1	1	2
1753	'I like the movie "I hate stories"'	1	1	2
1754	'I decided to watch movie after I heard claims that it is best film, the actors and the supporting cast is good as well. However, it can't hold up.'	2	0	1
1755	'He is a Doctor Zhivago. '	0	0	2
1756	'The story was monstrous. '	0	0	2

Figure 9. Sentiment of world knowledge feature after addressing challenge

Fields	phrase	finalcount_presence	finalcount_absence	finalsentiment
1748	'A muddle splashed with bloody beauty ...	0	0	2
1749	'The way the roundelay of partners funct...	0	0	2
1750	'But while the highly predictable narrativ...	0	0	2
1751	'Directed with purpose and finesse by En...	0	0	2
1752	'I hate the movie "I love stories"'	0	0	2
1753	'I like the movie "I hate stories"'	0	0	2
1754	'I decided to watch movie after I heard cl...	0	0	2
1755	'He is a Doctor Zhivago. '	1	0	1
1756	'The story was monstrous. '	0	0	2

personal feelings, views, emotions, or beliefs. Subjectivity detection aims at enhancing the performance of the system by filtering out the impact of subjective words on the overall sentiment. But this is not an easy task to do.

Consider the following examples:

I hate drama movies.

I hate the movie "I love stories".

I like the movie "I hate stories".

In the former example, an objective fact is presented whereas in the latter examples, opinion about a particular movie is depicted.

This challenge is addressed as:

i. **Step 1:** Create a knowledge base of subjectivity words.
ii. **Step 2:** Check for the presence of subjective words in a review.
iii. **Step 3:** On the occurrence of a subjective word, the effect of subjective word in the review is discarded by removing it from the review phrase.
iv. **Step 4:** Polarity (sentiment) of the updated review phrase is calculated based on the frequency (count) of positive or negative words in the phrase.

Figure 10. Sentiment of subjectivity detection feature before addressing challenge

Fields	phrase	finalcountpos	finalcountneg	finalsentiment
1749	'The way the roundelay of partners functions , and the interplay within partnerships and among partnerships and the general air of Gator-bashi...	1	0	1
1750	'But while the highly predictable narrative falls short , Treasure Planet is truly gorgeous to behold .'	1	0	1
1751	'Directed with purpose and finesse by England "s Roger Mitchell , who handily makes the move from pleasing , relatively lightweight commerci...	2	0	1
1752	'I hate the movie "I love stories"'	1	1	2
1753	'I like the movie "I hate stories"'	1	1	2
1754	'I decided to watch movie after I heard claims that it is best film, the actors and the supporting cast is good as well. However, it can't hold up.'	2	0	1
1755	'He is a Doctor Zhivago. '	0	0	2
1756	'The story was monstrous. '	0	0	2

Figure 11. Sentiment of subjectivity detection feature after addressing challenge

Fields	phrase	finalcount_pos	finalcount_neg	finalsentiment
1748	'A muddle splashed with bloody beauty as vivid as any Scors...	1	0	1
1749	'The way the roundelay of partners functions , and the interpl...	1	0	1
1750	'But while the highly predictable narrative falls short , Treasur...	1	0	1
1751	'Directed with purpose and finesse by England "s Roger Mitc...	2	0	1
1752	'I hate the movie "I love stories"'	0	1	-1
1753	'I like the movie "I hate stories"'	1	0	1
1754	'I decided to watch movie after I heard claims that it is best fil...	2	0	1
1755	'He is a Doctor Zhivago. '	0	0	2
1756	'The story was monstrous. '	0	0	2

v. **Step 5:** The sentiment thus obtained becomes another feature for the algorithm.

Figure 10 and 11 shows the sentiments of movie review dataset without handling the Subjectivity detection challenge (already existing method) and with challenge handled (proposed method) respectively.

Thus, to find the overall sentiment of an object (here review phrases), first the sentiment words (or opinion words) about the features of the said object are identified. Various features are extracted and then assigned weight on the basis of their polarity. Finally, the polarity weights of all the features of the object are aggregated in a feature set $\boldsymbol{Overall\_feature}$ .in order to get the overall opinion about the given object. This $\boldsymbol{Overall\_feature}$ .feature set is used for training the classifier.

17. **Classification:** Classification is the process of assigning documents to suitable categories. Here, the movie reviews are assigned to suitable pre-defined classes/categories on the basis of their overall sentiment. Classifiers like kNN, SVM, Naive Bayes, Logistic Regression, Stochastic Gradient Descent (SGD), Random Forest and many more can be used for this purpose. In this chapter, the authors have used two supervised machine learning models to validate the results for both the methods of Sentiment Analysis – one with challenges unhandled and the other with challenges handled (proposed method). These models are Naive Bayes classifier and k Nearest Neighbor classifier.
    a. **Naive Bayes Classifier:** Naive Bayes classifier is based on a probabilistic learning method and the assumption that terms occur independently of each other. The foundation Naive Bayesian was built so as to include unlabelled data. The undertaking of learning of a generative model is to appraise the parameters using labelled training data only. Using estimated parameters, the algorithm classifies new documents by ascertaining the given document belongs to which generated class. The working of Naive Bayes classifier (Govindarajan, & M., 2013) is as follows:
        i. **Step 1:** Consider a training set of samples having k classes $C_1, C_2, \ldots, C_k$ .ith the label of each class being T. An n-dimensional vector, $X = \{x_1, x_2, \ldots, x_n\}$, .which represents n measured values of the n attributes, $A_1, A_2, \ldots, A_n$ .respectively is associated with every sample.
        ii. **Step 2:** The given sample X .is classified by the classifier in such a way that it belongs to the highest posterior probability containing class. This implies X .is anticipated to be grouped to the class C_i .if and only if $P(C_i|X) > P(C_j|X)$ .for $1 \leq j \leq m, j \neq i$. .Thus the class that maximizes $P(C_i|X)$ .is found; this maximized value of $P(C_i|X)$ .for class C_i .is referred to as maximum posterior hypothesis.

In Naive Bayes technique, the basic idea to find the probabilities of categories given a text document by using the joint probabilities of words and categories. It is based on the assumption of word independence. In case of movie reviews, Naive Bayes classifier attempts to evaluate the probability of a document (review) being positive or negative, given its contents.

Bayes theorem for conditional probability is used as the initial point in this classifier, stating that, for a given data point x .nd class C .

$$P\left(C / x\right) = \frac{P\left(x / C\right).P\left(C\right)}{P\left(x\right)}$$

Now assuming that the probability of each of the attributes of a data point $x = \left\{x_1, x_2, \ldots, x_j\right\}$, .occurring in a given class is independent, we can estimate the probability of x as follows:

$$P\left(C / x\right) = P\left(C\right).\Pi P\left(x_j / C\right)$$

Thus, the conditional probabilities of each attributes occurring on the predicted classes are required to be estimated from the training data set to train a Naive Bayes classifier.

b. **k Nearest Neighbor (kNN) Classifier:** k Nearest Neighbor (kNN) is the simplest and the oldest classifier that can be employed for classifying text (Cover, & Hart, 1967). It is an interpretation of example-based method in which the decision on how to generalize beyond the training data is deferred as long as a new query instance comes across (Sebastiani, 2002). The principle on which kNN classifier works is that the closest points (reviews) in space, found by calculating a similarity measure between test review and each neighbor, are grouped to the same class (Patel, & Mistry, 2015). A reasonable distance or similarity measure, for example, Euclidean distance is selected for finding k-nearest neighbors of a new instance that needs to be classified. In other words, the k-Nearest Neighbor algorithm classifies a new occurrence by checking for its k closest instances called neighbors in the data set, and predicting the class of a new instance (Kalaivani, & Shunmuganathan, 2013) depending on classes that belong to the majority of its k neighbors.

Reasons for Choosing kNN and Naive Bayes Classifiers Over Random Forest, SGD and Logistic Regression:

i. KNN and Naive Bayes results are more interpretable than Logistic Regression and Random Forests.
ii. KNN is easier to explain than Logistic Regression, Naive Bayes is somewhat easier but Random Forests are very difficult to explain/interpret (since they are black boxes).
iii. Training speed of KNN and Naive Bayes is fast as compared to Random Forests. Whereas Logistic Regression has an average training speed.
iv. A Naive Bayes converges quicker than discriminative models like Logistic Regression, if conditional independence assumption holds, and hence minimum training data is required.
v. The speed at which Naïve Bayes perform prediction is fast as compared to Random Forests (owing to large number of trees).
vi. Lesser amount of parameter tuning is required for KNN than Random Forests.
vii. Naive Bayes performs well even with small number of observations as compared to Random Forests.
viii. Though both Naive Bayes and Random Forests perform well in separating noise from sound, Random Forests fail if noise ratio is very high. Logistic Regression has no such ability.

ix. KNN gives calibrated probabilities of class membership whereas Random Forests may have some possibility.
x. A large number of hyper parameters like the regularization parameter and a number of iterations are required in SGD.
xi. SGD is sensitive to feature scaling.
xii. Random Forests and Logistic Regression are highly biased.

c. **Cross Validation:** The predictive evaluation of the classifier is done by using a technique called Cross validation in which the original dataset is partitioned into a training set to train the model and a test set to access it. A 10-fold cross validation have been used with a sample size of 156060 and the ratio of training data to testing data being 80/20.

EXPERIMENTAL SETUP

This research work has been implemented in MATLAB R2014a serial update 2 (version 8.3.0.532).

Evaluation Criteria

Various standard evaluation measures have been used in this chapter to calculate the effectiveness of proposed method such as accuracy, precision, recall and Fscore. These metrics were estimated by making use of features like True Positive (t_p ., True Negative (t_n ., False Positive (f_p ., and False Negative (f_n . (Khan, Baharudin, & Khan, 2013) defined as:

- **True Positive (t_p .:** A test result is said to be true positive if it detects the condition when the condition is actually present. In other words, all extracted features that correctly match with the features annotated positive manually are known as true positive (t_p . features.
- **True Negative (t_n .:** A test result is said to be true negative if it does not detect the condition when the condition is absent. In other words, all non-positive features that the proposed method does not extract are called true negative (t_n . features.
- **False Positive (f_p .:** A test result can be called as false positive if it detects the condition when actually the condition is absent. In other words, all non-positive features that the proposed method includes in positive features are known as false positive (f_p . features.
- **False Negative (f_n .:** A test result can be called as false negative if it does not detect the condition when actually the condition is present. In other words, all positive features that the proposed method includes in non-positive features are called false negative (f_n . features.

These features are shown in Table 1.

Table 1. Various features for estimating evaluation measures of classification (Owais, Nafis, & Khanna, 2015)

Predicted Class (Observation)	Actual Class (Expectation)	
	Present	Absent
Positive	True Positive(t_p)	False Positive(f_p)
Negative	False Negative(f_n)	True Negative(t_n)

Results

The results of various performance metrics (parameters) of classification using Naive Bayes and kNN classifiers, of the method of Sentiment analysis without addressing the challenges like presence of Thwarted words, World knowledge and Subjectivity detection in sentiments and the novel proposed method of Sentiment analysis with all these challenges addressed, are given below:

18. **Accuracy:** Accuracy is a parameter of test that describes the proportion of true results (both true positives and true negatives) present in the total population. It can be used to estimate the efficiency of the framework employed and is defined as:

$$Accuracy = \frac{t_p + t_n}{t_p + f_p + t_n + f_n}$$

Comparison between accuracy in results of the two methods is shown in Figure 12 and 13.

19. **Precision:** Precision is a parameter of test that represents the ratio of true positives to all the positive results (both true positives and false positives) present in the total population. The exactness of a classifier can be measured by this parameter and is defined as:

$$Precision = \frac{t_p}{t_p + f_p}$$

Precision in results given by the two methods is depicted in Figure 14 and 15.

20. **Recall:** Recall can be referred to as the parameter of test that describes the proportion of the true positives against both true positives and false negatives present in the total population. It is used to measure the sensitivity of a classifier and is defined as:

$$Recall = \frac{t_p}{t_p + f_n}.$$

Figure 12. Accuracy without challenges addressed

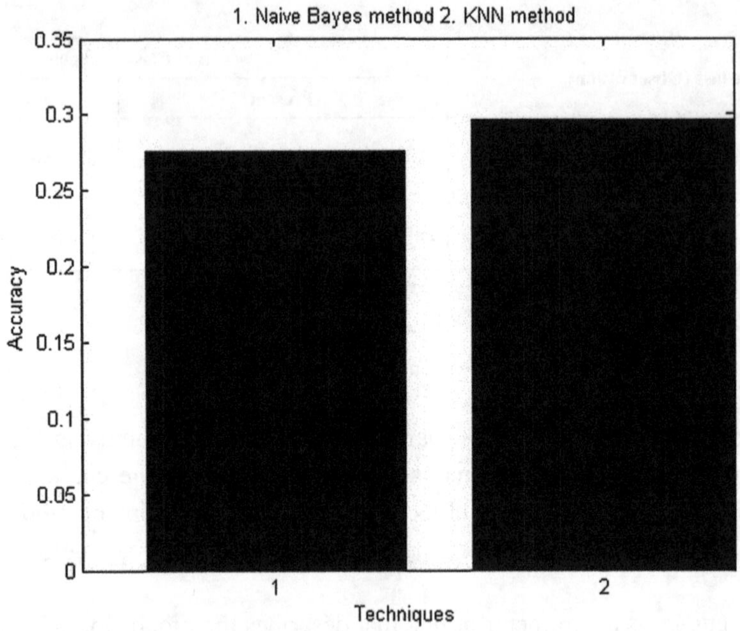

Figure 13. Accuracy with challenges addressed

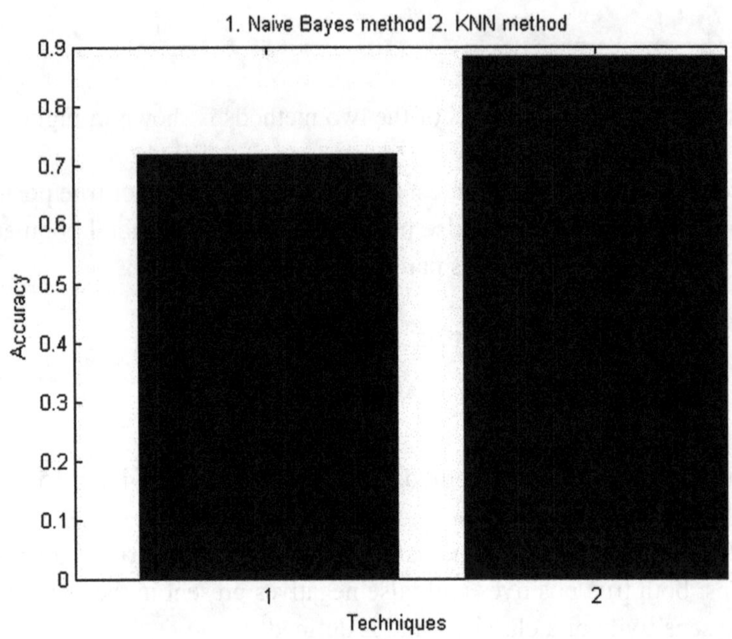

Figure 14. Precision without challenges addressed

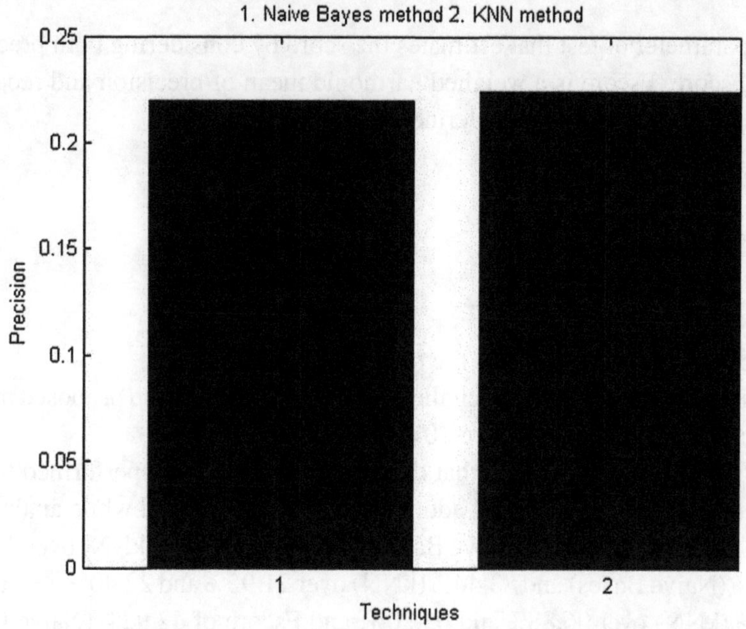

Figure 15. Precision with challenges addressed

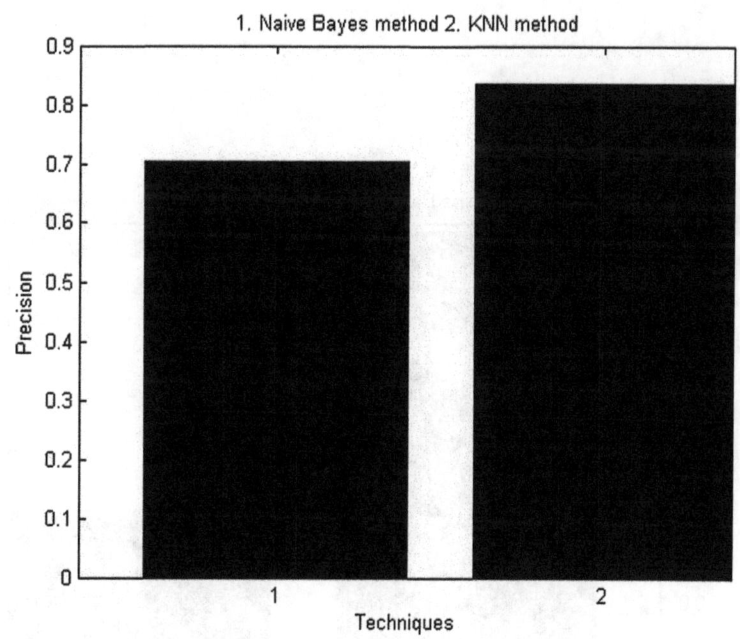

Recall calculated using the two mentioned methods is shown in Figure 16 and 17.

21. **Fscore:** The parameter of test that estimates the score by considering both precision and recall of test is called Fscore. Fscore is a weighed harmonic mean of precision and recall. This parameter measures the accuracy of test and is defined as:

$$F = 2.\frac{Precision.Recall}{Precision + Recall}$$

Figure 18 and 19 compares Fscore of the two methods.

Overall evaluation of the method where challenges are unaddressed and proposed methodology where challenges are addressed is shown in Figure 20 and 21.

It can be seen from Figures 20 and 21 that the proposed method outperformed the already existing method of sentiment analysis that does not address the challenges faced while analyzing sentiments. It achieved an accuracy of 71.75% (using Naive Bayes) and 88.38% (using kNN) over 27.56% and 29.61%, precision of 70.33% (Naive Bayes) and 83.44% (kNN) over 21.95% and 22.40%, recall of 31.43% (Naive Bayes) and 49.42% (kNN) over 06.88% and 03.20%, and Fscore of 42.92% (Naive Bayes) and 58.75% (kNN) over 20.00% and 32.88% respectively.

Figure 16. Recall without challenges addressed

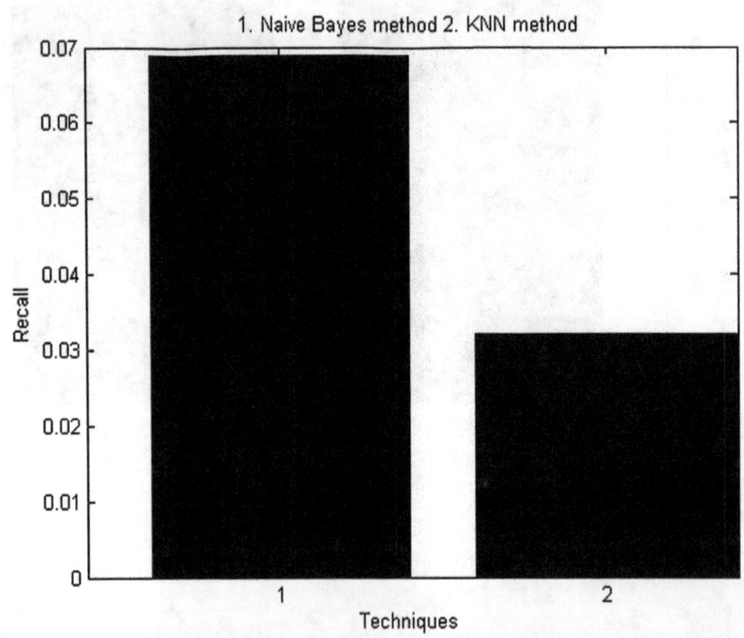

Figure 17. Recall with challenges addressed

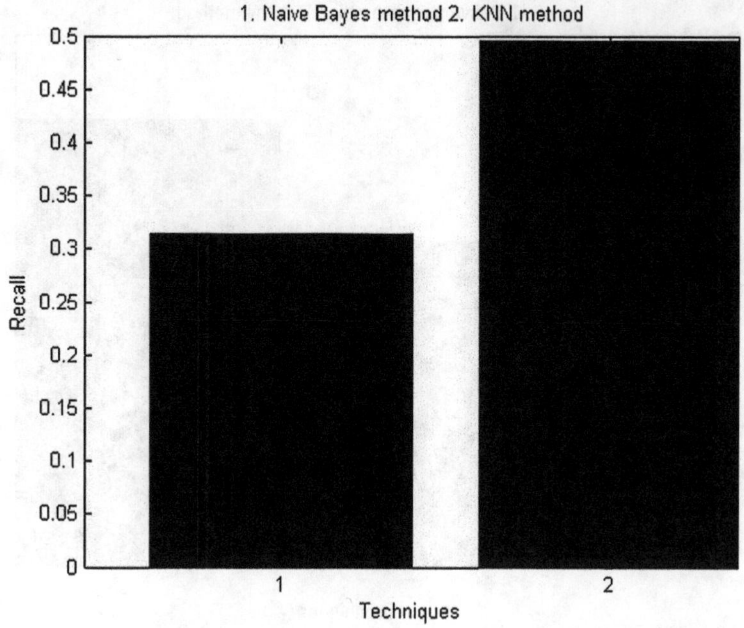

Figure 18. Fscore without challenges addressed

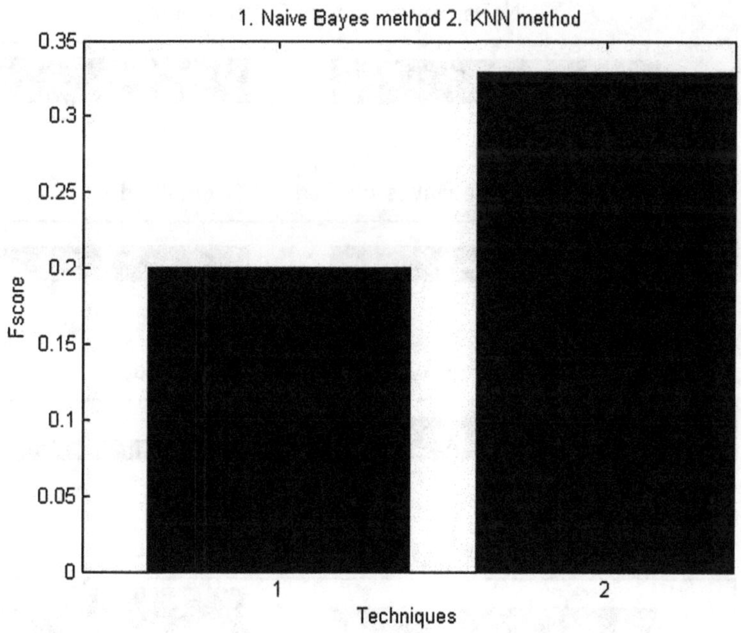

Figure 19. Fscore with challenges addressed

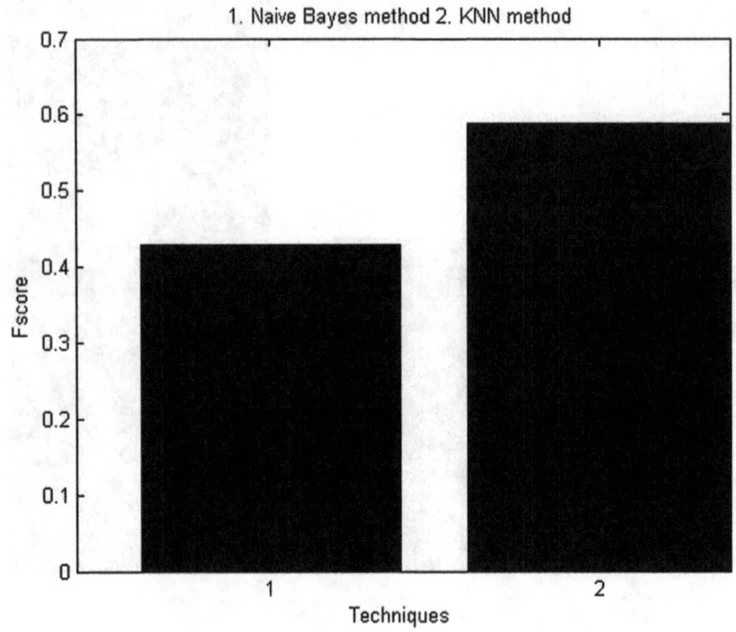

Figure 20. Results of method where challenges are unaddressed

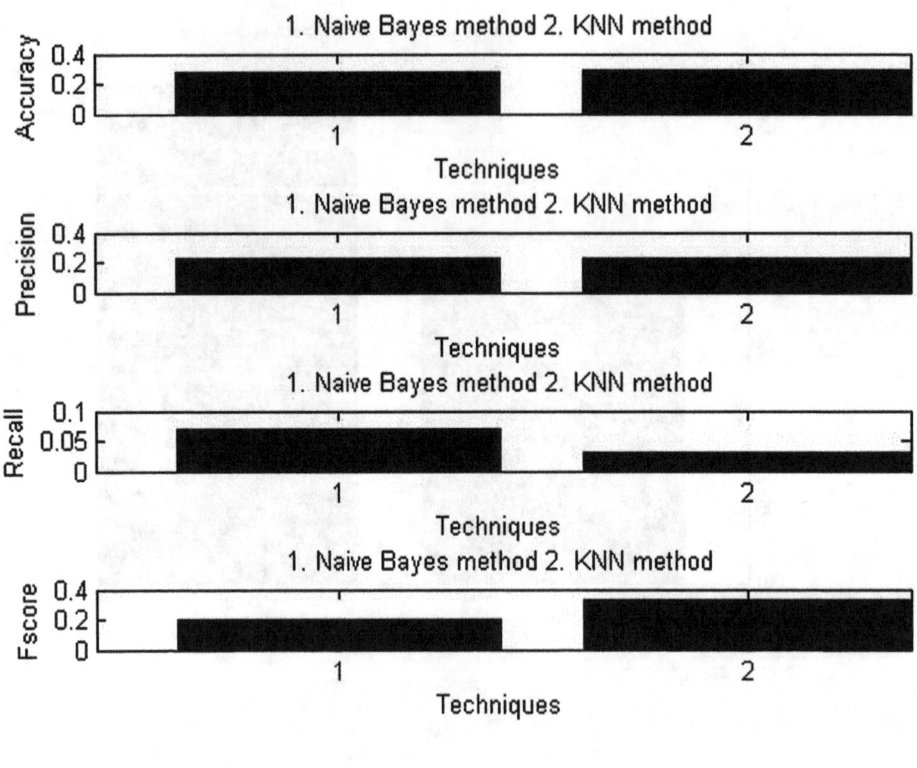

Figure 21. Results of method where challenges are addressed

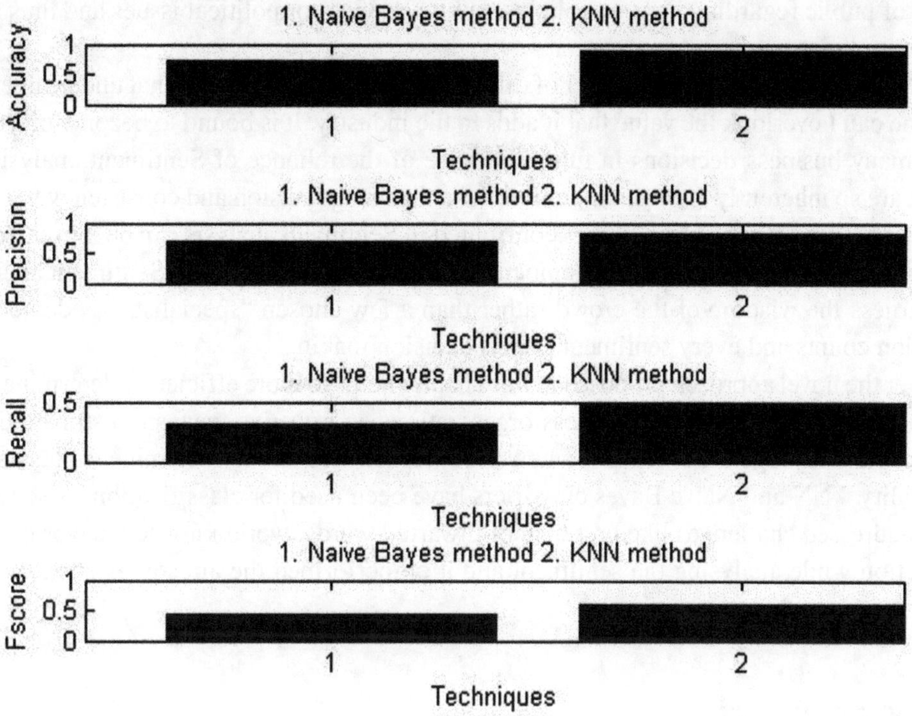

FUTURE RESEARCH DIRECTIONS

Although a lot has been done in the field of Sentiment Analysis and this research work presents novel ways of finding the sentiments of movie reviews as well as handling various challenges faced in analyzing sentiments, still a lot more can be done. In future, classifiers like Genetic algorithm and fuzzy classification can be applied on movie reviews dataset or reviews on any other subject area. In-depth concepts of Natural Language Processing (NLP) can be applied so as to predict the polarity of reviews posted online or of some document in a better way. Moreover, the proposed algorithm can be applied on other domains of opinion mining such as political discussion forums, newspaper articles and product reviews.

CONCLUSION

The field of sentiment analysis has emerged as an exciting new research direction since an ample number of real-world applications exist that rely on determining people's opinion for better decision-making. The need for analyzing opinionated content present online for various real-world applications has gained attention as more and more people have begun sharing their assessments and opinions about various products or topics on the web. Sentiment analysis of movie reviews deals with accessing the polarity of reviews that the users communicate, thereby enabling strategic decision-making for various business and commercial purposes. Sentiment analysis, in addition to analyzing movie reviews, can also be used for evaluating the reviews of many other products or services present on different social media and e-commerce websites. Likewise, it can be used to encourage politicians or policy makers to analyze the sentiments of public regarding various policies, public services or political issues and thus accordingly frame future policies.

Regardless of the considerable number of difficulties and potential issues that undermines Sentiment analysis, one can't overlook the value that it adds to the industry. It is bound to become one of the major drivers of many business decisions in future because of the reliance of Sentiment analysis results on factors that are so inherently humane. By enforcing enhanced precision and consistency in content mining procedures, some of the present issues confronted in Sentiment analysis can be minimized. Looking ahead, what one can see is a true social democracy that will be created using Sentiment analysis, where one can harness the wisdom of the crowd rather than a few chosen "specialists"- a democracy where every opinion counts and every sentiment affects decision making.

Moreover the novel approach proposed in this chapter helps to more efficiently determine the polarity of a movie review, thus providing business organizations an effective means to estimate the extent of product acceptance, judge the success of a new product launched and to determine strategies to improve product quality. kNN and Naive Bayes classifiers have been used for classification. Also the proposed algorithm addressed challenges like presence of thwarted words, world knowledge words, and Subjectivity detection while analysing the sentiment and it outperformed the already existing method where challenges are not addressed.

ACKNOWLEDGMENT

All praise be to Allah, Lord of the Worlds, and may the peace and blessings be on the most noble of Prophets and Messengers, our Prophet Muhammad, and on his family and all of his Companions. I offer to Him all praise and gratitude, and seek His assistance and forgiveness. I seek refuge in Allah from the evils of our souls and the wickedness of our deeds. Whomsoever Allah guides, none can misguide, and whomsoever Allah misguides, none can guide. I thank Allah, the Exalted, for the completion of this chapter. Alhamdulillah, Allah gave me enough strength and patience to tackle every problem with calm and ease.

I would like to express my profound gratitude to my research guide Dr. Farheen Siddiqui, Assistant Professor, School of Engineering Sciences and Technology (SEST), Jamia Hamdard, for her good guidance and direction, advice, strong support, highly-valued criticisms, deep insights and for providing resourceful information that contributed to the quality of this research.

I am highly thankful to my family for their love and support throughout my life and my studies. My parents, Mrs. & Mr. Mohammad Ismail Shah, raised me to believe that I could achieve anything I set my mind to. Thank you for your love, prayers, caring and sacrifices for educating and preparing me for my future.

Finally, my thanks go to all the people who have supported me to complete my research work directly or indirectly.

This research received no specific grant from any funding agency in the public, commercial, or not-for-profit sectors.

REFERENCES

Abbasi, A., Chen, H., Thoms, S., & Fu, T. (2008). Affect Analysis of Web Forums and Blogs Using Correlation Ensembles. *IEEE Transactions on Knowledge and Data Engineering*, *20*(9), 1168–1180. doi:10.1109/TKDE.2008.51

Abbasi, A., France, S., Zhang, Z., & Chen, H. (2011). Selecting Attributes for Sentiment Classification Using Feature Relation Networks. *IEEE Transactions on Knowledge and Data Engineering*, *23*(2), 447–462. doi:10.1109/TKDE.2010.110

Al-Moslmi, T., Albared, M., Al-Shabi, A., Omar, N., & Abdullah, S. (n.d.). Arabic senti-lexicon: Constructing publicly available language resources for Arabic sentiment analysis. Journal of Information Science, 1–18.

Aydoğan, E., & Akcayol, M. (2016). A comprehensive survey for sentiment analysis tasks using machine learning techniques. In *INnovations in Intelligent SysTems and Applications (INISTA), 2016 International Symposium on*. Sinaia, Romania: IEEE. doi:10.1109/INISTA.2016.7571856

Barzilay, R., & Lapata, M. (2005). Collective content selection for concept-to-text generation. In *Proceedings of the conference on Human Language Technology and Empirical Methods in Natural Language Processing* (pp. 331-338). Stroudsburg, PA: Association for computational linguistics.

Bholane Savita, D., & Gore, D. (2016). Sentiment Analysis on Twitter Data Using Support Vector Machine. *International Journal of Computer Science Trends and Technology*, *4*(3), 365–370.

Brindha, S., Prabha, K., & Sukumaran, S. (2016). A Survey on Classification Techniques for Text Mining. In *Advanced Computing and Communication Systems (ICACCS), 2016 3rd International Conference on*. Coimbatore, India: IEEE. doi:10.1109/ICACCS.2016.7586371

Buche, A., Chandak, M. B., & Zadgaonkar, A. (2013, June). Opinion mining and Analysis: A survey. *International Journal on Natural Language Computing*, *2*(3).

Carrillo de Albornoz, J., Plaza, L., Gervás, P., & Díaz, A. (2011). A joint model of feature mining and sentiment analysis for product review rating. In *ECIR'11 Proceedings of the 33rd European conference on Advances in information retrieval* (pp. 55-66). Berlin: Springer. doi:10.1007/978-3-642-20161-5_8

Chidananda, H. T., Sagnika, S., & Sahoo, L. (2017, February). Survey on Sentiment Analysis: A Comparative Study. *International Journal of Computers and Applications*, *159*(6), 4–7. doi:10.5120/ijca2017912952

Cover, T., & Hart, P. (1967). Nearest neighbour pattern classification. *IEEE Transactions on Information Theory*, *13*(1), 21–27. doi:10.1109/TIT.1967.1053964

Dave, K., Lawrence, S., & Pennock, D. (2003). Mining the peanut gallery: opinion extraction and semantic classification of product reviews. In *Proceedings of the 12th international conference on World Wide Web* (pp. 519-528). Budapest, Hungary: ACM. doi:10.1145/775152.775226

Deng, S., Sinha, A. P., & Zhao, H. (2017, February). Adapting sentiment lexicons to domain-specific social media texts. *Decision Support Systems*, *94*(C), 65–76.

Govindarajan, M., & M., R. (2013). A Survey of Classification Methods and Applications for Sentiment Analysis. *International Journal of Engineering Science*, *2*(12), 11–15.

Hu, M., & Liu, B. (2004). Mining and summarizing customer reviews. In *KDD '04 Proceedings of the tenth ACM SIGKDD international conference on Knowledge discovery and data mining* (pp. 168-177). New York, NY: ACM. doi:10.1145/1014052.1014073

Hussein, D. (2016). A survey on sentiment analysis challenges. *Journal Of King Saud University -. Engineering and Science*. doi:10.1016/j.jksues.2016.04.002

Jadhav, R., & Wakode, M. S. (2017, March). Survey: Sentiment Analysis of Twitter Data for Stock Market Prediction. *International Journal of Advanced Research in Computer and Communication Engineering*, *6*(3), 558–562. doi:10.17148/IJARCCE.2017.63129

Jo, Y., & Oh, A. (2011). Aspect and sentiment unification model for online review analysis. In *WSDM '11 Proceedings of the fourth ACM international conference on Web search and data mining* (pp. 815-824). New York, NY: ACM. doi:10.1145/1935826.1935932

Kalaivani, P., & Shunmuganathan, D. (2013). Sentiment classification of movie reviews by supervised machine learning approaches. *Indian Journal of Computer Science and Engineering*, *4*(4), 285–292.

Khan, K., Baharudin, B., & Khan, A. (2014). Identifying Product Features from Customer Reviews Using Hybrid Patterns. *The International Arab Journal of Information Technology*, *11*(3), 281–286.

Kim, S., & Hovy, E. (2004). Determining the sentiment of opinions. In *COLING '04 Proceedings of the 20th international conference on Computational Linguistics*. Stroudsburg, PA: Association for Computational Linguistics. doi:10.3115/1220355.1220555

Korkontzelos, I., Nikfarjam, A., Shardlow, M., Sarker, A., Ananiadou, S., & Gonzalez, G. H. (2016, August). Analysis of the effect of sentiment analysis on extracting adverse drug reactions from tweets and forum posts. *Journal of Biomedical Informatics*, *62*(C), 148–158. doi:10.1016/j.jbi.2016.06.007 PMID:27363901

Ku, L., Liang, Y., & Chen, H. (2006). Opinion Extraction, Summarization and Tracking in News and Blog Corpora. *AAAI Spring Symposium: Computational Approaches to Analyzing Weblogs*, 100-107.

Kummer, O., & Savoy, J. (2012). Feature Selection in Sentiment Analysis. In *CORIA 2012 Proceedings of the 9th Conference on Information Retrieval and Applications* (pp. 273-284). Bordeaux.

Liu, B. (2010). Sentiment analysis and subjectivity. In N. Indurkhya & F. Damerau (Eds.), *Handbook of Natural Language Processing* (2nd ed., pp. 627–661). CRC Press.

Liu, B. (2012). *Sentiment analysis and opinion mining*. San Rafael, CA: Morgan & Claypool.

Ma, C., Prendinger, H., & Ishizuka, M. (2005). Emotion estimation and reasoning based on affective textual interaction. In *Affective Computing and Intelligent Interaction* (Vol. 3784, pp. 622–628). Berlin: Springer. doi:10.1007/11573548_80

Matsumoto, S., Takamura, H., & Okumura, M. (2005). Sentiment classification using word sub-sequences and dependency sub-trees. In *PAKDD'05 Proceedings of the 9th Pacific-Asia conference on Advances in Knowledge Discovery and Data Mining* (pp. 301-311). Berlin: Springer. doi:10.1007/11430919_37

Ortony, A., Clore, G. L., & Foss, M. A. (1987). The referential structure of the affective lexicon. *Cognitive Science, 11*(3), 341–364. doi:10.1207/s15516709cog1103_4

Owais, S., Nafis, P., & Khanna, S. (2015). An Improved Method for Detection of Satire from User-Generated Content. *(IJCSIT). International Journal of Computer Science and Information Technologies, 6*(3), 2084–2088.

Pagolu, V., Reddy, K., & Panda, G. (2016). Sentiment analysis of Twitter data for predicting stock market movements. In *International Conference on Signal Processing, Communication, Power and Embedded System (SCOPES)*, 2016 (pp. 1345-1350). Paralakhemundi, India: IEEE. doi:10.1109/SCOPES.2016.7955659

Pang, B., Lee, L., & Vaithyanathan, S. (2002). Thumbs up? Sentiment classification using machine learning techniques. *Proceeding of the conference on empirical methods in natural language processing*, 79-86.

Pang, B., & Lee, L. (2008). Opinion mining and sentiment analysis. *Foundations and Trends in Information Retrieval, 2*(1-2), 1-135.

Patel, M., & Mistry, M. (2015). A Review: Text Classification on Social Media Data. *IOSR Journal of Computer Engineering, 17*(1), 80-84.

Pradhan, V. M., Vala, J., & Balani, P. (2016, January). A Survey on Sentiment Analysis Algorithms for Opinion Mining. *International Journal of Computers and Applications, 133*(9), 7–11. doi:10.5120/ijca2016907977

Rangel, F., & Rosso, P. (2016). On the impact of emotions on author profiling. *Information Processing & Management, 52*(1), 73–92. doi:10.1016/j.ipm.2015.06.003

Rimon, M. (2005). Sentiment classification: Linguistic and non-linguistic issues. *Proceedings of Israel Association for Theoretical Linguistics, 21.*

Rodrigues, R. G., Dores, R. M., & Camilo-Junior, C. G. (2016, January). SentiHealth-Cancer: A sentiment analysis tool to help detecting mood of patients in online social networks. *International Journal of Medical Informatics, 85*(1), 80–95. doi:10.1016/j.ijmedinf.2015.09.007 PMID:26514078

Salas-Zárate, M. P., Valencia-García, R., Ruiz-Martínez, A., & Colomo-Palacios, R. (2017, August 1). Feature-based opinion mining in financial news: An ontology-driven approach. *Journal of Information Science, 43*(4), 458–479. doi:10.1177/0165551516645528

Sebastiani, F. (2002). Machine learning in automated text categorization. *ACM Computing Surveys, 34*(1), 1–47. doi:10.1145/505282.505283

Sentiment Analysis on Movie Reviews. (2015). Retrieved February 09, 2017, from https://www.kaggle.com/c/sentiment-analysis-on-movie-reviews/data

Turney, P. (2002). Thumbs up or thumbs down? Semantic orientation applied to unsupervised classification of reviews. In *Proceedings of the 40th annual meeting of the association for computational linguistics* (pp. 417-424). Stroudsburg, PA: Association for Computational Linguistics.

Wang, H., Lu, Y., & Zhai, C. (2010). Latent aspect rating analysis on review text data: a rating regression approach. In *KDD '10 Proceedings of the 16th ACM SIGKDD international conference on Knowledge discovery and data mining* (pp. 783-792). New York, NY: ACM. doi:10.1145/1835804.1835903

Wilson, T., Wiebe, J., & Hoffmann, P. (2005). Recognizing contextual polarity in phrase level sentiment analysis. In *Proceedings of the conference on Human Language Technology and Empirical Methods in Natural Language Processing* (pp. 347-354). Stroudsburg, PA: Association for Computational Linguistics. doi:10.3115/1220575.1220619

KEY TERMS AND DEFINITIONS

Efficiency: Maximum productivity achieved with minimum waste of efforts or expense is called efficiency.

Euclidean Distance: Euclidean distance gives the measurement of length of a segment that joins two points, that is, distance between two points in a plane or three-dimensional space.

Feature Space: A hypothetical space which uses a point to represent each pattern sample in n-dimensional space is called feature space in pattern recognition. Dimensions of a feature space can be specified by the number of features utilized in portraying the patterns.

Harmonic Mean: The ratio of "number of the given values" and "sum of the reciprocals of the given values" is called harmonic mean.

Natural Language Processing (NLP): A branch of artificial intelligence that examines, understands, and creates languages used naturally by humans, thereby interacting with computers using natural languages of humans instead of computer languages in both written and spoken contexts is referred to as natural language processing (NLP). In other words, NLP is concerned with programming computers so that it can process large corpora of natural languages in an effective manner.

Opinion Mining: A sub-discipline of computational linguistics concerned with extraction of opinions, demeanors, and emotions expressed by users on the web towards different individuals, products, services, topics, and their features is called opinion mining.

Performance Metrics of Classification: The various measures that can be employed in assessment of performance or quality of classifiers or different learning methods and learned models are called performance metrics of classification.

Positive Predictive Value: In statistics and diagnostic tests, the proportion of positive results that are true positive results is called positive predictive value (PPV). Also called precision, it can be used to evaluate performance of a test.

Semantic Orientation: Classifying words as positive, negative, or neutral to identify the polarity of an opinion on a feature f is called semantic orientation.

Sensitivity: The measurement of proportion of correctly identified positives is called Sensitivity. In other words, it measures how good a test is at detecting the positives. It is also called true positive rate, recall, or probability of detection in some fields.

Supervised Learning: The machine learning task of analyzing labelled training data and hence inferring a function is called supervised learning. It can then be employed to map new examples.

APPENDIX 1

Accuracy, Precision, Recall and Fscore Results of Existing Method Using Naive Bayes Classifier

- Accuracy: 27.56%
- Precision: 21.95%
- Recall: 06.88%
- Fscore: 20.00%

APPENDIX 2

Accuracy, Precision, Recall and Fscore Results of Proposed Method Using Naive Bayes Classifier

- Accuracy: 71.75%
- Precision: 70.33%
- Recall: 31.43%
- Fscore: 42.92%

APPENDIX 3

Accuracy, Precision, Recall and Fscore Results of Existing Method Using kNN Classifier

- Accuracy: 29.61%
- Precision: 22.40%
- Recall: 03.20%
- Fscore: 32.88%

APPENDIX 4

Accuracy, Precision, Recall and Fscore Results of Proposed Method Using kNN Classifier

- Accuracy: 88.38%
- Precision: 83.44%
- Recall: 49.42%
- Fscore: 58.75%

Chapter 8
Authorship Attribution for Online Social Media

Ritu Banga
Jaypee Institute of Information Technology, India

Akanksha Bhardwaj
Jaypee Institute of Information Technology, India

Sheng-Lung Peng
National Dong Hwa University, Taiwan

Gulshan Shrivastava
National Institute of Technology Patna, India

ABSTRACT

This chapter gives a comprehensive knowledge of various machine learning classifiers to achieve authorship attribution (AA) on short texts, specifically tweets. The need for authorship identification is due to the increasing crime on the internet, which breach cyber ethics by raising the level of anonymity. AA of online messages has witnessed interest from many research communities. Many methods such as statistical and computational have been proposed by linguistics and researchers to identify an author from their writing style. Various ways of extracting and selecting features on the basis of dataset have been reviewed. The authors focused on n-grams features as they proved to be very effective in identifying the true author from a given list of known authors. The study has demonstrated that AA is achievable on the basis of selection criteria of features and methods in small texts and also proved the accuracy of analysis changes according to combination of features. The authors found character grams are good features for identifying the author but are not yet able to identify the author independently.

INTRODUCTION

Authorship Attribution is the way to identify the author of a given text or document by inferring their distinctiveness from the characteristic of a document written by that author (Juola, 2008). In this, documents are examined to determine stylistic details concealed in the text hence, concluding about the features

DOI: 10.4018/978-1-5225-5097-6.ch008

of the author of a text. It is useful in case of repudiation where no person is willing to state that whether a given text is written by him/her. This field has been taking advantages from research already pursued in areas like machine learning, natural language processing and information retrieval. The development of these areas influence authorship attribution technology in many ways as described below:

- Powerful machine learning techniques are becoming convenient to deal with higher dimensional and sparse data that permit more expressive representations.
- For representing and classifying a large amount of data or messages, efficient technologies like Information retrieval have been developed.
- To analyze the data or documents systematically, Natural Language Processing (NLP) tools are used that provides a new pattern of measures for illustrating the style.

Authorship attribution (AA) as a scholarly discipline has maintained a special connection to erudition in the digital humanities, where the authentication of disputed scholarly articles is of interest. For that reason, plenty of work in this field remains unexplored to researchers and professionals in digital forensics at large, in spite of accomplished efforts at outreach.

Authorship Analysis has four principal aspects:

1. **Authorship Attribution (or Identification):** Determine the particular document is written by which author among a list of known authors.
2. **Authorship Verification:** Determine the target document is written by that particular author or not.
3. **Authorship Profiling (or Characterization):** Determining the demographic characteristics/features of author (like age, gender, personality) from an anonymous document.
4. **Similarity Detection:** Compare multiple piece of writing and determines whether they were produced by a single author. Most research in this aspect is related to plagiarism detection. Plagiarism includes the full or partial replication of a piece of writing without owner's permission. To detect the plagiarism activity, plagiarism detection aim to investigate the similarity between two pieces of writing. Because writing styles of two authors differ in various aspects.

The problem of identifying the most appropriate author from the list of potential suspects, who are considered as classes, is a typical authorship identification and classification problem. A digital document can be used as an evidence to prove the guilt of a suspect involved in cybercrime or cyber-bullying. If the suspect or target authors are unknown, then we deal with an *authorship identification* problem.

Authorship analyses of online messages perform in various steps (Figure 1):

- **Data Gathering:** i.e. Messages are collected from prolific users in order to make relevant dataset to obtain better results. As we have more effective dataset thus, we have more information that can be extracted.
- **Preprocessing the Data:** In other words molding the raw data into an appropriate format. Data is cleaned using natural language processing techniques to make it more attractive or useful. Stylistic features are depicted from the individual writing styles and generate feature vectors which act as novel part in tracing the identity of an author.

Figure 1. Classification Steps for Authorship Identification

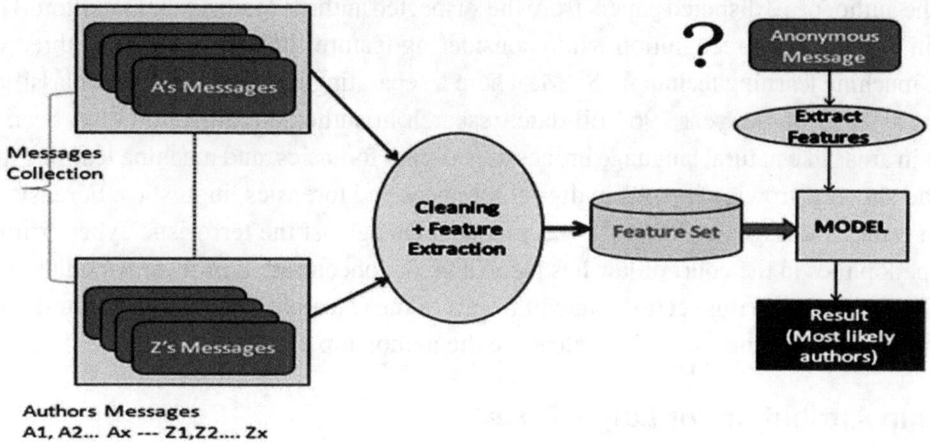

- **Training the Model:** The methods are trained by applying appropriate methods on feature sets. Different methods such as statistical, computational and machine learning methods can be applied to a dataset for authorship identification.
- **Authorship Identification:** Identify the anonymous author from the list of the known authors i.e. most likely author of a given anonymous tweet by extracting his/her features and validate these features on applied model.

Authorship Attribution has been performed to resolve dispute on short and long texts. Authorship identification is the problem from last six decades; when there were handwritten documents needed to be identified for the genuine author. Due to the technology advancement and increase in cybercrime and unlawful activities, this problem of AA becomes forth most important to trace out the author behind online messages. In this problem, given an anonymous text and a set of known candidate list, we have to find the most likely author of that text by extracting features from the literary style of authors by applying a suitable model. There are number of ways to extract features and numerous models that are applicable for short online texts.

Many research studies have explored the problem of authorship i.e. the author of unknown or disputed federalist's papers or a piece of text. In the field of digital and cyber forensic we need to analyze the documents and identify the individuality of a writer by preserving the data to get a true author of an anonymous message. This research is motivated on the factors such as Cyber bullying, Identity Theft, Masquerade, and Denial of Service Attacks, Phishing, Child Pornography, Drug trafficking, Terrorism and Suicide Notes.

STATE-OF-THE ART

The research on this area has been conducted from the 19th century. This section focuses on researcher's way of selecting features and what techniques they have approached to classify the text. Researchers gave different views on how to classify the documents. The authorship of disputed Federalist papers was claimed using statistical inference in the book of Mosteller and Wallace (1964) and Fung, G. (2003) predicted the author of 12 disputed papers from the suspected authors Madison or Hamilton. They tackled the problem of authorship recognition while considering features like frequencies of three words with the help of machine learning technique SVM, where a separating hyperplane clearly classified the data on Madison side. From the year 1964 till date, research in authorship attribution has been taking advancement in areas like natural language processing, digital forensics, and machine learning approaches. Recent trend shows a growing interest in digital forensics and forensics linguistics. Forensic authorship analysis on online messages brings out legal proceedings against the terrorists, cyber criminal, scammers, and pedophiles in the court of law has taken a great concentration in several studies and has been expanding in eminence. In this section, state of the art of the research on authorship identification shows most prominent features and methods to attribute the authorship of any document.

Authorship Attribution for Large Texts

Analysis has been performed on large amount of text such as novels, essay and newspaper. From the processed texts, there are numbers of features that has been selected to find the real author behind the long text. Seroussi, Y et al. (2011) used topic modeling to extract semantic features from document such as Latent Dirichlet Allocation (LDA) with classifier SVM which used topic distribution as features and Hellinger distance to quantify the similarity between the probabilities of document topic distribution. Their approach achieved high accuracy while reducing the run time and was useful for classification of ten to thousand authors. Later, author's proposed new model which aimed was to distinct two different words set that were document words set and author words set by originating them from two disassociate topic (word) sets of author topics and document topics. Disjoint Author-Document Topic Model (DADT) placed different importance on word distributions for document topics and author topics such as by assigning higher weights to stop-words in author topic rather than document topic and also found the ratio of document words to author words as per document (Seroussi et al., 2012).

To overcome the limitation of DADT and LDA model, Pratanwanich and Lio et al. (2014) introduced the concept of Author Topic (AT) model (unsupervised learning method) where words were assigned into topics, author interests, and author model. It was found that AT model was superior to LDA model to attribute authorship of the anonymous text. Seroussi, Y et al. 2012 showed DADT model which was restricted for single-author texts and dependent on various parameters regarding ratio of documents and author words and LDA model relied on the assumption that various type of response variable would arise from same underlying topic of interests, these issues that were not suitable for authorship attribution were overcome by Supervised Author Topic (SAT) model which was aimed to identify authorship of anonymous document where authors had different topic of interests based on topic-word distribution. Also, overcoming the limitation of AT model which assumed that document written by many authors had equity of author contributions. SAT model used supplementary Dirichlet distribution to model author contributions. They used perplexity function i.e. constantly diminishing the function of the text likelihood between two models SAT and AT, where SAT achieved the invariant state at lower perplexity which concluded that expanding the number of topics, upgraded the model fitness. They used random forest method as a discriminative classifier where the feature vectors were vectors of token counts. This technique was fast to train the data but quite slow to create predictions once trained. SAT model proposed was the generalized form of AT model in order to conclude particular topic word distributions, writer focus, and author contributions. They defined author contributions as the total number of words per document allotted to the author.

Topic modeling is performed when there are large lengths of documents but it fails on small texts such as tweets.

Authorship Attribution for Small Texts

Koppel, M et al. (2011) performed authorship attribution on a large number of candidate authors by considered the case of large (closed or open) candidate sets while ignoring the open candidate sets with limited text using n-grams features (lexical) where might be possible that actual author was not included. They represented each text as a vector for respective frequencies of character 4-gram that were space free and used a similarity-based method like cosine similarity which returns the author of snippet whose writing was similar to the snippet vector. They also adopted the approach of Koppel for authorship that permitted a response of Don't Know where attribution was uncertain.

Authors highlighted the three different views of stylometric features as character n-gram view, lexical view, and syntactic views and presented tri training method to repeatedly recognized authors of uncategorized data to improve the training set (Qian et al., 2014).They extended the existing approach of self-training and tri-training approach of two classifiers - Common n-gram (CNG) and SVM and additionally used Logistic regression (LR). Self-training for one view out of three used two classifiers and co-training method worked on two views using only one classifier. They evaluated self-training method using CNG+SVM and LR+SVM on all of the three views. Co-training methods used LR on character+lexical, character+syntactical, and lexical+syntactical views. LR outperformed SVM with a high margin of tri-training when iterations were less.

New features were used to attribute the authorship of short texts like Bag-of-features (BOW) And Style Markers (SM) such as characters, words punctuations, part-of-speech and frequency of characters and punctuations in each message that were extracted from the raw data and experimented using Sequential Minimal Optimization (SMO). They performed each experiment many times to record root mean squared error with values such that statistical significance was verified. The parallel experiments were performed on features BOW and SM and concluded that SM found to be more effective using these features instead of using semantic and word features.

Schwartz, R et al. (2013) recommended the idea of k- *signatures* where they indicated the k-*signatures* of an author A as a quality that came out in partially k% of A's training examples, while not turning out in the preparatory set of any other author. When the size of k was considerably large, such signatures pick up a rare style used by A. They trained an SVM method with linear kernel using 10 fold cross-validations with a set of character n-grams and word n-grams features and also applied a new set of features- *Flexible patterns* was a generalization of word n-grams in a way as they represented likely unseen word n-grams. Flexible Patterns collected fine-grained differences between writing styles of author's which composed of Content Words (CW) and High-Frequency Words (HFW). They used flexible patterns to check the improvement level when considering all the features under varying training set, two systems experimented were 1) with features character n-grams and flexible patterns and 2) with features character-grams, word n-grams and flexible pattern. Their demonstration had shown that if the flexible pattern was added then 2.9% average improvement achieved on the first system (character n-grams) and 1.5% averaged improvement achieved on a second system (with character n-gram and word n-gram together).

Later, Bhargava, M et al. (2013) used tweets in the group to obtain more relevant data. They grouped tweets of words 2 or 3 and extracted lexical and syntactical features with some additional features like Twitter specific features, the frequency of emojis, the number of emojis per word etc. They combined their model with other models like bag-of-words, maximum entropy classifiers, and n-gram language models and achieved precision up to 95.16% with SVM classifier using Radial Basis Function kernel.

To check that all character n-grams were equal, Sapkota, U et al. (2015) addressed some questions: Were all character n-grams uniformly important? Were character n-grams equally important for the cross domain? Were some of the character n-grams irrelevant? To answer these questions, they proposed a new approach to distinguish character n-grams into different categories. These categories were described three linguistic aspects for character n-grams: thematic syntax (word n-grams), morpho-syntax (affix n-grams) and style (punctuation n-grams). 10 categories were defined that were prefix, suffix, space-prefix for character grams, mid, whole, multi-word for word grams and beg, mid, end for punct that represented the top character n-grams and was used in experiments on the two corpora i.e. single domain and multi-domain where n chosen to be 3. Comparison of classifiers like SVM and Naïve Bayes with n equal to 3grams that occurred at least five times in the training data has been performed. From their experiment, they concluded that word n-grams feature was not capturing any additional information so it became unnecessary. On other hand, character n-grams feature was able to classify the text as they captured morphological information.

Rocha, A et al. (2017) worked on open set attribution problem in which they had various unknown samples in training set. To deal with this problem, they considered authorship verification via pair matching scenario using feature level fusion (combined individual features into a feature vector) to collect more information across samples. They proved their work on different dataset and author set using classifier Power Mean SVM (PMSVM) which can handle high dimensional data for large training datasets and SCAP. PMSVM combined features of both the kernels linear and non-linear which in turn made training so fast and avoid over-fitting to the training data with a gradient descent approximation. PMSVM outperformed the approach proposed by Schwartz, R et al. for 50 users nevertheless the size of the training set with character, word, and POS n-grams features.

Unsupervised Techniques for Authorship Attribution

Some of the researchers used unsupervised techniques to classify the data by extracting the stylistic information where each feature was converted into standard form using standard scalar in which data was to be centered at the origin and had unit variance and then they applied Spectral Clustering with Adjusted Rand Index (which was a general statistic for comparing two clusters that depended on matched-pair frequencies) (Berry & Sazonav, 2015). Hierarchical Clustering and Multidimensional Scaling applied on features by calculating the word frequency, then calculated the mean and standard deviation of frequencies of each word for the whole corpus and converted all the frequencies by their z-scores and obtained the distance between messages using delta measure (Nirkhi et al., 2016). Another research using unsupervised authorial clustering in which POS n-grams features were considered and determined the core elements that strongly represented authorship attributes of their respective clusters then clustered features using K-means and Spectral Clustering (Daks & Clark (2016)).

Syntactic Features for Authorship Attribution

Gimpel, K et al. (2011) introduced new Part of Speech (POS) tagger for Twitter data. They first annotated tweets and then included only English tweets that were correctly tagged. Basic features set included features for each word type such as suffix features up to length 3, and additional features were added like TWORTH: Twitter orthography-, NAMES: Frequently capitalized tokens- capitalized token likelihood, TAGDICT: Traditional tag directory, DISTSIM: Distributional similarity, METAPH: Phonetic normalization- as Twitter use alternate spellings of words, Metaphone algorithm was used to create phonetic normalization of words to simpler keys. Metaphone key used to denote current token. They trained the classifier on their own labeled data with features like words within a 5-word window, word shapes in a 3-word, prefix suffix length up to 3 and prefix/suffix pairs. Experiments were performed by removing one category of features from the features space. Some features were incorrect in a specific ablation but were corrected in full system. System struggled with the miscellaneous category, which covered obscure symbols artifacts of tokenization errors and rare tokens. System was successful on the whole, with in-domain lexical resources (DISTSIM), leveraging out-of-domain (TAGDICT) and sub-lexical analysis (METAPH). This study concluded that their proposed POS Tagger gave high accuracy as compared to Stanford POS Tagger. This approach was applied to many more linguistic analyses as there was a rapid change in linguistic conventions.

G. Sidorov et al (2014) showed how n-grams could be obtained from the syntactic trees based on the order in which elements appeared. They followed the path in the syntactic tree and generate n-grams and considered neighbors as words i.e. word follow one another in the path of the syntactic tree. Syntactic n-grams (sn-gram) were constructed using POS tags to get rid of surface language dependent information. They used both constituency (follow head nodes from the bifurcations) and dependency (follow the path in direction of arrows) representations using bigrams and trigrams to obtain sn-gram by ignoring stop words while parsing the tree. They traversed the tree node by node applying recursion in divarication. In this method, they followed the path represented by markers taken each word from the correlating nodes at each step and added them to n-grams sets. There were a variety of sn-grams used: - word sn-grams, character sn-grams, POS sn-grams and mixed sn-grams. They used 3 classifiers namely: SVMs, Naïve Bayes, and j48 in WEKA. SVMs found to more effective as compared to others and achieved good accuracy using bigrams and trigrams. Their approach was useful only for language-specific information for large data but not used for cross domain languages. Sn-grams has been overcome the problem of noisy data that was introduced by surface structure. But there was a disadvantage that it needed syntactic preprocessing that consumed significant time and also they used a set of lexical resources and syntactic parser that were not available for other languages.

Another study using POS showed by Pokou, Y et al. (2016) where part of speech skip-grams was constructed that permitted a skip distance or breach between adjoining POS tags which respond an author's behavior of using sentence structure. Skip grams were used to better capture the personal style of an author. They only have drawn out the top k skip-grams instead of computing the frequencies of all POS skip-grams which further reduced the processing time. The experiment was performed over 30 texts written by 10 authors. This approach used a training corpus C_m of m authors. This approach was composed of three phases which were data preparation and transformation, signature extraction, and author classification. This proposed algorithm was correctly identifying the authorship of a written piece of document with a small number of authors. They concluded that if the number of the pattern increases or go beyond 250, it did not provide better results. The experiment was also performed over three texts of each author from which 2/3 were correctly attributed.

Challenges

Identifying the author of online messages that do not have a considerable amount of content which makes it more challenging. Therefore, identification is much harder and complicated than other documents. Examining stylistics features of online messages can be a possible solution to a given problem. A person or author can be identified by extracting features or patterns from messages. Thus, text mining is performed on text to extract meaningful information. This is done by linguistic analysis of documents and by depicting writing patterns. Furthermore, the document is categorized into their class. There are some of the serious challenges or obstacles which occurred while identifying the author of given text are as follows.

- The writing style may change over time, peoples may change their styles according to the age, trends.
- Authors obfuscate their identity under different aliases. Users on a single platform creating multiple accounts with different names creating more troublesome to trace the identity of the genuine author. To overcome the problem of anonymity, Doppelganger finder was used (Afroz et al., 2014).
- Internets users use bombastic words or change their slang to internet slang, uses emoticons, punctuations in their tweets which make it difficult to extract meaningful information or valuable features from their tweets.
- Sometimes users use words or sentences of another user or we can say copying other authors writing style.
- Stylistic features may depend on demographic factors like age, sex education level etc.
- Authors use keywords with hashtags, URLs, stop-words that need to be removed while preprocessing the data, which leaves us with hardly 4-5 words for feature extraction.
- Tweets are of unstructured format, having a certain limit of the length of 140 characters which poses more problems while extracting information.

Scalability Issues

We focus on three main scalability issues that came in notice while attributing the authorship of a literary piece of writing are described below:

Short Text Authorship Attribution

It poses a specific challenge to the text categorization approach. Stylistic features are less presented in short texts thus; it requires a reliable and robust representation of machine learning techniques to work with limited data. Whenever the length of the dataset is reduced, it directly affects the results i.e. accuracy may degrade. In our dissertation, we use shorts texts such as tweets that allow us to investigate the scalability of our methods or techniques. Examine the scalability of an approach leads to a better insight in the merits of an approach in various conditions. By testing the approach, we can estimate how reliable it will perform on large scale.

Author Set Size

It is also a scalability issue i.e. how many authors are used for authorship attribution. When size of author set is small, we can easily predict the suspected author because we have to find genuine author from small list of authors. But in recent studies, Okuno, S et al. (2014) focused on large author set to predict the authorship of literary text. Some authors examined the impact of scalability of author set by varying number of authors.

Data Size

Many researches in authorship identification use large amounts of textual data per candidate author to determine the authorship which is not feasible. Schwartz, U et al. (2013) has focused on large data set sizes but they fail to prove the scalability of the approach. Sometimes, we cannot get large amount of data to attribute the authorship of a text like in Twitter. In this study, we investigate robustness of feature sets towards the data size and which machine learning algorithm gives best results with limited data.

FEATURES EXTRACTION AND SELECTION

Stylometric Features

Stylometry is the way to extract behavioral or stylistic features which a person exhibits while writing a piece of a document. It performs a statistical investigation of differences in literary style between one author and another. It helps to authenticate the authorship of an anonymous text.

From the 19th century, it has been used to solve the problem of authorship recognition. Standard stylistic features such as lexical, syntactical, the frequency of function words perform well with long textual data. For short texts, these features may not work well due to the certain length limit of a text.

Stylometric features are often used to attribute authorship of anonymous documents by labeling/classifying the content of online messages. It predicts the behavior or pattern of authors. Stylometry is used for stylistic purposes to extract features from documents or texts such as vocabulary richness, the frequency of words and frequency of characters. The combinations of these features can be used to identify the author of an anonymous message.

Syntactic Features

Syntactic information is more reliable, as they use indistinguishable patterns. The usage of function words which otherwise has less significant meaning, also known structural grammatical words includes pronouns (he, she, they), articles (a, an, the), conjunctions (and, or), interjections (Ahem, Boo, oops). Researchers can add style to the author writing. They found that female authors use fewer prepositions as compared to male authors. Using these words one can generate a profile of an author (according to the usage of function words by male or female authors). While identifying the analytical features of authors, the frequency of punctuations can also be measured. The usage of stop words can add more noise to the data there; they are removed before processing of natural language.

E.g. Text with stop words - 'She carries the world on her shoulders'.
Text without stop words - 'Carries world shoulder'

Part of speech (POS) tag is assigned to each word used in the sentence by POS tagger. Generally, NLTK Tagger is used for tagging. There are many others POS tagger available like Standard POS Tagger, Tagger. From morpho-syntactic information tag, a POS pattern is predicted like IN-DT-NN, highly used pattern in a document. Part of speech tag frequencies and Part of speech n-gram frequencies been used by researchers in the past to represent styles in the unrestricted text (Kumawat & Jain, 2015). Though, it provides a structural analysis of text, but it never reveals about how words merge to form phrases or in what manner phrases are put together to form high-level form (Rocha, A et al., 2017).

Structural Features

It represents the style that how an author molds the layout of a piece of a document. In online messages, paragraph indentation, paragraph length, greeting statements and signature related features contribute to the recognition of style. From the literature, it is noticed that female usually write longer sentences than males. While identifying the author's pattern, the length of sentence, a total number of the sentences and the average length of sentence can be extracted.

Lexical Features

These are the features for which a text is considered as a sequence of tokens and each token corresponds to a word. Thus, to attribute authorship, we simply measure the word length counts and sentence length counts. Further, Lexical features can be divided into character-based features and word-based features. The ratio of capital letters to the total number of characters, total number of special characters, the ratio of total number of short words to the total number of words is part of lexical features can be extracted easily. Vocabulary richness words are used to quantify the miscellany of the vocabulary of a text.

The vector of words frequencies is used to represent the texts i.e. a text is defined as a set of words and each word possess frequency ignoring the contextual information. This is also similar to the traditional or conventional Bag of Words representation which is used for topic-based classification.

The ratio of number of repetitive characters to the total number of words was adopted to predict the features (Bhargava, 2013). For stylistic purposes, character n-grams were more accountable than word n-grams. Sapkota, U et al. (2015) concluded that character n-grams alone were novel features for attribution.

Content Specific Features

This is the most discriminating features for online messages. Selection of such features depends on specific application domains. One user may post a tweet on relatively small range of topic but others may distribute tweets on different topics (Li et al.,2014). Due to this, words or characters are tightly coupled to a specific topic may provide a hint about the identity of the author. For example, offender selling pirate software may use such words as "for sale", "deal", "offer" and someone who posts pornography stuff on the web may use words like 'sexy' or 'hot' for the same.

Linguistic Features

In online messages, uses of jargons quickly increase. On Facebook chats, SMS, instant message, commonly used words are 'BRB', 'BTW', 'WTF', which make it more difficult to obtain the pattern over writing style. The writer may use idiomatic expressions like 'break a leg', 'hit the sack' in a tweet which can be considered as a feature for authorship identification. An acronym is kind of shortened formed by the basic or primary components of a word or phrase like 'Mr.', 'Dr.' and so on. A number of acronym words over a total number of words can be adopted as features. Emoticons have gradually entered in cyberspace with an emotional and human touch (Silva et al., 2011). It is a typographic version of paralinguistic features. Users often used an emoticon in end of the sentence to show the emotional state of the author. Eg- *"that's a lot of pizza for a little dog. I'll come help:-P", "I'm getting bored ☹ ".*

Twitter Specific Features

These are the features that are unique to Twitter. These features along with URLs based features are used to detect phishing in cyberspace. Features used are #hashtags per tweet, @mentions per tweet, the number of URLs used over a number of words is taken into consideration for AA. Most of the research that has taken place has deleted retweets because it adds to the data redundancy and duplicity (Gimpel et al.,2011).

Collected dataset cannot feed directly to any machine learning algorithms for classification because this results in poor classification and consume more time for training of large corpus. Therefore, it's better to transform the dataset into a set of features using feature extraction methods. Feature extraction reduces the required amount of resources to describe the large set of data hence reducing large amount of memory and computation power. It also helps in reducing the problem of over-fitting to the training samples and provides results of classification with sufficient accuracy. Some of the algorithms expect numerical features as feature vectors rather than raw text. Features are characteristics properties of writing patterns that help in differentiating between the classes or suspected authors. It gives a representation of linguistics items or terms present in the text for the purpose of classification.

Feature Extraction

N-Grams

From the past research, it is clearly depicted that n-grams based models alone are very significant for text categorization (Schwartz, Tsur, Rappoport & Koppel, 2013). N-Gram is a sequence of n-words, n-characters, n-tags etc. N-grams can be used as skip-grams that are in a discontinuous way. It has the ability to capture linguistic information from the stylistic features such as lexical, syntactical liking of an author. For text representation, we use n-gram technique as it effectively represents stylistic information of any text. N-Grams model such as bigram models, trigram models used for developing a language model (Keselj, Peng & Thomas, 2003). In the field of machine learning, n-grams are used for creating features. N-gram analysis is widely used to extract writing styles as it has the ability to capture both low-level and high-level features. Some of the n-grams that are widely used for extracting features are:

Character N-Grams

As we discussed earlier that Character n-grams is very important feature in the field of text mining (Layton, Watters & Dazeley, 2010). It is being able to capture phonology (the study of the organization of sounds) and morphology (the study of words, their formation, and how they are related to other words) significant information from the text related to suffix, affix and prefix character n-grams. Phonology and morphology are the branches of linguistics deals with phoneme and morphemes respectively. The value of n could be any number if n is small then character n-grams would be able to capture syllable information (Stamatatos, 2009). The value of n chose to be very effective as it directly affects the accuracy. With the previous studies in the survey, Character-4 grams show the best performance as compared to all other n-grams (Sapkota et al., 2015) and we considered this as a feature. We also consider character-3-grams as they are also contributing most towards features. Sapkota, U et al., 2015 also proved that character 3-grams were considered as a novel feature for authorship identification. From the 20th century, Character n-grams have been widely used for document similarity or document classification. This feature was used by authors to find clusters using spectral or hierarchical clustering (Smita, 2016).

Word N-Grams

Word n-grams which contain words in groups of one, two three are referred as word unigram, word bigrams, word trigrams respectively. Word n-grams approach has been used earlier for long texts for authorship analysis (Schwartz et al., 2013). This feature has the ability to capture syntax and semantic information as they are organized into specific word order and structures. In our work, we consider word unigrams and word bigrams counts but ignoring word trigrams as in tweets we rarely found users use the same three words in their tweets. For word unigram, there are many words that are hapax legomena i.e. that a word only occurs once in the whole document so these words are removed. Some authors used frequencies of word n-grams. Word n-grams are used for lexical phrases and structures of the sentences. These lexical features provide thematic syntax information and from word n-grams, Schwartz et al. introduced the new concept flexible pattern (a generalization of word n-grams) that can capture likely unseen words from the text. For micro-messages, word n-grams would not consider as a novel feature because of length restriction.

POS N-Grams

Part of speech (POS) is used to categorize a word in accordance with its syntactic operation and that are similar in linguistic terms. For Standard English, 9 parts of speech are: noun, pronoun, verb, adverb, conjunction, preposition, determiner, adjective, and interjection. POS categories are elementary building blocks that play an important role in many natural language processing tasks, from machine translation to informal extraction. POS tags have the ability to overcome the problem of noisy texts as they reduce the feature space into a limited dimensional space. POS tagging is a process of classifying the words in a sentence according to their types.

Table 1. N-grams (character n-grams and word n-grams) representation of a given text – "she will meet you"

Character Bigrams	Character Trigrams	Word Unigrams	Word Bigrams
'sh', 'he' 'e ', ' w', 'wi', 'il', 'll', 'l ', ' m', 'me', 'ee', 'et' ….	'she', 'he ', 'e w', ' wi', 'wil', 'ill', 'll ', 'l m', ' me', ' mee', 'eet' …	'she', 'will', 'meet', 'you'	'she will', 'will meet', 'meet you'

POS tagging is an automated linguistic annotation of text where an exact part of speech tag is assigned to the current word based on previously tagged words. Tagset is the collection of tags which tagger is expected to select to assign to the suitable word. Each tagger has its own standard tagset to tag the corresponding word. POS tagging can be used for Linguistic-text Pre-processing before semantic analysis (Pratanwanich & Lio, 2014).

Part of speech statistics are modeled in the form of part of speech (POS) n-grams, which are contiguous sequences of parts of speech, extracted from text. POS n-grams help in obtaining sensitive or morphological information. POS tags are generated as shown in the following the example.

Tweet: 'happy valentine's day almost 28 years always feels new'
Pos Tags: 'JJ NNS NN RB CD NNS RB VBP JJ'

Feature Selection

There are a number of features extracted from the tweets from which some are relevant features and remaining are irrelevant features that may affect the accuracy. Therefore, it is desirable to select some relevant features from the features set. Feature selection methods are used for selecting the informative, selective and independent features in text classification. These methods are used for making models more straightforward towards users by reducing the training times of models. Feature selection methods are used for reduction in dimensionality and the problem of overfitting. It simply creates subsets of features by removing redundant and irrelevant features. Here we use Feature selection methods do univariate statistical tests in which a statistical test is applied to each feature separately.

PCA

It is a statistical technique that transforms the correlated variables into uncorrelated variables into a linear form. It simply decomposes a multivariate set in a set of orthogonal components using singular value decomposition where each component denotes a maximum amount of variance. It mainly used for higher dimensional data where the matrix is symmetrically correlated having numeric values. PCA can be performed by a decomposing eigen value of a correlated matrix (or covariance matrix) where each value of data matrix has to mean centered. It projects the high dimensional data into a lower dimensional space. It helps in dimensionality reduction where data matrix is transformed by a set of p- dimensional vectors of weights $W_k = \left(w_1, \ldots, w_n\right)_{(k)}$ where it maps each row vector $x\left(i\right)$ of X to a new principal component vector. Here we kept only first few principal components using only the first j weights.

$$T_j = XW_j \tag{1}$$

where T_j matrix consists of n-rows only having j columns. PCA learns linear transformation of data matrix where it orthogonally transforms the j features that are uncorrelated and preserving the variance of data at the same time. Here we used randomized solver as it drops the most singular vectors and kept only few components that are most efficient. While performing PCA on dataset, n_components is always less than or equal to the number of features.

Chi-Square Test

It is a popular feature selection method in which a chi2 test is applied on features to test the independence of two features. Chi2 are constructed using sample variance or through the sum of squared errors. It simply computes the statistics between positive features and classes. We used chi2 test with SelectKBest method where it keeps the k features which gives highest scores. It measures the dependency between stochastic variables so after using weeds out function it removes the irrelevant features from the feature set without any assumption about the distribution of the population. It compares two variables in a contingency table to check the correlated variables. The chi2 statistical test can be calculated as in Equation 2.

$$\chi^2 = \sum \frac{\left(observed\,values - expected\,values\right)^2}{expected\,values} \tag{2}$$

It is a way to check the relationship between two categorical values. It computes the chi2 for i^{th} position value of matrix in a contingency table.

METHODOLOGY

Authorship attribution is a process of identifying the real author of an anonymous text given a set of candidate authors by extracting features from the author's writing style. Earlier, statistical methods were used to discriminate the authors of a given message. But in recent work, computational methods have been used; machine learning techniques are taking advantage over all methods by predicting an accurate author with high frequency. Integrated summary of existing techniques based on features that are extracted is given in annexure.

In every authorship attribution problem, there is a set of known authors and a set of training data which consists of text/message sample. The testing data set consists of text samples of unknown authors which should be attributed separately to each applicant author. Authorship identification approaches are distinguished according to training data that was treated individually. Cumulative representation of author is extracted from the huge file (where all the training data are concatenated). In such cases the researchers ignoring the differences between the texts written by same author. This approach is known as Profile based approach. It is also noticed that each of the training data features are different from the extracted stylometric features of a concatenated file. The profile based approach uses training set, consists of extraction of profiles for all applicant authors. Differences of profile of unseen message and profile of each author are computed based on distance function. In this approach, tweets can be considered as text source for classification and large documents of tweets were created by joining tweet. To classify the text, Bayesian classifier is used.

To develop an accurate profile, multiple training text samples were required. The known authorship text sample is taken as an instance and every text sample as a unit. Each text sample is represented as vectors of attributes and classification model is trained based on set of known authorship, which requires more training instances per class. The text samples represent author's style very appropriately. This approach is known as Instance based approach. In this approach, different features can be combined easily as compared to profile based approach. To classify the unknown text, machine learning classifiers (SVM) are used.

Probabilistic Models

Probabilistic model is one of the earliest approaches that are still used in many modern researches. Probabilistic methods seek to maximize the probability for a text over known author (P(text/known author)). A variant of such classifiers is Naïve Bayes (supervised learning method) which is used in topic-based text categorization. It is a conditional probability model; where an instance is to be classified having some independent features. It assigns to this instance probabilities for each of x possible outcomes. This classifier uses feature like character n-gram and word n-gram. It is a powerful algorithm for predictive modeling mainly for multiclass problems (Almishari et al., 2014). This probabilistic classifier has secure independence assumptions as it is based on Bayes Theorem. It computes the probability of feature vector of a text represented by t_j to a class c_i. P (t_j) is the probability of the text picked randomly and P (c_k) is the probability of a text t_j belongs to c_k. Construct the posterior probability for the event c_k among a set of possible outcomes C= { $c_1, c_2, \ldots, c_k \ldots\ , c_i$ } using Equation 3.

$$P\left(c_k, t_j\right) = \frac{P\left(c_k\right) P(t_j \mid c_k)}{P\left(t_j\right)} \tag{3}$$

Or it can also be written as

$$p(c_k | t_1, t_2, t_3, \ldots, t_j) \propto p\left(t_1, t_2, t_3, \ldots, t_j | c_k\right) p\left(c_k\right) \tag{4}$$

The assumption of Naïve Bayes is that all features are independent; to go beyond this assumption, Markov models are used for authorship attribution. This extension can capture contextual information by calculating probabilities of word or character transitions, and place them into probability transition matrix.

Probability of unknown text is calculated by a particular transition matrix. Probabilistic models are faster than compression models as they quickly classify the given text.

Compressional Models

These models follow the profile based approach, which do not generate a concrete vector description of authors' profile. All text of known authors are concatenated to form a big file and compression model is used to generate a compressed file. Then the unknown text is inserted into each text of big file and compression model is called again for each known text including unknown text. The difference in bitwise size of compressed files, i.e. difference between text having known text and unknown text and text with known text, indicates the similarity of unknown text with each author. Basically, it calculates the cross entropy between the two texts. PPM (prediction by partial matching) algorithm uses compression model to classify the text using character sequences.

Machine Learning Approaches

In recent work, computational methods have been used for authorship analysis. As machine learning techniques are taking advantage of all methods by predicting an accurate author with high accuracy. These techniques learn how to automatically make predictions based on the past observations. This technique is used for pattern matching or data mining. These classification methods are used to find separate line among all the classes which in turn minimize loss function. It is used as predictive analysis for identification of the author. These techniques are classified into supervised learning and unsupervised learning.

Unsupervised Techniques

In this technique hidden structure or pattern is inferred from unlabeled data. Unsupervised methods used for authorship attribution are clustering, multidimensional scaling, NN nearest neighbour and Hierarchical clustering.

1. **Clustering:** It is used to show the similarity between two messages. Given an open set of open set of authors and unlabeled messages, group of authors is formed corresponds to the messages. Most used clustering is Hierarchical Clustering. This algorithm constructs a hierarchy of clusters. The cluster formation process is of two types, the agglomerative way and the divisive way. In the agglomerative clustering is bottom up approach where the hierarch goes one step up and merged with clusters. On, other hand, Divisive hierarchical clustering is based on top-down approach where all the elements will remain in same cluster, when hierarchy goes down the clusters get splitted into smaller level clusters. Both the approaches make the merging and splitting decisions based on the measurement value of the dissimilarity between the sets of observations. This can be achieved by using an appropriate metric and a linkage criterion. In agglomerative approach, small groups of closely related messages are formed using n-gram features; these groups are then combined to produce larger groups till all messages are connected into a single large cluster. The message written by single author is place into neighboring cluster.
2. **Multidimensional Scaling (MDS):** If we could see how the various texts are arranged in feature space, we get to know the intention how style markers group the texts of authors. This can be performed by using multidimensional scaling in which it maps the text into 2-D space. It takes input of matrix of distances between points, and manages to put all the points into an n-dimensional

space while maintaining distances as much as possible. A 2-D MDS plot gives an appropriate visual presentation of distances between texts, and shows that if points are close together in plot then they are closely related in feature space.

Supervised Learning

In Supervised learning, a function is inferred from the labeled data and classification is performed by selecting the suitable class label for a given text. Some of the supervised machine learning approaches support multi-class classification problem, in which one instance may have more than two classes. In this technique training sets are represented in numerical form i.e. each corresponding tweet has exactly one assigned label in numeric form.

In supervised machine learning method, the machine is trained using the training dataset and then apply on texting dataset to get the desired output. In this, training set containing the exact label of all the tweets. Then data is randomized and predicted the class label for new text using trained classifier model as shown in Figure 2.

TF-IDF

Tf-idf is used in the selection of word as it depicts the importance of a word to a message. It simply assigns weight to a word, work as a weighting factor. Different online social network (Twitter, Facebook) are used by people with various motives, and posting procedure of posts or tweet are possible to be thematically different. To overcome this problem, one should look at user's language models not in seclusion, but in comparison to the languages models of everyone else. In other words, analyze features of a particular language model that are characteristic to its corresponding user, and then use these characteristics to calculate closeness between different accounts. This problem can manage with Term Frequency-Inverse Document Frequency, or TF-IDF, in combination with cosine similarity. TF-IDF is a process of transforming text into numbers so that it can be represented meaningfully by a vector. TF-IDF is the result of two statistical terms, Term Frequency (TF) and Inverse Document Frequency (IDF). Term Frequency computes the number of times a word appears in a document. Normalization is performed to

Figure 2. Machine Learning Phases

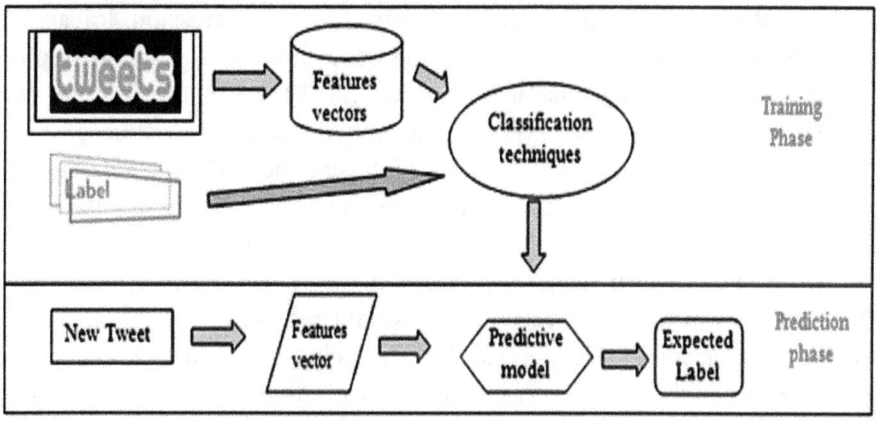

normalize the documents according to their size. This can be achieved by dividing the number of times a token appears in a document (TF) by the total number of words.

$$TF\left(t,d\right)=\frac{Number\,of\,times\,a\,token\left(t\right)appear\,in\,any\,document\left(d\right)}{Total\,number\,of\,tokens\,in\,the\,document} \tag{5}$$

TF examines all words as equally important; however, certain words that appear commonly should have little impact (for ex, the word \An"). And reversely, words that appear rarely in a document can be more effective. Thus, there is need of Inverse Document Frequency which integrates the weights of words according to their importance like words that appear commonly in a document, it lowers down the weight and words that appear rarely it increases the weights. Therefore, words that rarely occur in a document are not neglected and all the words that are effective weighing accordingly. The Inverse Document Frequency simply represents the words importance or words that provide information according to their occurrence in a document.

$$IDF\left(t\right)=\log\left(\frac{Total\,number\,of\,documents}{Number\,of\,documents\,with\,token\,t\,in\,it}\right) \tag{6}$$

Using TF-IDF, a vector is derived from the dataset of each account and computes the likeness between two documents using cosine similarity. Combining Equation 5 and 6, we get TF_IDF of each term in a document as shown in Equation 7.

$$TF\_IDF\left(t,d\right)=TF\left(t\right)*IDF\left(t\right) \tag{7}$$

Support Vector Machine

Support Vector Machines is another popular classification technique that analyzes data. SVM was first developed by Vladimir Vapnik based on statistical learning. SVM is supervised learning techniques used in computational and linguistics field. It simply constructs a hyperplane or set of hyper-planes in n-dimensional space. It is mostly used in case of classification and regression. It learns to classify the data based on the labeled training dataset. SVM come out as a method of authorship attribution that addresses the problem of high dimensional feature vectors. SVM was mainly used for two class binary classification. Later it was used for multiclass classification of texts. SVM's concept of maximum edge leads to better generalization and thus better accuracy for binary and multi-class classification problems. Linear SVM is a method of inferring by dividing the hyperplane with a highest potential margin of error (Rocha eta al., 2017). It uses the features like content-based, idiosyncratic, stylistic and character-word level n-gram. These techniques are potentially stronger but they can easily overfit the training data when kernelized. SVM can easily manage sparse data that was extracted from BOW features and style markers, hence achieved the highest accuracy (Koppel et al., 2011). To classify the data, choose the best hyperplane with a large margin between the two classes so that distance between the data point and hyper-plane is maximized. SVM depends on kernel function as kernel helps in projecting data points in n-dimensional space for higher results. Kernel a similarity function which accepts two input and in return provides similarity between the samples. Kernel plays an important role for SVMs in the classification process. Some of the kernels used for classification as described below:

Linear Kernel Classifier

It linearly separates the data points by plotting straight line with a margin. For multi-class classification, this kernel separates the data trained from the model and new data points or features are mapped and classified based on their respective position with respect to the model.

For linear kernel

$$K\left(X_i, Y_j\right) = X_i \,.Y_j \tag{8}$$

where Xi represents the data points and Yj represents the classes that are in numeric form.

Nonlinear Kernel Classifier

Other than linear classification, non-linear classification has been applied using kernel trick with kernel methods polynomial, radial basis function and sigmoid. In this dot product of data points and classes is replaced by a non-linear kernel function. This classifier is usually fit the hyperplane in a transformed feature space.

- **Radial Basis Function (RBF):** The radial basis function network is based on the artificial neural network where RBF use as activation functions. It mainly used to classify nonlinear data points. It uses normal curves around the data points and sums up all the curves to get a good decision boundary. With a large number of training samples or we can say with a large number of features in input space, RBF performs well. RBF use fewer hyper-parameters that affect the complexity of selected method. It simply maps a single vector to a vector of higher dimensionality by adapting a form of a function x.

For Radial Basis Function Kernel

$$K\left(X_i, X_j\right) = \exp\left(-\gamma \left|X_i - X_j\right|^2\right) \tag{9}$$

where $\left|X_i - X_j\right|^2$ is squared Euclidean distance between the two feature vectors of data points and classes. The value of γ should be greater than zero.

Sigmoid Kernel

It is also used in a neural network such as perceptron and also similar to the logistic regression model where a logistic function generates curves where it gets larger value than some other value.

$$K\left(X_i, Y_j\right) = \tanh\left(ZX_i \,.Y_j + c\right) \tag{10}$$

where the value of Z and c must be greater than zero and X_i , Y_j represents features and classes respectively.

Logistic Regression

It is a regression model which uses one vs rest if using in a multiclass case. Logistic regression works as a linear model for classification. This model uses parameters like a penalty for specifying the norm and for sparse matrix feature it uses confidence score. It also provides multinomial classification by fitting the data to a logit function. This method is suitable when there are one or more independent variables that find out an outcome. Logistic regression uses the logistic equation in which it generates coefficients ($b_0, b_1, ..b_k$) to predict a logit transformation using Equation 11.

$$ln\left(\frac{p}{1-p}\right) = b_0 + b_1X_1 + \ldots + b_kX_k \tag{11}$$

where p is the probability of occurring of an event Y (dependent variable value must be 0 or 1 i.e. only two possible values) and $ln\left(\frac{p}{1-p}\right)$ is the log odds ratio (logit). Estimated probability of likelihood of any event must lie between 0 and 1. Independent variable ($X_1, X_2, \ldots, X_k$) are those categorical values in our case features that influence the values of Y classes. This model is used to predict the probabilities of the all unique possible outcomes of categorical values (X) on the basis of independent variables (Y). It is also known as Maximum entropy classifier, used to classify the weights that are maximized using maximum a posteriori estimation. It is the process for predicting the value of weights and the interpreted score. Here we use L2 regularization for multiclass problems which minimizes the following constant function:

$$min\frac{1}{2}w^T w + C\sum_{i=1}^{n}\log\left(\exp\left(-Y_i\left(X_i^T w + c\right)\right) + 1\right) \tag{12}$$

For multiclass and sparse problems, we used lbfgs solver which is an optimization problem that optimizes the Broyden–Fletcher–Goldfarb–Shanno using limited memory.

Multilayer Perceptron Classifier

It is a supervised learning technique used for classification where there are one or more non-linear layers (hidden layers). It is a feed-forward neural network where data flows in one direction from the input layer to the output layer. It is generalization model of perceptron and can separate data which is non-linear. It has an activation function which maps the weighted input to the output of each neuron. It learns a function $f(.) : X^i \rightarrow X^o$ by training on a dataset with i number of dimensions for input and O number of dimensions for output. It is trained using back-propagation technique where weights are adjusted based on the error computed by difference in output feedback and desired output.

$$e_k(m) = D_k(m) - O_k(m) \tag{13}$$

where D_k is the desired output and O_k is the output feedback or resulted feedback of k node in the m data point and this error is minimized by adjusting the weights of the nodes given in Equation 14.

$$\varepsilon(m) = \frac{1}{2}\sum_k e_k^2(m) \tag{14}$$

Using stochastic gradient descent, weights are changed based on the Widrow-Hoff delta learning rule in which weights are adjusted according to the mean square error of output feedback to the input samples. Multilayer perceptron consists of hidden layers between the input layer and output layer. Here we use constant learning rate with initial learning rate used to control the change in weights using stochastic gradient descent solver. It trains the dataset iteratively and at each step, parameters are updated accordingly. The tuning of hyper-parameters such as hidden layers (neurons), learning rate and iterations are selective. It is very sensitive towards features scaling.

CONCLUSION

From the past research on authorship attribution, it can be concluded that AA is an interesting realistic problem. There are various ways through which authorship analysis can be performed. AA depends on so many factors like dataset (which dataset is choosing for authorship analysis), how to gather data from online social media, in what contribution author and data size are distributed, and length of the given text etc.

It mainly depends on the stylistic features that are extracted from the training and testing set and how these features are used to train the model. Stylistic features are highly impactful for both small and large texts to attribute the authorship of any document. More the valuable features to classy the text less the chances of misclassification. It is clearly reflected from the investigation that combinations of different features were effectively contributing to authorship identification hence improved accuracy. Stylometric features which make authorship attribution possible are lexical and syntactical features. N-grams features make most of the contribution towards features distributions to identify the author of given message. Some of the features that play a crucial role in authorship identification are character n-grams, POS n-grams, prefix and affix n-grams. Though character n-gram feature performs well but features in combination yields better results as compared to a single feature. Character n-gram has the utility or ability in capturing morphology (Sapkota,U et al., 2015). For small texts, especially tweets, other features such as Twitter specific features, a number of emojis per tweet can be extracted and for a better result, tweets can be combined if their length is less than 3 or 4 words. From the past research, it was depicted that lexical and character features have been proved efficient for small data sets, whereas syntactic features gave better results with large data sets.

Features extracted are in n-dimensional space which takes too much time for evaluation, so researchers reduced dimensions of features using Principal Component Analysis (PCA), Latent Discriminant Analysis (LDA). Another way to reduce dimensionality is feature selection methods like Chi-Square, Euclidean distance, Information Gain etc.

Some of the classifiers like SVM, SCAP outperformed even with restriction of information. SVM with its default kernel yields best results with the small training set. Random Forests performed well with numerical features (Khonji, Iraqi & Jones, 2015). Some techniques gave better results even with a large set of suspected authors. In this article, authors presented the concept of cross-linguistic features across domain and languages, and procedure to marks POS tags.

FUTURE WORK

With our contribution to the domain, we have just been able to scratch the surface, in future investigation of authorship identification will be performed with large author size and variations of author size on the same dataset using more robust machine learning algorithms. Also, we will try to expand the scope of our work to any platform or cross-linguistics platform. Thus to come up with an application which is independent of dataset and platform. This research will be further investigate on features related to specific platform, also group of different stylometric features based on parsed text. This analysis can be extended for classifying the tweets/ messages with labels as correctly classified, misclassified and unknown or unpredictable tweets.

Another interesting point for further research is that distribution of data over the classes can be weighted or imbalanced instead of balanced data distribution. Also, this application can be applied where a candidate author may not in known author suspected list i.e. open set recognition problem. As we used sparse features and then reduce the dimensionality of sparse features set with the help of PCA and select features using a Chi-Square method which sometimes does not give effective features set as this technique failed to converge.

For Further research, messages with fewer length and images will be considered to increase the information quality by exploring new ways of extracting features and extend approaches beyond just stylometry.

REFERENCES

Afroz, S., Islam, A. C., Stolerman, A., Greenstadt, R., & McCoy, D. (2014, May). Doppelgänger finder: Taking stylometry to the underground. In *Security and Privacy (SP), 2014 IEEE Symposium on* (pp. 212-226). IEEE.

Almishari, M., Kaafar, D., Oguz, E., & Tsudik, G. (2014, November). Stylometric linkability of tweets. In *Proceedings of the 13th Workshop on Privacy in the Electronic Society* (pp. 205-208). ACM.

Azarbonyad, H., Dehghani, M., Marx, M., & Kamps, J. (2015, August). Time-aware authorship attribution for short text streams. In *Proceedings of the 38th International ACM SIGIR Conference on Research and Development in Information Retrieval* (pp. 727-730). ACM. doi:10.1145/2766462.2767799

Berry, D., & Sazonov, E. (2015, April). Clustering technical documents by stylistic features for authorship analysis. In SoutheastCon 2015 (pp. 1-5). IEEE. doi:10.1109/SECON.2015.7132936

Bhargava, M., Mehndiratta, P., & Asawa, K. (2013, December). Stylometric analysis for authorship attribution on Twitter. In *International Conference on Big Data Analytics* (pp. 37-47). Springer International Publishing. doi:10.1007/978-3-319-03689-2_3

Daks, A., & Clark, A. (2016). Unsupervised Authorial Clustering Based on Syntactic Structure. *ACL, 2016*, 114.

Fung, G. (2003, October). The disputed Federalist Papers: SVM feature selection via concave minimization. In *Proceedings of the 2003 Conference on Diversity in Computing* (pp. 42-46). ACM. doi:10.1145/948542.948551

Ge, Z., Sun, Y., & Smith, M. J. (2016). *Authorship Attribution Using a Neural Network Language Model.* arXiv preprint arXiv:1602.05292

Gimpel, K., Schneider, N., O'Connor, B., Das, D., Mills, D., Eisenstein, J., & Smith, N. A. (2011, June). Part-of-speech tagging for Twitter: Annotation, features, and experiments. In *Proceedings of the 49th Annual Meeting of the Association for Computational Linguistics: Human Language Technologies: short papers-Volume 2* (pp. 42-47). Association for Computational Linguistics.

Green, R. M., & Sheppard, J. W. (2013, May). Comparing Frequency-and Style-Based Features for Twitter Author Identification. *FLAIRS Conference.*

Juola, P. (2008). Authorship attribution. *Foundations and Trends® in Information Retrieval, 1*(3), 233-334.

Juola, P., & Mikros, G. K. (2016). Cross-linguistic stylometric features: A preliminary investigation. *International Conference on Statistical Analysis of Textual Data.*

Keretna, S., Hossny, A., & Creighton, D. (2013, October). Recognising user identity in Twitter social networks via text mining. In *Systems, Man, and Cybernetics (SMC), 2013 IEEE International Conference on* (pp. 3079-3082). IEEE. doi:10.1109/SMC.2013.525

Kešelj, V., Peng, F., Cercone, N., & Thomas, C. (2003, August). N-gram-based author profiles for authorship attribution. In *Proceedings of the conference pacific association for computational linguistics, PACLING* (Vol. 3, pp. 255-264). Academic Press.

Khonji, M., Iraqi, Y., & Jones, A. (2015, May). An evaluation of authorship attribution using random forests. In *Information and Communication Technology Research (ICTRC), 2015 International Conference on* (pp. 68-71). IEEE. doi:10.1109/ICTRC.2015.7156423

Koppel, M., Schler, J., & Argamon, S. (2009). Computational methods in authorship attribution. *Journal of the American Society for Information Science and Technology*, *60*(1), 9–26. doi:10.1002/asi.20961

Koppel, M., Schler, J., & Argamon, S. (2011). Authorship attribution in the wild. *Language Resources and Evaluation*, *45*(1), 83–94. doi:10.1007/s10579-009-9111-2

Kumawat, D., & Jain, V. (2015). POS Tagging Approaches: A Comparison. *International Journal of Computers and Applications*, *118*(6).

Layton, R., Watters, P., & Dazeley, R. (2010, July). Authorship attribution for Twitter in 140 characters or less. In *Cybercrime and Trustworthy Computing Workshop (CTC), 2010 Second* (pp. 1-8). IEEE. doi:10.1109/CTC.2010.17

Li, J. S., Monaco, J. V., Chen, L. C., & Tappert, C. C. (2014, November). Authorship authentication using short messages from social networking sites. In *e-Business Engineering (ICEBE), 2014 IEEE 11th International Conference on* (pp. 314-319). IEEE. doi:10.1109/ICEBE.2014.61

Nirkhi, S., Dharaskar, R. V., & Thakare, V. M. (2016). Authorship Verification of Online Messages for Forensic Investigation. *Procedia Computer Science*, *78*, 640–645. doi:10.1016/j.procs.2016.02.111

Okuno, S., Asai, H., & Yamana, H. (2014, October). A challenge of authorship identification for ten-thousand-scale microblog users. In *Big Data (Big Data), 2014 IEEE International Conference on* (pp. 52-54). IEEE. doi:10.1109/BigData.2014.7004491

Peng, J., Choo, R. K. K., & Ashman, H. (2016, August). Astroturfing detection in social media: Using binary n-gram analysis for authorship attribution. In Trustcom/BigDataSE/I SPA, 2016 IEEE (pp. 121-128). IEEE.

Pokou, Y. J. M., Fournier-Viger, P., & Moghrabi, C. (2016). Authorship Attribution Using Small Sets of Frequent Part-of-Speech Skip-grams. In *FLAIRS Conference* (pp. 86-91). Academic Press.

Pratanwanich, N., & Lio, P. (2014, December). Who wrote this? Textual modeling with authorship attribution in big data. In *Data Mining Workshop (ICDMW), 2014 IEEE International Conference on* (pp. 645-652). IEEE. doi:10.1109/ICDMW.2014.140

Qian, T., Liu, B., Chen, L., & Peng, Z. (2014, January). Tri-Training for Authorship Attribution with Limited Training Data. ACL, (2), 345-351. doi:10.3115/v1/P14-2057

Rocha, A., Scheirer, W. J., Forstall, C. W., Cavalcante, T., Theophilo, A., Shen, B., & Stamatatos, E. (2017). Authorship attribution for social media forensics. *IEEE Transactions on Information Forensics and Security*, *12*(1), 5–33. doi:10.1109/TIFS.2016.2603960

Sapkota, U., Bethard, S., Montes-y-Gómez, M., & Solorio, T. (2015, May). Not All Character N-grams Are Created Equal: A Study in Authorship Attribution. In HLT-NAACL (pp. 93-102). Academic Press. doi:10.3115/v1/N15-1010

Schwartz, R., Tsur, O., Rappoport, A., & Koppel, M. (2013). Authorship attribution of micro-messages. In *Proceedings of the 2013 Conference on Empirical Methods in Natural Language Processing* (pp. 1880-1891). Academic Press.

Seroussi, Y., Bohnert, F., & Zukerman, I. (2012, July). Authorship attribution with author-aware topic models. In *Proceedings of the 50th Annual Meeting of the Association for Computational Linguistics: Short Papers-Volume 2* (pp. 264-269). Association for Computational Linguistics.

Seroussi, Y., Zukerman, I., & Bohnert, F. (2011, June). Authorship attribution with latent Dirichlet allocation. In *Proceedings of the fifteenth conference on computational natural language learning* (pp. 181-189). Association for Computational Linguistics.

Sidorov, G., Velasquez, F., Stamatatos, E., Gelbukh, A., & Chanona-Hernández, L. (2014). Syntactic n-grams as machine learning features for natural language processing. *Expert Systems with Applications*, *41*(3), 853–860. doi:10.1016/j.eswa.2013.08.015

Silva, R. S., Laboreiro, G., Sarmento, L., Grant, T., Oliveira, E., & Maia, B. (2011, June). 'twazn me!!!('automatic authorship analysis of micro-blogging messages. In *International Conference on Application of Natural Language to Information Systems* (pp. 161-168). Springer Berlin Heidelberg. doi:10.1007/978-3-642-22327-3_16

Stamatatos, E. (2009). A survey of modern authorship attribution methods. *Journal of the American Society for Information Science and Technology*, *60*(3), 538–556. doi:10.1002/asi.21001

KEY TERMS AND DEFINITIONS

Alias: A false name, especially one used by a criminal.

Anonymity: The condition or fact of being anonymous.

Classification: It is a division or category in a system that divides things into groups or types.

Clustering: It is a data-mining technique used to place data elements into related groups without advance knowledge of the group definitions.

Data Mining: A process used to extract usable data from a larger set of any raw data.

Plagiarism: The practice of taking someone else's work or ideas and passing them off as one's own.

Stylometry: A statistical method of analyzing a text to determine its author.

Chapter 9
Business-Oriented Analytics With Social Network of Things

Pawan Kumar
Government of India, India

Adwitiya Sinha
Jaypee Institute of Information Technology, India

ABSTRACT

In the modern era of technological advancements, internet of things (IoT) and social network of things (SNoT) have gained vitality with the extensive application of sensors for accumulation of socially relevant data. A colossal amount of social data collected becomes unfeasible to process and deliver with progress in time and domain. Therefore, a major problem lies in analysis, interpretation, and understanding of the huge amount of social data. This challenge has been greatly leveraged by context-aware computing, which permits storing context information so that meaningful analysis of data can be achieved. Also, the importance of context-aware social networking and network diffusion is elaborated with the aim to develop effective solutions to issues in this domain. The main concept here is people around a person share common experiences with that person, which in turn can be made interactive, thereby leading to collective and quick resolving of problems. Social network of things is closely coupled with context awareness to make interpretation of big data easier and compatible to recent trends.

1. INTRODUCTION

Social media and networking provides a platform for sharing content, opinions and views for interaction and building influential communities. The chapter is organized into four sub-sections to deal with several research oriented challenges and recent trends. The chapter would begin with a complete systematically introduction of fundamental concepts of social networking, business applications & analytics, social network of things. This is followed by explanation of tools, statistics and services of social networking with business perspective. In next section various categories of context is discussed along with their individual relevance. The basic definitions of context and context-enabled features are detailed. Later characteristics of context aware systems would be considered with deeper insight of context aware systems which further will lead to various usages of such systems in various fields.

DOI: 10.4018/978-1-5225-5097-6.ch009

1.1. Social Networking

Social network portals are gaining popularity via vast usage of mobile internet in present day scenario. It offers a massive ground for exchange of multimedia, entertainment, news, opinion, communication, microblogging, media sharing, bookmarking etc. Some of the major social network sites include, MySpace, Facebook, Hi5, Bebo, Friendster, LinkedIn, StudiVZ, Xing, YouTube, Imeem, Twitter, Digg, StumbleUpon, Delicious, Scribd, Flickr, SecondLife etc. are used for various applications such as photo, audio, video, virtual worlds, online gaming, social news, blog etc. for creating public or semi-public profile for social media users.

Information present on social network include contact, location, associations, personal information, work history, preferences, friendship etc. Social media promote brand or product to the potential customers and connects an individual with their friends. Advertisement in the social media connect consumer and company to share information about their products in community group who share same interest or ideas. The online advertisement in social media attracts mostly the younger population (Normally age between 18 to 30 years). The electronic messages generate more interest about a product due to internet rather than exposure to information provided by marketers.

Due to the popularity of online social network sites, people communicate with each other for communication, create and share content, give and receive recommendations. Social media changed the existing communication method. A social network is a social structure between actors, people, groups, organizations, information or knowledge processing entities through some links that shows relationship among them. The primary purpose of social network is for communication and exchange of ideas or interest among peer groups or communities.

Social network consists of a graph $G = \left(V, E\right)$ in which vertices represent node or individual and edges represent social link or relationship between them. The graph made by the social network is represented by adjacency list or matrix internally having binary values. If there is a relationship between two nodes, value is one otherwise it is zero. Social network analysis focuses on the relationship between people and groups of people. Social network analysis combines mathematical models with organizational theories to help the organizations and groups dynamics in which patterns can be discovered from which valuable conclusions can be drawn.

A social network consist individuals or organizations connected by kinship, friendship, beliefs, common interests, financial exchange and many other relationships. Inter network relationship of individuals in the social group access more knowledge or information rather than intra network relationship. These sub network are also connected by some type of relationship and acts as a connecting node or bridge. Social network provides a platform for the users to share and use information in all fields due to revolution in the digital world. With the increasing numbers of social network user, a large volume of dynamic raw data (structured, semi-structured and unstructured) is generated, which is parsed and interpreted to get reports and results with the help of several data mining tools. Social network analysis provides a media for knowledge sharing and helps in determining various results such as how the information flows with in nodes in an interconnected network, finding important or higher degree nodes, information popularity and other network metrics. Business intelligence tools analyse huge amount of data for getting patterns, recommendation, predicting future trends and forecasting possible opportunities from social media data that helps in decision making for business organizations to get better results and profit. It also provides possibility for a node or an individual to join a certain group or a particular community in near future (Vibhav et al, 2015).

Social networking sites are now used for building and managing relationship, communication and online opinions/blogs for extracting more information and knowing more about their business. Social network and business analysis is a large multidisciplinary area of study which is evolving very fast. The number of social network users increased exponentially in last few years. Facebook and MySpace are most commonly used social network site. Younger respondents spend more time than older respondents. Reuniting with old friends, maintaining long distance friendship, and sharing photos are greatly simplified by social network sites.

Social media changed business process, politics, entertainment and other areas to a great extent. Most of the internet users prefer to connect with brands via social media ("Nielsen Social Media Report", 2012).

Social media spread message or information in very less time in the entire network to their users. Social media has become popular in last few years. Now a days organizations use online social media for brand awareness and marketing to find out the potential customers. Social network analysis has various applications such as finding potential customers and promotional scheme based on their past purchase history, identifying loyal customers who are vocal, active and passionate. They can be characterized as brand ambassadors, identifying central Connectors, determining the likelihood and impact of activity, detecting patterns, establishing linkage between individuals.

1.2. Business Application

The use of social networking services has become popular and integral part of daily communication in the world. Social media acts as a viral marketing of the new information with the help of new users, direct/indirect friends and interested group. People create community or network with unknown/known users in the social network all over the world. The content posted on social network include uploading photos, audios and videos, install application, messaging friends, writing a blog, dating, promoting a brand, currently occurring events, posting status message and comment, joining several groups that belong to same interest. The number of users on social network is location dependent. Percentage of active users on social networking site vary from country to country.

Social network sites provide real time behavioural data. The data from social network sites can be collected through the use of tools or directly from the company data warehouse or repository. Social media can be used for internal communication as well as for existing and potential customer interactions. Social media is growing rapidly with web and mobile based technologies.

Social media is used in several fields like as increasing brand awareness, product promotion and development, knowledge sharing and feedback mechanism. By the use of social media, companies perform better in creating brand awareness and image. Social media helps in determining marketing strategy. With the creation of profile, page and group social media provides a way for users to connect with others virtually. Individual share information about themselves and identify others in the network. Online social media provides collaboration and communication, instant informal commenting and feedback.

Social media has impact on brand recognition and business revenue. Users can freely create content and transmit information irrespective of its location instantly to a large population in online social media. Twitter is a micro-blogging site allow users to share news, information or thoughts with other user (followers) with 140 characters or less known as tweets within their network. Twitter share information or news faster to a large audience online. In LinkedIn, company or business organization access user information through their profile data for advertisement and reaching towards their members. All group members write at least one tweet message for solving problem for teaching and learning purpose. Social media acts as an extension for marketing strategy.

The business organizations increase awareness about their product by engaging customers on the social media and forms virtual communities. Global as well as local companies are adopting online advertisement, campaign and marketing using online social network sites rapidly. Organizations generally use social media data to understand customer behaviour and their needs with respect to the organization current and future services or products. The combination of network and text mining reveals new insights into customer behaviour in social media which is not possible by using any one of these techniques alone.

1.3. Business Analytics

The main objective of business analytics is to explore data for generating knowledge, understanding and learning support for decision making and performance management. It focus on discovery, interpretation and communication of meaningful pattern in data. Decision making in business today, replace the traditional process of performing action first then examining working of process. Now a days, business organizations first understand the process and make intelligent business decisions. Historical data can be used to predict the happening of an event in future.

Individuals with prior knowledge and experience make decision by collecting, integrating and analysing data. Decision making is dynamic, contextual and personal/group activity. Artificial intelligence and machine learning technology reduce the effort to search patterns, identify relationships and patterns from historical data to influence performance in the business environment. A large amount of data is available on the social media, the main task is to find out the usable information and pattern.

Business analytics use data mining and prediction techniques for gathering, storing and analysing data to make better and strategic decisions, likelihood of an event occurrence, identify relationships and patterns, what is happening today and what will happen in future. Analytic tools and techniques include statistical, quantitative and mathematical models, finding information, decision making and visualization methods for improving business operations (Evans, 2013). Data collected from different sources for business intelligence and analytics is described by figure 1.

Data mining tools extract hidden and predictive information from large database. Data is collected from facts and figures as a collection of files. Several metrics are used to quantify the performance (Evans, 2013). Business analytics software include tools and applications for tracking, storing, visualizing,

Figure 1. Data Source for Business Analytics and Intelligence

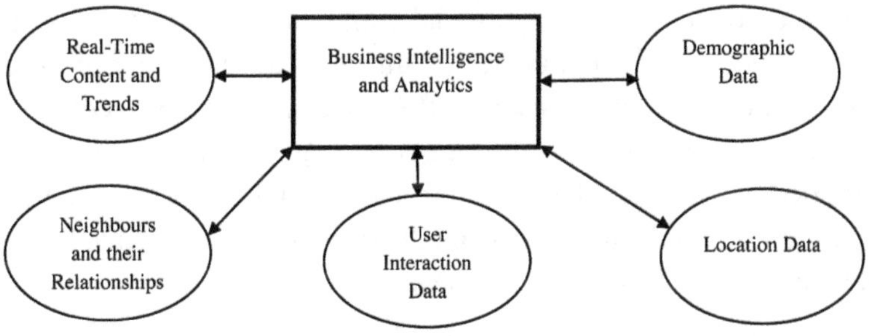

analysing, and modelling data for decision making process. Business analytics process improve business performance and determine strategies to achieve competitive advantages in sales, pricing, coupons and advertisement. Business intelligence users find out followers, todays trend, ideas and feelings of a people so that information provide business value.

Combining business intelligence and social media together helps in attracting target audience and cost reduction to the business firms via online advertisement and campaigns. Business intelligence system analysed real time data from social media. Various tools fetch data from online social media in easy and readable formats on the basis of certain input parameters. Business intelligence software retrieve, analyse, transform and report data. The process of analysing social network business data is described as:

- Data collection and processing
- Data modelling and information retrieval
- Analysis and prediction

Social media have various types of services and communications simultaneously taking place throughout the cyberspace. Social media attains new customers rapidly that has been previously a tough task. It creates a series of links for connecting customers to the companies or organizations. Social media analytics analyse comments and data related to product or brand to find out opinions, targeted followers and audience. Social media provides a platform for interlinking social internet with business process for the current and potential customers knowing their requirements, interest, problems and feedback.

Natural language processing algorithms based on social network analysis, data mining techniques and sentiment analysis filters the data on the basis of blogs. Influencing individuals for brand reputation and voice of targeted customer helps in deriving critical decisions to the business. Web community focuses on the real-time sentiments and opinions of a new product advertisement or campaign via messages or video sharing while they are released/launched across the globe. Business analytics software automates business process for an organizations to monitor, capture and analyse the huge amounts of data and optimize the process of strategic and tactical decision. Business analytics is used in several fields like as in managing customer relationships, financial and marketing activity, supply chain management, human resource planning, decision making in pricing etc. Business analytics is associated with profit, shareholders returns, understanding of data, competitiveness with other business firms, generating information reports. Business analytics use descriptive, predictive and prescriptive analytics methods to understand present and past data, analyzing past performance and optimization method.

Social business analytics access unstructured text data from social media communities, blogs, forums, online comments to analyse and integrating it to their organization data to deliver better results, profit and decision making process. Sentiment analysis optimize marketing campaigns, building customer and employee relationships, product services from social communities very fast. Social media and predictive analytics tools give better results in business from sales, development of product, marketing and financial operations. Most department stores clear their seasonal stock by reducing price and discount on the basis of historical data to maximize sale and profit. They change the scheme and discount offer time to time, it is decided by analyzing the previous data. Social business analytics provides opinions, preferences, new opportunities, hidden patterns and trends in the social media. Social business analytics transform business processes in several areas such as:

- **Marketing:** Social media provide information about campaigns details for future plans by Integrating and implementing end to end social media strategy.
- **Sales:** Social media develop promotional offers and discount to increase sale on the basis of user data.
- **Product Management:** Find out new consumers and their choice in the market.
- **Customer Service:** Helps in identifying real customer issues and resolving them before they become major problem to business.
- **Human Resources:** Identify potential customers and thoughts of people about company and product.

User data from different online social media is collected to analyse social conversation to build a model for prediction and recommendation. Self-social media network is created for collaboration and sharing important business information to the users. Business Analytics process is described by the figure 2.

1.4. Impact of Social Network on Business Application

Social media analytics provide various types of information such as sales marketing, customer and public relations, product development, effectiveness of promotional campaigns, customer needs, preferences, feedback and market trend data (Ruhi, 2014). Social media is a web based technology mechanism that transmit information to a large number of users quickly. It increase the number of people who visit the company website by mentioning the uniform resource locator (URL) in the social media web page. In other words, online social media directly connect customers with the business organizations.

Figure 2. Business Analytics Process

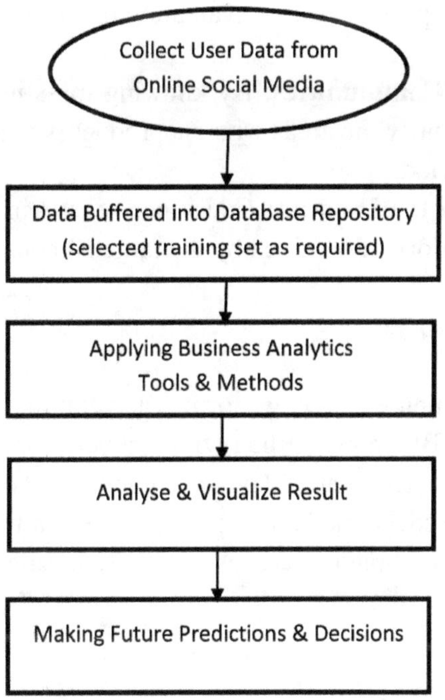

Social media reduce the budget to search and reveal target audience for online shopping etc. Now a days, business organization update product information through social media so that it is directly visible to their followers or users. Informal communication in the viral marketing promotes product, services and brands among social media users. The information propagation depends on the manners and user interaction and the type of relationship they share in the social graph. Diffusion mechanism increase the adoption rate of product or service. People often tend to use online social media for collaboration, communication and sharing information rapidly. Advertisements in social media about newly launched products easily attracts a large number of users or customers. Social media generates higher revenues, assisted with online feedback for better customer retention.

Social media network in the business perspective helps to find out answers for several queries such as which sections/regions are targeted for acquisition and growth, Who influences brand or product, emerging business related topics or themes, brand perception among users, brand comparison against rivals, knowing best social media channels for discussion/advertisement/ promotion. Social networking sites such as Facebook creating data centers around the globe to collect and process business related data of their users which can be used to assist in decision making particularly in marketing and brand management (Ruhi, 2014). It helps in identifying potential customers and new market prediction and forecasting outcome helps in growth opportunities of business to their customers. Social network affect business application in several areas, including:

- **Consumer Trends and Opinions:** Several API are used to aggregate and collect comments from online communities to find out keywords for gaining information about frequently purchased items on the basis of past or historical data.
- **Ratings:** On the basis of numerical value of product rating, this information is used for sentiment analysis purpose.
- **Desires for Improvements:** Reviews and comments about a particular product helps in improvements to be taken further. It provides a real evaluation of a product given by the interested groups of people.
- **Location and Density of Communities:** By knowing mass users and their geographical location helps companies to identify the areas where a product is to be launched first for their product popularity in short time period.
- **Degree of Involvement in the Product:** Consumer behaviour can be find out from small and detailed review feedback information given by the targeted consumers.

1.5. Social Network of Things

Social media data present on communities, blogs, forums and comments on social network sites provide business value to a great extent. By knowing the reviews about product or services from customers or employees, effective decision and action are taken for competitive advantage. Social business analytic tools fetch, measure and analyse social media and provide solution for the experts for taking decision. The higher correlation to customer, brand awareness, increase in sales and revenue find out the factors which attract public attention.

1.6. Social Media Networking and Services

Social media is a tool for advertising, marketing, creating brand awareness, to find out new customers, innovation, customer service, problem resolution in the business to attract and engage their customers, employees and other stakeholders. There are several benefits and application of social networking services usage such as formal and informal education, learning, innovation, self-identity, building relationships, communities and participation.

1.6.1 Advantages

Various advantages associated with social media in context of business usage and applications, are enlisted as:

- **Feedback Analysis:** Business organizations get fair feedback to improve the quality of product from people across the globe.
- **Marketing:** Social media has become hub for marketing and branding product services with mobile and internet technology. All E-Commerce sites use this method for product advertisements and sale.
- **Connection With Customers:** Several E-Commerce and business firm created their own forum or web space for directly connecting customers or users providing latest offers and product information. A lot of customers have a registered account on their sites. Their feedback and review increase the popularity of product in the media.
- **Reduction in Overall Marketing Expenses:** Most of the social network sites are free, we can post create page or profile of our product on social network site so that it enables to identify peer groups or influencers in the network. Social media can capture target market segment through network effect in very less time with cheaper cost as compare to traditional advertising methods for a small business firms.
- **Professional Networking:** LinkedIn interconnects professionals throughout the world and acts as a job portal. Social media has become an important tool for recruiting top talent employee for desired profile. Professional people used online social network sites to increase their visibility, profile seen by others, telling about their company services and getting more clients etc.
- **Entertainment:** Individual joins a social network to get connected with his friends irrespective of geographical or cultural barriers.
- **Polls:** Opinions and polls help in decision making having for diverse topics.
- **Knowledge Pool:** Experts collect data based on their customer experience and feedback.
- **Education:** Educational institutes have existence on social networking sites mainly aiming at academics, extra-curricular activities, achievements, highlights etc.

1.6.2. Disadvantages

Certain disadvantage of social media networking are in perspective of security and false personification, are detailed as following:

- **Security:** There are still some chances of committing online crimes or fraud activities using personal information of user present on the social media. Only the authorised or valid user can access the information and various security level should be implemented to stop hacking.
- **Online Harassment and Stalking:** On social networking sites, Personal information of user is easily available. There is a risk of misuse of information, posting humours, photo downloading and morphing.
- **Fake Identity:** Some people make their online profiles with fake information for making real users fool. It is not easy to determine whether the profile of any person is real or not, if you do not know personally.
- **Addiction:** People physically interact in the community but in online social media it is virtual and having addiction of using these sites.

2. SOCIAL NETWORK TOOLS IN BUSINESS PERSPECTIVE

Social network analysis tools used to identify, analyse, visualize and represent individuals and their relationships from various types of input data. Individuals are represented by nodes or vertices and their relationship is shown by links or edges in the social network graph (Kumar et al, 2016) Output data is further analysed and can be saved in external files.

2.1. Business Analytical Tools

Analysis tools explores network of small size to very large network such as family, team, disease transmission, internet, web link etc. These tools include mathematical and statistical methods to analyse the social network graph (Kosorukoff, 2011). Social network analysis, in business perspective, support various activities such as customer interaction, information analysis, marketing and business intelligence requirements.

2.1.1. NetMiner

NetMiner mainly used for visualization and analysis of large social network data to discover pattern and structure. It can be used for research and teaching social networks. Python programming script language used for transformation, analysis, statistics, and visualization of network (Kosorukoff, 2011). NetMiner data file format is .NMF. It Import/export data in various file formats such as .txt, .csv, .xls, .xlsx, .ntf, .dl, .da, .net, .vec, .clu, .per, .dat, etc.

2.1.2. iPoint

iPoint aggregate news and topics with sentiment and demographics, monitor and analyse social media data from all levels. Analysed data can be viewed and managed from worldwide, state and local neighbourhood level.

2.1.3. Inflow

Network data can be entered from CSV files, different databases, spreadsheets, automated survey tools etc. and calculate various network metrics. InFlow attracts many business users due to its simplicity.

2.1.4. KeyHubs

Keyhubs is a simple online tool for informal networks, permitting business managers for mapping interactions in a business organization.

2.2. Network Visualization Tools

Network visualization offers an integrated interface with rich graphics to display results from experimental analysis in a more meaningful and interpretative way (Kosorukoff, 2011).

2.2.1. Sentinel Visualizer

Sentinel Visualizer is a Comprehensive network analysis and visualization tool that generates dynamic link chart, timeline and geospatial view for temporal analysis and individual relationship in social network. It has a multi-user knowledge base for storing analysed data efficiently.

2.2.2. NodeXL

NodeXL is an open source network analysis and visualization tool for Microsoft Excel. It imports data from various online social media such as Facebook, Twitter, Flickr, web hyperlinks, YouTube, Microsoft Exchange Server, Google+ etc. via application programming interface to collect, analyze and visualize network data (Kosorukoff, 2011). NodeXL contains library of network metrics parameters such as centrality, clustering coefficient, diameter, average path length, giant component etc. for both directed and undirected network (Kumar et al, 2016). Different community detection algorithms are applied to find out clusters in the social network. The network graph contains edge lists or adjacency matrices representation in various file formats. NodeXL also imports UCINet, GraphML files, Excel spreadsheets etc. data.

2.2.3. KXEN Social Network (KSN)

KXEN social network analysis extract, integrate and exploit social network attributes from database storage. It has several important features such as classification, regression, segmentation, time series, product recommendation, prediction, finding group of individuals with similar behaviour and pattern.

2.2.4. ORA

ORA is an assessment and analysis tool for dynamic meta network consist of hundreds of social networks. It finds out dynamic network and trail metrics, cluster nodes, local pattern and change detection techniques from dynamic meta network. It examines how network changes with time. ORA can handle multimode, multiplex and multilevel networks and identify main influencing players and groups (Kosorukoff, 2011)

2.2.5. Sonamine

Sonamine is a scalable network and analyse millions of nodes and billions of edges. It is used for improving data mining prediction method for marketing. It retrieves the functioning of neighbouring nodes of the current user in a very less time period, improves social advertisement through clicks and speed up initial user adoption in the social network.

2.3. Social Media Analytical Tools

The social media analytics tools assess volume, sentiment and trends from online social media sources across the globe.

2.3.1. IBM Social Media Analytics Tool

IBM analytics contains users search items, feedback about product, brand, services, employee, partners, etc. data for a certain time period. Analytic results in charts and dashboards are easy to understand for a business organization. Information obtained from these tools can be used for marketing campaigns, enhancing reputation and market share, improving customer service and experience, product development, resolve problems, new opportunities etc.

2.3.2. IBM SPSS Predictive Analytics

Data from social media interactions is analysed for customer behaviour to attract new customers and boosting marketing campaigns. Social media and predictive abilities build advertisement and campaigns to a particular customer group through right channel delivering and accepting the offer at the right time. It predicts user desires and expectations in the future about a product.

2.3.3. IBM Cognos Business Intelligence

It provides dashboard, scorecard and report analysis, planning and accounting abilities on social media for achieving better business output in present and future time for an organization. All relevant stakeholders know what is happening on social media for decision making and customer satisfaction.

2.3.4. IBM Connections

IBM Connections build co-operative social networks, share business process and respond to evolving opportunities from professional networks and communities with various applications. It connects organization and customers to provide exact business outcome. It reduces the guesswork in finding trends and decision making in the business process.

2.3.5. SAS

SAS is a statistical analysis tool for business intelligence, predictive analytics, data management and multivariate analysis for mining, altering, managing, retrieving data from a variety of sources (web, social media) to find out customer, predict their behaviour, manage and optimize communication.

2.3.6. Microstrategy

Microstrategy is a business intelligence tool for query, generating report, dashboard and scorecard to make decision.

2.4. Network Statistics

Network parameters are calculated from graph build by social network data set. Higher degree or central nodes (Hub Nodes) are important in social network analysis for diffusing information at a fast rate (Kumar et al, 2016). On deleting these nodes from graph, various sub graphs are generated (Kosorukoff, 2011) Let $l(i,j)$ is the shortest path from node $i\, to\, j$. Let the total number of nodes in a graph is

N. Network metric parameters for a graph $G = (V,E)$ are defined below, where V and E represent nodes and edges respectively.

2.4.1. Diameter

The maximum distance between any two nodes in a graph.

$$Diameter = Maximum\, l(i,j) \tag{1}$$

2.4.2. Average Path Length

Average path length for a network graph is calculated as:

$$Average\, Path\, Length = \frac{\sum_{i \geq j} l(i,j)}{N(N-1)/2} \tag{2}$$

2.4.3. Centrality Measure

It defines the relative importance of a node in the network. It indicates how well they connect the network and to what extent they are central (Kosorukoff, 2011) Centrality is classified into degree, betweenness and closeness centrality.

2.4.4. Degree Centrality

Total number of nodes directly connected to a node is defined as degree centrality. In-degree and out-degree is defined for a directed graph. For an undirected graph, an edge acts as both in-degree and out-degree. For node i, degree centrality can be expressed as:

$$C_D(i) = \frac{Degree(i)}{N-1} \tag{3}$$

2.4.5. Closeness Centrality

It measures the degree to which a node is close to all other nodes in the network graph. For a node i, closeness centrality is defines as:

$$C_C(i) = \frac{N-1}{\sum_{i \neq j} l(i,j)} \tag{4}$$

2.4.6. Betweenness Centrality

It analyses the extent to which a node lies among rest of the nodes in the network graph. It determines importance of a node connectivity in the network structure. If the node is eradicated, it divide the network into sub networks. Let $P(i,j)$ is the total shortest paths that exist between node i and j; and $P_k(i,j)$ is the total shortest paths that exist between node i and j, including node k. Betweenness centrality is calculated as:

$$B_k(i,j) = \sum_{i \neq j, k \notin \{i,j\}} \frac{\frac{P_k(i,j)}{P(i,j)}}{\frac{(N-1)(N-2)}{2}} \tag{5}$$

2.4.7. Clustering Coefficient

It measures how neighbours of a node are linked to each other. Higher value of clustering coefficient represents well connected group. The value of clustering coefficient exist between 0 to 1. Clustering coefficient is defined as:

$$Cl(G) = \frac{3 * No.of\ triangles\ in\ the\ network}{No.of\ connected\ triples\ of\ nodes} \tag{6}$$

2.4.8. Density

It is the ratio of total number of edges present in network to number of edges for a complete graph.

$$Density = \frac{No.\ of\, edges\, present\, in\, the\, network\, graph}{N\left(N-1\right)/\,2} \tag{7}$$

2.4.9. Bridge

An edge which connects two or more different networks. Its end point lies in different components of graph.

3. CONTEXT AWARENESS AND SOCIAL NETWORK OF THINGS

Context awareness is evolved from various application ranging from web and desktop application, mobile and pervasive computing to Internet of things (IOT) in last few years (Perera et al, 2014). The communication and interaction among users regarding various products and objects enables several applications in various smart domains to operate as Internet of things. With the increasing popularity of Internet and social media, colossal amount of data is generated from users' activities from social networking sites. User identity is identified by social network profile. In Internet of things, data collected from a large number of intelligent sensors is analysed and interpreted with the impact of context-awareness. The sensors and handheld electronic devices communicate to each other via internet without requiring too much human involvement at any instant of time and independent of their location. Various types of sensors (homogenous or heterogeneous) are interconnected to perform cross-disciplinary functionalities. Data from various sensor nodes is collected by the sink node and further it is transmitted to computational devices. Context is used for fusing sensor data to get novel information and knowledge with reference to situational awareness that surrounds the region of interest. Middleware technology is used to impart context awareness to Internet of things.

Worldwide interconnection of object such as sensors, actuators, RFIDs (Radio Frequency Identification) and smart applications forms the internet of informative resources (Perera eta l, 2014). Data collected from social media is analysed by various contextual reasoning and decision models such as decision tree, naive bayes classifier, hidden markov model, regression analysis, support vector machine, k-nearest neighbours algorithm, neural network, fuzzy logic, supervised and unsupervised learning. Preprocessing methods are further applied to remove ambiguous and interpolate missing values.

The context information collected from various online social network sites aligned with context information collected by mobile and network-enabled devices, enhances applications for prediction, recommendation and personal assistance. These applications use location data, user preference and schedules, likes/dislikes and other information to apply the contextual essence.

3.1. Context

Context is an information which is used to describe the state of an entity for interaction between user and application. An entity can be person, place, software and application services, objects or any handheld electronic devices which significantly enable for interaction between user and application. Context information gets generated by processing the raw data gathered from group of intelligent sensors deployed in the region of interest (Perera eta l, 2014). The context types are described below:

- **Primary Context:** Information generated without using sensor data fusion method and existing context.
- **Secondary Context:** Information is computed from primary context and data retrieval operations.

3.2. Context-Aware Systems

Context-aware system uses context information to provide appropriate service and information to users on the basis of application specific task. These systems have presentation, execution and tagging features. The context information is presented to user on the basis of location and time. Some actions are taken dynamically on an automated basis with contextual information. Context data is tagged with multiple sensor data for processing (Perera et al, 2014b). Various charts, graphs and other visualization methods are used to present information in desired form.

Context awareness is classified into three levels including, personalisation, active and passive, depending user interactivity. Context lifecycle is divided into four phases that involves acquisition, modelling, reasoning and diffusion of context. The context awareness communication and computing play an important role in ubiquitous computing and Internet of things (IoT) systems, thereby creating an intelligent interaction (Perera et al, 2014). People and things are now connected with anything from anywhere at any time by the Internet of things (IoT) systems.

3.3. Applications Coupled With Context-Awareness

Normally in sensor-based applications, several sensor nodes are deployed in bulk around a certain geographical area to monitor and capture the description of environmental situation. The captured sensor data is further processed and fused to generate information that could be eventually used for decision making purposes (Perera et al, 2014) There exists certain intelligent sensor devices (for instance - Nest thermostat) that has ability to understand user behaviour and preferences over a particular time and control temperature efficiently. This can enable real-time remote monitoring of patients, thereby making eHealth intelligence a reality. All smart applications tend to make use of contextual data such as location, time and other surrounding detail to build an intelligent system. These systems are capable of processing real-time data and approach with dynamic solution. Voice triggered IoT solutions can answer common questions by processing natural language and semantic technology. Users can easily interact with IoT based solutions through voice, gesture and touch screen method. Mostly, the centralized hubs are managed and controlled by smart phone, tablet and computers. The intermediate nodes exist between sensors/actuators and centralized node that assists in coordinating the operation intelligence.

Generally, IoT solutions are categorized into smart wearable, smart home, smart city, smart environment and smart enterprise. These IoT systems use information and communication technology to provide smart services. In smart home environment user can switch on their appliances apart from home. In the supply chain management system, SenseAware use context information such as location, temperature, humidity, pressure and other parameters for processing. Another such IoT based application is Mimo, a baby monitoring product that notifies parents about abnormal health conditions (Perera et al, 2014).

Internet of things is used in various applicable areas widely spanning over waste management, parking slot management, street lighting, fire safety, indoor localization, manufacturing process management, concrete structure, health monitoring, environmental monitoring, air quality monitor, smart farming, smart river management, weather monitor, smart home, smart cities, smart water, security automation systems etc.

3.4. Social Network of Things in Contextual Business Network

Social network is considered to be perhaps the richest source of variety of user information, including location coordinates, personal identity, addresses, preferences and user neighbourhood statistics. Online users interact with each other through social structure formed owing to capabilities and extensibilities of electronic gadgets, thereby forming social network of things. Owing to tremendous development in sensor & digital domain, the electronic devices are well-equipped with networking, computational, sensing and buffer capabilities.

A global network of interconnected objects represents an intelligent end to end system based on communication protocol stack. Social Internet of things add an essence of sociality and smartness to the manner electronic devices interact without intervention of humans. The network relationship and interactions among the electronic objects is similar as per social network services. The real-time requests for an event are made to extract facts from social profiles of the users with application of several natural language processing techniques. By analysing the user profile, an application send notification to mobile device having relevant services and objects, for further processing on contextual basis.

With the rapid development in networking infrastructure, systems can access application and services on demand anytime from anywhere, pervasively. The contextual information of an individual at a particular time is collected from heterogeneous data such as personal, applications, devices, entities and other networking components. On occurrence of a particular scenario, the aggregated outcome is published to social media and an event is triggered to a nearby location area in social Internet of things (SIoT). Certain components of the contextual information can be static as well as dynamic in nature (Moore et al, 2013).

4. DIFFUSION AND INFLUENCE IN BUSINESS

The diffusion of information, ideas, virus, disease, innovation, influence and cascading behaviour exist in social and information networks (Gomez-Rodriguez et al, 2010). Diffusion model mainly includes threshold, cascading and epidemic model. In threshold-based models, an individual who diffuse information or transmit it to their neighbours depends on the threshold value. Threshold value is chosen as per network structure and connections. In the cascading model, the nodes who already adopt the information or idea (activated node), influence or activate other nodes which are currently in inactive state (nodes which have no information) that are directly connected to them. This process stops when all nodes participate for active state in the network. Cascading process initially start from some source nodes on the basis of degree centrality or distance value. The tendency of a node to become active increases as most of its neighbour node are in active state (Kempe et al, 2003). A node becomes inactive to active state but active to inactive transition is not allowed. In the business perspective point of view, the brand promotion or advertisement will go in a single direction progressively.

An epidemic model describes propagation of infectious disease in a community network. In epidemic model, there are susceptible, infected and recovered state. The disease spreads in the community through some agents like as fungi, bacteria, virus etc. when a people comes in contact of a person which is infected, then there are chances of people which are connected to the infected one to become infectious. It will depend on immunity power of a person. Information like as news, rumours and innovation ideas in the social media network follows epidemic model for transmission of information from one node to other through some relationship between them. The spread of virus or malware in computer network also follows epidemic model. The network metrics parameter value affect the rate of information diffusion. Consumers adopt the behaviour of an early adopter if they are closely related or distance between them is less. Lesser distance nodes will diffuse information first and they will forward the information to their connected neighbours. A social network is an interaction graph of individuals that plays a major role in diffusion of information, idea and influence in the network.

Influence Maximization choose most potential individuals to diffuse information so that maximum number of users adopt the product, news or information in the network (Huiyuan et al, 2014) In the last few years, exponential increase in users of online social network site (Facebook, Twitter, GooglePlus etc.) provide a best platform for information diffusion and exchanging information (Huiyuan et al, 2014). Influence maximization in information diffusion process will depends on the seed set (initially chosen) nodes. Viral marketing, recommendation system and information diffusion process can be seen in many forms on online social network and follow social influence phenomena. The adoption of new ideas, technology and information is affected by the decision of their friends, colleagues, neighbours and word of mouth phenomena.

The network structure and information content jointly affect the path of diffusion process in the network. It predicts how rapidly an individual is aware about news or information will depends on strength and ties of communication media. Initially the diffusion process is fast and after some time it will become constant (follow S shape pattern). Information spread between individuals via behaviour, word of mouth effect, marketing, innovations and social groups in the industrial organisation. Different types of information diffuse in a different manner. The user creates and share information with each other for their mutual understanding. Spread of information is dependent on the degree or connection of an individual to others in the network. Highly or strongly connected nodes increase the possibility of accepting information as compare to loosely connected nodes.

Higher degree and clustering coefficient value in the network increase the number of adopted population or users to follow their behaviour or information who have already adopted the information, news and product. The network parameters identify influencers and predict the adoption probability of the users that have not adopted till now. A highly connected sub group in the network have a strong influence on its members. Innovation ideas are key factors for business growth. It enhances the competitiveness in the business environment. Without diffusion process, an innovation has no impact on business economy. The parameter that influence the business is the rate of diffusion and it is different for different products, news and information. It is affected by social, political and economic chrematistics. Diffusion predicts the rate and pattern of innovation adoption over time and space. It increases the productivity in the business process.

4.1. Diffusion in Social Network

Diffusion in the social network is the spread of information from one place to another. A social network is dynamically changing and continually evolving in nature. Such evolution is attached with the spread of information on top of the network. The network connection affects the diffusion of information. A node can adopt a new behaviour or technology, it will depend on how many neighbours an agent has (Degree), cost, threshold value and communication media. Individuals receive multiple types of information during communication in the social media. Diffusion in social network analysis is applied in many areas such as diffusion of innovations, health care, organizational studies, social media, trend prediction, business and marketing, community detection, content sharing, epidemic model. Innovation is generally considered as a progressive model, making communication a medium for adoption. At each time instant the number of users who adopt the innovation increases.

4.2. Influence of Diffusion in Online Social Media

Diffusion in online social media is a process that explains how, why, and at what rate new ideas, technological events, information or news propagate through certain mediums among individuals for a certain time period is given by figure 3. Information, communication medium, time, social system (media) are important parts of the diffusion process. The information spread from one node to another node through influence of external sources (Myers et al, 2012). The external influence process affects the information adoption process to some extent time to time. External influence increases the brand popularity in the business network.

Diffusion of information in online social media is affected by direct or indirect connections and by some external factors such as newspaper, television, radio etc. In the business perspective product popularity is also affected by its features, quality, price etc. and by other sources like as comparison with respect to competitors.

Online social network sites such as MySpace, Facebook influence the customer decision in the business environment and an organisation explores about their marketing strategy. Friends of individual have dense connection with each other i.e. average distance between individual to any other on this planet

Figure 3. Elements of Diffusion Process

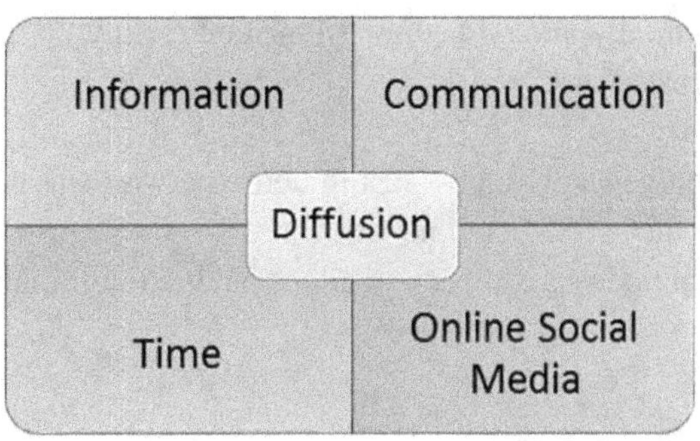

is six (Six degree of phenomenon). Highly connected members have strong influence on adoption as compared to sparsely connected members in the network.

4.2.1. Viral Marketing

Spread of information and ideas in online social network where individual act as the motivation for the others. It will predict the future popularity based on the early adopter and the connections between them. If we post any news/advertisement on any social media with initially on a central or highest degree node, then how much time it takes to become popular among the social media. Viral marketing is a technique for increasing brand awareness. People choices are also affected by decision of their friends, colleagues and neighbours.

Initially, viral marketing choose small number of influential members to convince other users to adopt new product. Adoption is increased to a great extent by advertisement and recommending product to their friends. Influence maximization problem finds out key individuals for maximizing spread of influence (Huiyuan et al, 2014). Online social networking sites attract mass number of people for influence maximizing in viral marketing strategy (Huiyuan et al, 2014). In viral marketing, people adopt particular behaviour or product without knowing the key influencers for adoption process (Gomez-Rodriquez, 2010). Strong communities in the network have more relevance for word of mouth effect.

4.2.2. Market Basket Analysis

While getting the relevant dataset of opinions or blogs from online social media and applying several pre-processing and mining techniques, we finally get the list of products that are purchased by the customer frequently/most of the times. Normally, there exists certain products, news and some kind or source of information that is highly associated with other one. Such commonness acts as the basis for this analysis so that we get the list of these associated items sorted by their value, rank or popularity.

4.3. Discovering Trends in Business

The mass media play an important role in spreading information from one vertex to another. In figure 4, vertex number represents the distance from source vertex and the connection between them.

Mass communication consists of two parts. In the first part, mass media nodes inform and influence initiator nodes. In the second part, initiator nodes influence potential adopters within their communities and so on. The second part of diffusion is important in spreading of information because it sees the high degree network connections. First, less number of people adopt an information/news/product, but after some time it increase exponentially, then it becomes constant (follows S shape pattern).

Some facts related to diffusion are:

- Diffusion of information/news/product is fast in dense networks as compared to sparse networks
- Diffusion rate is low in an unconnected network
- Higher degree or central nodes are chosen to adopt innovation initially

Figure 4. Random Network with 100 Nodes

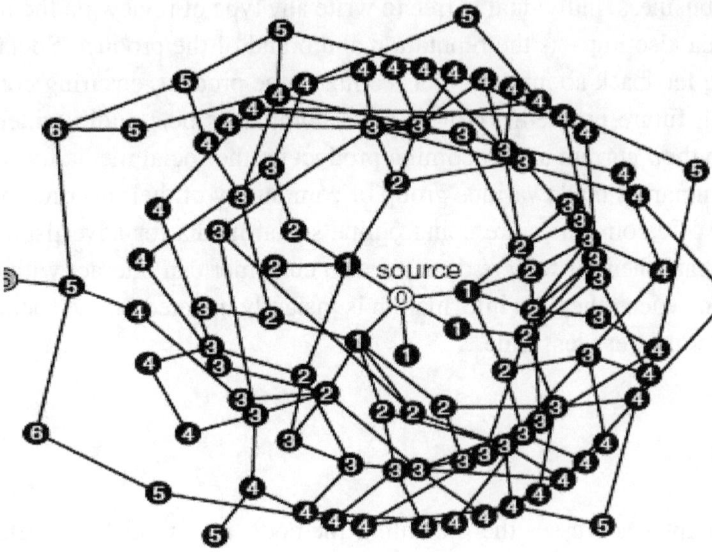

Network parameters play important role in information propagation at each time instant. Diffusion model is used in prediction, forecasting in various areas in taking decision. Node with high degree and centrality act as a vast source of spreading information to their connected neighbours.

4.4. Business Strategy and Marketing Communication

Many business organization communicate to their customers through social media. Social media provides direct communication interface to connect customer and business organization. By knowing target audience profile factors such as age, likes, dislikes, interest, income etc. then it is easy to locate them on the social media. Social media strategy relies on type of content, frequency of posting and time at which content is posted. Social media advertisement increase the competition in business which is beneficial for the consumers.

Communication in social media helps companies to know their clients, services required by them, communicating to a larger group of community, sales and building reputation over the globe. Communication in marketing includes several mode such as advertisement, sales offer, publicity, direct and interactive marketing, word of mouth etc. social media is communication tool which exchange various types of information among users and customers in the business.

Social media include activities of interaction about companies brand and connecting firm to their target audience. Customer reviews about product or services helps companies to take corrective actions. The presence of huge number of people on the social media increase brand awareness and interaction among people. Social media is an easiest method for communicating and listening their customer requirements. Online social media have interactive communication with its target audience for spreading short information message while increasing sales and adding new customers in the business. Business organizations increasing their network towards social media users.

Social media helps in managing consistency, sales, exposure, marketing expenditure, ranking, position and customers in the business. Individual is free to write any type of review on the internet, so negative review on social media also impacts the reputation and brand of the product. Social media provides a platform for receiving feedback about customer feeling to the product, ensuring companies to respond quickly from avoiding future problems. Now a days, companies post audio, video, image and other information related to their current and upcoming product on the social media for reducing the time of knowing features. Companies made various group of community of their user to know their behaviour and reviews. Fortune 500 companies are using online social media for advertisement and campaign. Companies communicate their customers directly, also customer can interact with other on the social media without knowing each other. An information is instantly updated on the social media and can be seen by a lot of people in a very less time.

5. CONCLUSION

To summarize, the chapter addresses the prevailing methods, new models, current trends and future projections of research in business social network. This would foster the understanding of formidable challenges confronted and expanding scope in developing business analytical standards. The chapter is designed with the aim to serve as the leading reference for those who seek broad knowledge with in-depth conceptualization on impact of networking in business perspective with social network of things.

REFERENCES

Evans, J. R. (2013). *Business Analytics Methods, Models and Decisions*. Pearson Education, Inc.

Gomez-Rodriguez, M., Leskovec, J., & Krause, A. (2010). Inferring Networks of Diffusion and Influence. *Proceedings of the 16th ACM SIGKDD International Conference on Knowledge Discovery and Data Mining*, 1019-1028. doi:10.1145/1835804.1835933

Kempe, D., Kleinberg, J., & Tardos, E. (2003). Maximizing the Spread of Influence through a Social Network. *Proceedings of the 9th ACM SIGKDD International Conference on Knowledge Discovery and Data Mining*, 137-146. doi:10.1145/956750.956769

Kumar, P., & Sinha, A. (2016). Real-Time Analysis and Visualization of Online Social Media Dynamics. *IEEE International Conference on Next Generation Computing Technologies*, 362-367. doi:10.1109/NGCT.2016.7877442

Malviya, V., & Gupta, G. P. (2015). Performance Evaluation of Similarity Based Link Prediction Schemes for Social Networks. *IEEE International Conference on Next Generation Computing Technologies*, 654-659. doi:10.1109/NGCT.2015.7375202

Moore, P., Sharma, M., Xhafa, F., & Barolli, L. (2013). Context and the Cloud Situational Awareness in Mobile Systems. *IEEE International Conference on Network-Based Information Systems*, 551-558. doi:10.1109/NBiS.2013.92

Myers, S. A., Zhu, C., & Leskovec, J. (2012). Information Diffusion and External Influence in Networks. *Proceedings of the 9th ACM SIGKDD International Conference on Knowledge Discovery and Data Mining*, 33-41. doi:10.1145/2339530.2339540

NielsenS. M. R. (2012). Retrieved from http://blog.nielsen.com/nielsenwire/social/2012/

Perera, C., Liu, C. H., Jayawardena, S., & Chen, M. (2014). Context-aware Computing in the Internet of Things: A Survey on Internet of Things from Industrial Market Perspective. *IEEE Access: Practical Innovations, Open Solutions*, *2*, 1660–1679. doi:10.1109/ACCESS.2015.2389854

Perera, C., Zaslavsky, A., Christen, P., & Georgakopoulos, D. (2014). Context Aware Computing for the Internet of Things: A Survey. *IEEE Communications Surveys and Tutorials*, *16*(1), 414–454. doi:10.1109/SURV.2013.042313.00197

Ruhi. (2014). Social Media Analytics as a Business Intelligence Practice: Current Landscape & Future Prospects. *Journal of Internet Social Networking & Virtual Communities*.

Zhang, Mishra, & Thai. (2014). Recent Advances in Information Diffusion and Influence Maximization of Complex Social Networks. In *Opportunistics Mobile Social Networks*. Taylor and Francis Group.

Chapter 10
Social Aware Cognitive Radio Networks:
Effectiveness of Social Networks as a Strategic Tool for Organizational Business Management

Anandakumar Haldorai
Akshaya College of Engineering and Technology, India

Arulmurugan Ramu
Bannari Amman Institute of Technology, India

Suriya Murugan
Velammal College of Engineering and Technology, India

ABSTRACT

The mobile networks seem to have a steady future in the direction of the recent emergence of socially aware cognitive mobile networks. Their style and design are specifically made in improving shared spectrum space access, in cooperative spectrum sensing, and in enhancing device-to-device communications. Socially aware mobile networks do have enough potential to amass sufficient returns in the efficacy of the spectrum and also to march and gain a considerable amount of increase in the capacity of the network. Even though there are lot of gains in its potency to be reaped yet, still there seems to be enough challenges that are both business- and technical-related that have to be taken care of. This chapter delves into the cognitive radio (CR) and its social relations and also makes sufficient exploits in establishing a scheme that will be based on social-based cooperative sensing scheme (SBC).

INTRODUCTION

These current days seem to have an imposing problem in its face which is the dire need of wireless spectrum as there is a ubiquitous growth in the use of wireless portable devices. A definite amount of structured spectrum has been allocated only to the licensed users as per the recent rules and regulations of

DOI: 10.4018/978-1-5225-5097-6.ch010

spectrum allocation. The licensed users are for example the military, and others and therefore the rest of the customers with wireless devices are forced to make use of only the unlicensed spectrum. This system Burbank, J., Chimento, P., Haberman, B., & Kasch, W. (2006) which is known as the static spectrum access or in other terms this type of spectrum is permanently kept open only for the licensed clients. Although it is not made use of by the licensed users at all times, this licensed spectrum is inaccessible to rest of the customers and this leads to deficit in utilization of the entire spectrum supply.

A key investigation done by the Federal Communications Commission (FCC) reveals that the utilized portion of the licensed spectrum area is quite uneven and it also remains at a very constant stumpy of 15% . This inefficacy in spectrum management has to be seriously dealt with to meet the increasing necessities of the wireless spectrum. Joseph Mitola put forth the idea of Cognitive Radio or the CR in the year 1999. This is nothing but the intelligence of a wireless radio which is able to counter use the frequency band on the basis Dynamic Spectrum Access (DSA). A cognitive radio (CR) is quite efficient in Juarez, J., Dwivedi, A., Hammons, A., Jones, S., Weerackody, V., & Nichols, R. (2006) detecting the channels of frequencies that are available in its immediate neighborhood. Then it actually changes its broadcasting constraints as per the availability so as to not create disturbance to the original licensed users and also the rest of the secondary clients.

The parameters of the dynamic spectrum access states that when a licensed primary user (PU) do not make use of its spectrum area and do not relay any data through it then the secondary user (SU) can have access to that particular unused spectrum channel. Although whenever the PU decides to make use of their particular channel, then the SU have to clear their way and immediately vacate the spectrum. In an opportunistic spectrum access, a spectrum hole is made use of by the users when their wireless machines have permission to make use of a free standing frequency band.

The SU makes use of spectrum sensing in order to find out whether a particular spectrum is in use or stands free, so that unwarranted interference into a PU's transmission can thus be avoided. Spectrum sensing tentatively tests a signal of the PU and based on its analysis, arrives at a conclusion about the condition of the PU as per the characteristic features of the sample signal. An unused or a free frequency is used for testing or tracing by the SU, as long as the PU restarts to work on the band again. On the other hand, whenever the SU senses the functions of a PU it immediately leaves the area and continues its Kamal, A. E. (2006) quest for any other free and unused channels. The DSA proves its worth by providing a much competent and resourceful means to improve spectrum utilization and the CRs makes reuse of the free licensed frequency bands. This helps greatly to alleviate the swarming crowd of the unlicensed channel.

The usage of cooperative spectrum sensing makes a marked difference in calculating or deciding the accuracy of PU channel when compared to sensing by using a local spectrum sensing. This is clearly shown in a previous study. A CR perceives the PU frequency on its own in a local sensing and comes to a conclusion about the condition of the PU relying on the results of its own perception. On the other hand, a cooperative spectrum sensing implies multiple perception of man CRs which sense the PU channels in common. A default mode on the basis of previous cooperative sensing is perceived where CRs totally wills to cooperate even if this condition does not stay the same always. Most of the wireless instruments are powered through batteries and the CRs are constantly in requirement of energy consumption in a much better efficient method. In spite of all this, performances of unrestricted cooperation activities are definitely are completely safe and secure.

To launch a Social Based Cooperative sensing scheme (SBC), the different social relations of the CRs are thoroughly utilized and this subject is precisely dealt in this Chapter. To be accurate, all of these social relationships do belong to the clients who hold the cognitive radio machines with them. As a result, most of these devices are made use of by individual people and so there is a definite pattern in the communication and transmission of these wireless devices because of the social influence of the people who use them. The natural understanding and cooperative tendency of two individual CRs is Egele, M., Stringhini, G., Kruegel, C., & Vigna, G. (2017) decided by their mutual social bindings. Any particular CR will naturally incline to cooperate with a mutually understandable partner than a complete stranger, which reveals the human social characteristic feature and its coincidence. In addition to this, the impression created by a diversified social input is analyzed on the CRs sensing or perceiving ability.

BACKGROUND

Any social network for instance is a collective set of performers who are bound by the social interactions with each other. The major two factors that are in play in social networks are the individual persons or the organization and the other one is the social binding that exist among them. Social Network Analysis (SNA) is a specialized plan to unravel the network infrastructure that lies beneath. More specifically, SNA concentrates on the concept on the characteristic nature of the performers and the nature of data which is the output derived from these social contacts. SNA is absolutely a competent device which allows an altogether different concept to the network designer.

These recent decade have seen a totally enormous improvement and growth of the various online Internet social networks like that of Twitter, Facebook and Instagram and so on. This Xiao, M., Wu, J., Huang, L., Cheng, R., & Wang, Y. (2017) increases the need to make additional researches on social relationships. The SNA on its own has brought forth immense and deep attention to a variety of research branches in the fields of information science, economics, communication studies, anthropology, biology, geography, developmental studies, organizational studies and many others to continue. This results in the conclusion that social media has an immediate and important position in the designing of a complete and thoroughly result oriented network protocol.

Social Incentives for Cooperative Spectrum Sensing

To understand and comprehend CRNs, Cooperative Spectrum Sensing or the CSS plays a crucial role and as a technology it helps the SUs to occupy the empty or free spectrum bands without creating any untoward damage and disturbance to the PUs. The CSS Anandakumar. (2014) aims to improve the performance of spectrum sensing by scrutinizing the diverse nature of the available space compared to the observations made about the different SUs who are located in varied spaces. By cooperating with one another, the SUs will reveal to one another the information of their individual sensing and it helps a great deal to make a combined decision which is by far more precise rather than that of individual decision making.

On the other side, a unanimous assumption is made by all the CSS that there is a common consensus among the SUs to willingly cooperate. There are a few individual SUs who refuse in sharing the results of their local sensing so that they may save transmission time or energy but still they make use of others' sensing results. These individual character and activities of certain SUs pose a great detriment to the performance of the CSS. On the whole, one particular SU who is not willing to cooperate Li, J., Yan, H., Liu, Z., Chen, X., Huang, X., & Wong, D. S. (2017) who do not directly benefit out of it will be the cause of failure to a very well constructed CSS design. Finally all this rests in the manner where an effective and efficient way is found to address these individual CRNs' problems and this in turns will find a solution to the more challenging cause in achievement of better performance of the CSS.

An incentive method of a differential service approach appears to be more yielding. A game theory is used in the CSS where this kind of an approach is used. In Guimaraes, R. G., Rosa, R. L., De Gaetano, D., Rodriguez, D. Z., & Bressan, G. (2017), the CSS was modeled to be an N-player horizontal infinite game by its authors and made use of the Carrot and Stick line of attack. This ended in mutual cooperation with the Nash equilibrium of the game. In Chen, X., & Wang, L. (2017), a different strategy using Nash equilibrium to be the solution of the non-cooperative game between the SUs for cooperative spectrum sensing was used by the authors. In Sharma, V., You, I., Kumar, R., & Kim, P. (2017), the authors created a much more interactive session on the frequency of selfish SUs as a non cooperative game, and the more reliable and result oriented Nash equilibrium corresponding to a specific frequency profile.

The SUs are then prompted to receive an excellent distributed algorithm, so that they can benefit a particular and desired frequency over the other. In Chenlong Liu, Jing Liu, & Zhongzhou Jiang. (2014), the framework of the cooperative sensing was designed to be an evolutionary play where every SU has the allowance to decide on the basis of its history of usage and utility, and therein is prompted to act repeatedly on a more recurrent manner while this action yields a greater utility value. Anyway, all these game theory work under the impression that it is directly played among a particular set of players for any number of times. Whenever there is a change of place or situation, the customers tend to inform their counterparts about this transformation so that the performance is much better with advance knowledge. This denotes that one particular set of players have only a limited set of times to interact with the specific knowledge of time frame which is known to both or one of the players Xia, F., Jedari, B., Yang, L. T., Ma, J., & Huang, R. (2016). To add to this woe, many of the existing frameworks of these game theories are particularly connected to the central network spectrum, and they in turn a difficult set of mathematical analytics and computations. In CRNs which are widely distributed over space, the SUs usually are limited to their capacity of computation skills. So this complex theory of carrot and stick games are most definitely not the answer to the imposing challenges.

Socially Aware Information Dissemination in Mobile Networks

A brief or transient network which is self-configured with a few mobile instruments without the help of any infrastructure that is centralized in nature is known to be a mobile ad hoc network. These ad hoc networks involve mobile units which are able to transmit to each other with the use of short range wireless communication parameters like that of the Wi-Fi and the Bluetooth. With the infusion of all these mobile units like smart phones, tablets, pocket PC and other specific sensors have seen a fast growth, and these have resulted in development Anandakumar, H., & Umamaheswari, K. (2017) of newer mobile applications for these mobile ad hoc networks. This also sees the emergence of higher and piqued interest of these devices and they hone towards these mobile service and support. In any mobile ad hoc network and its mobile application, there is an important feature of data dissemination like that of the event sharing, notification and advertisements. Wi-Fi and Bluetooth is expected to be used overtly by these mobile customers and they depend on these technologies more and more to share their knowledge and content which has personal and biased preferences. In a university or college, students usually make use of these technologies with their mobile devices to share their study material or entertainment info with the rest of their peers within the campus grounds.

Without the use of proper and concrete network infrastructure, a direct method for data disposal through mobile ad hoc networks is used and it is found to be flooded. Hereby, each mobile unit found in then network acts as a node and retransmit the data dissemination packets as received by it. Usually the user preference Stepan, T., Morawski, J. M., Dick, S., & Miller, J. (2016) and satisfaction is ignored in this process. So while this dissemination process of data packets many of the mobile units who are not interested in these details also receive and thus results in unnecessary transmission of data. Lately, many of the social networks have developed their analysis and have designed a data dissemination method where they receive data packets as per their interests which are socially recognized.

The uncontrollably increase in new and advanced mobile devices and wireless communication technology development, the recent years seems to zoom in on the concept of data dissemination in mobile ad hoc networks. In addition to this, 3G cellular networks have been associated with these mobile ad hoc networks helps a great deal in reducing the traffic load in broadcasting of advertisements and dissemination of data packets. As there is no infrastructure for a fixed communication network or a Torra, V., Shafie, T., & Salas, J. (2016) centralized one, the manner in which these data are broadcasted through mobile ad hoc network is entirely different from that of the information that is broadcasted through fixed and centralized wired networks. A very inquisitive and detailed interest seems to be dispatched to the concept of Flooding as a ground level process for dissemination of data in mobile ad hoc network. When probed in a detailed manner, it is seen that there is one serious issue in flooding with an increased amount of retransmissions which are redundant as they are sent to those who are not interested in the content. This leads to unwarranted consumption of basic resources like power, bandwidth or frequencies and as well as broadcast storm problems which are quite scarce.

Socially Aware Routing and Forwarding Protocols

As there is a continuous process of movement in the mobile instruments used, it is always a disturbing fact to zero in on the exact location of start to end of the communication (source to destination) during the initiation of the process itself. The presently available routing details always share a paradigm which is store-carry-and-forward. They make use of this and continue to interact in intermittent and disturbed networks like DTN or delayed tolerant networks and networks that are opportunistic in nature. Abbas, F., Rajput, U., & Oh, H. (2016) It is always crucial and dire in nature about relaying selection and forwarding decisions which should be determined by the node which is in the current location with its base founded on a particular routing strategy. The method and style of effective protocols for routing and forwarding has one specific issue which seems to be the prediction of contact opportunity. The social features are taken into consideration by the SAN in the process of routing and forwarding data in a particularly designed protocol in order to achieve better forwarding decisions.

Based on the destination of the data to be delivered, routing is divided into both unicast and multicast routing. When the data is specifically destined to be sent to one single point the focus is on Unicast routing. On the other hand, when multiply varied destination is there for the distribution of data to collective members of a group, Multicast routing is used. This area of the chapter deals with the protocols of both unicast and multicast routing on their basis of social characteristics. Broadcasting congestion is yet another challenge which has to be dealt with as it is also a vital factor that will make an impact in the designing of routing parameters. .

Unicast Routing

Selection of the best nodes that will relay transmission with highest prospects to reach the delivery point or destination which will ensure maximum ratio of delivery with minimal delay and message overhead is the crucial factor in the protocol of routing mechanism. For example, relationships like communal relations in relative and stable social factions of the clients prove to be ideal and reliable data to foretell any contact possibilities in the future. The entire social network can be envisaged in its three basic formats: individual, community and an entire network. Among these, community is the one which is extensively made use in routing parameters and protocols. The nodes or mobile points of a same society or group are prone to make more and frequent contact other than that from varied communities.

Multicast Routing

Where there is a disturbed and divided network which is changing frequently, there lies the problem of multicast routing and it is considered as a newbie and equally challenging issue. Usually multicast routing is permitted to transmit and deliver data to a number of destinations and they are categorized as one single community or society. Patra et al. looked upon this issue and divide all these multicasting strategies of DTNs based on their fundamental working procedures. They are mainly the flooding multicast routing, probability based multicast routing, tree-based multicast routing, and intelligent multicast routing.

Cognitive Communication and Spectrum Sharing

The heavy increase of traffic or transmission of data has made the availability of radio spectrum extremely lesser. But on the other hand, there are studies done on spectrum usage measurements and their results show that there are still a lot of underutilized spectrum bands due to the temporal and variance in space or even the sudden rush of wireless traffic which comes under the static spectrum allocation policy Anandakumar, H., & Umamaheswari, K. (2017). The fresh emergence of cognitive radio technology has opened innovative paradigms in communications and it permits access to dynamic spectrum to improve spectrum usage efficacy.

Cognitive radio is nothing but a wire free communication method which can identify and analyze the condition of its environments and energetically accustoms its operating strategy and settings like the modulation, frequency bandwidth, coding schemes and also access protocols Li, T., Liu, A., & Huang, C. (2016) as per the need and change of the situation. Even though cognitive radio is seen with interest of late, this is not an entirely new concept and this cognitive interaction or communication has been followed by wireless communication networks from long back. In a CSMA protocol, it is seen that a transmitter has to make an attempt to find if there is any other active transmitter in the nearby area and also has to make use of the feedback from a receiver before another active transmission can be done. This "Sense before Transmit" protocol or capacity creates an exclusive arena around the transmitter which is in use and prevents other nodes in the vicinity from making use of any active transmission simultaneously.

Also cognitive communication permits the use of the available spectrum to share in a much controlled manner between various individual users and networks. Both the primary user and the secondary user (cognitive) both make use of the same available spectrum bands and share them through a hierarchical spectrum sharing network. This strategy thus makes it possible for both the PUs and SUs to coexist, wherein the primary users have more likeliness to make use of the spectrum. The secondary users Suganya, M., & Anandakumar, H. (2013) are parallel to them in communication on the same spectrum with an awareness of the controlled and less effect over the functioning of the PUs. This process implies that the SUs should be constantly aware of their functions and use of the same spectrum and be cautious enough not to disturb the primary users which might lessen the performance level of the PUs. Hierarchical sharing of the same spectrum is quite common and is considered by many as an application of the Cognitive Radio Technology.

There is a much known and conventional method to arrange the sharing of the spectrum in a hierarchical way. The spectrum holes which are resource frequencies unused by the PUs are found out by the SUs and in turn they make use of these bandwidths for their own transmission of information. This Zhang, M., Yang, P., Tian, C., & Tang, S. (2017) in fact affects the accuracy of spectrum sensing and the efficacy of hierarchical sharing of spectrum as it is mainly based on the capacity of the SUs' decision making skill. It is nothing but seeking out the most sensible access method which rests on the results of the sensing skill. Also there is another means to avoid this by formulating a PER (Primary Exclusion Region) which closes the perimeter of the active PU, its transmitters as well as the receivers. This prevents the SUs to make use of the same spectrum simultaneously and results in avoiding interference from the Secondary users.

The same amount of interest is carried over toward the capacity of extremely big hierarchical networks of spectrum sharing which the spectrum sensing and techniques of access to it receives. Today many studies reveal that the same standard of scaling law of a single lone wireless network which allows both the primary and secondary users to actively share the same spectrum can be achieved if only more care in shelved into the protocols designed for the secondary users is considered. To achieve this, the capacity of the transmission as well as the density of the area in a large spectrum sharing network is taken into calculation and this is where both the primary and secondary users are seldom disturbed by each other with less impact on their performance too. It is assumed that the secondary network has more on their skill set with the capacity to tune the transmission density. This is done to face the limitations of the primary users' outage probability and reveal that the functioning of the secondary network will be greatly increased with consecutive cancelling of the interference as well as find the most advantageous transmission power or the transmission distances.

COGNITIVE SOCIAL AWARE NETWORK MEDIA MARKETING

Social Media Examiners released a report of Xia, W., Cao, M., & Johansson, K. H. (2016) report emphasizes that increase in exposure and increase in traffic are the two highest benefits reaped out of the social media marketing. It is shown that a 92% of the marketers agree to the fact that they have seen an immense increase of business exposure due to their social media efforts. Also with 80% positive results, increase of transmission traffic tends to be the second best benefit. This is also the age of social media where almost everyone who use a mobile unit punch their presence in any one of the social interactive medias like that of the as Facebook, Twitter, Tumblr, LinkedIn, Instagram, Google+ and Pinterest. The index at March 2017 shows that there are nearly 3415 billion users who are very active in Facebook, and over 688 million users in Twitter. Even though many of the corporate setups and giant organizations have their page and presence in these types of social interactive groups, they do not make use of it. They are completely unaware of the wide opportunities they offer to business and many are unfocussed, no strategy or inclination to indulge in the online market which opens into a virgin business arena. This is because of their innocence to the buzzing possibilities of such a vibrant presence of online social media. Bacon has directed to the four major areas which could act as the basis for a more yielding and beneficial online and cognitive social media.

- **Contents:** Any social media finds its content to be the entire backbone of it. Constant and continuous updation of fresh and relevant content should be published for the consumers. This will help to build up more traffic to the site through online and social media. If there is no fresh content churned out regularly, it is considered to be dead and invalid.
- **Engagement:** The next important point to keep a smooth and successful media campaign seems to be better audience participation. When the audience is kept engaged through various means, and the companies or individuals are perceived as responsible and friendly. These perceptions are considered as improvements in sales, goodwill, brand affiliation, loyalty and there are also a group of ambassadors for a particular organization who will reach out to any length to maintain the positivity of their name, brand, product, service or the cause.
- **Skills:** Behind the scene, there are numerous skills which have to be applied to maintain the roaring and successful scenario of the social media. They range from research, backend management, designs, graphic scales, optimization, analytics, constant monitoring and many more. If there is no competent knowledge about the utilization of all these skills as to when, where, how and why or if they are misused it is a definite path to disability or disaster to the social media and its functions.
- **Consistency:** Apart from all the above mentioned facts which are key to success, there is one more to the set of it. All the knowledge about what to do and when to do, do not pay the effort unless it is done painstakingly at all times. The constant part or the consistency yield much more and could definitely avoid failure. There are many examples worldwide of companies and personalities who have failed even though they have all the facility, means, power and finance in the whole wide world, just because that they lacked consistency. They did not have any or nil activity in their social media network and in course of time they have been simply forgotten by their audience or customers.

Colliander et al have made a powerful remark that the social media is used by most of the marketers to increase their fan base loyalty which is at 72% and also receive 71% of market place knowledge. The changes since the study of 2017 indicate to reports from marketers about improved profits and benefits in all the areas. There was a drastic improvement in development of fan base loyalty which saw a hike to 72% from 65% in 2017 and there was also sales increased due to this which ran from 43% to 50% in the same 2017. These study thereby gives raise to many more questions like, “Will I get an even better results if I spend more time in social media?”, “If those who are using social media for an even longer period are benefitting more?”, and also “ Do B2B and B3C have any difference in between them?”. All the above mentioned queries are dealt by Drury and Dean who confronts them vigorously.

- **Improved Sales:** To see great results in connection to this factor, it definitely takes time which is needed to develop relationships. Those who painstakingly spend enough time are the ones who reap good results. The marketers of the recent past, who have spend at least a minimum of three years in the social media finds that their sales have been improved greatly. Also those who spend at least 5 to 6 hours per week get the same benefits and those who make use of nearly 40+ hours in the social media find new business areas which are a result of their efforts. To the contrary the remaining half or 50% of the marketers have no improvement in their sales in spite of making use of the social media. This might be due to their negligence and lack of the required machinations that help track the sales survey.

- **Increased Exposure:** Dean seems to confirm with his study that the marketers who have spend nearly six hours per week on social media have agreed to the fact that their business have received the due exposure. Almost all of the marketers who spend time on their efforts in social media marketing for more than a period of one year confirm that this effort have done a great to increase exposure to their business.
- **Grew Business Partnerships:** Business partnerships are gained by the use of time spent in social media networking. The more they put in time and effort, the more they benefit. Those who have put in their time for more than a year have concluded that they had gained new partnerships as like those of who have spent at least six hours in a week. These partnerships are the ones where they sell to other business marketers instead of selling to consumers.
- **Generated Leads:** With putting in as little as six hours in a week, more than 66+% of the marketers agree that they can visualize leads or new directions for their business as a benefit of using social media. This stands to agree with those who have spent the amount of time consistently for a period of more than a year in these social platforms online.
- **Reduced Marketing Expenses:** The same could be said to the expense incurred for marketing. This is reduced considerably for those who spend at least six hours on social network platform in a week and for at least a year at that. Those marketers who have less than 10 employees or fewer agree to reduction in marketing expenses to a 57% and those who have more than 1000 employs agree at a rate of 40% only.
- **Improved Search Rankings:** When a marketer uses the social platform for his business promotions for more than a year, there is a report which says that nearly 58% agree to have improved search engine rankings. Even it extends to 60% for those who spend a minimum of six hours in a week, and they have seen greater increase of their businesses in search engine rankings.
- **Increased Traffic:** There seems to be a greater increase of traffic in their business when the participants spend more than six hours per week in their social media platforms. And it is the same for those who have at this for more than a year consistently, as they agree to improved results than their lesser counterparts.
- **Provided Marketplace Insight:** A greater understanding and insight into their businesses have been gained by those participants who have at least one year experience in their investment of time in social media platforms is the result of a study by Kietzmann. This reaches to 69% and much more to 74% who spend regularly a good six hour in a week in their venture into the social media network.
- **Developed Loyal Fans:** B2C marketers seem to develop a greater fan base loyalty with the help of the time spent in social media than that of the B2B marketers. Those who have been using the social media for a period of one year are likely a 69% in the process of developing loyal fan base, but in connection to the time spent it is a 78% increased loyal fan base to those who make use of the online social media for at least six hours in a week. For those who spend less than five hours a week the result stands just at 56% of result in developing a loyal fan base.

SOCIAL AWARE COGNITIVE MEDIA NETWORKS

A social network platform or site can very well be understood as a service that is web based. This allows the participating persons or companies to build a public or quasi-public profile about them within the constraints of the system and secondly Jiang, C., Chen, Y., & Liu, K. J. R. (2014) it makes a list of their co personalities or users with whom they would communicate and finally they see and navigate through their connections and the ones that are made by their friends and co-users within the platform.

MAJOR SOCIAL MEDIA NETWORKS

Facebook: Mark Zuckerberg is the founder of Facebook and it has become one of the widely used social platforms and is the largest social media network at present. Initially, this was designed for the students of Harvard University only. This is a free social network and is a very popular one. It allows the users to register for free, to create profiles, upload video, audio and images as well. Users make use of it to send messages and it helps to link with family, friends and mates despite the time and distance each one may be. This network is translated into as many as 37 languages and it has many unique features in it. They include as follows:

- **Marketplace:** A place to post ads, read and respond to them.
- **Groups:** It allows the users with common ideas and interests to track and communicate.
- **Event:** It permits the members to make an event known to all, send invites and also identify those who will attend it.
- **Pages:** It also makes it easy for its users to design new pages and promote these public pages which revolve around a particular title or idea.
- **Presence Technology:** It allows its users to view who are online in their contact list and can chat with them.

The following are the precise data or statistics released by the Facebook:

- 864 million daily active users on average for September 2014
- 703 million mobile daily active users on average for September 2014
- 1.35 billion Monthly active users as of September 30, 2014
- 1.12 billion Mobile monthly active users as of September 30, 2014
- Approximately 82.2% of the daily active users are outside the US and Canada

Facebook is also a social network which involves in business relationships with various organizations and their brand campaigns. In 2011 April, a new portal was initiated by Facebook to aid marketing companies and their creative agencies in building brand promotions Liu, C., Ling, H., Zou, F., Yan, L., Wang, Y., Feng, H., & Ou, X. (2014) with the use of Facebook as their platform. Today one can boldly say that there are no organizations which do not have an account with the Facebook. This social media network is now identified in both fronts of society and business and for both individuals as well as business front. It is also yet has another face and acts as a portal or opening for political interface and access.

Any business or relation thrives on the very fact when it is recommended personally by word of mouth. This is a very influential and important strategy in marketing and many companies rely very much on this particular method. This is the very basis of strategy used in Facebook as it helps improve businesses where they magnify their technique in the very places the users tend to spend most of their time, be it in Internet or in online mobile instruments.

Given below is another set of information which shows the level where people interact with their mini businesses in USA using Facebook.

- An average of above 2 billion interactions happens between people and local business.
- Any average week sees that over 645 million views passes through and 13 million comments are given in local business Facebook Pages.
- There are about 70% monthly active users of Facebook in both the US and Canada who are connected to one another with regard to their local business through the Facebook.

In April 2012, these results were derived from a study conducted by Nielsen's Global Trust in Advertising Survey done with the platform of 28,000 internet users in about 56 countries who make use of the Facebook for their wide reach of small and local businesses.

Twitter: It was created by Dorsey, Williams, Stone and Glass and saw its launch in March 2006. This is also an online micro blogging service and an online social interactive network which encourages its users to read and post short messages with a maximum of 140 characters to it. These text messages are known as tweets and they are read by other registered users and post their own tweets in response to what they have read. Unregistered users can only read these tweets. Twitter aims at giving the opportunity to invariably empower everyone to post and share information, ideas at any given moment instantly without any hurdles. It holds its place among the top 10 of the best social media network. In June 2014, Twitter holds over 500 million registered users of it with nearly 271 million active customers per month. Almost 500 million tweets are seen to be sent every day and 77% of the Twitter accounts are registered outside of US and this media also supports more than 35 plus languages as per the data given in any home page of Twitter.

Twitter allows its users with multiple choices and options to retweet, post a favorite or reply to any particularly interesting tweet seen earlier and also to follow any new trending topic with the user's own individual thoughts. This helps any particular organization or forum to learn what is the current favorite of the public and their opinion with regard to it. There is a very intense and direct communication between any individual and the company or group. Many organizations are allowed to buy advertisements on Twitter to attract the users. This is very much different from buying ad space in a newspaper. Newspapers tend to charge according to the area that is allocated in any page of the newspaper which may or may not be chosen to be read by the customer. On the other hand, purchase of ads in Twitter is buying space of an individual's timeline. After April 2013, an even more attractive and unique feature was made available to the advertisers where in they can send post their ads to targeted users who use specific key words in their communications or tweets. These keywords may be related to their product or service and they are immediately identified by the data search engines and alerted Hu, X., Chu, T. H. S., Leung, V. C. M., Ngai, E. C.-H., Kruchten, P., & Chan, H. C. B. (2015) to the advertisers. This helps the advertisers to best identify, target and notify their posts to specific people and almost can make a reliable amount of prospective customers to them. Another yet interesting feature available in Twitter is the introduction of the "hash tag". This creation helps the users to post their tweets in connection to the event attached to the hash tag sign and also anyone who sees this can go and view the other person's view with regard to the post bearing the same hash tag.

YouTube: This is particularly a visual social media network. This promotes free video sharing and uploading or downloading of it. Many of the videos can be shared and the content of YouTube ranges to anything that is shot in any camera like music videos, movies, demonstrations on any topic and there is no end to the content of it. To make use of its specific features, registration is a must and a user can access through this account. As per the news augmented in BBC in 2006, YouTube is now Google's subsidiary and was bought for an awesome sum of $1.65 billion. Three big visionaries Hurley, Chen and Karim laid the founding stone for YouTube. Woda in 2014 states the characteristic features of YouTube as follows:

1. It is the third most visited site on the internet (behind Google and Facebook)
2. Worldwide, there are nearly 2,000,000,000 Video viewed per day.
3. Videos uploaded each day amounts to 829,440 on an average number.
4. The average internet user spends 900 seconds on You Tube per day.

The YouTube provides with a Comment Box section below the uploaded video. This ensures that communication is established. This is a new experience to the advertisers who post their ads and get a direct feedback from the customers immediately. The interaction becomes more personal and therefore ensures better understanding. Initially what was done to bring alertness to the individual consumers who use the social network media was found by the advertisers as a golden opportunity to perceive Masson, A. R., Hayel, Y., & Altman, E. (2017) what is the exact reaction and perception of the user. This also has a negative aspect because the advertisers has to face the immediate backlash of the customers if something inappropriate or wounding to the feelings of the public was seen in connection to racism, gender or political and social issues were seen. So great care undertaken by the advertisers ensure that nothing goes wrong with the advertisements before they are aired in the YouTube. Actually this is a healthy environment by all means and the YouTube users communicate with one another also with the comment box available. Other forms of communications are:

- They post comments on a video and respond to others' comments.
- They also record a video response to something they watched.
- They also share videos thru email, embedding the video on their blog, or using Twitter or Facebook.
- Comments are posted directly to a person's channel.
- Finally, they can also privately message the owner of any particular channel.

Famous brands like the Sony have become prone to make use of the YouTube to build their brand reputation using this platform for their social media interaction with their client base. The new era of online video dominates everything in the advertising arena using different means to publicize their messages. The pre-roll ads that come during any visuals on the YouTube will allow an option to SkipAd, and the advertisers pays only if a minimum of 30 seconds have been viewed by the user. The bottom of the screen will ensure few display advertisements during a video promotion and this space can be bought by the advertisers.

CONCLUSION

This article deals with the current scenario of cooperative sensing of the cognitive radio undertakes researches where invariably a uniform conclusion that the CRs or cognitive radio users are always cooperative willingly and unconditionally. It is not always the situation and has been failed to understand by one and all. The CR may not agree to cooperate due to various personal issues like energy deprivation or security reasons. This chapter proposes the SBC or the social based cooperative spectrum sensing scheme, which analyzes the possibilities of the social relations between the various CRs to act upon cooperative sensing. CRs usually are specific in choosing their cooperators keeping in view their social bindings. Previous sensing functions and possibilities will be taken into consideration in the selection of cooperators as it ensures a learning strategy. In fact, the CRs are perfectly capable of identifying solid and perfect cooperators on the basis of their own previous experiences in the field of cooperative sensing function.

This current chapter has put together two major areas of research: social network and the cognitive radio. Initially the backdrop of the cooperative sensing in cognitive radio and social network analysis was introduced to the readers. Specifically, the classification of cooperative sensing and the major techniques used in cooperation has been summarized. In addition to that, the benefits and overhead of the cooperation behavior brought forth is also discussed in a brief manner. An illustration of the classical metrics used in our model has been used for the analysis of the different social network. Finally, a discussion in relation to the works which exploits social awareness in socially aware cognitive radio as well as the wireless networks was done along with a discussion of various applications of the available social aware networks.

On the whole, this chapter provides a different perception to the modeling of CR as it intends to take advantage of the social network in cooperative sensing of cognitive radio. With the intention to make sufficient improvements on the model of the CR which is social based one and which would be authentic and more convincing to encourage the future growth to this innovative direction of research.

REFERENCES

Abbas, F., Rajput, U., & Oh, H. (2016). PRISM: PRivacy-Aware Interest Sharing and Matching in Mobile Social Networks. *IEEE Access: Practical Innovations, Open Solutions*, *4*, 2594–2603. doi:10.1109/ACCESS.2016.2564985

Anandakumar, H., & Umamaheswari, K. (2017). Supervised machine learning techniques in cognitive radio networks during cooperative spectrum handovers. *Cluster Computing*, *20*(2), 1505–1515. doi:10.1007/s10586-017-0798-3

Anandakumar, H., & Umamaheswari, K. (2017). An Efficient Optimized Handover in Cognitive Radio Networks using Cooperative Spectrum Sensing. *Intelligent Automation & Soft Computing,* 1–8. doi:10.1080/10798587.2017.1364931

Anandakumar. (2014). Energy Efficient Network Selection Using 802.16g Based GSM Technology. *Journal of Computer Science*, *10*(5), 745–754. doi:10.3844/jcssp.2014.745.754

Burbank, J., Chimento, P., Haberman, B., & Kasch, W. (2006). Key Challenges of Military Tactical Networking and the Elusive Promise of MANET Technology. *IEEE Communications Magazine*, *44*(11), 39–45. doi:10.1109/COM-M.2006.248156

Chen, X., & Wang, L. (2017). A Cloud-Based Trust Management Framework for Vehicular Social Networks. *IEEE Access: Practical Innovations, Open Solutions*, *5*, 2967–2980. doi:10.1109/ACCESS.2017.2670024

Egele, M., Stringhini, G., Kruegel, C., & Vigna, G. (2017). Towards Detecting Compromised Accounts on Social Networks. *IEEE Transactions on Dependable and Secure Computing*, *14*(4), 447–460. doi:10.1109/TDSC.2015.2479616

Guimaraes, R. G., Rosa, R. L., De Gaetano, D., Rodriguez, D. Z., & Bressan, G. (2017). Age Groups Classification in Social Network Using Deep Learning. *IEEE Access: Practical Innovations, Open Solutions*, *5*, 10805–10816. doi:10.1109/ACCESS.2017.2706674

Hu, X., Chu, T. H. S., Leung, V. C. M., Ngai, E. C.-H., Kruchten, P., & Chan, H. C. B. (2015). A Survey on Mobile Social Networks: Applications, Platforms, System Architectures, and Future Research Directions. *IEEE Communications Surveys and Tutorials*, *17*(3), 1557–1581. doi:10.1109/COMST.2014.2371813

Jiang, C., Chen, Y., & Liu, K. J. R. (2014). Graphical Evolutionary Game for Information Diffusion Over Social Networks. *IEEE Journal of Selected Topics in Signal Processing*, *8*(4), 524–536. doi:10.1109/JSTSP.2014.2313024

Juarez, J., Dwivedi, A., Hammons, A., Jones, S., Weerackody, V., & Nichols, R. (2006). Free-Space Optical Communications for Next-generation Military Networks. *IEEE Communications Magazine*, *44*(11), 46–51. doi:10.1109/MCOM.2006.248164

Kamal, A. E. (2006). Algorithms for multicast traffic grooming in WDM mesh networks. *IEEE Communications Magazine*, *44*(11), 96–105. doi:10.1109/MCOM.2006.248171

Li, J., Yan, H., Liu, Z., Chen, X., Huang, X., & Wong, D. S. (2017). Location-Sharing Systems With Enhanced Privacy in Mobile Online Social Networks. *IEEE Systems Journal*, *11*(2), 439–448. doi:10.1109/JSYST.2015.2415835

Li, T., Liu, A., & Huang, C. (2016). A Similarity Scenario-Based Recommendation Model With Small Disturbances for Unknown Items in Social Networks. *IEEE Access: Practical Innovations, Open Solutions*, *4*, 9251–9272. doi:10.1109/ACCESS.2016.2647236

Liu, C., Ling, H., Zou, F., Yan, L., Wang, Y., Feng, H., & Ou, X. (2014). Kernelized Neighborhood Preserving Hashing for Social-Network-Oriented Digital Fingerprints. *IEEE Transactions on Information Forensics and Security*, *9*(12), 2232–2247. doi:10.1109/TIFS.2014.2360583

Liu, C., Liu, J., & Jiang, Z. (2014). A Multiobjective Evolutionary Algorithm Based on Similarity for Community Detection From Signed Social Networks. *IEEE Transactions on Cybernetics*, *44*(12), 2274–2287. doi:10.1109/TCYB.2014.2305974 PMID:25296410

Masson, A. R., Hayel, Y., & Altman, E. (2017). Posting Behavior Dynamics and Active Filtering for Content Diversity in Social Networks. *IEEE Transactions on Signal and Information Processing over Networks*, *3*(2), 376–387. doi:10.1109/tsipn.2017.2696738

Sharma, V., You, I., Kumar, R., & Kim, P. (2017). Computational Offloading for Efficient Trust Management in Pervasive Online Social Networks Using Osmotic Computing. *IEEE Access: Practical Innovations, Open Solutions*, *5*, 5084–5103. doi:10.1109/ACCESS.2017.2683159

Stepan, T., Morawski, J. M., Dick, S., & Miller, J. (2016). Incorporating Spatial, Temporal, and Social Context in Recommendations for Location-Based Social Networks. *IEEE Transactions on Computational Social Systems*, *3*(4), 164–175. doi:10.1109/TCSS.2016.2631473

Suganya, M., & Anandakumar, H. (2013). Handover based spectrum allocation in cognitive radio networks. *2013 International Conference on Green Computing, Communication and Conservation of Energy (ICGCE)*. doi:10.1109/ICGCE.2013.6823431

Torra, V., Shafie, T., & Salas, J. (2016). Data Protection for Online Social Networks and Stability for Graphs. *IEEE Transactions on Emerging Topics in Computing*, *4*(3), 374–381. doi:10.1109/TETC.2015.2433923

Xia, F., Jedari, B., Yang, L. T., Ma, J., & Huang, R. (2016). A Signaling Game for Uncertain Data Delivery in Selfish Mobile Social Networks. *IEEE Transactions on Computational Social Systems*, *3*(2), 100–112. doi:10.1109/TCSS.2016.2584103

Xia, W., Cao, M., & Johansson, K. H. (2016). Structural Balance and Opinion Separation in Trust–Mistrust Social Networks. *IEEE Transactions on Control of Network Systems*, *3*(1), 46–56. doi:10.1109/TCNS.2015.2437528

Xiao, M., Wu, J., Huang, L., Cheng, R., & Wang, Y. (2017). Online Task Assignment for Crowdsensing in Predictable Mobile Social Networks. *IEEE Transactions on Mobile Computing*, *16*(8), 2306–2320. doi:10.1109/TMC.2016.2616473

Zhang, M., Yang, P., Tian, C., & Tang, S. (2017). You Can Act Locally With Efficiency: Influential User Identification in Mobile Social Networks. *IEEE Access: Practical Innovations, Open Solutions*, *5*, 136–146. doi:10.1109/ACCESS.2016.2632900

Chapter 11
An Experimental Evaluation of Link Prediction for Movie Suggestions Using Social Media Content

Anu Taneja
Jaypee Institute of Information Technology, India

Bhawna Gupta
Jaypee Institute of Information Technology, India

Anuja Arora
Jaypee Institute of Information Technology, India

ABSTRACT

The enormous growth and dynamic nature of online social networks have emerged to new research directions that examine the social network analysis mechanisms. In this chapter, the authors have explored a novel technique of recommendation for social media and used well known social network analysis (SNA) mechanisms-link prediction. The initial impetus of this chapter is to provide general description, formal definition of the problem, its applications, state-of-art of various link prediction approaches in social media networks. Further, an experimental evaluation has been made to inspect the role of link prediction in real environment by employing basic common neighbor link prediction approach on IMDb data. To improve performance, weighted common neighbor link prediction (WCNLP) approach has been proposed. This exploits the prediction features to predict new links among users of IMDb. The evaluation shows how the inclusion of weight among the nodes offers high link prediction performance and opens further research directions.

INTRODUCTION

Social Networks are the most popular way to model the interactions among users in the network-users can communicate among users through online social platforms like Twitter, Facebook etc to exchange information. The data in social networks can be considered in the form of links between objects. This can

DOI: 10.4018/978-1-5225-5097-6.ch011

be modeled as graph where objects represent nodes and edges correspond to links. But social networks are not static; they are dynamic in nature as nodes and links that connect the nodes keeps on increasing which led to evolution of network i.e. nodes may enter or exit the network and interaction among the nodes represented by links may weaken or strengthen over time. This dynamic nature of social networks makes the task of link prediction a very challenging task in analysis of social networks. The links can be predicted using various social network analysis and mining techniques. Most network models capture global information (user profile) but do not capture local information (attended events, check-in status). Local information covers details about links to be formed and this type of information is more important for various applications such as event recommendation, next check-in location prediction etc. Link prediction approach helps in forming network of users on the basis of local information. In this chapter, author focuses on real environment problem which can be resolved through link prediction.

The dynamic and sparse nature of social networks makes difficult to predict links across a network. Though the task of link prediction is important as it forms the entire network, depict the relationship between individuals but is a highly challenging task. So, can more links be predicted on social networks? The research on this can be beneficial to assess the relationship among individuals and resonate the social behavior of individuals.

Although link prediction has been applied on wide variety of areas like bibliographic domain (Yu, 2012), molecular biology (Hammond, 2001; Setubal, 1997; Stamenkovic, 1989) criminal investigations (Chen, 2004; Huang, 2009), prediction of unknown information on protein networks (Link, 1997; Marcotte, 1999; Roy, 2010; Smith, 1996; Zuker, 1999) and recommender systems (Barbieri, 2014; Chen, 2005; Emanuelsson, 2000; Guns, 2014; Li, 2013; Liu, 2010; Tang, 2015) then also more effort is required in order to investigate link prediction area. While recommendation, the most popular and successful approach of recommendation is collaborative filtering (Ekstrand, 2011) which takes user-item rating matrix as input and generate recommendations by identifying similar users on the basis of rating patterns. But the main limitation with this approach is sparse nature of user-item rating matrix. To reduce the degree of sparsity, the recommendation problem is viewed as task of predicting links known as link prediction problem. Therefore the main motivation behind this work is to reduce sparsity as it leads to the formation of incomplete links among nodes than the number of links that should exist in the network using link prediction during recommendation and prediction. Another motivation is that generally people trust on friends more, so there is a need to find social patterns formed across user network and combine it with the network structure information.

This chapter contributes in the following manner:

1. Extracted data by querying Twitter API which results in tweets containing movie ratings originating from IMDb.
2. Discovered general pattern like common movies watched by the users in the network-common neighbors, ratings fetched from tweets which forms the basis of link formation in online social network-Twitter.
3. Analyzed the general pattern discovered and propose a weighted common neighbor link prediction approach (WCNLP) which incorporates the discovered general patterns into a network.
4. Improvised prediction performance through weighted common neighbor link prediction approach (WCNLP) and validated the accuracy against classic evaluation metrics like in terms of precision, recall and AUC.

Organization

The rest of the chapter is organized as section 2 presents the literature and state-of-art in link prediction, section 3 introduces the background of link prediction, section 4 presents proposed approach including dataset description and evaluation of experimental results and section 5 concludes the chapter and discusses future research directions.

1. **Related Work:** This section presents the literature and state-of-art techniques in link prediction.
2. **Background:** This section discusses the relevant background required for link prediction in which authors presents formal definitions of link prediction, discusses about link prediction issues and link prediction approaches.
3. **Dataset Description:** In this section authors gives the detailed statistics of dataset used. The authors fetched the data by querying Twitter API which results in tweets containing movie ratings originating from IMDb.
4. **Experimental Evaluation and Results:** This section presents a novel weighted common neighbor approach for link prediction to deal with sparse movie network-IMDb and comparative analysis of common neighbor link prediction (CNLP) and weighted common neighbor link prediction (WCNLP) is being done.
5. **Conclusion:** The author concludes in this section and provides the potential future research directions for link prediction.

RELATED WORK

A large amount of work has been done in the area of recommendation systems using link prediction techniques. It is no surprise that recent literature includes a number of different linkage measures for network analysis. Here in this chapter, authors propose a novel weighted common neighbor link prediction approach (WCNLP) to deal with sparse IMDb-movie network. According to authors' knowledge, their work differs in this way that no one applied this type of approach on tweet based IMDb dataset. The authors' research is motivated by the fact to make efficient use of user-generated content on social web to drive recommendation systems. To this end, it is useful to consider two related areas of research-understanding the form, function and background of link prediction and applicability of link prediction algorithms to recommend user-generated content. But here authors' summarize the work that is most relevant to the study. Therefore, authors mainly focus on research work which is going on all around this domain.

Firstly authors' did an extensive study of link prediction in social networks. (Wang, 2015) did a thorough survey of link prediction in social networks. The authors review link prediction techniques, analyze problems, state-of-art, its applications, various challenges and future research directions in this area. (AI Hasan, 2011) classify link prediction methods on the basis of model so discuss various existing link prediction models and analyze their strength and weakness and conclude the survey with a discussion on recent developments and future research direction. They considered three types of models: firstly, the traditional (non-Bayesian) models to extract a set of features to train a binary classification model, second, the probabilistic approaches to model the joint-probability among the entities in a network by Bayesian graphical models and finally the linear algebraic approach to compute the similarity between the nodes in a network by rank-reduced similarity matrices. In this, authors (Lu, 2011) extract missing information, identify spurious interactions and evaluate network evolving mechanisms using link prediction algorithms. The recent progress about link prediction algorithms is summarized, emphasizing on the contributions from different approaches, such as the random-walk-based methods and the maximum likelihood methods and also introduce three typical applications: reconstruction of networks, evaluation of network evolving mechanism and classification of partially labelled networks.

Secondly applicability of link prediction algorithms to recommend content and users has been studied like in this paper; authors (Chen et. al., 2005) extended the idea of user-item interactions by analyzing it as graphs and employ link prediction approaches for making collaborative filtering recommendations. A wide range of linkage measures are used for making recommendations. The experimental results based on a book recommendation dataset show that some of these measures achieved significantly better performance than standard collaborative filtering algorithms. Similarly, authors (Chiluka, 2011) applied link prediction algorithms on flickr dataset to recommend relevant content from vast repositories of user-generated content systems as classic collaborative filtering techniques do not perform well due to data-sparsity and scalability issues. The results show that link prediction algorithms are more scalable and accurate in context of user-generated content systems.

Singh, A. P et. al. (Singh, A. P, 2008) further extended the idea and propose a collective matrix factorization model to simultaneously factorize several matrices, sharing parameters among factors when an entity participates in multiple relations. Each relation can have a different value type and error distribution; so nonlinear relationships between the parameters and outputs are allowed using Bregman divergences to measure error. The standard alternating projection algorithms is extended to their model, and derived an efficient Newton update for the projection. Furthermore, stochastic optimization methods are proposed to deal with large, sparse matrices-movie dataset. Then, Matrix Factorization concept is further extended to tensor factorization to model multiple dimensions by Yu et.al. (Yu, 2007) in which Gaussian process (GP) framework is proposed, stochastic relational models via tensor interaction of multiple GPs, each defined on one type of entities. It offers a discriminative approach to link prediction, namely, predicting the existences, strengths, or types of relationships based on the partially observed linkage network as well as the attributes of entities on a toy problem and a user-movie preference link prediction task and very prominent results are achieved.

Similarly, Rossetti et. al. (Rossetti, 2011) studied the problem of Link Prediction, i.e. the problem of predicting new upcoming connections in the multidimensional network i.e. multiple connections may reside between any two nodes and introduce several predictors based on structural analysis of the networks. The results obtained on real networks-DBLP and IMDb, shows that the performances of both the introduced multidimensional versions of the Common Neighbors and Adamic-Adar improves the accuracy. The researchers (Dong, 2012) extended the work of link prediction in a single network to heterogeneous network by proposing a ranking factor graph model (RFG) for predicting links in social network based on the assumption that people make friends in different social network with similar principles. Then transfer-based RFG model is developed and results show that transfer of general social patterns helps in prediction of links.

In this authors (Yang, 2015) focus on local information instead of global information as local information plays an important role in link prediction by proposing a new measure- Local Neighbor Link (LNL) in which cohesion between common neighbors and predicted nodes is considered in addition to local information that consists of node's attributes or small amount of topology information about common neighbors. The LNL method is implemented by researchers in both Map-Reduce and Spark and results shows that implementing by Spark has higher efficiency and accuracy than Map-Reduce. (Hannon, 2010) works on followee recommendation by creating relationship between users on social web-Twitter in which users can follow other users, for which various profiling and recommendation strategies have been evaluated on large dataset of Twitter users and their tweets for efficient followee recommendation. Scellato et. al. (Scellato, 2011) further explored prediction features on the basis of places visited by a user by proposing a supervised learning framework to predict new links among friends-of-friends and place-friends for online location-based social networks. The evaluation shows how the inclusion of information about places and related user activity offers high link prediction performance. This shows prediction space can be made 15 times smaller, while still 66% of future connections can be discovered.

In this chapter, authors propose a weighted common neighbor link prediction approach (WCNLP) in which weights are assigned to the nodes on the basis of number of common movies watched, ratings given by users to movies and other node and structural features. The comparative analysis of common neighbor and weighted common neighbor link prediction approach is carried out. The experimental evaluation is done on tweet based movie dataset of IMDb to prove its efficiency which is the main aim of this chapter and is presented in detail in the next subsequent sections.

GENERAL DESCRIPTION AND FORMAL DEFINITIONS OF LINK PREDICTION

Link prediction task is considered as classification, where two entities are given in a network, and it has to be defined if there would be a relation between them? Classification is based on features of entities: entity attributes and relational features.

- **Entity Attributes:** It represents identity of nodes for example node can be a user, movie, event, interests, topic model, affiliations, demographic data etc. Figure 1 depicts a user-movie network; user and movie are entity attributes which are depicted by nodes. There can be various criteria to assign weight to node like in figure 3 movie node's size signifies weight given to a movie in terms of rating and user node's size signifies number of movies rated by a particular user.
- **Relational Features:** It captures dependencies between links and is depicted by forming an edge between nodes. In figure 2, relation among movies is presented by edge, an edge exist in two movies if both movies are seen by a user. Edge weight among two movies presents strength of the relationship for example edge weight keeps on increasing if there are large number of users that are rating both movies. Graph-Based statistical measure which are used to compute relational features are length of shortest path, neighborhood overlap, relative importance, mean first passage time etc.

Social Network

A social network is defined as set of nodes and edges that connect the nodes and is represented as G= {V, E} where V represents the set of vertices/nodes and E represents the set of edges/ links that captures the interaction between nodes. The graph in form of user-movie network is shown in figure 1, V={U1, U2, U3, U4}, {M1, M2, M3, M4}, E={(U1, M1), (U1, M2), (U1, M3)} where {U1, U2, U3, U4} is set of users and {M1, M2, M3, M4, M5} is set of movies and an edge exists between two nodes if movie is rated by a particular user.

Figure 1. User-movie network

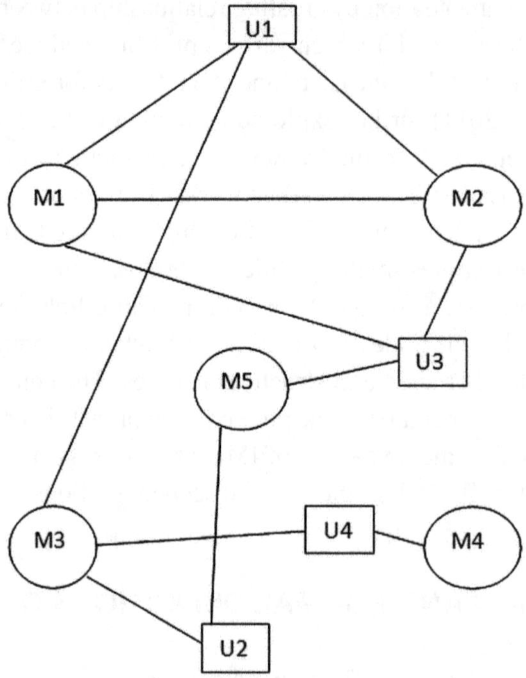

Figure 2. Movie network

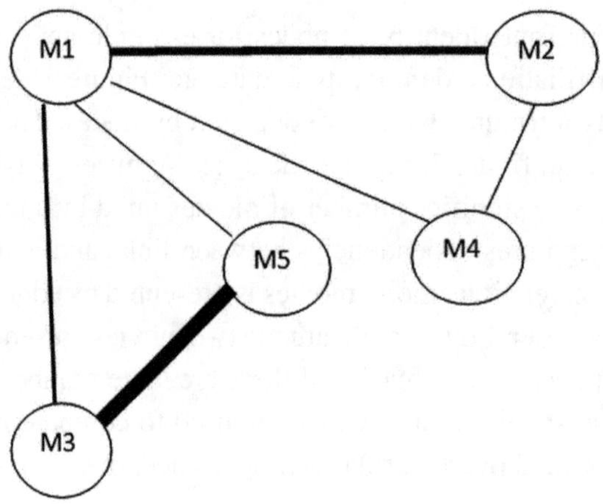

Movie Network

Consider a movie network M= {V, E}, where V is the set of movie nodes and E is the set of edges between the movie nodes which exists if both the movies are rated by a particular user, having a particular genre/ actor etc. The problem of link prediction is the task to predict how likely a new link $e_{ij} \notin E$ will exist between a pair of existing nodes in the network (mi, mj).

Figure 3. Weight assignment to nodes

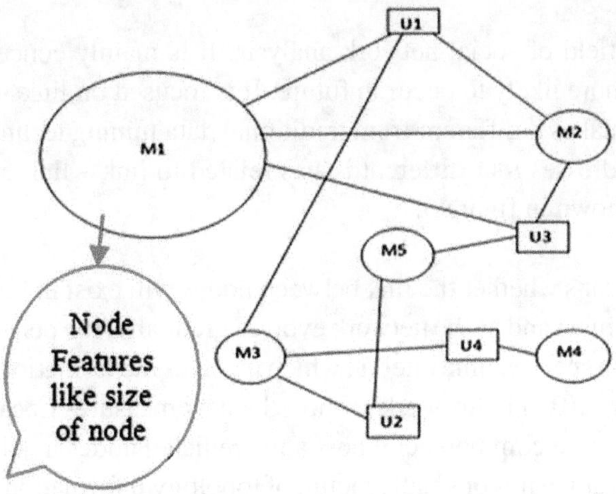

Figure 2 shows a movie network where V= {M1, M2, M3, M4, M5}, E= {(M1 M2), (M1, M3), (M1, M4), (M1, M5)}.

Figures 1, 2, 3 and 4 detail entities and their relationship features including weight assignment to nodes and relationship in significance of their properties.

- Figure 1 shows an original user-movie network i.e. which movies are rated by which users.
- Figure 2 shows a movie network with edge weight on the basis of two similar movies rated by more number of users.
- Figure 3 shows assignment of weight to an entity (node) according to node features. For example if rating is considered as a node feature for movie node then node size of a movie will become larger if having more rating than movie having less rating like size of node M1 is larger than M2 as it gets more rating.
- Figure 4 depicts assignment of edge in between nodes on the basis of their structural (relationship) feature such as if two users have given rating to a movie then relationship will exist in between these two nodes and weight of edge depicts strong relationship in between users according to their movie interest.

Figure 4. User-user relationship

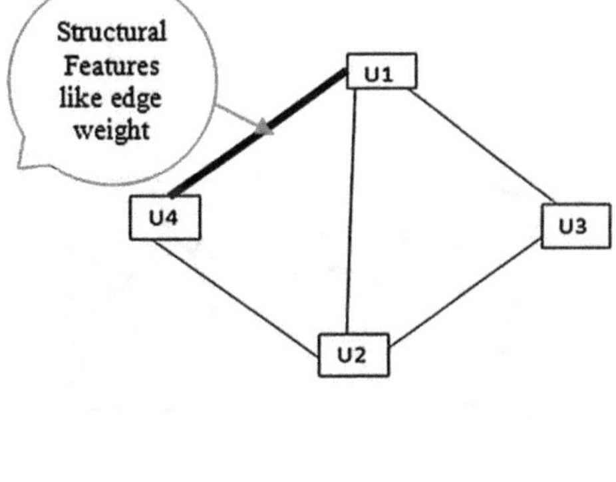

Link Prediction Issues

Link Prediction is a sub-field of social network analysis. It is mainly concerned with the problem of predicting links that are more likely to occur in future. It is focused on links between nodes rather than nodes themselves which makes it different from traditional data mining techniques as they mainly focus on nodes. Therefore it addresses four different issues related to links- link existence, link weight, link cardinality, link type as shown in figure 5.

- **Link Existence:** It means whether the link between nodes will exist in future or not. Figure 6 shows the social network at time t and as the network evolves gradually; the periodic snapshot of network is taken at time t+1 after a specific time interval which involves the formation of new links that are likely to be predicted. (Yang, 2015) in his work proposed a new measure- Local Neighbor Link (LNL) to consider cohesion between common neighbors and predicted nodes in addition to local information that consists of node's attributes or small amount of topology information about common neighbors.
- **Link Weight:** It means links can have different weights associated with them as shown in figure 7 which depicts bold weights are highly weighted in comparison to regular weights. For example user U1 has given more rating to movie M1 in comparison to movie M2 and M3; therefore the link between U1 and M1 is bold weighted. (Zhang, 2007) proposed a novel recommendation method based on diffusion of opinions expressed by a user over the object-to-object network of movies. When data is processed from all users, contributions from all users are accumulated to obtain an aggregate representation of the input data and converted to a weighted movie-to-movie network.
- **Link Cardinality:** It states that more than one link can exist between same pair of nodes as shown in figure 8 where more than one link exists between nodes M1 and M2 which signify that 3 users have rated both movies. (Li, 2016) works on link cardinality aspect by proposing a novel utility-based link recommendation method based on Bayesian network that recommends the links with highest

Figure 5. Link prediction issues

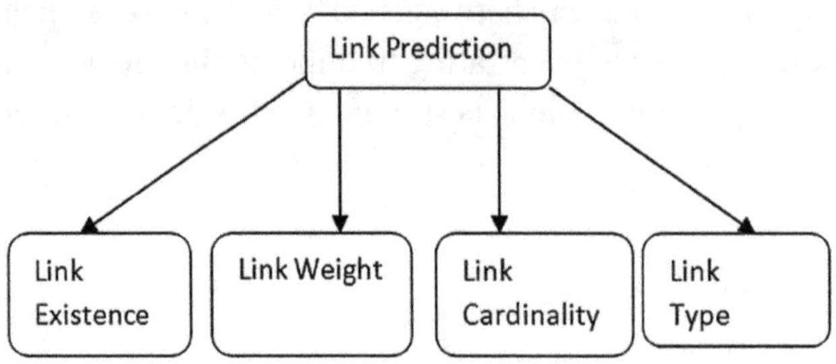

Figure 6. Link existence

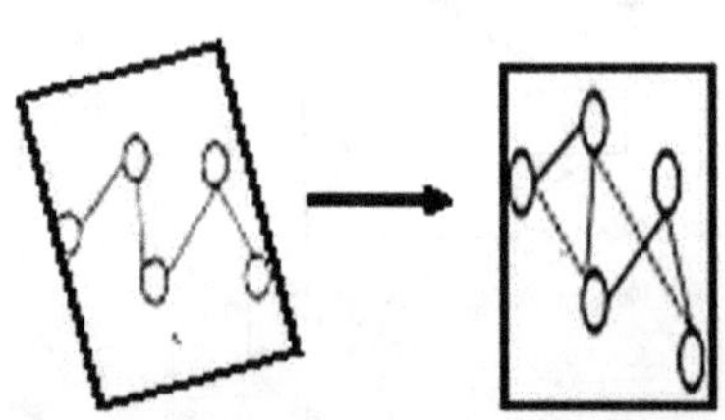

Figure 7. Link weight

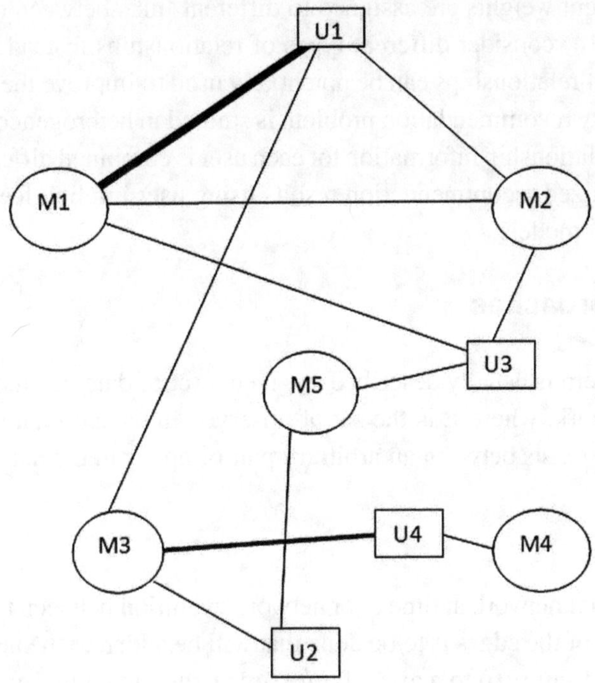

Figure 8. Link cardinality

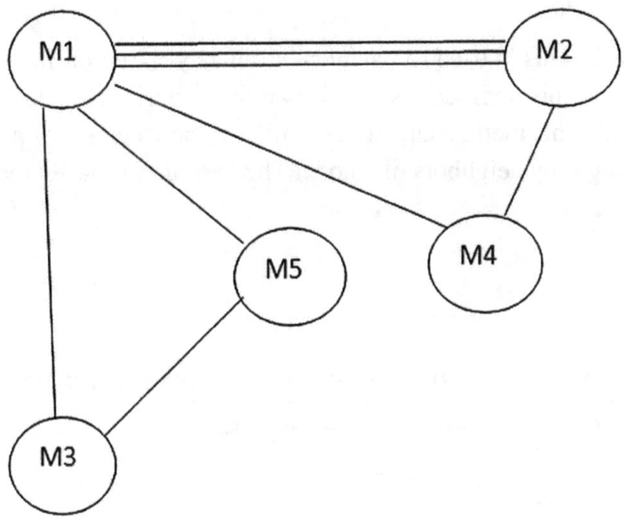

probabilities. (Gimenes, 2014) also works on link cardinality by presenting a methodology based on the use of multiple topological metrics in order to achieve prospective link recommendations considering time constraints which acts as an input to binary classification algorithms that state whether two pairs of authors will/should define a link.

- **Link Type:** It means assignment of different roles to relationship between two nodes as shown in figure 9 where different weights are assigned to different links between nodes M1 and M2 by different users. (Yu, 2014) consider different types of relationships instead of single relationship i.e. friendship as different relationships can be potentially used to improve the recommendation quality. In this paper, the entity recommendation problem is studied in heterogeneous information networks. The heterogeneous relationship information for each user is combined differently and aims to provide high-quality personalized recommendation results using user implicit feedback data and personalized recommendation models.

Link Prediction Approaches

The link prediction problem is usually described as given a set of data instances, which is organized in the form of a social network, where L is the set of observed links and then the task is to predict how likely an unobserved link exists between an arbitrary pair of nodes in the data network.

Link Prediction

Given a snapshot of a social network at time t_i (or network evolution between t_i and t_j) as shown in figure 4 and accurate prediction of the edges is to be done that will be added to the network during the interval from time t_i (as shown in figure 10) to a given future time t_j (as shown in figure 11).

Link prediction approaches have been broadly classified into three categories namely neighborhood based, path based and higher level approaches (AI Hasan, 2011), (Liben-Nowell, 2007) as shown in figure 12.

- **Neighborhood Based:** This is used to calculate similarity based on node's neighbors properties. The main advantage of this approach is that it is quite generic in social networks, so no domain knowledge is required. This method calculates similarity between every pair of nodes in a network rather than considering only neighbors of a node. The various similarity measures are explained as:

Figure 9. Link type

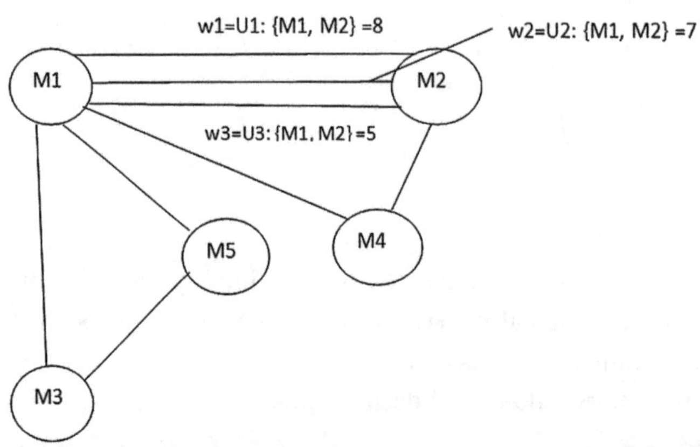

Figure 10. Network at time ti

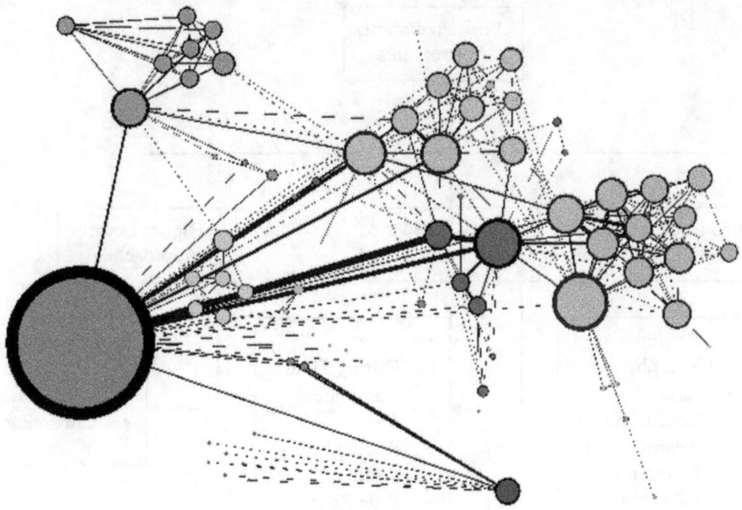

Figure 11. Network at time tj

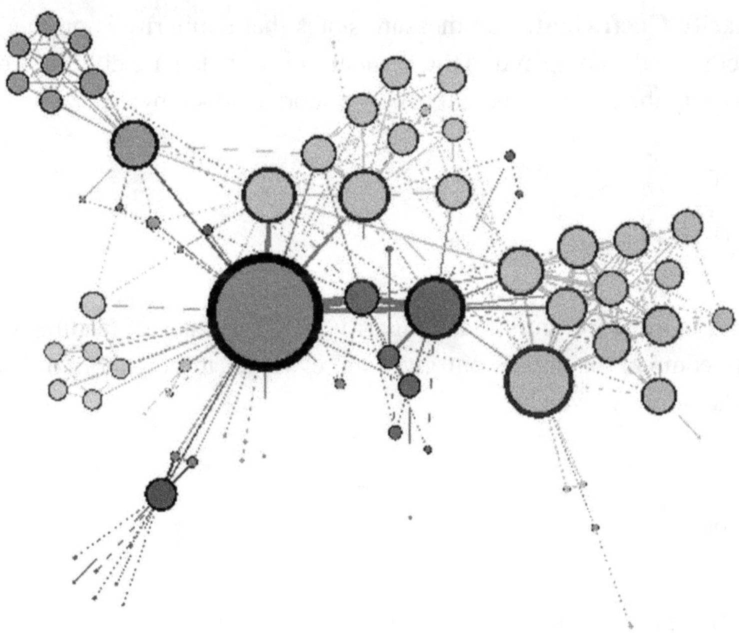

- **Common Neighbors:** The measure states that the number of common neighbors of x and y represent the similar nodes like more are the common neighbors, more the nodes are similar. This method is based on the assumption that two nodes with many common neighbors will be connected in the future. It is mainly used to compare the performance of other methods with this as benchmark. The score is given by:

$$Score\ (\mathrm{x},\ \mathrm{y}) = \left|\tau(x) \cap \tau(y)\right|$$

Figure 12. Link prediction approaches

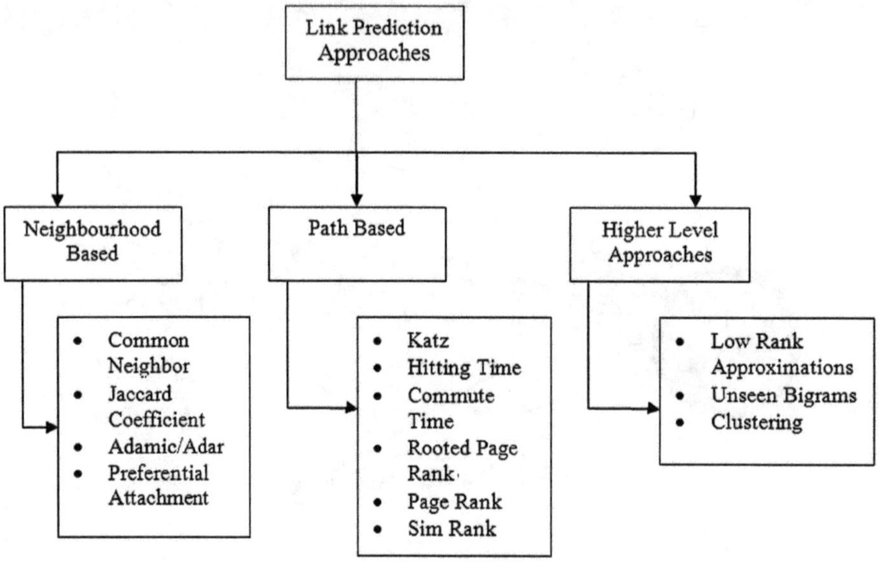

- **Jaccard Similarity Coefficient:** The measure states that similarity is on the basis of number of neighbors of both x and y compared to the number of nodes that are either x's or y's neighbors i.e. rate of common neighbors in their neighbors. The score is given by:

$$Score(x, y) = \frac{|\tau(x) \cap \tau(y)|}{|\tau(x) \cup \tau(y)|}$$

- **Adamic/Adar:** The measure states that similarity is on the basis of features shared by nodes and allows counting common neighbors but gives more weight to neighbors that are not shared with many others. The score is given by:

$$Score(x, y) = \sum \frac{1}{\log|\tau(z)|} \text{ where } z \in (\tau(x) \cap \tau(y))$$

- **Preferential Attachment:** This measure states that similarity is on the basis of item's popularity and to how much extent is the user involved in the system is measured by the product of their degree. The score is given by:

$$Score(x, y) = |\tau(x)|.|\tau(y)|$$

- **Path Based:** In this method similarity is based on shortest path distance as it also influences the formation of links in a social network. The various similarity measures are explained as:

- **Katz:** This method takes path lengths between every pair of nodes; then number of paths between every pair of nodes is calculated with path length l and then multiplied by factor that is used to adjust the weight of path of length l. It measures by summing the weights of all paths between two nodes exponentially. Katz is a prediction method based on the topology of whole network and thus its calculation is more complex than other methods.
- **Hitting Time:** A random walk start at a node u and moves to a neighbor of u say v, chosen randomly. Hitting time measures the number of steps required to move from node u to node v. Lesser is the hitting time, more similar are the nodes.
- **Commute Time:** It is more symmetric form of measuring similarity between nodes than hitting time because hitting time is small whenever v is a node with stationary probability.
- **Rooted Page Rank:** It overcomes the limitation of hitting time as it is able to include only few nodes so rooted page rank has the ability to reset the random walk at node u after specific time with a fixed probability at each step.
- **Page Rank:** It measures similarity between two nodes as the stationary probability of v in a random walk that returns to u with probability $1 - \beta$ in each step, moving to a random neighbor with probability β.
- **Sim Rank:** In this two nodes are similar to the extent that they are joined to similar neighbors.
- **Higher Level Approaches:** These approaches can be used with any of the above methods.
- **Low Rank Approximation:** The adjacency matrix M is used to represent the graph but to simplify the representation low-rank matrix Mk can be generated that best approximates M where k is chosen to be very small. This can be done using Singular Value Decomposition (SVD) method which forms the basis of many information retrieval techniques such as Latent Semantic Analysis.
- **Unseen Bigrams:** It is used to estimate the frequencies for unseen bigrams that appear in test data but not in training data. The score (x, y) can be increased by using the value of score (z, y) where z are the nodes that are similar to x.
- **Clustering:** Clustering is mainly used to improve the prediction performance by deleting the fragile edges and re-computing the score which will result in more accurate prediction of links.

MOVIE RECOMMENDATION USING LINK PREDICTION APPROACH

The initial impetus has been performed to predict links using neighborhood based link prediction approach which is 'Common Neighbor Link Prediction Approach (CNLP)'. The authors' have applied CNLP approach on movie tweets posted through IMDb by users to recommend movies according to rating posted by users to a specific movie. Further, authors' have enhanced CNLP approach and propose a weighted common neighbor link prediction (WCNLP) which includes a weight factor on the basis of rating assigned to movie and recommend accordingly. Finally, authors' perform comparative analysis of results of both the approach (CNLP and WCNLP) which shows improvement and better accuracy in WCNLP approach.

Data-Set Description

The data available through the Twitter platform is enormously abundant. Twitter users post an average of 500 million tweets every day, thereby exchanging opinions, ideas, links, jokes and many other types of information. In this work, author mine rating datasets by filtering and extracting relevant preference indicators contained in these tweets. The authors' avoid dataset ambiguity by focusing on structured tweets originating from the social share feature integrated on many popular online platforms.

Movies – IMDb, the first online platform which focuses on movies. IMDb (Internet Movie Database) is one of the biggest and most popular websites concerning movies. It offers a wide variety of movie content information and lets users' rate movies on a 10-star scale. Although users have the option to make their ratings public but few users actually do this, so individual rating information is usually not accessible (Dooms, 2014). IMDb provides an option to users that they can publicize their provided movie rating on twitter. It proposes a pre-formatted tweet with the following structure.

I rated <Title> <Rating> /10 # IMDB
<Link to IMDB Movie Page>

By querying the Twitter API for the term 'I rated #IMDb' will result in tweets containing movie ratings originating from IMDb. From the tweet the following data fields can be extracted as shown in figure 13:

- User-ID (Twitter User Identifier)
- Movie-ID
- Rating (10-star scale)
- Rating Timestamp
- IMDb URL of the movie: The URL contains the unique IMDb identifier for the movie, which allows easy disambiguation of the movies and furthermore enables extraction of additional meta-data from the movie's IMDb page.

Table 1 shows the statistics of dataset:

The authors' implemented proposed approach on IMDb platform which results in large number of tweets but for consistency of data structured tweets are retained and ratings are collected of different users towards various movies on weekly basis as shown in figure 14.

Common Neighbor Link Prediction

Social networks are highly dynamic and sparse in nature. In social networks like Twitter a user "follows" other users to their tweets. The important way to sustain and grow twitter is to help users to discover the connections. Link Prediction helps in finding that whether the links between nodes can exist or not.

Figure 13. IMDb data format

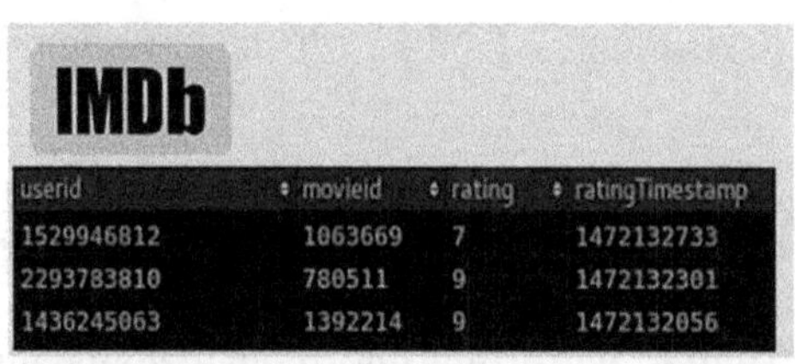

userid	movieId	rating	ratingTimestamp
1529946812	1063669	7	1472132733
2293783810	780511	9	1472132301
1436245063	1392214	9	1472132056

Table 1. IMDb dataset statistics

Metric	Value
Number of Ratings	3909
Number of unique Users	1504
Number of Unique ratings	1006
Min. number of Ratings per user	1
Average Rating	7.29
Max. number of Ratings per user	32
Min. number of Ratings per item	1
Average Rating per item	6.8
Max. number of Ratings per item	25

Figure 14. Collection of ratings from IMDb platform

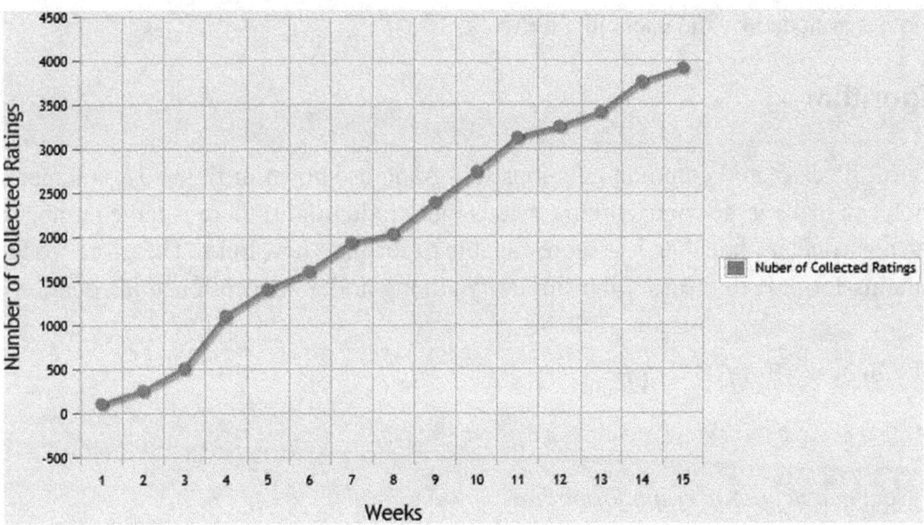

A user may be interested in following other users based on shared interests like they follow many of the users in same profile; common connections like a user interested in movies may follow @stargold and number of other factors but two users are similar if they have similar interest in movies and due to homophily principle (which states that similar users have more tendency to correlate with each other as shown in figure 10) similar users get good suggestions. Thus link prediction algorithms are based on node's features or network information to find the probability of occurrence of links. The algorithm is implemented for the future link suggestion between the users on the basis of the common movies they have watched. In this algorithm, common neighbor metric is implemented by taking common movies watched by a particular user as the common neighbors. The graph formed is a property graphs in which nodes are not of same nature.

Definition

Given a IMDb movie graph G (V, E, X) where V is set of movie and user nodes, E is set of links among nodes which gives complete information about data, X is set of node and structural features such as size, weight etc. For a particular user, links are to be predicted such that movies can be recommended to the users on the basis of common neighbors. The predictive function can be defined as:

$$f:(V,E,X,U)\rightarrow Y$$

where V = {M1, M2, …, Mn} and {U1, U2, …, Un} is set of movie and user nodes; E = { (U1, M1), (U1, M3), (U2, M7)…, (Ui, Mj)} is set of links among nodes; X is set of node and structural features like size, weight etc, U ={ u1, u2, …, un} is set of users in a movie network and Y= {y1, y2,…, yn} is the set of common neighbors out of the list of users U with which the links can be created.

The structure of graph is as shown in figure 15 in which arrow tail depicts pointing to user tweet id and arrow head pointing to movie id. This shows the common neighbor graph formation on the basis of common movies watched by the users in a network.

CNLP Algorithm

The density of the extracted common neighbor sub-graph as shown in figure 15 is larger so nodes in the sub-graph can make large contribution towards link prediction. If there is large number of common neighbors to a particular node then it is more capable of forming new links. Therefore we formulate the score calculating formula to measure the similarity among nodes as mentioned in equation (1):

$$Similarity\_Score=\left\|\left(M_{(ui)}\cap M_{uj}\right)\right\| \tag{1}$$

Figure 15. Common neighbor graph formation

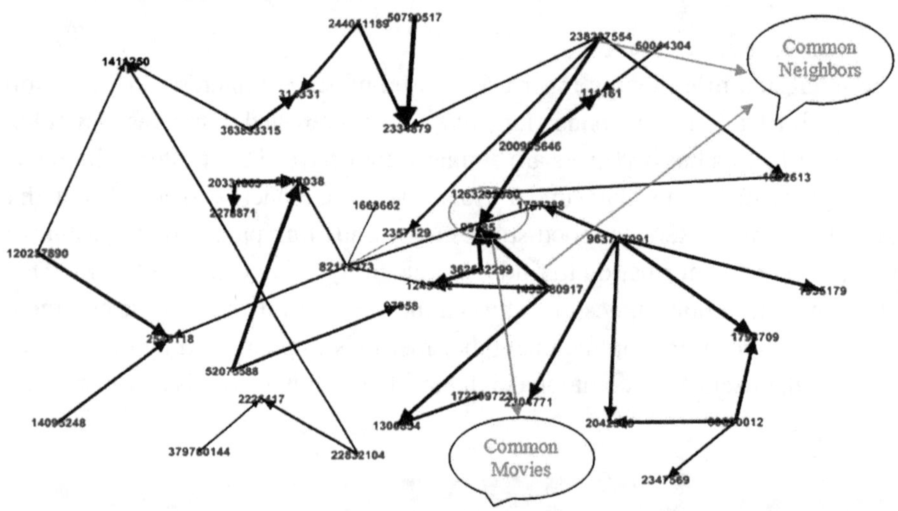

where M (ui) represents the movies rated by a user ui and M(uj) represents the movies rated by a user uj and their intersection gives the common movies.

The similarity score measures the count of number of common movies watched between every node pair. The more is the value of the score more are the chances of formation of links between the users in future.

With this similarity score as measure, the detailed description of CNLP algorithm is given as in table 2.

Weighted Common Neighbor Link Prediction (WCNLP)

By introducing the weight factor in traditional common neighbor approach, enhanced weighted common neighbor link prediction (WCNLP) approach is applied to predict the links on the basis of node's attributes like ratings given by users to movies, number of common movies watched among different users. The reason for assigning weights is to consider neighbor of neighbors too instead of considering only immediate neighbors and to further improve the efficiency of the suggestion for a particular user, a weight measure is included in the above common neighbor formula as mentioned above in equation 1.

Definition

Given a IMDb common neighbor movie graph G (V, E, X) where V is set of common neighbors, E is set of links among nodes which gives complete information about data, X is set of node and structural features such as size, weight etc. For a particular user, links are to be predicted which have more weightage so that more relevant movies can be recommended to the users on the basis of weighted common neighbor link prediction approach. The predictive function can be defined as:

$$f : (V, U, E, X, w) \rightarrow Y$$

where V = {V1, V2, ..., Vn} is set of user nodes; U ={ U1, U2, ..., Un} is set of common neighbors in a user-movie network; E = { (V1, U1), (V1, U10), ..., (Vi, Uj)} is set of links among nodes; X is

Table 2. CNLP algorithm

CNLP Algorithm
Input: IMDb Movie Graph G = (V, E), node u, node v
Output: Similarity of node u and node v
Description
Step 1: Fetch the tweets posted through IMDb platform containing movie ratings by querying twitter API.
Step 2: Form the graph database using Neo4j visualization tool.
Step 3: Find the common neighbor set of the node pair by finding the common movies watched through the formation of two set of nodes and taking pair of users from the first set and matching the common movies from other set.
Step 4: Extract the sub-graph containing tested node-pair and their common neighbors.
Step 5: Repeat step 6 till common neighbor set is not null.
Step 6: Calculate the similarity score between every node pair using equation 1 as mentioned above.

set of node and structural features like size, weight etc, w is a weighting factor assigned on the basis of ratings given to a particular movie and number of common movies watched among node pairs and Y= {y1, y2,..., yn} is the set of weighted common neighbors out of the list of users U with which the links can be created.

The structure of graph is as shown in figure 16 which depicts the weighted common neighbors. This shows the weighted common neighbor graph formation on the basis of rating given by a user compared to its all other common neighbors and then weight is assigned on edges according to rating scale which is explained in next section.

WCNLP Algorithm

The weighting factor is taken as a metric to evaluate the proposed WCNLP approach. The weight, w (u, l) is calculated for each connected relation <u, l> where u is a particular user and l is a link. This measure serves as a degree of possibility for a link to establish between < u, l> for future recommendations. The weighted common neighbor approach is motivated by the idea that if node u has more links with predicted nodes; then more weight will be assigned to node u.

The weight of link, w (l) is formulated as in equation (2):

$$Weight(l) = 1/n\left(\sum Average\ \text{Rating}(M_{(ui)} \cap M_{(uj)})\right) \tag{2}$$

where n is number of common movies i.e. uj)) $\left\| M(u_i) \cap M(u_j) \right\|$.

With this weighting factor as measure, the detailed description of WCNLP algorithm is given as in table 3.

Figure 16. Weighted common neighbor graph formation

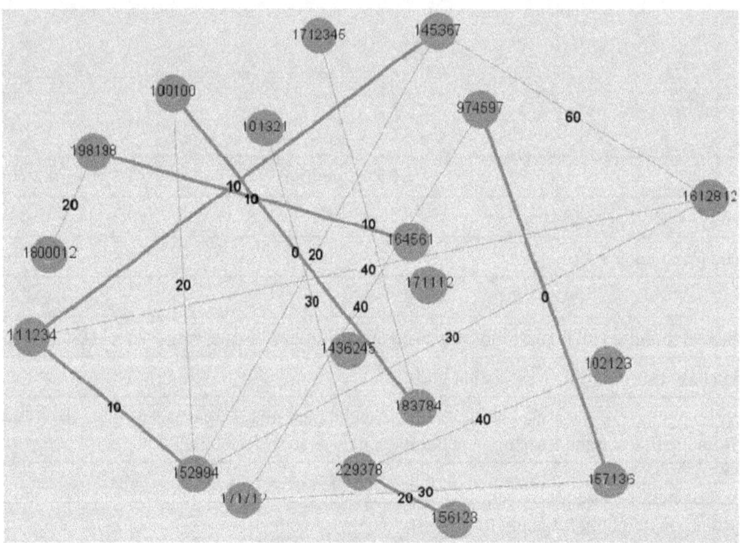

- **Pseudo Code:** The pseudo code of the proposed approach is discussed as in table 4.

The figure 17 shows a graph depicting that weighted common neighbor approach satisfies the homophily principle which states that similar users have more tendency to associate with each other. As shown in figure 17, larger are the number of common neighbors, more is the probability of formation of new links.

EXPERIMENTAL RESULTS

In this experiment, authors' used Twitter-based IMDb-Movie dataset to verify the performance of the proposed weighted common neighbour link prediction approach against common neighbour link prediction approach as benchmark. This data set is real as we fetch tweets corresponding to the IMDb platform for 15 weeks. The algorithm is evaluated by actually implementing it and used Neo4j tool for visualization of graph database. Figure 18 shows the common neighbors of a particular user according to node attributes like common movies watched by a user.

The above graph shows the enlarged view of the resultant graph as shown by the algorithm. The edges represent the rated relationship between the users and movies where nodes towards the headed side of the arrow represent the movie-id and on the tail sides are the user-id. To clearly understand the graph structure, a graph with a closer view is represented in the below figure 19.

Figure 20 shows a graph with less number of nodes to have a clear pictorial representation.

Table 3. WCNLP algorithm

WCNLP Algorithm
Input: Common Neighbor IMDb Movie Graph G = (V, E), node u, node v
Output: Weight Assigned to Links and suggestion of movies
Description
Step 1: Find common neighbors and calculate similarity score among node pairs using equation 1.
Step 2: Extract the sub-graph containing tested node-pair and their common neighbors.
Step 3: Repeat step 4 till common neighbor set is not null.
Step 4: Calculate weight of all connected relations using equation (2) on the basis of rating scale table.
Step 5: If calculated weight > threshold weight *Then retain those node pairs* *Else* *Discard the node pairs* Threshold Weight is calculated as average score of a particular user to all the other users as mentioned in equation (3): $Threshold\ \text{Weight}= avg(Score(U_i)) / Avg(Score(U_i \cap U_j))$ (3)
Step 6: Calculate updated similarity score of node u and node v as: $Updated\_Similarity(u,v) = w(l) * CNLP.Similarity\_Score(u,v)$
Step 7: Recommend movies according to updated similarity score.

Table 4. Pseudo code of proposed WCNLP approach

Input: IMDB Dataset Nodes: User-Id, Movie-Id Links: Rating
Output: Graph, Similarity Score, Recommendation List
Declare: Global Variables: String DBPath // variable to store Neo4j graph database path String User-Id=1, String Movie-Id=2 Data Structures: Array: String [] rating // to store all the data i.e. rating [0] stores rating of first user-id Hash Maps Class: Node, Pair, Score Evaluator

Begin:
//Process1: Initialization
1. Uid← user_id
2. Mid← movie_id
3. Graph_Object← Db path
4. Graph of user and movie nodes is formed and visualized using Neo4j.
//Process2: Compute Node relationships (Edges)
1. Relationship between two node types is stored in hash map with custom nodes.
2. Declare the hash map and variables as:
a. Initialize Source=NULL // node type variable to store source
b. Initialize Destination=NULL // node type variable to store destination
c. String UserId=rating[0]
d. String MovieId=rating[1]
3. IF hashmap contains UserId
Source=UserId
ENDIF
ELSE
Source= userid node from the neo4j graph
Put it in hashmap
END ELSE
4. IF hashmap contains MovieId
Destination=MovieId
END IF
ELSE
Destination = movieid node from the neo4j graph
Put it in hashmap
END ELSE
//Process3: Score Calculation
1. Compute similarity score using CNLP and WCNLP algorithms.

Figure 17. Homophily principle

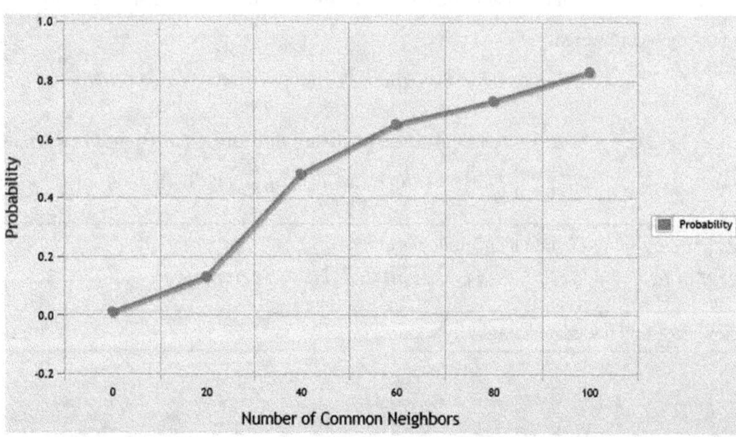

Figure 18. Common neighbor graph formation

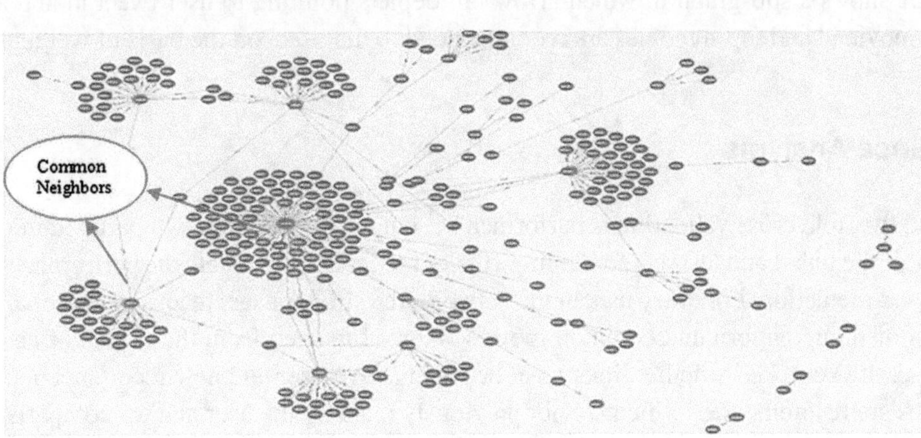

Figure 19. Closer view of common neighbor graph formation

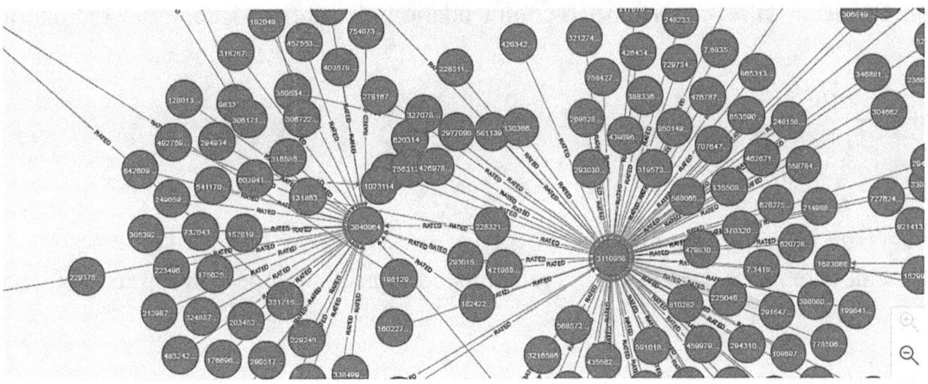

Figure 20. Graph with less number of nodes

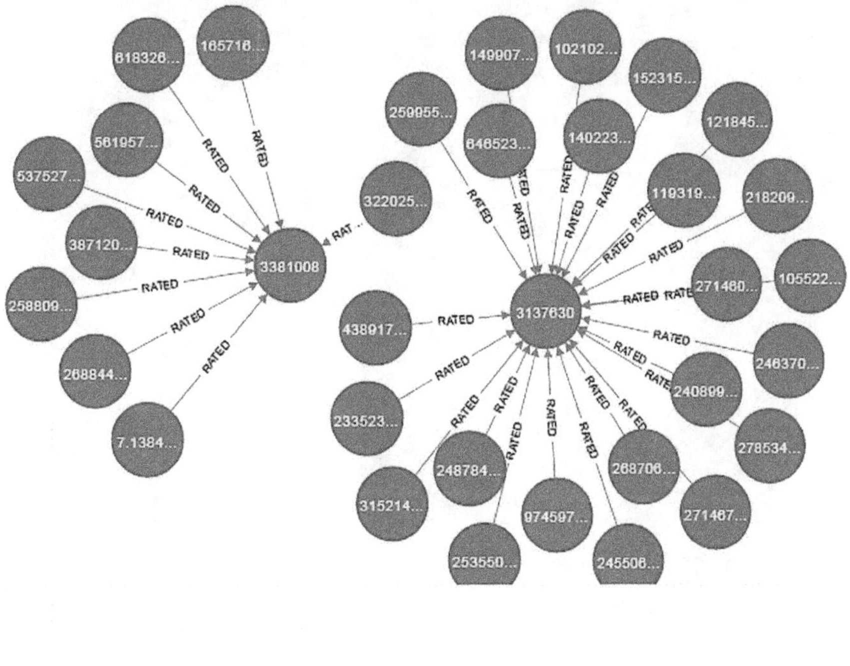

Figure 21 shows a sub-graph in which arrow tail depicts pointing to user tweet id and arrow head pointing to movie id and top-n movies are recommended to the users on the basis of weighted common neighbors.

Performance Analysis

In this work, two-fold cross validation is performed i.e. data is divided into two parts: training set (containing 90% of the links) and test set (containing 10% of the links) to evaluate the performance of recommendation and prediction. For every user in the network, the similar users to an active user are predicted on the basis of rating pattern and common movies watched fetched from the tweets of an active user and in test set, it is checked whether links form between active user and new recommended users. The top-n movies are recommended which are not previously rated by the user and for comparison purpose proposed weighted common neighbor approach (WCNLP) is compared against non-weighted common neighbor approach (CNLP) as benchmark. The performance is evaluated in terms of precision, recall and area under ROC curves (AUC) (Yang, 2015) at different timestamps.

Precision: Precision is the proportion of recommendations that are good recommendations. It is given as:

$$\Pr ecision = \frac{|TP|}{|TP| + |FP|}$$

where TP- True Positives and FP-False Positives

Recall: Recall is the proportion of good recommendations that appear in top recommendations.

Figure 21. Recommendation of movies on the basis of weighted common neighbors

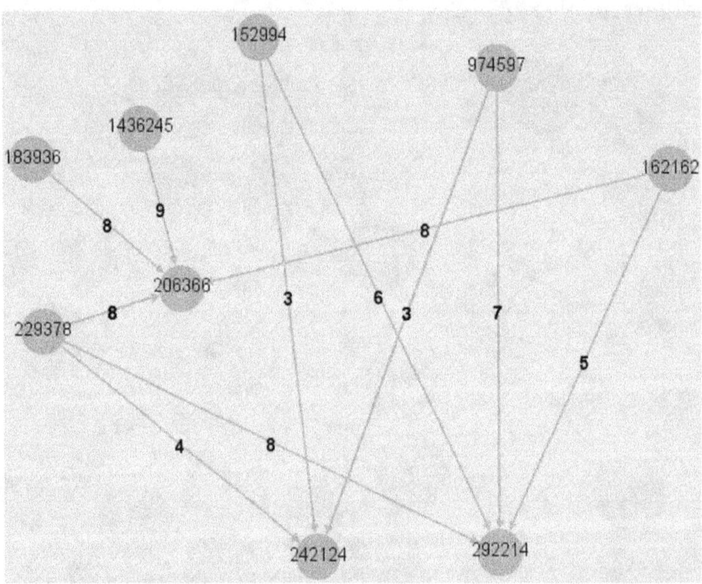

$$\mathrm{Re}\,call = \frac{|TP|}{|TP| + |FN|}$$

where TP- True Positives and FN-False Negatives

AUC: AUC is a scalar measure of performance over all timestamps and is used as a measure of performance in link prediction. The AUC indicators are used to evaluate the experimental results. The AUC index refers to the area under ROC curve. The point in the curve corresponds to the performance of the algorithm under each time-stamp. The greater is the AUC value, more is the performance.

The recommendation quality for each measure is listed below in table 5 and table 6 for CNLP and WCNLP respectively and shown pictorially in Figure 22 and Figure 23. The results indicate that link prediction approaches are useful for local network analysis.

Table 5. Performance analysis of common neighbor link prediction approach

CNLP	t1	t2	t3	t4	t5
Precision	0.05	0.1	0.275	0.481	0.6
Recall	0.1	0.1	0.198	0.35	0.5
AUC	0.1	0.175	0.325	0.496	0.63
Time-Stamp (in Days)	30	60	90	120	150

Figure 22. Performance analysis of common neighbor link prediction

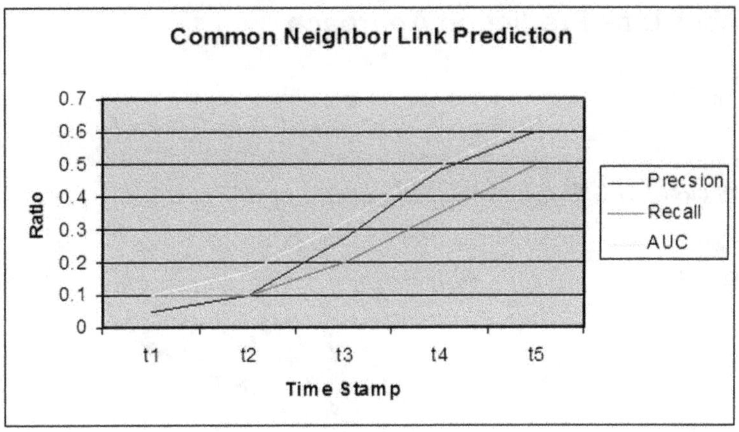

Table 6. Performance analysis of weighted common neighbor link prediction approach

WCNLP	t1	t2	t3	t4	t5
Precision	0.1	0.21	0.327	0.571	0.696
Recall	0.1	0.195	0.293	0.477	0.52
AUC	0.1	0.223	0.398	0.682	0.75
Time-Stamp (in Days)	30	60	90	120	150

Figure 23. Performance analysis of weighted common neighbor link prediction

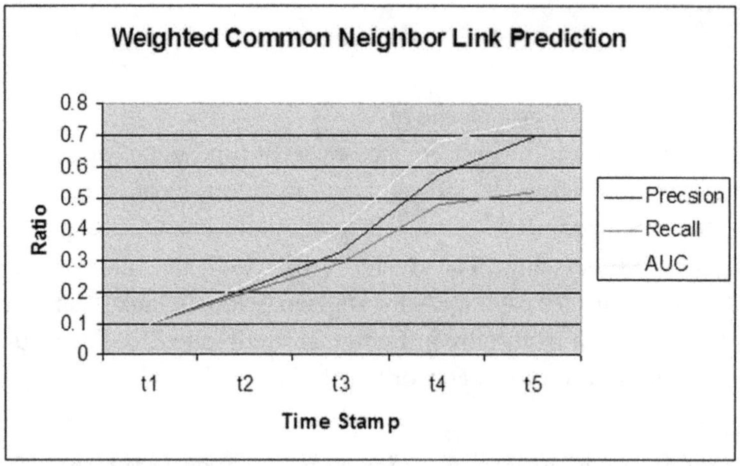

The algorithms take into account the time attribute information and topology information of the network. At different time-stamps, the true positive rate and the false positive rate is calculated respectively. Then the corresponding Precision, Recall and ROC curves are drawn for the common neighbor and weighted common neighbor link prediction approach. It can be seen from Figures 24, 25 and 26 that the prediction performance of weighted common neighbor approach is more than common neighbor link prediction approach.

Comparative Analysis of Common Neighbor and Weighted Common Neighbor Link Prediction Approach

See Figures 24, 25 and 26.

Figure 24. Precision curve of CNLP and WCNLP

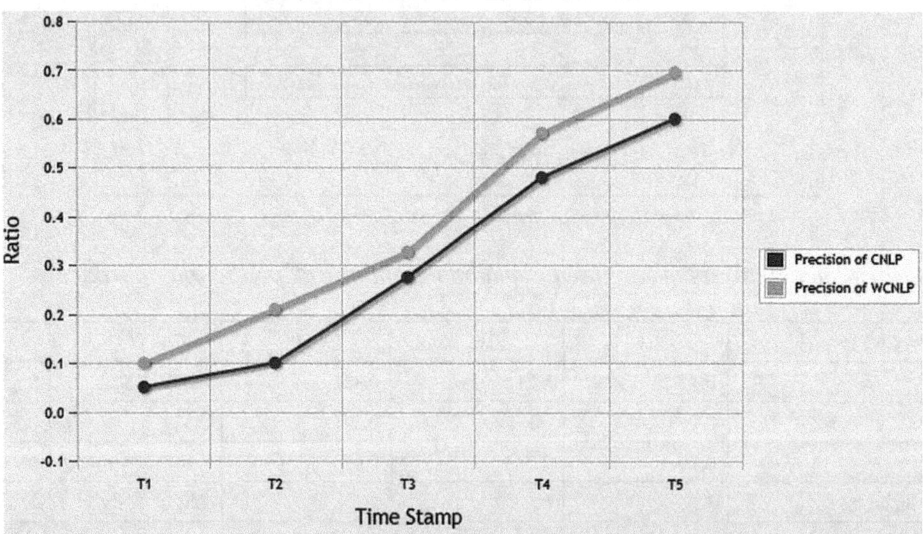

Figure 25. Recall curve of CNLP and WCNLP

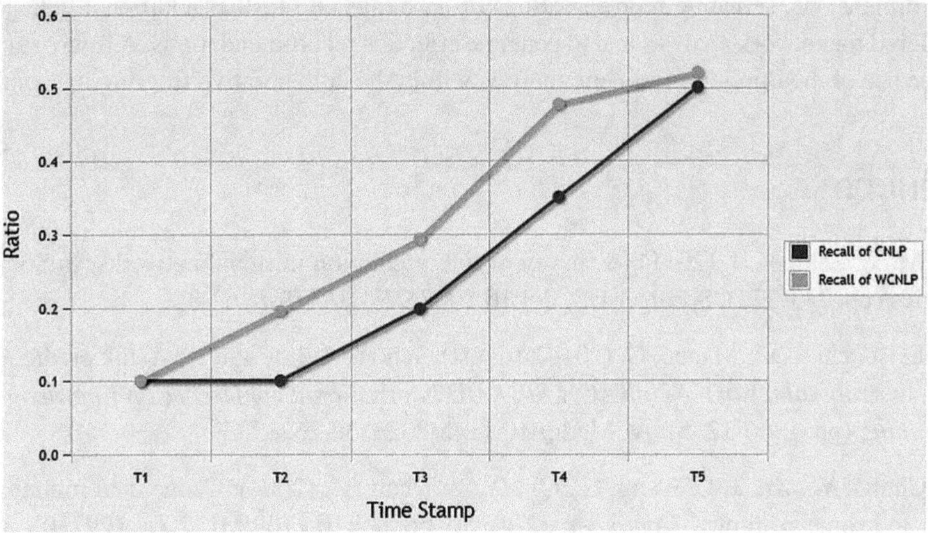

Figure 26. AUC curve of CNLP and WCNLP

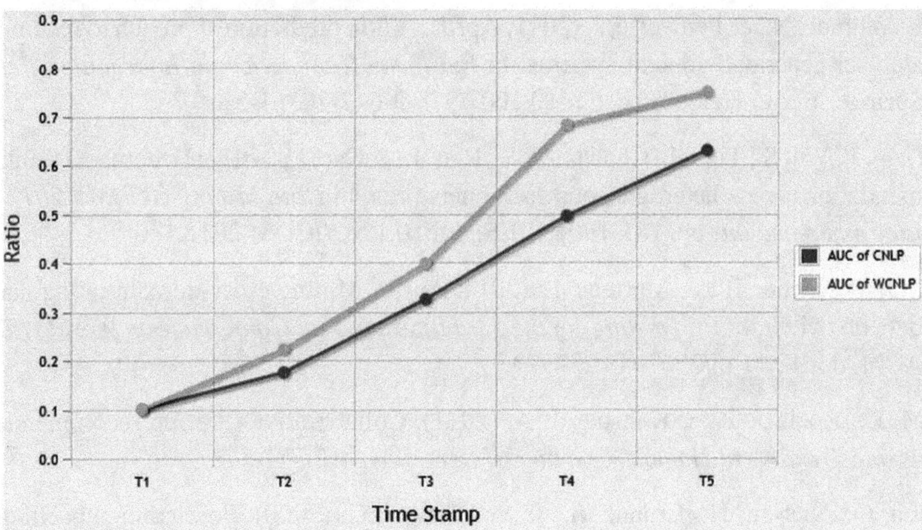

CONCLUSION

In this chapter, the authors have described a movies recommender system for tweet-based IMDb platform. Firstly the concept of link prediction, its importance and its approaches have been discussed. The authors work emphasizes the use of link prediction to improve the performance of the recommendation process. The authors have defined a novel weighting function that takes into account common movies and user interests. This technique allowed building more complete user profiles than traditional content-based approaches. The experimental results show that the proposed approach significantly improves the prediction performance by comparing it with non-weighted common neighbor approach In future, some other contextual dimensions, semantic representations of hash tags and further additional linkage measures can be explored for network analysis and to generate effective recommendations. A future study will also focus on the use of the implicit sentiment analysis within the collaborative filtering in social networks.

REFERENCES

Al Hasan, M., & Zaki, M. J. (2011). A survey of link prediction in social networks. In Social network data analytics (pp. 243-275). Springer US. doi:10.1007/978-1-4419-8462-3_9

Barbieri, N., Bonchi, F., & Manco, G. (2014, August). Who to follow and why: link prediction with explanations. In *Proceedings of the 20th ACM SIGKDD international conference on Knowledge discovery and data mining* (pp. 1266-1275). ACM. doi:10.1145/2623330.2623733

Chen, H., Chung, W., Xu, J. J., Wang, G., Qin, Y., & Chau, M. (2004). Crime data mining: A general framework and some examples. *Computer*, *37*(4), 50–56. doi:10.1109/MC.2004.1297301

Chen, H., Li, X., & Huang, Z. (2005, June). Link prediction approach to collaborative filtering. In *Digital Libraries, 2005. JCDL'05. Proceedings of the 5th ACM/IEEE-CS Joint Conference on* (pp. 141-142). IEEE.

Chiluka, N., Andrade, N., & Pouwelse, J. (2011, April). A link prediction approach to recommendations in large-scale user-generated content systems. In *European Conference on Information Retrieval* (pp. 189-200). Springer Berlin Heidelberg. doi:10.1007/978-3-642-20161-5_19

Dong, Y., Tang, J., Wu, S., Tian, J., Chawla, N. V., Rao, J., & Cao, H. (2012, December). Link prediction and recommendation across heterogeneous social networks. In *Data Mining (ICDM), 2012 IEEE 12th International Conference on* (pp. 181-190). IEEE. doi:10.1109/ICDM.2012.140

Dooms, S., De Pessemier, T., & Martens, L. (2014, April). Mining cross-domain rating datasets from structured data on twitter. In *Proceedings of the 23rd International Conference on World Wide Web* (pp. 621-624). ACM. doi:10.1145/2567948.2579232

Ekstrand, M. D., Riedl, J. T., & Konstan, J. A. (2011). Collaborative filtering recommender systems. *Foundations and Trends® in Human–Computer Interaction, 4*(2), 81-173.

Emanuelsson, O., Nielsen, H., Brunak, S., & Von Heijne, G. (2000). Predicting subcellular localization of proteins based on their N-terminal amino acid sequence. *Journal of Molecular Biology*, *300*(4), 1005–1016. doi:10.1006/jmbi.2000.3903 PMID:10891285

Gimenes, G. P., Gualdron, H., Raddo, T. R., & Rodrigues, J. F. (2014, March). Supervised-learning link recommendation in the DBLP co-authoring network. In *Pervasive Computing and Communications Workshops (PERCOM Workshops), 2014 IEEE International Conference on* (pp. 563-568). IEEE. doi:10.1109/PerComW.2014.6815268

Guns, R., & Rousseau, R. (2014). Recommending research collaborations using link prediction and random forest classifiers. *Scientometrics*, *101*(2), 1461–1473. doi:10.1007/s11192-013-1228-9

Hammond, S. M., Boettcher, S., Caudy, A. A., Kobayashi, R., & Hannon, G. J. (2001). Argonaute2, a link between genetic and biochemical analyses of RNAi. *Science, 293*(5532), 1146–1150. doi:10.1126/science.1064023 PMID:11498593

Hannon, J., Bennett, M., & Smyth, B. (2010, September). Recommending twitter users to follow using content and collaborative filtering approaches. In *Proceedings of the fourth ACM conference on Recommender systems* (pp. 199-206). ACM. doi:10.1145/1864708.1864746

Huang, Z., & Lin, D. K. (2009). The time-series link prediction problem with applications in communication surveillance. *INFORMS Journal on Computing, 21*(2), 286–303. doi:10.1287/ijoc.1080.0292

Li, X., & Chen, H. (2013). Recommendation as link prediction in bipartite graphs: A graph kernel-based machine learning approach. *Decision Support Systems, 54*(2), 880–890. doi:10.1016/j.dss.2012.09.019

Li, Z., Fang, X., Bai, X., & Sheng, O. R. L. (2016). Utility-based Link Recommendation for Online Social Networks. *Management Science*.

Liben-Nowell, D., & Kleinberg, J. (2007). The link-prediction problem for social networks. *Journal of the Association for Information Science and Technology, 58*(7), 1019-1031.

Link, A. J., Robison, K., & Church, G. M. (1997). Comparing the predicted and observed properties of proteins encoded in the genome of Escherichia coli K-12. *Electrophoresis, 18*(8), 1259–1313. doi:10.1002/elps.1150180807 PMID:9298646

Liu, W., & Lü, L. (2010). Link prediction based on local random walk. *EPL, 89*(5), 58007. doi:10.1209/0295-5075/89/58007

Lü, L., & Zhou, T. (2011). Link prediction in complex networks: A survey. *Physica A, 390*(6), 1150–1170. doi:10.1016/j.physa.2010.11.027

Marcotte, E. M., Pellegrini, M., Thompson, M. J., Yeates, T. O., & Eisenberg, D. (1999). A combined algorithm for genome-wide prediction of protein function. *Nature, 402*(6757), 83–86. doi:10.1038/47048 PMID:10573421

Rossetti, G., Berlingerio, M., & Giannotti, F. (2011, December). Scalable link prediction on multidimensional networks. In *Data Mining Workshops (ICDMW), 2011 IEEE 11th International Conference on* (pp. 979-986). IEEE. doi:10.1109/ICDMW.2011.150

Roy, A., Kucukural, A., & Zhang, Y. (2010). I-TASSER: A unified platform for automated protein structure and function prediction. *Nature Protocols, 5*(4), 725–738. doi:10.1038/nprot.2010.5 PMID:20360767

Scellato, S., Noulas, A., & Mascolo, C. (2011, August). Exploiting place features in link prediction on location-based social networks. In *Proceedings of the 17th ACM SIGKDD international conference on Knowledge discovery and data mining* (pp. 1046-1054). ACM. doi:10.1145/2020408.2020575

Setubal, J. C., Meidanis, J., & Setubal-Meidanis. (1997). *Introduction to computational molecular biology*. PWS Pub.

Singh, A. P., & Gordon, G. J. (2008, August). Relational learning via collective matrix factorization. In *Proceedings of the 14th ACM SIGKDD international conference on Knowledge discovery and data mining* (pp. 650-658). ACM. doi:10.1145/1401890.1401969

Smith, L. J., Bolin, K. A., Schwalbe, H., MacArthur, M. W., Thornton, J. M., & Dobson, C. M. (1996). Analysis of main chain torsion angles in proteins: Prediction of NMR coupling constants for native and random coil conformations. *Journal of Molecular Biology*, *255*(3), 494–506. doi:10.1006/jmbi.1996.0041 PMID:8568893

Stamenkovic, I., Amiot, M., Pesando, J. M., & Seed, B. (1989). A lymphocyte molecule implicated in lymph node homing is a member of the cartilage link protein family. *Cell*, *56*(6), 1057–1062. doi:10.1016/0092-8674(89)90638-7 PMID:2466575

Tang, J., Chang, S., Aggarwal, C., & Liu, H. (2015, February). Negative link prediction in social media. In *Proceedings of the Eighth ACM International Conference on Web Search and Data Mining* (pp. 87-96). ACM. doi:10.1145/2684822.2685295

Wang, P., Xu, B., Wu, Y., & Zhou, X. (2015). Link prediction in social networks: The state-of-the-art. *Science China. Information Sciences*, *58*(1), 1–38.

Yang, J., Yang, L., & Zhang, P. (2015, June). A New Link Prediction Algorithm Based on Local Links. In *International Conference on Web-Age Information Management* (pp. 16-28). Springer International Publishing. doi:10.1007/978-3-319-23531-8_2

Yang, Y., Lichtenwalter, R. N., & Chawla, N. V. (2015). Evaluating link prediction methods. *Knowledge and Information Systems*, *45*(3), 751–782. doi:10.1007/s10115-014-0789-0

Yu, K., Chu, W., Yu, S., Tresp, V., & Xu, Z. (2007). Stochastic relational models for discriminative link prediction. In Advances in neural information processing systems (pp. 1553-1560). Academic Press.

Yu, X., Gu, Q., Zhou, M., & Han, J. (2012, April). Citation prediction in heterogeneous bibliographic networks. In *Proceedings of the 2012 SIAM International Conference on Data Mining* (pp. 1119-1130). Society for Industrial and Applied Mathematics. doi:10.1137/1.9781611972825.96

Yu, X., Ren, X., Sun, Y., Gu, Q., Sturt, B., Khandelwal, U., & Han, J. et al. (2014, February). Personalized entity recommendation: A heterogeneous information network approach. In *Proceedings of the 7th ACM international conference on Web search and data mining* (pp. 283-292). ACM. doi:10.1145/2556195.2556259

Zhang, Y. C., Medo, M., Ren, J., Zhou, T., Li, T., & Yang, F. (2007). Recommendation model based on opinion diffusion. *EPL*, *80*(6), 68003. doi:10.1209/0295-5075/80/68003

Zuker, M., Mathews, D. H., & Turner, D. H. (1999). Algorithms and thermodynamics for RNA secondary structure prediction: a practical guide. In *RNA biochemistry and biotechnology* (pp. 11–43). Springer Netherlands. doi:10.1007/978-94-011-4485-8_2

Chapter 12
Knowledge Discovery Using Data Stream Mining: An Analytical Approach

Prasanna Lakshmi Kompalli
Gokaraju Rangaraju Institute of Engineering and Technology, India

ABSTRACT

In recent years, advancement in technologies has made it possible for most of the present-day organizations to store and record large streams of data. Such data sets, which continuously and rapidly grow over time, are referred to as data streams. Mining of such data streams is a unique opportunity and also a challenging task. Data stream mining is a process of gaining knowledge from continuous and rapid records of data. Due to increased streaming information, data stream mining has attracted the research community in the recent past. There is voluminous literature that has been published in this domain over the past few years. Due to this, isolating the correct study would be grueling task for researchers and practitioners. While addressing a real-world problem, it would be difficult to find relevant information as it would be hidden in data streams. This chapter tries to provide solution as it is an amalgamation of all techniques used for data stream mining.

INTRODUCTION

Innovation in IT has given birth to huge amounts of data. Day to day activities like credit card transactions, web browsing, mobile usage, network traffic also generate huge amount of flowing data. Streams of data so produced contains valuable information. This information can be used in decision making, development of better quality products, finding new relations among existing items etc. As it is not conceivable to manually study all the data, automated techniques must be developed with good computational power for finding valuable and relevant information.

Data Mining deals with design of algorithms that help computers to identify valid and useful patterns, take quick and clever decisions based on empirical data. Data mining approaches work well with large amounts of static data stored in system but does not address the problem of continuously flowing data.

DOI: 10.4018/978-1-5225-5097-6.ch012

Usually, a model created from training data of *i* instances using data mining cannot be updated with the newly arriving data. For every newly arriving $(i+1)^{th}$ instance of data the whole training process must be repeated. So data mining techniques will be inefficient for addressing the problem of streams of flowing data. Mining data streams for gaining knowledge is a progressive discipline. The difference between Data mining and Data Stream Mining is illustrated in Table 1.

Data Stream mining is an archetype addresses the issues related to continuously arriving data. Handling and processing data steams require single examination of data, fast processing with minimum space utilization, availability of results on the request of user (K.Prasanna, 2015).

This chapter introduces the methodology and constraints of data stream mining, algorithms developed by well-known researchers. Processing streaming data also needs summarization. Several summarizing techniques used with streaming data are also discussed. It is hoped that the chapter will greatly help and provide a reference to researchers, practitioners and students interested in the emerging domain of data streams.

BACKGROUND

Studying and formulating new techniques for data stream mining is a challenge encountered by researchers. In data streams data arrives like a stream and if not processed immediately it will be lost forever. Furthermore, assumption is made that data arrives rapidly so it is not practical to store this data in active storage media for longer period of time.

As technology has advanced the methods of collecting data continuously have been simplified. Extraction of knowledge from data streams is becoming a key task for several researchers (K.Prasanna, 2010). Mining data streams have multitudinous applications with many daunting research issues. Archetypal applications include monitoring of network, web mining, public health surveillance, telecommunication, and financial transactions etc., all these applications are characterized by mining data streams to discover knowledge, which are crucial for strategic decisions. As the entire data stream will not be available at once, processing needs a sequential strategy. The algorithms designed for working with data streams must sometime deal with data sizes which exceed the main memory of system. New methodologies are designed by extending the existing techniques of data mining by including the constraints posed by data streams. Before proceeding to further discussion, a study of the features related to data streams is presented.

Table 1. Differences between Data Mining and Data Stream Mining

Criteria	Data Mining	Data Stream Mining
Number of iterations	Multiple	Single
Processing Time	Limitless	Restricted
Memory Used	Limitless	Restricted
Access	Random	Sequential
Data	Persistent	Transient

Features of Data Streams

The following features act as constraints over a model built for working with streaming data.

1. Voluminous data arrives continuously and rapidly. Hence not feasible to store it completely. Concise summary generated by modelling data streams can be stored.
2. Streams arrive fast, so each stream must be processed and discarded within limited amount of time.
3. Streams may change over time. Some applications like fraud detection may need complete knowledge gained from the beginning of data stream and some other applications like sensor data stream may need only current knowledge of data streams. Thus, past knowledge gained may be relevant or may be irrelevant based on the application.

Constraints presented in 1 and 2 features limit the processing time of streaming algorithm. Intense research is being carried out for developing algorithms which take minimal amount of time for processing each data element. 3 feature presents a constraint, for which data stream mining algorithms must sometimes work with recent data and some other time must work with whole data (K.Prasanna, 2015), (Odysseas et al., 2015).

Research Issues

The main research issues to be addressed while developing an efficient and operative data stream mining algorithms are as follows:

1. **Improved Performance:** Generation of appropriate methodologies to provide accurate results by balancing the time complexities and quality of mining. (K.Prasanna, 2015).
2. **Computation With less Time Complexity:** Data stream mining process must be completed with minimum time complexity as permitted by application. (Yang et al., 2016).
3. **Working With Unknown data Streams:** Proposed techniques must be estimated not only on real datasets but also on synthetic datasets. Algorithms so developed must capture unseen data structures from data streams which are evolving in nature. (K.Prasanna, 2010)
4. **Concept Drift:** This occurs when the concept of the data changes over time. In order to address concept-drift, a data stream model must continuously adapt itself to the most recent concept. (Mohammad M Masud et al., 2011)
5. **Concept Evolution:** This occurs when arriving streams flows in with a new concept. Concept evolution can be addressed when the data stream model automatically detects the new concept when they appear in data streams. (Masud et al., 2013)

The following section explicates the concepts related to selection of data from data streams and methodologies used to process them.

DATA SUMMARIZATION TECHNIQUES

In data streams data selection mostly depends on statistical and computational approaches. These approaches usually work with examining and analyzing a subset of complete data or transforming the whole data to a representation with an estimated smaller size. This process is called data summarization. It is an important area of study due to evolving nature of data streams, which pose constraints on resources. Summarization always helps in mining with accurate results. There are wide variety of summarization techniques. The strategy of selecting a particular summarization technique depends on the type of problem to be solved. Applicability of these structures over data streams must even sort the constraints of space and time complexities. These techniques can be divided into summarization based on data and summarization based on task. Summarization based on data is called as data reduction techniques which employ stream filtering with the help of sampling, load shedding and sketching. It even includes synopsis construction techniques. Data reduction techniques help by selecting a subset of incoming data stream to be analyzed. Summarization based on task are the methods used for addressing computational challenges by modifying the existing techniques or by designing new methodologies. Task based techniques include windowing, approximation and granularity techniques.

Summarization Based on Data

Random Sampling

Sampling is one of the oldest technique which makes probabilistic choice of data for processing. It provides an unbiased estimate of data.

Definition: Simple random sampling is a sampling design in which *k* distinct items are selected from the *n* items in the population in such a way that every possible combination of *k* items is equally likely to be the sample selected (Thompson et al., 2012).

Random sampling works well with applications with multi-dimensional data. Selection of the sample along with its bounds can be done using probabilistic approaches. These approaches use inequalities like Markov inequality, Chebyshev inequality, Chernoff bound, Hoeffding bound (Charu C Aggarwal et al., 2007).

In probability, Markov's inequality provides an upper bound for the random variable *X*. For any $a > 0$, it can be succinctly shown using mathematical notation as

$$P(X \geq a) \leq \frac{\mu}{a} \tag{1}$$

Where μ is expectation of probability distribution.

Markov inequality is a large deviation bound. Applying this on a random variable $(X-\mu)^2 / \sigma^2$ generates an inequality called Chebyshev inequality which is noted as

$$P(| X - \mu |> a) \le \frac{\sigma^2}{a^2} \tag{2}$$

Where σ is variance.

Chernoff bounds are tighter than Markov's and Chebyshev bounds. The basic requirement of Chernoff bound is that the variables with which it works must be independent. It contains lower as well as upper tail bounds which are as follows

$$P(X < (1 - \delta)\mu) \le e^{-\mu\delta^2/2} \tag{3}$$

$$P(X > (1 + \delta)\mu) \le \max\{2^{-\delta\mu}, e^{-\mu\delta^2/4}\} \tag{4}$$

Another important inequality which is more general than Chernoff bound is Heoffding inequality. This inequality is very widely used in applications related to classification and query estimation (Domingos.P et al., 2000). Hoeffding inequality bounds the sum of k independent random variables. Let X be the sum of k independent random variables and for any $\delta > 0$, then according to hoeffding bound X must satisfy:

$$P(| X - \mu) |> \delta) \le 2e^{-2k^*\delta^2/(r)^2} \tag{5}$$

Data selection using sampling techniques can reduce data size dramatically by providing probabilistic error bound using the above inequalities. These fail to work properly for applications which include outliers. So they cannot be applied directly to anomalous detection applications. Sampling over data streams cannot have fixed or predefined size of sample as the size of streams is unknown. At the same time the probability of including a data point in the random sample cannot be fixed in advance, it varies as data stream progresses. To handle such type of streams, reservoir based sampling, concise sampling methods are applied.

Reservoir Sampling

Reservoir sampling is an archetypal algorithm for maintaining an online random sample. It randomly choosing a sample of k items called a reservoir from a list S containing n items, where n is either a very large or unknown number. The probability of replacing an old data item with new data item is always k/n. The algorithm used for working with reservoir sampling is presented below (Jeffrey Vitter et al., 1985).

ReservoirSample(S[1..n], R[1..k])

for i = 1 to k

R[i]:= S[i]

```
for i = k+1 to n

j:= random(1, i)

if j <= k

R[j]:= S[i]
```

The algorithm creates an array and stores first *k* items from total *S* items. This array was named as "reservoir". The next step revolves through remaining elements of *S* till the last element of *S*. At i^{th} element, a random number between *1* and *i* is generated dynamically called *j*. If this *j* is less than or equal to *k* then j^{th} element is replaced with i^{th} element of *S*. Reservoir sampling algorithm takes *O(n)* as time complexity. This methodology suits very well for multi-dimensional sampling.

Concise Sampling

For single dimensional applications concise sampling is more effective. Concise sampling helps by increasing the sample size in the available limited memory. Concise sampling works with the fact that the size of data stream is much bigger when compared to the number of distinct values of an attribute. The size of sample will be increased based on repeated occurrence of same value.

Definition: A concise sample is a uniform random sample of data stream such that values appearing for the first time are stored as singleton and appearing more than once in a sample are represented as <value,count>

The number of elements in concise sampling are represented as footprint. This footprint value must be always less than or equal to sample size. As the data arrives in data stream, it will be added to the sample with a probability of *1/p* where *p* is threshold parameter which defines the probability of successive sampling of stream. If arrived data is already existing in sample then its count is incremented, otherwise inserted as a singleton which will increase the value of footprint. This increase may require the removal of an element from the concise sample *S*.

Load Shedding

Load shedding refers to removing a batch of sequence of elements from data streams without processing them for reducing the system load. This is required at times where the accuracy of solving a query drops. Algorithms must be designed properly to determine at what area of query solution the load shedding must be performed and what amount of load must be shed in order to maximize the accuracy of query answers. Load shedding operation is performed by operators called load shedders. This summarization technique also has similar problems as sampling. Applications related to time series analysis must be designed without load shedding as it may remove batch of data streams that might represent a pattern of interest. This technique is best when applied on aggregate queries of data stream flowing through windows (B. Babcock et al., 2003). Applications involving continuous monitoring of data streams must even apply load shedding.

The load shedder operator used for removing unwanted stream of data must be run throughout the flow of data stream. Periodically, existing load must be measured and compared with system capacity. If the load is found to be more than the capacity then the load must be shed by activating the stream removal methodology in query. If the load is found to be less than the capacity then stream removal methodology must be deactivated. Therefore, load shedding approach must have methods for activating and deactivating load shedders as part of design based on current load due to changing data stream arrival rates.

Sketching

Sketching (Babcock et al. 2002), is a process which involves summarization of stream of data in a concise and small amount of memory. The main strength of sketching is its simplest and fastest update procedures. This technique is generally used for comparing various streams and in applications which need aggregation of queries. It is a single pass methodology which works with vertical sampling of data streams. It summarizes the data points of data streams into a small random variables using random functions. Sketching if generalized can provide approximate answers to complex and aggregate queries (Dobra et al., 2002). Applications build for distributed computation on multiple streams works well with sketching technique. Main drawback of sketching is the computational accuracy.

Synopsis

Synopsis data structures is another methodology for holding summarized information over streams. They are based on idea of using small space and providing approximate solution to huge data streams. Query estimation is the most widely used applications of synopses structures (Garofalakis et al., 2016). Complexities calculated cannot be $O(N)$ where N can be space/time cost per element to solve a problem. Some solution which gives results closer to $O(poly(logN))$ are needed. Synopsis data structures are developed which use much smaller space of order $O(log^k N)$(K.Prasanna, 2010). Synopsis structures are constructed using a number of techniques which are briefly discussed

Histograms

Histograms are widely used for capturing distribution of data. Arriving data streams are represented in the form of relations. Data is divided into one or more attributes of a relation by grouping attribute values. This attribute data is maintained in "buckets" along with count for each bucket. Space required for histogram is defined by number of buckets used for storing data. Histograms are comparatively simple for applications with query estimation. Solutions need to examine only the set of buckets. Main concern in histograms usage is the distribution of data in buckets. The distribution is assumed to be uniform as it is not retained. This drops the accuracy of processing through histograms for the estimation at the query boundaries. Applications working with histograms must have a proper design for buckets. As an illustration, if data points are disseminated unevenly through different buckets and if such buckets contain range boundary of a query then it may lead to inaccurate estimations of queries. Sometimes, this inaccuracy can be maximized to twice the count in any bucket. Solution to such cases can be shown using V-optimal histograms which states that the bucket boundaries must be minimizing the cumulative weighted variance of buckets. Time complexity needed for the work will be $O(n^2k)$ and space complexity will be $O(n)$, where k is number of buckets.

Wavelets

Hierarchical data decomposition and summarization use the well-known technique called wavelets. In this technique the data characteristics are decomposed into set of wavelet functions and basic functions. They provide multi resolution view of data so will be versatile for using it with more than one dimension. Wavelets are mathematical tool used in signal and image processing applications. Haar wavelets have emerged to provide effective solution to data reduction.(Dobra et al., 2016). The rule of wavelet method is that broad trends of data can be found using high order coefficients and lower order coefficients provide localized trends present in data. Efficiency of processing with wavelets raises due to reduced representation of data. As a result, the accuracy also increases since the small coefficients are discarded.

Micro-Clusters

It is a method of maintaining statistical information about the data locality. This technique works well with evolving data streams. Micro clustering is a density based clustering. The data structures which can be used for summarizing stream using micro-clusters are presented below.

- **Feature Vector:** BIRCH algorithm (Zhang et al, 1997) was the first algorithm which used this feature vector. Zhang named it as clustering feature (CF) which had three components: Number of data objects *N*, linear sum of data objects *LS* and sum of squared data objects *SS*. Zhang computed cluster mean using these three components. The equations used for this job are

$$centroid = \frac{LS}{N} \tag{6}$$

$$radius = \sqrt{\left(\frac{SS}{N} - \left(\frac{LS}{N}\right)^2\right)} \tag{7}$$

$$diameter = \sqrt{\left(\frac{2N * SS - 2 * LS^2}{N\left(N-1\right)}\right)} \tag{8}$$

As the data arrives CF vector values are computed and the closest micro-cluster is selected to absorb it otherwise a new micro-cluster is created. The nearness between new object and cluster is found using Euclidean distance.

- **Prototype Array:** This structure was used in Stream (Guha in 2000) which used an array of prototypes by splitting the arriving data stream into a chunk of size *m* which is N^{ε}, $0 < \varepsilon < 1$. Using k-medoids algorithm, each chunk of *m* objects is summarized in *2k* representative objects. The process of reducing the description of data objects is done recursively till an array of *m* prototypes is obtained.

- **Coreset Tree:** This summarized structure is a binary tree where each node contains components like E_i set of objects, x^{pi} a prototype of E_i, N_i number of objects in E_i and SSE_i sum of squared distances of objects in E_i. This was employed in StreamKM++ (Ackermann et al, 2012). This tree reduces the objects to half of its count. All these components are used in the construction of the tree. The steps involved in the construction are as follows. Firstly, the tree has a root node *t*, which includes all *2m* objects from E_t. x^{pt} is chosen randomly from E_t and $N_t=2m$. Next, as the tree is binary tree, 2 child nodes are created t_1 and t_2. An object that is very far from x^{pt} is selected using probability proportional called *P*. An object with highest *P* is selected namely x^{qt}. Equation for *P* is as follows

$$P = \frac{Dist(x^{j_t}, x^{p_t})^2}{SSE_t}, \forall x^{j_t} \in E_t \tag{9}$$

The next step is generation of E_{t1} and E_{t2} from E_t using

$$E_{t1} = \left\{ x^{it} \in E_t \mid Dist(x^{it}, x^{pt}) < Dist(x^{it}, x^{qt}) \right\} \tag{10}$$

$$E_{t2} = \frac{E_t}{E_{t1}} \tag{11}$$

This data of t_1 child is updated as $x^{pt1} = x^{pt}$, $N_{t1} = |E_{t1}|$ and the data of t_2 child is updated as $x^{pt2} = x^{qt}$. When the tree grows in size then a decision about which child to expand first must be taken. Selection of a child for expansion is done by traversing from root node with probability proportional to $\frac{SSE_{child}}{SSE_{parent}}$. This expansion is stopped when the number of leaf nodes reach to *m*.

Summarization Based on Task

Task based summarization techniques use some standard modifications in the designed algorithms for achieving time and space efficiency.

Approximation Algorithms

Gaber et al., in 2005 stated that approximate algorithms have their roots in algorithm design for computationally hard problems. Results given by these algorithms are approximate and error bound. The problems like data rates with available resources could not be solved using these algorithms. Additional tools are required along with these algorithms for working with available resources.

Windowing Algorithms

A Windowing technique maintains a portion of entire data using a window. The size of the window can be set based on sequence or timestamp (Vladimir Braverma et al., 2009).

- **Sequence Window:** The size of window based on sequence is fixed to *t* transactions. It is also called as fixed size window. These are used in applications where the rate of arriving data stream is uniform.
- **Timestamp Window:** Size of time stamp window is based on the time duration. The size of window is arrived from a fixed interval of time. This window is also called as bursty window. It is used in applications where the rate of arriving data stream is non-uniform.

According to stream data processing model, the research of data selection models are classified as three categories: Sliding Window (Odysseas Papapetrou et al., 2015), Damped Window (Niu Q et al., 2009) and Landmark Window (K.Prasanna, 2015). These techniques are described in brief as follows.

Landmark Window (K.Prasanna, 2015)

In this model, all data starting from a fixed point called landmark till recent data will be available. The window grows as streams flow into the system. Each older data element is given same importance as the current data element. Summarization is done using data structure. Landmark window is shown in Figure 1. which explains the instances of landmark window. Window W_1 denotes all transactions from T_i till T_j i.e., $W_1 = \{T_i, T_{i+1}, T_{i+2}, \ldots\ldots\ldots, T_j\}$, while window W_4 contains transactions from T_i till T_{j+3} and so on.

Sliding Window (Odysseas Papapetrou et al., 2015)

In this model, recent data is only available for the entire work. The simplest approach is a window of fixed size. This window restricts and limits the length of data. Sliding window uses the concepts of timestamp or sequence for setting the window size. Restriction on size can be based either on recent *n* data elements or by recent *t* time units where *n* and *t* are constants. In this type of window, on the arrival of a new data element, the oldest element from the window is lost. Sliding window is depicted in Figure 2. The size of the window depends on the application and available resources. Window W_1 denotes all transactions from T_i till T_{j-2} i.e., $W_1 = \{T_i, T_{i+1}, T_{i+2}, \ldots\ldots\ldots, T_{j-2}\}$, while window W_3 contains transactions from T_{i+2} till T_j and so on.

Figure 1. Landmark window

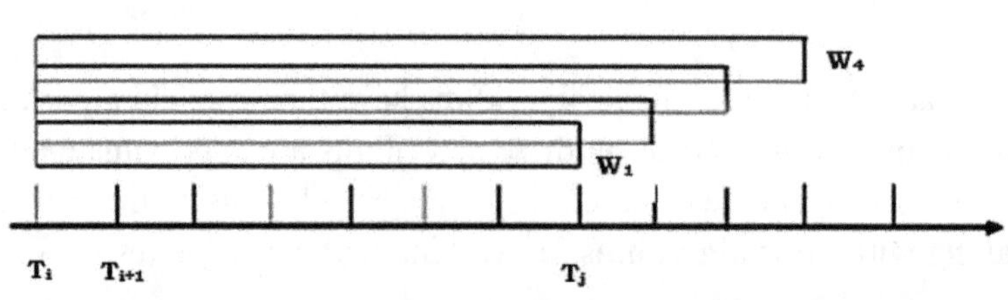

Figure 2. Sliding window

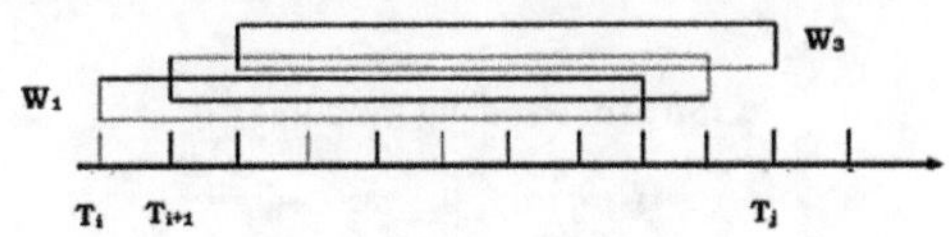

Damped Window (Niu Q et al., 2009)

In this model, all data elements are associated with weights. These weights are relative to time. Recent stream data elements will have higher weight than past data elements. As time passes stream will get damped continuously. Varieties of different weighted models are available like linear, log linear (Niu Q, 2009) etc. A better methodology for streams of data will be exponential method, in which the weight assigned to the data element declines in an exponential manner with time. Damped window is same as sliding window as it also works on recent data.

Output Granularity Algorithm

Output Granularity algorithms are resource aware data analysis algorithms. These can work very well with fluctuating data with very high rates using the limited memory. They have three stages: Mining the data, adaptation to resources and rates of data streams and finally merging the generated results to cope up limited memory (Gaber et al., in 2005).

DATA STREAM MINING FRAMEWORK

All the features of data streams studied, calls for designing of new methodologies to replace traditional data mining techniques. The data stream mining framework is presented in Figure 3. It consists of all components needed for generating solution for stream mining.

The algorithms designed for data streams must process every element in real time otherwise the opportunity of processing them is lost. Processing must also happen in limited memory as data streams are unbounded in nature. The framework, includes stream handling module and stream mining module. Figure 4 depicts the Stream handling module and Figure 5 illustrates the stream mining module.

Figure 3. Data Stream Mining Framework

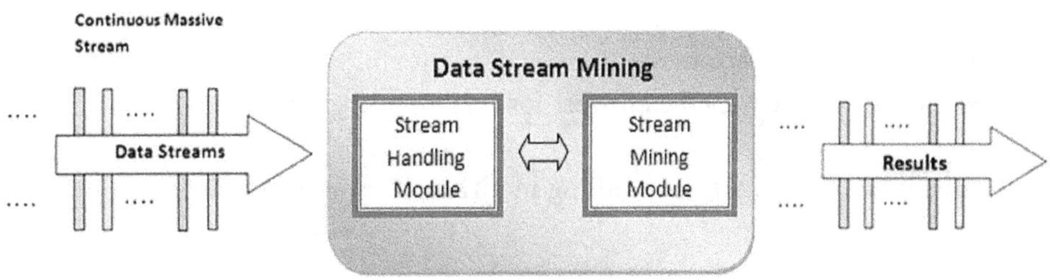

Figure 4. Data Stream Handling Module

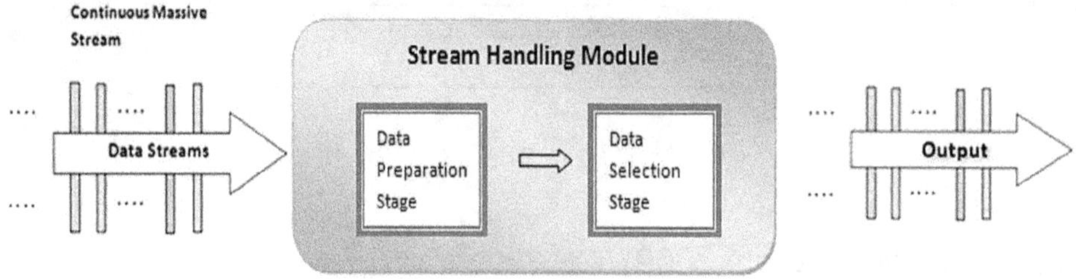

Figure 5. Data Stream Mining Module

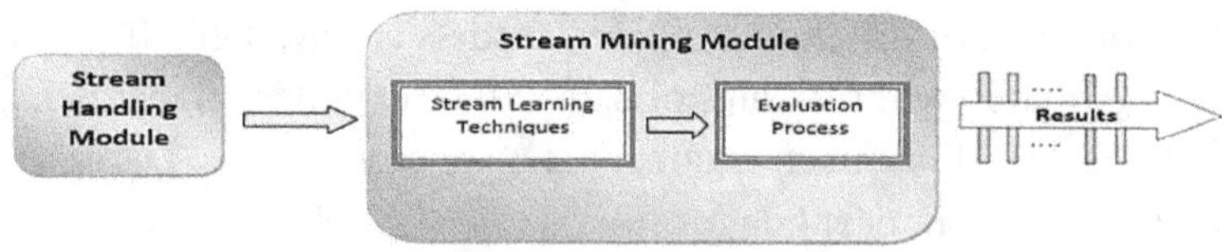

TECHNIQUES OF STREAM MINING

Owing to the nature of streaming data, developing an efficient mining algorithms has become a dominant goal of stream research. A generic approach would be to choose techniques from data mining concepts, convert them according to the need of stream mining and apply them to streaming data.

Data Stream Mining Using Clustering

This technique is used in applications where grouping of similar data is needed. These applications include multimedia data, sensor networks, intrusion detection and stock market analysis. The main cause for so many algorithms in clustering technique is due to the fact that concept of cluster is not precisely defined. Every algorithm designed works with different induction principle. For dealing with infinite length streams, applications adapt windowing summarization techniques which are discussed in section 3. Windowing summarize the flowing stream of data by preserving the meaning of original stream without storing them. Algorithms designed with clustering concept are single scan algorithms and they must employ a mechanism to differentiate between actual data, evolving data and outlier data. The methodologies applied for clustering technique can be broadly classified into four approaches. These are Hierarchical stream approach, Partitioning stream approach, Density Based stream approach, Grid Based stream approach. The algorithms so designed using them processes the stream data in two phases

- Online process which summarizes the flowing data stream.
- Offline process which generates the clusters for further processing.

Figure 6 depicts the various algorithms falling in different approaches designed for clustering.

Figure 6. Clustering Algorithms

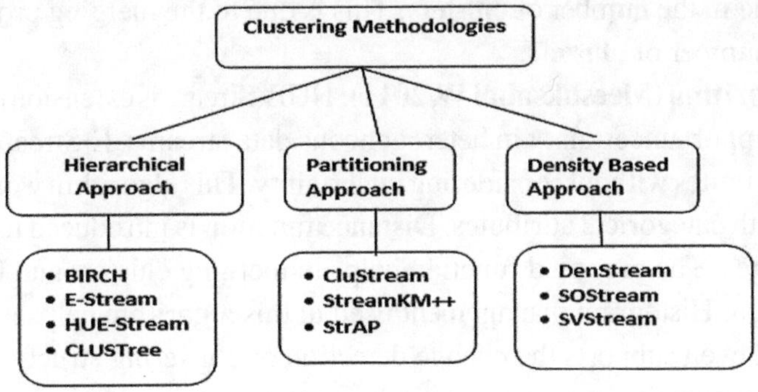

Hierarchical Stream Approach

In Hierarchical stream approach, the clusters are built by splitting the instances of data stream recursively either in bottom-up fashion or in top-down manner. The resulting solution by top-down fashion varies from bottom-up approach (Agarwal et al., 2013). Flowing instances of data streams are grouped into a tree of clusters. This tree is represented using binary tree based data structure called dendrogram. Different clustering solutions can be obtained by dividing the tree at different levels without executing the algorithm again and again. Hierarchical clustering is a single phase clustering technique which can be improved for the quality by including multiple phase. The algorithm so generated is called BIRCH designed by Zhang et al. in 1997.

- **BIRCH Algorithm (Zhang et al., 1997):** Balanced Iterative Reducing and Clustering using Hierarchies (BIRCH) is a dynamic clustering algorithm which incrementally clusters the data and yields the best quality clusters with limited resources. BIRCH created a data structure called CF which was discussed in section3.1.4.3. This CF is an efficient technique for creating clusters from the entire data set. CF is a height balanced tree in which every node contains CF information. BIRCH uses K-means algorithm for creating clusters. According to Zhang et al, BIRCH works in two stages. In the first step, CF tree is built in memory using the dataset. In second step, all the sub-clusters in the leaf nodes are grouped into global cluster.
- **E-Stream Algorithm (Udommanetanakit et al., 2007):** E-Stream is an evolution based algorithm that monitors and changes the detection of clustering structures. Udommanetanakit classified the evolving data streams into five categories: appearance, disappearance, self-evolution, merge and split. E-Stream uses histograms named as α- bin histogram as summarization technique. Each cluster is denoted as Fading Cluster Structure (FCS) which maintains the feature values. Features extracted by histogram of cluster data is used for splitting cluster. E-Stream algorithm starts with empty. Based on the radius threshold a newly arriving data stream is mapped onto one of the existing clusters. If the data stream is not mapped into existing cluster then a new cluster is created using it. Number of data elements in a cluster are counted as weight of that cluster. Based on the pre-specified density level a cluster is either considered as active or inactive. If the weight of a cluster is not meeting the density level then that cluster is considered as inactive and it remains isolated until its weight meets the desired value of density. If a cluster remains inactive for certain time it may be deleted. Accord-

ing to Udommanetanakit et al. E-Stream exhibits linear runtime in the number of dimensions but polynomial runtime in the number of clusters. This is due to the merging procedure, which requires $O(k^2)$ time in the number of clusters.

- **HUE-Stream Algorithm (Meesuksabai W, 2011):** HUE-Stream is extension of E-Stream by Meesuksabai in order to support uncertainty in heterogeneous data streams. E-Stream algorithm works only with numerical attributes without considering uncertainty. This algorithm works well with numerical attributes along with categorical attributes. Distance function is introduced to identify uncertainty in categorical attributes. The proposed function helps in merging clusters and finds closest cluster for the incoming stream. Histogram management used in this algorithm helps in splitting the cluster in categorical data. It even supports the change detection of clustering structures that can evolve over time. The algorithm exhibits linear runtime in number of data points.
- **ClusTree Algorithm (Kranen et al, 2011):** This algorithm is used for applications which report outliers, concept drift and novelty of data. According to Kranen et al it is anytime algorithm that works with micro-clusters in a tree structure for fact access and adapts size of micro-clusters based on variance of assigned data points. It works dynamically even for setting the size of cluster. It is a parameter less stream clustering algorithm. Based on the request of user the results can be delivered at any point of time without any delay.

Partitioning Stream Approach

This approach allocates instances of data streams by moving data objects from one cluster to other. Each cluster is the representation of a partition. These clusters are formed based on k-means algorithm using distance function. The clusters so formed usually will be in spherical shape.

- **CluStream Algorithm (Aggarwal et al. 2003):** CluStream uses micro-clusters for summarizing the data streams. In CluStream algorithm a new data stream point is assigned to its closest micro-cluster based on Euclidean distance. If this distance between new point and a nearest cluster centroid is within a maximum boundary then the point is stored in that cluster. If the point is placed in any existing clusters then a new cluster is created with new point. At any point of time only *n* clusters are maintained where *n* is input parameter.
- **StreamKM++ Algorithm (Ackermann, 2012):** This StreamKM++ algorithm maintains summarized data using merge-and-reduce technique which creates a coreset tree that maintains data as a binary tree. According to Ackermann the time complexity for a single step of merge-and-reduce technique is $O(m^2n)$ where *m* is number of objects stored. This algorithm is a two phase algorithm in which first phase is online phase in which coreset tree is constructed and the second step is offline phase in which k-means++ algorithm is applied. K-means++ is an extension procedure of k-means algorithm that provides better results.
- **StrAP Algorithm(Zhang, 2008):** This algorithms works well with applications related to outlier detection. It is an extension to Affinity Propagation (Frey et al., 2007) algorithm which uses reservoir sampling for summarizing data streams. The steps involved in this algorithm are
    - Extends the algorithm given by Frey et al. to weighted items with no loss of generality.
    - This step is concerned with reducing the quadratic complexity of affinity propagation (AP) algorithm.
    - Deals with changes in data distribution to catch drifting data.

The first batch of data stream is used to initialize the first cluster in the model. As the data stream flows each data point is checked for its exemplar, if it is found then the data point of stream is added to reservoir otherwise the model is updated. This algorithm is an improvement over k-means algorithm.

Density Based Stream Approach

Algorithms in this approach consider dense areas of objects in the data space as clusters.

- **DenStream Algorithm (Cao et al., 2006):** DenStream uses CF vector of micro-clusters for data summarization. When a new data point arrives, it is inserted into closest micro-cluster based on radius. If the data point is found to be outlier then the point is inserted into a new outlier micro-cluster. Before insertion into a micro-cluster a cluster is selected with a distance less than or equal to radius. Main drawback of this algorithm is that it does not release the memory by either removing a micro-cluster or merging two old clusters into one.
- **SOStream Algorithm (Isaksson et al., 2012):** Self Organizing Density Based Clustering Over Data Streams identifies structures in evolving data streams by using density threshold. The threshold used by SOStream is dynamically generated for each cluster based on the idea of building neighborhoods with minimum number of points. Clusters are merged if their spheres in *d*-dimensional space defined by radius of each cluster overlap. When two clusters are merged then the radius of the merged cluster will be the largest radius of two clusters. Dynamically generated threshold value defines the number of clusters.
- **SVStream Algorithm (Wang et al., 2013):** Support vector based stream clustering (SVStream) algorithm is based on support vector clustering (SVC). According to Wang et al. data points of streams are mapped from data space to feature space using Gaussian kernel. Cluster boundaries are constructed using support vectors.

Data summarization technique and clustering methodology used by the discussed algorithms is presented as a summary in Table 2. In this chapter, discussion has been confined only to a few algorithms, while there are many more existing in clustering domain for mining data streams.

Table 2. Summary of the algorithms pertaining to clustering technique.

Sno	Algorithm	Data Summarization Technique	Clustering Methodology
1	BIRCH	Feature Vector	K-Means
2	E-Stream	Histograms	K-Means
3	HUE Stream	Histograms	K-Prototypes
4	CLUSTree	Feature Vector	K-Means
5	CluStream	Feature Vector	K-Means
6	StreamKM++	Coreset tree	K-Means
7	StrAP	Reservoir Sampling	AP
8	DenStream	Feature Vector	DBSCAN
9	SOStream	Micro-clusters	DBSCAN
10	SVStream	Support Vector	SVC

Frequent Itemset Stream Mining

Frequent pattern mining of data streams is one the most important and challenging task (J.Han et al., 2007) for applications related to network analysis, telecommunication, stock market data analysis, sensor data analysis, supply chain analysis. Associative mining helps in extracting correlated features present in data streams (K.Prasanna, 2015). The two versions of frequent pattern mining are

- **Mining for Frequent Items:** In a single pass over data streams all frequent 1-items are identified and store in this type of mining. This can be applied to streams which are repetitive in nature, finite and comparatively small in size. Data summarization is done using sketches which creates compressed data structure with approximate counts of items.
- **Mining for Frequent Itemsets:** This type of mining is a challenging task as it works with data streams which are unique in nature, infinite in length. It is assumed that the number of distinct elements called items are very large. The main hurdle in this case is computation, quality of identifying frequent itemsets, memory and time needed for computation.

Based on the results generated, various techniques related to finding frequent itemsets in data streams are classified into exact algorithms and approximate algorithms. Figure 7 presents the various algorithms falling in different approaches designed for frequent itemset mining.

In exact algorithms, the support threshold of all selected frequent itemsets will be greater than or equal to user specified support. The results so obtained will be accurate but definitely incur more cost as the data to be processed is large and continuous. Exact algorithms are based on maintaining either closed or maximal itemsets in place of storing all itemsets. Approximate algorithms produce approximate results with or without error. The algorithms in this category work in two approaches: false-positive and false-negative. False-positive approach includes some patterns which are not frequent and false-negative approach misses some patterns which are frequent. Almost all algorithms use windowing techniques presented in section 3.2. The underlying methodologies of various algorithms pertaining to frequent itemset mining over data streams are discussed in further sections.

Lossy Counting Algorithm

This algorithm was the first single pass algorithm proposed by Manku, for finding all frequent itemsets over data streams. Lossy counting was a false-positive approximate algorithm. It guarantees the quality

Figure 7. Frequent Itemset Mining Algorithms

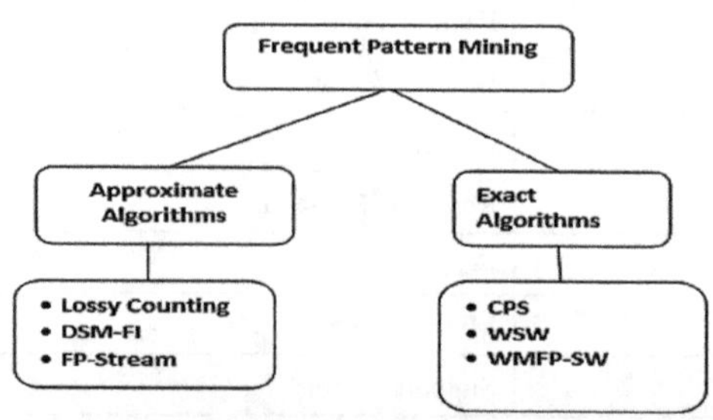

with a user specified error parameter ε for a given support level of θ (Manku et al., 2002). A batch of streams are divided and placed initially in buckets denoted as b_c. Each bucket is identified with a unique id. Support threshold and error rate are the two inputs to this algorithm. A prefix-tree is constructed with the stream of data in lexicographic order. Each node of the tree maintains frequency count of the item and maximum error rate. When the arriving stream is found existing in the prefix then the tree is updated with frequencies. When the arriving stream is a new stream then a new branch is created in the tree. The algorithm was designed with three modules called Buffer, Trie and SetGen. Buffer module filled the memory with arriving stream of data. Trie module constructed and maintained the prefix-tree. SetGen module generated the itemsets. Approximate frequent itemsets are collected over the entire data stream flowing through landmark window. Tedious job here is setting the value of error parameter. If the value for error parameter is small then a lot of frequent sub items are generated with more accurate results. This process takes more CPU time and more space of storage. The time complexity for the working of Lossy counting algorithm is $O(1 / \varepsilon \log(\varepsilon \mid D \mid))$ where D is length of data stream.

DSM-FI Algorithm

Data Stream Mining for Frequent Itemsets is used for fining all frequent itemsets over the entire data stream flowing through landmark window. Main features of DSM-FI are single scan of data, extended prefix-tree representation of data in compact manner and finally top-down approach for identifying frequent itemsets. The performance of DSM-FI is over and above Lossy Counting algorithm (Li et al., 2004). This algorithm works with user defined support threshold *ms* falling in between 0 and 1 and maximum error rate threshold ε lying between 0 and *ms*. It is an online incremental algorithm over continuous streams of online transactions. Each arriving transaction from the stream is inserted into a summarized data structure called Summary frequent itemset forest (*SFI-forest*). SFI tree holds all the frequent itemsets present in the stream of transactions. An efficient top-down frequent itemset selection (*todoFIS*) was also developed for retrieving all frequent itemsets from SFI-forest. The space complexity in the worst case for constructing SFI forest is $O(2^m)$ where m is number of frequent items. DSM-FI periodically pruned all those itemsets whose support is less than *ms*. SFI-forest is more compact then prefix-tree. This compactness lead to more number of tree traversals.

Compact Pattern Stream Tree Based Algorithm

Using CPS Tanbeer et al., introduced a novel concept for dynamically restructuring the tree for handling streaming data. A novel compact prefix-tree based structure called CPS tree was proposed to store all recent frequent itemsets (Tanbeer et al., 2009). This algorithm works in two phases. First phase was called insertion phase in which items from arriving data stream is inserted into each node of CPS tree based on item order. *I-List* was maintained by the algorithm for ordering the items. Second phase was called restructuring phase in which *I-List* was arranged based on descending order of frequency counts. Based on the *I-List* the CPS tree is restructured. The two phases are repeated till the end of data streams. The data flowing from data streams is processed as pane of transactions. With the transactions present in pane CPS tree is constructed using insertion phase. Algorithm functionality starts with insertion phase and ends with restructuring phase. CPS Tree algorithm follows sliding window concept and works with recent data. The main problem with this technique was utilization of more space and time for restructuring phase. Overall performance of CPS tree based algorithm was more efficient in terms of memory and time complexities when finding recent frequent pattern from data streams (Tanbeer et al., 2009).

FP-Stream Algorithm

FP Stream algorithm uses a FP-tree based data structure for maintaining time sensitive frequent itemsets (Chris Gianella et al., 2004). This FP-Stream algorithm has an in-built frequent pattern tree and works with titled time window table for each frequent pattern. Complete frequent itemsets are extracted with the help of an approximate error bound. The model used fine granularity to mine the recent data and coarser granularity to mine historical data. The entire data stream was divided into frequent, sub frequent and infrequent itemsets. The functionality of tilted window was just like sliding window concept where only recent data was given more importance than old and past data. A drawback with this approach is that as time passes FP-Stream can become very large due to which updating and scanning such structures may reduce the mining throughput.

Weighted Sliding Window Algorithm

Tsai et al., in 2009 proposed an approach based on weighted slide window model with the help of two algorithms called WSW and WSW-Imp. These two algorithms are based on Apriori algorithm. This algorithm needs inputs like number of windows, size of window, minimum support threshold and weight for each window. The window used here was based on time. Different weights are provided to windows based on the importance of data in that window. Highest weight was always given to window with recent data. The algorithm works with weighted sliding window. The main advantage of this algorithm is, it is a single pass algorithm. As the size of window increases the time taken by algorithm decreased. The main problem is with generation of candidate itemsets with the help of smaller sized window. This candidate itemset generation will definitely take more time and space (Tsai et al.,2009).

Weighted Maximal Frequent Pattern Mining Over Data Streams Based on Sliding Window Model (WMFP-SW)

Lee et al. in 2014 proposed a methodology for efficiently compressing the frequent patterns generated from data streams flowing through sliding window. The contributions of this research are

- A novel tree structure called WMFP-SW-tree was also proposed for WMFP mining task. WMFP-tree was used to manage with WMFP information and even used it for subset checking work. Along with these two an array called WMFP-SW-array was created for improving efficiency of mining operation.
- WMFP-SW uses support count and weights as two metrics for extracting frequent patterns. Pruning strategy was introduced to prune unnecessary operations causing meaningless pattern generation.

Algorithm employs branch sorting method for maintaining compactness in the trees. This algorithm is scalable in nature as it finds maximal frequent itemsets (Lee et al., 2014).

Most of the algorithms designed for frequent itemset mining employ task summarization techniques for retrieving data from flowing data streams. Analysis of various algorithms in the domain of frequent pattern or itemset mining is presented in Table 3. This chapter has detailed only a few of the algorithms, where in reality there are many more algorithms in the domain of frequent itemset mining.

Data Stream Mining Using Classification

Classification of data streams is the process of building a model based on past data to be applied to new data. The model is built with the arriving data stream using learning phase and applying this model over new data to assign a class label for unlabeled data is done using testing phase. Model prepared by learning phase of classification helps in predictive analysis. The applications for this technique range from very crucial geophysical applications to decision support systems in business applications. Figure 8 depicts the various algorithms designed for classification.

Decision Tree

Algorithms designed based on decision trees can be either incremental or batch processing algorithms. In a batch processing algorithm the decision of branching is taken with the help of heuristics like gini index or information gain. Incremental processing algorithms use hoeffding bound concept. These bounds are used to select optimal splitting attribute. Decision tree based classifiers work very well when compared with other classifiers. The leaf nodes of the tree provide the results based on the decision taken by root node of the tree. Each non-leaf node has a test on a particular attribute that distributes the data into

Table 3. Summary of algorithms for frequent pattern mining

Sno	Algorithm	Task Summarization using window model	Type of algorithm
1	Lossy Counting	Landmark Window	Approximate
2	DSM-FI	Landmark Window	Approximate
3	CPS	Sliding Window	Exact
4	FP-Stream	Tilted Time Window	Approximate
5	WSW	Sliding Window	Exact
6	WMFP-SW	Sliding Window	Exact

Figure 8. Data Stream Mining algorithms using Classification

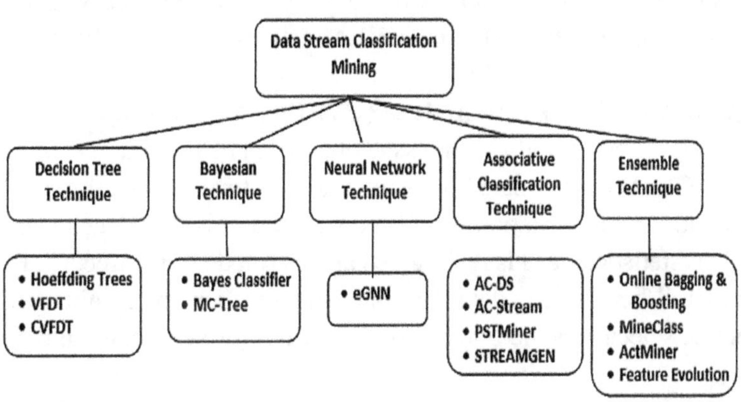

various sub-trees. Tree is constructed in learning phase with nodes based on attributes that do the best split. During testing phase, as a new stream to be classified arrives, a traversal on the tree happens and the result is obtained using leaf node. The new stream is assigned with class label.

- **Hoeffding Trees:** Hoeffding tree algorithm is an incremental algorithm. Decision tree is constructed from data streams by spending very limited amount of time on each data element. The stream is used to update the tree which is stored in memory. The leaf nodes of the tree contain the class label of the classifier. Hoeffding tree algorithm is an incremental algorithm so it cannot access all the data. Hoeffding bound is an innovative methodology applied to decide how many data points has to be seen for deciding the split for a branch in the tree learning phase. For a random variable r whose range is R, assume n observations are made and mean of r is computed as $\bar{r}$ then Hoeffding bound states that, with a probability of $1-\delta$, the mean of the variable is at least $\bar{r}-\varepsilon$ where

$$\varepsilon = \sqrt{\frac{R^2 \ln(1/\delta)}{2n}}$$

The random variable is selected as difference between gains of the two best attributes. Let the best attributes for X_i be X_a and X_b after observing n items, then random variable is taken as $\Delta\bar{G} = \bar{G}(X_a) - \bar{G}(X_b) \geq 0$. The random variable must be chosen only if $\Delta\bar{G} > \varepsilon$ (Domingos et al., 2000). Hence the algorithm must wait till n samples having $\Delta\bar{G} > \varepsilon$ to decide on an attribute to split. After which the algorithm splits on the selected attribute. For every arrival of stream, the algorithm uses the Hoeffding bound to check whether the best splitting attribute is obtained to create the next level of tree node. The performance of this algorithm is very high in terms of accuracy and works well with infinite length. Main drawbacks of this algorithm are it fails to performance well with concept drifts, spends lot of time in case of ties for selecting splitting attribute.

- **Very Fast Decision Tree (VFDT) Algorithm:** VFDT is based on Hoeffding tree. VFDT works efficiently when compared to Hoeffding tree in case of ties for selection of splitting attribute $\Delta\bar{G} > \varepsilon$. Approximate ties are broken using a user defined threshold with acceptable error measure. Limited memory usage is facilitated by removing the least promising leaves and by ignoring poor attributes. Identification of this poor attribute is done by the difference between splitting criteria of highest and lowest attributes. If this difference is more than a pre-specified value then the attribute with lowest splitting value is removed from memory. Compared to Hoeffding tree VFDT is better in terms of time and memory. Time taken by VFDT is $O(n^2)$. Main problem with VFDT is that it cannot handle concept drifts.
- **Concept Adapting Very Fast Decision Tree (CVFDT) Algorithm:** CVFDT algorithm is an extension of VFDT algorithm to address the issue of concept drift (Hulten et al., 2001). The previous decision taken by CVFDT is validated by using the statistical information maintained by CVFDT algorithm. This statistical information is updated with the arrival of data and decremented with the outdated data. This statistical data is maintained at every node of the tree. CVFDT works with sliding window model. When drifting data arrives in streams then some splits which were previously selected will not be selected as the other attributes will have more gain on the new stream. Due to

this CVFDT creates a new sub tree with the new best attribute at the root. It continuously monitors the quality of newly arriving data for understanding the concept drifts. Processing time taken by CVFDT is *O(logn)*.

Bayesian Classification Technique

Bayesian technique is an important tool for modelling probabilistic relationships among problem variables. It explores the mutual dependencies among the features in a particular domain. This is a statistical approach.

- **Indexing Density Model Using Bayes Classifier:** Seidl proposed index based classifier called Bayes classifier which works on kernel density estimators. A novel tree called Bayes tree is automatically constructed with hierarchy of mixture of densities that represent kernel density estimators at successively coarser levels (Seidl et al., 2009). Every node of the tree contains linear sum, quadratic sum, number of data objects and minimum bounding rectangle for all data objects. This algorithm is an incremental algorithm. A new probability density query is designed for descending the tree based on strategies favoring the accuracy of classification. A new evaluation technique called Poisson streams was also proposed for anytime classification. Every class has a bayes tree constructed. Refinement of Bayes tree takes more time.
- **Multi Class-Tree (MC-Tree) Based Algorithm:** MC-tree combines all classes in a multi-Gaussian tree and needs only one step to refine all class models simultaneously rather than many steps of bayes tree refinement (Kranen et al., 2010). For transformation of data space this algorithm employs multi-dimensional scaling. This transformation is done during tree construction to optimize the condition of the tree with respect to multiple classes. This algorithm outperforms Bayes tree in terms of accuracy constantly by up to 15% (Kranen et al., 2010).

Neural Network

Leite et al., 2010 proposed an evolving granular neural network (eGNN) supported by granule based learning algorithms to classify data streams. eGNN works in two phases. Firstly, eGNN constructs information granules of incoming data using T-S neurons. Secondly, neural network is built using information granules. Fuzzy aggregation neurons was used as processing units in eGNN structure. eGNN is an incremental learning methodology capable of processing online granular data. Problem like lack of transparency of black box neural network model was taken care by fuzzy hyperbox representations. These representations are interpretable and transparent in nature. eGNN combined functional and linguistic fuzzy models into a single model. This algorithm operates on recursive learning which requires only features of fuzzy rules. Main issue of concern in eGNN is the time taken for training phase due to which eGNN is only chosen while working with small data streams.

Associative Classification

Association and Classification (AC) are two widely used tools in the domain of data mining. Amalgamation of these two techniques helps in creation of efficient associative classifier (Baralis et al., 2012),

(K.Prasanna, 2015). AC is a rule based classification technique which prepares a classifier with class based association rules. Classification finds all possible correlations between attributes values and their classes called rules and constructs a larger size classifier using them. The generated classifier is bigger as this approach aims at producing additional useful knowledge missed by traditional approaches which definitely improves the accuracy of prediction in various applications. Hence, the accuracy of the generated knowledge is higher than conventional classification approaches and acumens decision makers.

- **AC-DS Algorithm:** LiSu in 2011 proposed an AC technique based on estimation mechanism of lossy counting and landmark window model. AC-DS uses single rule for predicting a new data stream in testing phase. Support count threshold is the given input to the algorithm. This algorithm was the first algorithm designed in the domain of AC. AC-DS uses Apriori concept for building a classifier using associative classification rules in learning phase. This is biased towards general rule and is not suitable for streams that are slowly changing from time to time and streams with concept drift.
- **AC-Stream Algorithm:** AC-Stream was proposed by Saengthongloun in 2013 which works with multiple rules. It is based on support threshold and works with landmark window. It is designed to work in two steps. In the first step AC-Stream generates strong Class Association Rules (CARs). Initially all frequent itemsets are generated using Apriori algorithm. These itemsets are incrementally updated and stored in T-tree. Infrequent itemsets are pruned from T-tree and CARS are generated. In the second step, these CARs are ranked based on precedence rule. AC-Stream uses the first k ranked rules for prediction process of unlabeled data stream. It determines best k-rules for predicting unseen data stream. Hoeffding bound was used as a gain to separate the best class from other classes to determine k number of rules (Saengthongloun et al. 2013). AC-Stream algorithm out performs the existing single rule predictive algorithms.
- **PSTMiner Algorithm:** In 2015 an efficient single pass algorithm called PSTMiner was developed by K.Prasanna. This algorithm is efficient in terms of accuracy of prediction and time consumed for prediction. The algorithm works in three steps in learning phase. They are construction of PSTree, generation of frequent itemsets containing class label and building classifier with rules. Prediction of class label for the unseen data streams is the part of testing phase. A compact tree structure called PSTree was built with a single pass of data streams (K.Prasanna, 2015). Arriving data stream was inserted into the tree in batches. Each batch had fixed number of transactions. AC techniques generate huge number of rules which consume a lot of space and takes more time for execution. In the era of data evolution as data keeps growing on hourly basis, there is a need for optimization techniques for reducing the size of vast amount of rules generated by Associative Classification algorithms. Pruning techniques are the best optimization techniques used for discarding redundant and ambiguous rules. The surviving rules after pruning techniques are used for preparing classifier. PSTMiner uses chi square as pruning technique for building a quality classifier.
- **STREAMGEN Algorithm:** StreamGen proposed in 2009 by Chuancong. is the other efficient algorithm to mine frequent itemsets. It is designed using sliding window concept. It works with a novel enumeration tree structure to maintain the generated frequent itemsets. The infrequent itemsets are pruned from the tree. Insertion of a transaction into enumeration tree is performed using operation called ADD and deletion of old transaction is performed using REMOVE operation (Chuancong et al., 2009). REMOVE operation helps in working with recent stream of data. ADD operation helps in maintaining the frequent itemsets when a new transaction arrives as part of stream. Remove op-

eration removes the information of old transactions from the stream. This algorithm uses the rules generated from complete set of transactions in the current window. Empirical results show that this algorithm performs well when compared with other algorithms.

Ensemble Classification

Ensembles have modular construction so they can integrate new data elements. This integration can happen with the help of new component creation into the ensemble, updating the existing components of ensemble. Ensemble based algorithms are generally designed for working with blocks of data or for online data. Most of the block based ensembles work with component classifiers with the newest data block and replace the worst ensemble with the new data block classifier. Almost all the time the size of the block is fixed to a size specified by end user. Ensemble algorithms can be updated efficiently and very easily they can adapt to changes in streams. In the learning phase, the arriving data stream is divided into equal blocks. Each of these blocks is used for training a classifier. In testing phase, an ensemble of *N* such classifiers are used to label unlabeled data stream with class label.

- **Online Bagging and Boosting Algorithm:** Online Bagging and Boosting algorithm was the first design which used traditional bagging and boosting over data streams. In data streams applications recurrence of data objects can be *k* times in the classifier based on probability *p(k)* which may tend to Poisson distribution as the length of data stream is infinite (Oza et al., 2005). Oza et al. proposed online bagging which assigns weights to data objects based on Poisson distribution. This can be considered as a new summarization technique replacing sampling method.
- **MineClass Algorithm:** Mining novel Classes in data streams was proposed by Masud et al., in 2009 for finding novel class in presence of concept drift by providing cohesion among unlabeled test instances. The latest data stream in the form a chunk is provided as input to MineClass algorithm. This algorithm tries to find for existence of novel class in the chunk of stream. In absence of novel class the algorithm classifies the stream with the help of ensemble (Masud et al., 2009). In the learning phase ensemble of classifiers is prepared using two algorithms called K-NN and decision tree. Using these ensembles an inventory of used space and unused spaces is maintained using pseudo points of clustering. In testing phase, these pseudo pints are used to detect outliers and declare the existence of a novel class if there is a strong cohesion between outliers.
- **ActMiner Algorithm:** Masud et al., proposed ActMiner in 2010, which mainly addressed challenges like concept drift, concept evolution and limited labeled data. ActMiner is an extension of MineClass and tries to work with limited labeled data stream. ActMiner uses a hybrid batch incremental process (Masud et al., 2010). It divides the stream into chunks of equal size and prepares *M* ensembles where each ensemble is a classification model for each chunk of stream. When a new chunk arrives, a new model is trained and one of the old model is replaced with new model. Selection of old model is based on the accurate latest labeling of unlabeled chunk of stream. In the testing phase, ACTMiner collects all the test instances which are well separated from training data stream for the sake of identification of novel class. All these test instances are named as raw outliers. Data streams falling in raw outliers are due to concept drift or noise. A novel class is assumed to have appeared if sufficient amount of cohesion is found between raw outliers. These streams with strong cohesion are filtered and called as F-outliers. F-outliers are then classified as novel class instances. ActMiner solves the limited labeled problem by using only few selected instances to be labeled. The

instances with highest expected error for classification model are only selected by which 90% time and cost are saved when compared with traditional approaches that use all instances for labeling unknown data stream (Masud et al., 2010).

- **Adaptive Novel class Detection of Feature Evolving Algorithm:** Masud et al., improvised outlier detection of ACTMiner in 2013 using slack space outside the decision boundary of each classification model and adaptively changed this slack space based on characteristics of evolving data stream. Gini Coefficient was also adapted to find novel class. This probabilistic coefficient helped in identifying the reason for outliers namely noise, concept drift and concept evolution. More over a graph based approach was used to detect the appearance of more than one novel class simultaneously and to separate the instances of one novel class from other. For identifying feature evolution Masud et al., used Lossless conversion technique in which when a test instance is to be classified using a model, both model and the instance are made to expand their feature sets and an union operation is applied which was called as lossless homogenizing since the model and instance preserve their dimensions. In this technique no useful features are lost. It is even very easy to identify a newly evolved feature.

Analysis of various techniques in the domain of Classification in terms of advantages and limitations are presented in Table 4. This chapter has presented only a few of the algorithms, where, in reality there are many more algorithms in the domain of classification for mining data streams.

FUTURE DIRECTIONS

Research in the domain of data streams started a decade ago. There are still many research issues of major concern which have to be explored. Few of them are presented in this section

- **Dynamic Feature Selection:** Feature evolution occurs when new features emerge in the flowing streams. Most of the existing algorithms assume that the feature space of the data points in stream is static. In real world the features of data streams are dynamic in nature. New methodologies must be designed to handle this dynamic nature of features.
- **Cluster Evolution:** In many applications, it is necessary to keep track of cluster evolution over time so as to analyze the nature of the data streams. Evolution of clusters must be tracked by preserving the cluster transitions still remains as a challenge.

Table 4. Advantages and Limitations of various techniques in classification

Sno	Technique	Advantages	Limitations
1	Decision Tree	Easy to understand, works well with redundant attributes, low computational cost,	Suffers from the problem of over fitting
2	Bayesian Classification	Simple, effective and efficient	Unrealistic Assumptions
3	Neural Network	Generalizing capability is good	Interpreting the learned model is difficult
4	Associative Classification	High accuracy, Easy to implement,	Generates huge amount of mined rules
5	Ensemble Classification	High accuracy	Vulnerable to high dimensional data, lack of solid theory

- **Mining Text Streams:** Social networking is an emerging trend and efficient algorithms need to be designed for email spam filtering, target marketing, sentimental analysis and many more. Text streams generated by social media are rich with surprising events and complex topic generation over time so that mining text streams is still a tedious task.
- **Online Monitoring Systems:** Network monitoring systems must be efficiently designed. Such system must monitor a variety of continuous data streams that may be characterized as unpredictable and arriving at a high rate containing packet traces and network performance measurements.
- **Designing Compact Data Structure:** Due to the bounded memory size and huge amount of data streams coming continuously, efficient and compact data structure is needed to store, update and retrieve the collected information.

CONCLUSION

Data stream Mining has emerged as a new area of research. Stream data analysis in real time is becoming an important task for allowing organizations to solve the problems that appear for improving their performance. This aims at extracting knowledge from data generated continuously. It is difficult to analyze large amounts of data streams without using an automated technique. Developing an efficient methodology with accurate results for this data streams is an interesting area of work. Mining data streams have multitudinous applications with many daunting research issues. As the entire data stream will not be available at once, processing needs a sequential strategy. The algorithms designed for working with data streams must sometime deal with data sizes which exceed the main memory of system. New methodologies are designed by extending the existing techniques of data mining by including the constraints posed by data streams. Algorithms used for processing streaming data must also involve summarization techniques. Various summarization techniques related to data streams are discussed. This chapter provides an overview of various state-of-art algorithms for data stream clustering, association and classification. This chapter also focused on various issues of concern like real time response, bounded memory, concept drift, concept evolution and feature evolution. Finally, this chapter explored future research directions which will definitely push the boundaries and increase the impact of data stream mining.

REFERENCES

Ackermann, M. R., Martens, M., Raupach, C., Swierkot, K., Lammersen, C., & Sohler, C. (2012). StreamKM++: A clustering algorithm for data streams. *ACM Journal of Experimental Algorithmics*, *17*(1), 173–187. doi:10.1145/2133803.2184450

Aggarwal, C. C., Watson, T. J., Ctr, R., Han, J., Wang, J., & Yu, P. S. (2003). A framework for clustering evolving data streams. In *VLDB* (pp. 81–92). Berlin: VLDB Endowment. doi:10.1016/B978-012722442-8/50016-1

Aggarwal & Yu. (2007). A Survey of synopsis construction in data streams. Advances in Database Systems, 31, 169-207.

Babcock, B., Babu, S., Datar, M., Motwani, R., & Widom, J. (2002). Models and issues in data stream systems. *Proceedings of PODS*. doi:10.1145/543613.543615

Babcock, B., Datar, M., & Motwani, R. (2003). Load Shedding Techniques for Data Stream Systems. *Proceedings of 2003 Workshop on Management and Processing of Data Streams.*

Baralis, E., & Garza, P. (2012). I-prune: Item Selection for Associative Classification. *International Journal of Intelligent Systems*, *27*(3), 279–299. doi:10.1002/int.21524

Braverma, V., Ostrovsky, R., & Zaniolo, C. (2009). Optimal Sampling from sliding windows. *Proceedings of 28th ACM SIGMOD-SIGACT-SIGART symposium on Principles of database systems*, 147-156. doi:10.1145/1559795.1559818

Dobra, A. (2016). *Sketch-Based Multi-Query Processing over Data Streams*. Data Stream Management. Springer Berlin Heidelberg.

Dobra, A., Garofalakis, M., Gehrke, J., & Rastogi, R. (2002). Processing Complex Aggregate Queries Over Data Streams. *Proceedings of SIGMOD*. doi:10.1145/564691.564699

Domingos, P., & Hulten, G. (2000). Mining high-speed data streams. *Proceedings of the 6th ACM SIGKDD international conference on knowledge discovery and data mining*, 71–80.

Frey, B. J., & Dueck, D. (2007). Clustering by passing messages between data points. *Science*, *315*(5814), 2007. doi:10.1126/science.1136800 PMID:17218491

Gaber, M. M., Zaslavsky, A., & Krishnaswamy, S. (2005). Mining data streams: A review. *SIGMOD Record*, *34*(2), 18–26. doi:10.1145/1083784.1083789

Garofalakis, M., Gehrke, J., & Rastogi, R. (2016). *Data Stream Management: A Brave New World. In Data Stream Management* (pp. 1–9). Springer Berlin Heidelberg. doi:10.1007/978-3-540-28608-0

Guha, S., Mishra, N., Motwani, R., & O'Callaghan, L. (2000). Clustering data streams. In *IEEE Symposium on Foundations of Computer Science*. IEEE Computer Society.

Hulten, G., Spencer, L., & Domingos, P. (2001). Mining time-changing data streams. *Proceedings of the seventh ACM SIGKDD international conference on knowledge discovery and data mining*, 97–106. doi:10.1145/502512.502529

Isaksson, C., Dunham, M. H., & Hahsler, M. (2012). SoStream: Self organizing density-based clustering over data stream. In *MLDM* (pp. 264–278). Berlin: Springer Berlin Heidelberg. doi:10.1007/978-3-642-31537-4_21

Kranen, P., Assent, I., Baldauf, C., & Seidl, T. (2011). The ClusTree: Indexing micro-clusters for anytime stream mining. *Knowledge and Information Systems*, *29*(2), 249–272. doi:10.1007/s10115-010-0342-8

Kranen, P., Günnemann, S., Fries, S., & Seidl, T. (2010). MC-tree: Improving Bayesian anytime classification. Lecture Notes in Computer Science, 6187, 252–269.

Lee, G., Yun, U., & Ryu, K. H. (2014). Sliding window based weighted maximal frequent pattern mining over data streams. *Expert Systems with Applications*, *41*(2), 694–708. doi:10.1016/j.eswa.2013.07.094

Leite, D., Costa, P., & Gomide, F. (2010). Evolving granular neural network for semi-supervised data stream classification. In *The 2010 international joint conference on neural networks* (pp. 1–8). IEEE. doi:10.1109/IJCNN.2010.5596303

Li, Lee, & Shan. (2004). An efficient algorithm for mining frequent itemsets over the entire history of data streams. *Proceedings of the international workshop on knowledge discovery in data streams.*

Li, Liu & Song. (2011). A new classification algorithm for data streams. *Int. J. Modern Education and Computer Science, 4*, 32–39.

Manku, G. S., & Motwani, R. (2002). Approximate frequency counts over data streams. In *Proceedings of the 28th international conference on very large data bases*, (pp. 346–357). Academic Press. doi:10.1016/B978-155860869-6/50038-X

Masud, M. (2009). *Integrating novel class detection with classification for concept-drifting data streams.* Machine Learning and Knowledge Discovery in Databases. doi:10.1007/978-3-642-04174-7_6

Masud, M. M. (2010). Classification and novel class detection in data streams with active mining. In *Pacific-Asia Conference on Knowledge Discovery and Data Mining*. Springer Berlin Heidelberg. doi:10.1007/978-3-642-13672-6_31

Masud, M. M., Chen, Q., Khan, L., Aggarwal, C. C., Gao, J., Han, J., & Oza, N. C. et al. (2013). Classification and adaptive novel class detection of feature-evolving data streams. *IEEE Transactions on Knowledge and Data Engineering, 25*(7), 1484–1497. doi:10.1109/TKDE.2012.109

Masud, M. M., Gao, J., Khan, L., Han, J., & Thuraisingham, B. (2011, June). Classification and Novel Class Detection in Concept-Drifting Data Streams under Time Constraints. *TKDE, 23*(6), 859–874.

Meesuksabai, W., Kangkachit, T., & Waiyamai, K. (2011). Hue-stream: Evolution-based clustering technique for heterogeneous data streams with uncertainty. *Advanced Data Mining and Applications - 7th International Conference*, 27–40. doi:10.1007/978-3-642-25856-5_3

Niu, Q., Xia, S., & Zhang, L. (2009). Association Classification Based on Compactness of Rules. *2009 Second International Workshop on Knowledge Discovery and Data Mining*. doi:10.1109/WKDD.2009.160

Oza, N. C. (2005). Online bagging and boosting. IEEE international conference on systems, man and cybernetics, 3, 2340–2345. doi:10.1109/ICSMC.2005.1571498

Papapetrou, O., Garofalakis, M., & Deligiannakis, A. (2015). Sketching distributed sliding window data streams. *VLDB Journal, 24*(3), 345-368.

Prasanna & Reddy. (2010). A Survey on Different Trends in Data Streams. *Proceedings of 2010 IEEE International Conference on Networking and Information Technology.*

Prasanna & Reddy. (2015). Efficient mining of Data Streams using Associative Classification Approach. *International Journal of Software Engineering and Knowledge Engineering, 25*(3), 605-631.

Saengthongloun, B. (2013). Ac-stream: Associative classification over data streams using multiple class association rules. *Computer Science and Software Engineering (JCSSE), 2013 10th International Joint Conference on*. doi:10.1109/JCSSE.2013.6567349

Seidl, T., Assent, I., Kranen, P., Krieger, R., & Herrmann, J. (2009). Indexing density models for incremental learning and anytime classification on data streams. *Proceedings of the 12th international conference on extending database technology: advances in database technology*, 311–322. doi:10.1145/1516360.1516397

Tanbeer, S. K., Ahmed, C. F., Jeong, B.-S., & Lee, Y.-K. (2009). Sliding Window-based frequent pattern mining over data streams. *Elsevier, Information Sciences*, *179*(July), 3843–3865. doi:10.1016/j.ins.2009.07.012

Tsai, P. S. M. (2009). Mining frequent itemsets in data streams using the weighted sliding window model. *Elsevier, Expert Systems with Applications*, *36*(March), 11617–11625. doi:10.1016/j.eswa.2009.03.025

Udommanetanakit, K., Rakthanmanon, T., & Waiyamai, K. (2007). E-stream: Evolution-based technique for stream clustering. ADMA, 605–15. doi:10.1007/978-3-540-73871-8_58

Wang, C., Lai, J., Huang, D., & Zheng, W. (2013). SVStream: A support vector-based algorithm for clustering data streams. *IEEE Transactions on Knowledge and Data Engineering*, *25*(6), 1410–1424. doi:10.1109/TKDE.2011.263

Yang, J., Yang, C., & Wei, Y. (2016). Frequent Pattern Mining Algorithm for Uncertain Data Streams Based on Sliding Window. *Intelligent Human-Machine Systems and Cybernetics, 2016 8th International Conference on, 2*. doi:10.1109/IHMSC.2016.293

Zhang, T., Ramakrishnan, R., & Livny, M. (1997). BIRCH: A new data clustering algorithm and its applications. *Data Mining and Knowledge Discovery*, *1*(2), 141–182. doi:10.1023/A:1009783824328

Zhang, X., Furtlehner, C., & Sebag, M. (2008). Data streaming with affinity propagation. In *ECML/PKDD* (pp. 628–643). Springer Berlin Heidelberg.

Chapter 13
Trust and Credibility Analysis of Websites:
Role of Trust and Credibility in Evaluating Online Content

Himani Bansal
Jaypee Institute of Information Technology, India

Prakhar Shukla
Jaypee Institute of Information Technology, India

Manav Dhar
Jaypee Institute of Information Technology, India

ABSTRACT

Trust on any online information is psychosomatic and hidden by nature. The choice is in the hands of the information seeker to consider, evaluate, and confirm the contents of the websites before using it. This makes a sharp concern for websites dealing with sensitive topics like health, research, or academics. There is no benchmark or tool that tells or characterises about making these "trust" decisions. Although web users make such decisions after considering numerous factors, still there are no such criteria to fulfil the underlying principle to deal with such decision making. This chapter is an effort to resolve the problem of how to measure the content provided by any website in terms of its credibility. Various models have been projected in this chapter to identify several factors pertaining to the credibility of content and users' trust on any website and accordingly analyse the identified factors to assess the websites.

INTRODUCTION

In today's age of 'Information era', information is available to any user on a press of a button. He/she is returned with several website's links which claims to have a relevant information. It is a concern of TRUST and CREDIBILITY for him/her to decide that which data can be relied on from the huge pool

DOI: 10.4018/978-1-5225-5097-6.ch013

of data and information. The credibility of information promotes trust of an individual. It is said that trust is a primary and central virtue which is assessed and acquired while evaluating any organization. This is also necessary for web associations. A web association refers to the development of information and the data-searching through websites which are provided by the search engine on a relevant search query. We can describe it in following steps (also depicted in Figure 1):

1. Entering a search term in search box of a search engine.
2. The search engine returns websites which are associated with the search term entered by the user.
3. User shortlists these websites according to his/her own needs.

Mostly search engines use many complex and unrevealed algorithms with best mechanisms to define and store all these websites for easier retrieval, but none of these factors and task ensures that web links provided on the top are more trustworthy or credible than the links which are appearing in the last.

Previous studies have declared that there is no such controlling legalization on all the information and data available on the web links because of their enormous size (*Marchand, D. 1990, Alexander, J. E., Tate, P. 1999, Hernon, P. 1955, & Calvert Phillip J. 2001*). Mostly the users and the internet consumers of information do not have sufficient time to cross check and validate the contents provided by any web page. This is a matter of great concern when the searched topic is related to sensitive areas and terms like medical or health symptoms. Based on a renowned study, "eight out of 10 Internet users have, at one time or another, searched for health info on the Web, in part because they feel their healthcare needs are not being adequately addressed by increasingly busy physicians" (*Prescient Digital 2015*). Pew Internet and American Life Project reported that 50% of the people who have used the Internet for health and medical symptom analysis informs that the acquired information has improved the way they take care of themselves (*Prescient Digital 2015*).

Studies also create a significant question mark on the security and faith while using this information by stating that "identifying quality patient information isn't always easy (*Lewis, T. 2006, Baker, L., Wagner, T. H., Singer, S., & Bundonf, M. K. 2003, Eastin, M. S., & Guinster, N. M. 2006*)". They point that the health seekers don't follow any search strategy before consuming the overwhelming information; which one has to take care of, if it isn't assessed medically, as there might be some business profits rolling in the darkness.

For concern in information evaluation when the query is related to academics or about gaining some information for taking an important decision, many surveys were conducted on the various group of people to understand their perspective towards TRUST and CREDIBILITY of websites. A survey was conducted on students to know: "How students evaluate information and sources when searching the World Wide Web for information" (*Walraven, A., Brandgruwel, S., & Boshuizen, H. 2009*). Figure 2 presents the average time one student spends on searching (44%), scanning(31%), processing (16%) and organising (9%) while analysing the website.

Figure 1. A web association

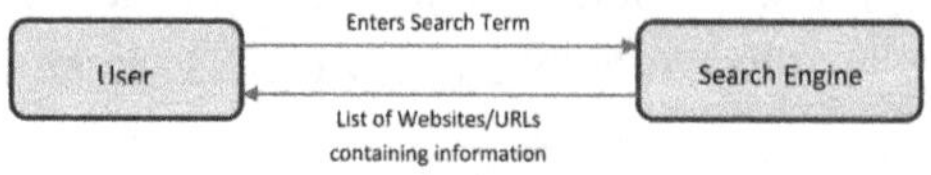

Figure 2. Time (%) Spent per Constituent Skill

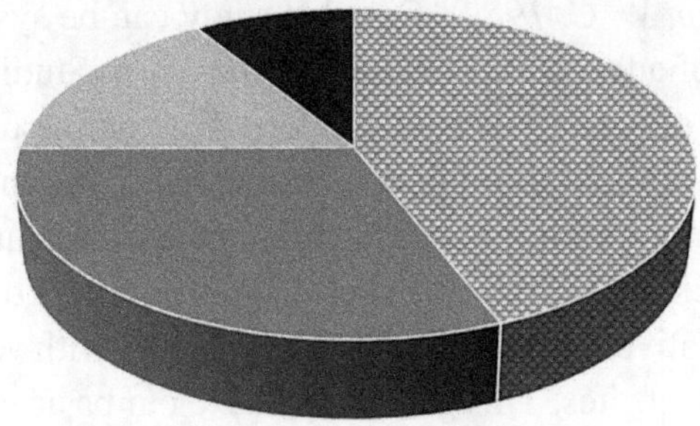

Further a survey was conducted on employees of a company who were not told about the purpose of the survey. Participants were asked to give their opinion on one Wikipedia article, without even specifying on what aspect of the article their opinion belongs. The facts and figures of some web pages were altered to check the attention a person pays on the figures. The users with less domain knowledge were not able to properly spotlight on the content characterized to access credibility. This implied that manipulating the accuracy of the data does not influence the trust and credibility judgment of these users.

"When people rely on the web to gather and distribute information, they can build a sense of trust in the websites with which they interact" (*Cheshire, C., Antin, J., Cook, K.S., & Churchill E. 2007*). This sense comes from the decisions taken based on prior knowledge or past personal experience by the users. As there are a lot of sources relevant to a given query and all the sources claim themselves to be the most credible source of information, these decisions are made regularly. "The onus is to exploit this decision-making power of humans to understand the correlates of trust which is essential for constructing better models of trust and online behaviour and at the same time identify the factors which impact the credibility of any given information on web which in turn builds TRUST of an individual" *(Singal, H., & Kohli, S. 2016)*. This study investigates into the fact that how credibility and trust are closely related and at the same time how credibility of information acts as a stepping stone towards building trust of an individual.

BACKGROUND

The outset of trust in information complies with relational model of trust (*Chopra, K., & Wallace, A. W. 2002*). Generally, research findings highlight direct precursors or individual characteristics of trust such as reputation, authority, prior familiarity, competence, reliability, openness, integrity, benevolence and institutional safeguards (*Jarvenpaa, J. S., Knoll, K., & Leidner, D. E. 1998, Paul, D. L. 2000, Gefen, D., Karahanna, E., & Straub, D. W. 2003, Mayer, R. C., Davis, J. H., & Schoorman, F. D. 1995*). This elucidates trust akin to the construct itself. Circumplex theory is used (*M. S. Pooleet al. 2004*) to identify factors that lead to interpersonal interaction in the world of web, especially in context of telemedicine. Circumplex takes 16 personality traits based on different degrees of Dominance, Control and Affiliation. Circumplex theory states that these sixteen personality traits influence trust and the cognitive processes that cause them (*Carson, R. C. 1969, Wiggins, J. S., Phillip C. K., & James N. B. 1982, Gains*

Jr., S. O., Lyde, M. D., Panter, A. T., Steers, W. N., Rusbult, C. E., Cox, C. L., & Wexler, M. O. 1997, Johnson-George, C. J., & Swap, W. C. 1982). Detailed study can be systematically tabularized (Table 1) for assessing the sequence of advancements in evaluating trust. Studies convey the active participation of researchers in the field of trust in web, also referred as 'online trust'. It can also be assimilated from the studies that trust in an online content is of particularly importance in websites related to health in any manner, as this is the area which directly impacts the humans and society using the internet to quench their knowledge regarding any kind of issues. Moreover, most of the research has been carried out to measure trust in collaborative world, virtual or social media with very few directed towards actual online content supplied by the websites. This gives impetus to our basic goal of research: 'How trust can be effectively measured in a website?' In slake of finding an answer to this question; the authors have carried out the study on the websites dealing with sensitive information in any manner.

To support the general idea of credibility acting as a stepping stone towards building online trust of users, a model has been proposed after identifying certain factors which affect the credibility of information on the web which ultimately becomes the deciding criterion for TRUST.

RESEARCH METHODOLOGY

Web Analytics tools deliver us with an enormous size of analytical data (web metrics); for all kind of web links even including all types of content-driven websites; but the question arises how to change that data into fruitful information, which will increase the business returns according to the business form is the problem which has not been solved successfully yet today (Kaushik, A. 2007).The work on TRUST and credibility has tried to focus on many factors. Many models are there to present, evaluate and symbolize the TRUST for various websites, but to the best of understanding there is very limited study to calculate trust (*Singal, H., & Kohli, S. 2016, Singal, H., & Kohli, S. 2015, Singal, H., & Kohli, S. 2014*), which is based on web metrics for health related web links or websites which are content driven; which is one of focal point of this study. So, the purpose is to resolve this breach by conceptualising a new model, which will try to calculate the TRUST maintained for the content driven web links over the time phase. This can only be done by modelling and masking the behaviour of visitors on the website and web users into trustworthy value, which one perceives about any website. This study conducted by one of the authors previously (*Singal, H., & Kohli, S. 2016, Singal, H., & Kohli, S. 2015, Singal, H., & Kohli, S. 2014*) has been extended and the later part probes into finding the factors which affect the credibility of online content and analyses them to come up with a quantitative measure of credibility of any given website.

The objective of the research was to find an assessing criterion for websites to help search engines to re-rank search results based on criteria like TRUST and CREDIBILITY. The initial part of this research objective was met using three major modules i.e. Desk Research, Factual Survey & Perceptual Implementation, all combining to form the Model-1 (The TRUST Model) by scientifically developed analysis and ranking process (Figure 3). The later part of this research was carried out in three phases which focused on CREDIBILITY being the criterion for ranking of websites. This formed the Model 2 (The CREDIBILITY Model). In the end, a comparative study of Model-2 (The CREDIBILITY Model) was done with existing tools. At the same time, a survey was conducted in a closed group to perform a face validity test of the credibility model(MODEL-2) to determine the similarity between the human responses and the results obtained from the CREDIBILITY Model.

Figure 3. Research methodology

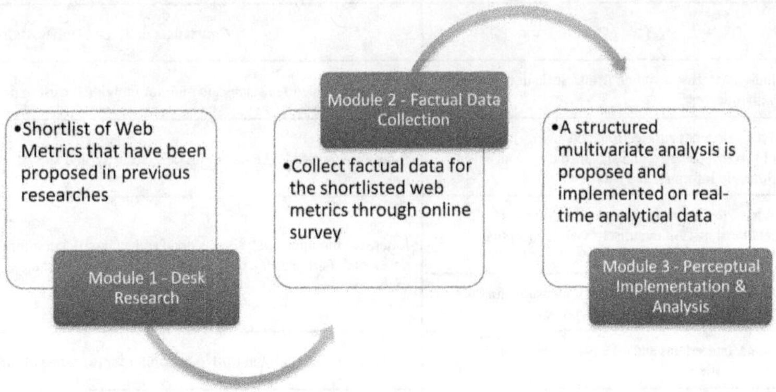

MODEL-1 (THE TRUST MODEL)

The initial part of this research which basically focuses on TRUST building and its related factors has been proposed through this model. The work has been carried out in three phases forming the respective modules which are as follows (Figure 3):

- Desk Research
- Factual Survey
- Perceptual Implementation

MODULE 1: DESK RESEARCH

The module 1 was a secondary research module. A comprehensive list of web metrics was generated with the help of research papers, articles and other publications. There are many web metrics suggested in the literature. Since the difference between measurable outcomes of these web metrics is small, conceptual clustering (*McKnight, D. H., & Choudhury, V. 2002*) was used to group them into different categories as tabularized in Table 1.

Table 1. Literary assessment of trust

S. No.	Author Name	Title of Study	Constructs of Trust Studied/Referred
1.	*Cheskin Research & Studio Archetype/ Sapient (1999)*	e-Commerce Trust Study	Antecedents of TRUST were studied to come up with six mechanisms for building web merchant trust.
2.	*Dayalet al.(1999)*	How to build trust online?	Qualitative analysis is done for ascertaining six elements and four stages of trust building.
3.	*Hoffman et al. (1999)*	Building consumer trust online	Surveyed issues for exchanging personal information in online relationship to monitor trust.
4.	*Jarvenpaa et al. (2000)*	Consumer trust in an internet store	Proposed strategies to develop trust, particularly in e-commerce websites.

continued on following page

Table 1. Continued

S. No.	Author Name	Title of Study	Constructs of Trust Studied/Referred
5.	*Bhattacherjee, A. (2002)*	Individual trust in online firms: Scale development and initial test	Proposed a scale to measure and monitor individual trust in online enterprises.
6.	*Belanger et al. (2002)*	Trustworthiness in electronic commerce: The role of privacy, security, and site attributes. Journal of Strategic Information Systems	Strongly supported "the role of privacy, security, and site attributes in e-Commerce".
7.	*McKnight et al. (2001)*	What trust means in e-commerce customer relationships: An interdisciplinary conceptual typology	Extensive literature analysis was done and a classification for cross-disciplinary trust was developed. Further, they proposed an instrument to measure typology of trust constructs found in their study.
8.	*McKnight et al. (2002)*	Developing and validating trust measures for e-commerce: An integrative typology	
9.	*Ridings et al. (2002)*	Some antecedents and effects of trust in virtual communities	Surveyed and established trust as an arbiter for exchange of information.
10.	*Shankar et al. (2002)*	Online trust: A stakeholder perspective, concepts, implications, and future directions	Proposed a model for "understanding antecedents and consequences of online trust" after an extensive literature survey.
11.	*Gefen et al. (2003)*	Managing user trust in B2C e-services	An extensive study was done and it was determined that social presence impacts consumer trust and found that repeated customers have different perceptions of trust than new customers.
12.		Inexperience and experience with online stores: The importance of TAM and trust.	
13.	*Kim et al. (2003)*	Trust-related arguments in internet stores: A framework for evaluation	Gave a pioneer direction in the study of TRUST among websites by developing a model that classifies major issues among trust.
14.	*Cline et al. (2001)*	Review consumer health information seeking on the internet: the state of art	Presented a pertinent analysis advocating that civic health inspectors should be alarmed about online health seeking, consider impending benefits and discover criterion for appraising online health information.
15.	*Eysenbach et al. (2002)*	How do consumer search for and appraise health information on the World Wide Web? Qualitative study using focus group usability tests and in-depth review	Systematically evaluated health Websites and established that the common quality criterion included "accuracy, completeness, and design (visual appeal, readability)". 70% of their studies concluded that "the quality of health-related Web content is low".
16.	*Sillence et al. (2004)*	Trust and mistrust of online health sites	Studied the impact of design and content on the trust and mistrust induced by health Websites. They conducted a study of small number of subjects engaged in "structured and unstructured search sessions". They found that "aspects of design appeal stimulated mistrust, whereas the credibility of information and personalization of content engendered trust".
17.	*Kohli et al. (2009)*	Certainty Factor Based Analysis for Measuring Users Satisfaction with Search Engine	Evaluates user satisfaction with a search session based on heuristic. It appraised sources of uncertainties in a search session and their impact on user satisfaction.
18.	*Kohli et al. (2011)*	Evolution of user dependent model to predict future usability of a search engine	Presents a 'user dependency' model which showed that psychological satisfaction level of the
19.	*T. Lewis (2006)*	Seeking health information on the internet: lifestyle choice or bad attack of cyberchondria?	Confers the growing trend towards the general public looking for health-related information online. They performed a qualitative study into young peoples' use of the Web for health material indicating that people are often sceptical consumers of Web-based health material.
20.	*Baker et al. (2003)*	Use of Internet and e-mail for health care information: results from a national survey	Probes the prevalence of Web and email use for healthcare, and their effects on users' knowledge of healthcare matters and their use of the healthcare system.
21.	*Eastin et al. (2006)*	Worried and wired: effects of health anxiety on information seeking and healthcare utilization behaviors	Probing the relationship between online health information searching and health care utilization (visiting a general practitioner). Their findings suggested that an individual's health anxiety regulates the relationship between online health information searching and healthcare.
22.	*Xiong et al. (2003)*	A Reputation based Trust Model for Peer-to-Peer e-Commerce communities	Proposed a TRUST model which considers the TRUST related factors that affect the reputation of entity in a system.
23.	*English et al. (2004)*	Engineering Trust based collaborations in a global computing environment	Provide an insight of the relationship between TRUST and risk.
24.	*Lam et al. (2005)*	Trading in Open Marketplace Using Trust and Risk	Gave a model that enable agents to use TRUST and risk as tools to evaluate the trustworthiness of potential agents.
25.	*Bin et al. (2010)*	A method for Evaluating Initial Trust Value of Direct Trust and Recommender Trust	Aims to get initial trust value of direct trust and recommender trust.
26.	*Aljazzaf et al. (2011)*	Towards a Unified Trust Framework for Trust Establishment and Trust Based Service Selection	Proposed a framework to build trust for services and to select services based on trust criteria. The main purpose is to move towards a unified framework that includes the main trust components to have a complete trust solution based on trust definition and trust principles.
27.	*Nafi et al. (2012)*	An advanced Certain Trust Model using Fuzzy Logic and Probabilistic Logic Theory	Proposed an extension of Certain TRUST Model based on probabilistic and Fuzzy logic.
28.	*Xin et al. (2013)*	A Dynamic Trust Conference Algorithm for Social Network	Proposed an algorithm for inferring dynamic trust based on trust chains and interactions for social networks.

Five categories were picked for conceptual clustering that appeared most relevant. Those five categories are:

1. Website Quality
2. Conversion Rate
3. Dwell Time
4. Bounce Rate
5. Overall Traffic

The pie-chart in Figure 4 depicts the share of each of these categories.

These five categories or web metrics formed the basis of our first research model. These kind of metrics supported by numerous theories (*Fishbein, M., & Ajzen, I. 1975, Ajzen, I. 1991, McKnight, D. H., & Choudhury,V. 2002 Chen, S. C., & Dhillon, G. S. 2003, Chen, Kong,W., & Hung,Y. T. C. 2006, Salo, J., & Karjaluoto 2007, Pan, B., Hembrooke, H. A., Gay, G. K., Granka, L. A., Feusner, M. K., & Newman, J. K. 2004, Sutcliffe, A. 2002, Peterson, E. T. 2006*) helped to formulate the research hypotheses, whose detailed findings can be referred in one of our author's previous work (Singal, H., & Kohli, S. 2014). The hypothesis modelled showed a direct relationship between perceived trustworthiness and web metrics which could be easily collected through Web Analytics tools.

MODULE 2: FACTUAL DATA COLLECTION

Based on the research hypotheses formulated by authors, a questionnaire was created and circulated amongst them to collect data about how internet users observe the significance of these factors to calculate the trustworthiness of web, the information or content they mostly gather from the websites. This closed survey was conducted online with the convenience sampling of size 100. In all, 106 responses were collected out of which three responses were not able to pass the validation phase, thus providing the final sample size as 103. The detailed analysis of this survey done by the authors can be found in (Kohli, S., & Singal, H. 2015). It was found that the hypotheses perceived almost fell in line with the

Figure 4. Share of each Web Metrics after conceptual clustering

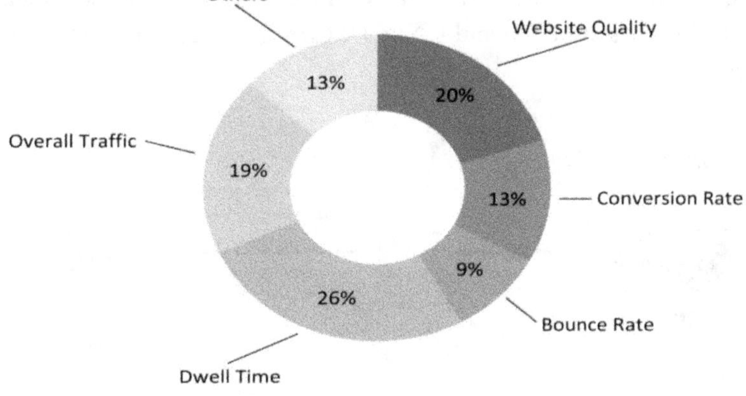

data collected from actual web users. Based on its outcome, following web metrics were decided to be used as antecedents of TRUST for information-driven websites: Bounce Rate, Average Daily Visits, Pages/Visit and Average Time on the Website.

- **Average Time on Website:** This is just an average amount of time all visitors spend on a particular page.
- **Pages/Visit:** Average number of web pages visited in a single session by the user.
- **Average Daily Visits:** This gives the number of visitors who have visited the website.
- **Bounce Rate:** The percentage of visitors to a particular website who navigate away from the site after viewing only one page; particularly in less than 30 seconds.

As a result of the detailed study done by the authors, further to benchmark the model for trust evaluation, real-time data was gathered from Similar web Ltd. which provides services in data mining, web analytics and business intelligence for international corporations (*Similarweb 2015*). It uses big data techniques to corroborate analytical data world wide and analyse it. Since the main aim is to evaluate trust in content driven websites or information led websites related to health, data of roughly 100 medical websites were collected over the time of six months from June 2014 to November 2014, for the web metrics identified (Bounce Rate, Average Time on Website, Pages/Visit, Average Daily Visits) and Rank, under the list of health type which covers medical sub-fields as following:

Dentistry, Education & Resources, Healthcare Industry, Pharmacy, Products & Shopping, Conditions & Diseases, Alternative and Natural Medicine, Addictions, Child Health, Senior health, Women's health, Public health & Safety, Reproductive health, Medicine, Men's Health, Mental Health and Nutrition.

These web links were chosen in such a way so that they can easily be classified into 3 trust categories as direct studies in (*Nurse, JRC, Agrafiotis, I., Goldsmith, M., Creese, S., & Lamberts, K. 2014, Idris, NH, Jackson, MJ, & Abrahart RJ. 2011*) powerfully suggest that trust should not have more than 3 categories. This information was gathered in the month of December 2014.

MODULE 3: PERCEPTUAL IMPLEMENTATION AND ANALYSIS

Perceptual implementation of real-time data collected is depicted in Figure 5. Implementation was done in two ways to analyze data: on monthly basis for all six months and six months as a whole using R software. R is an open-source software which supports most of the strong statistical computationsand graphics. It supports Windows, Mac OS and UNIX (*R Core Team 2014*). We have used R version3.1.2 – "Pumpkin Helmet".

Figure 5. Data Implementation Plan

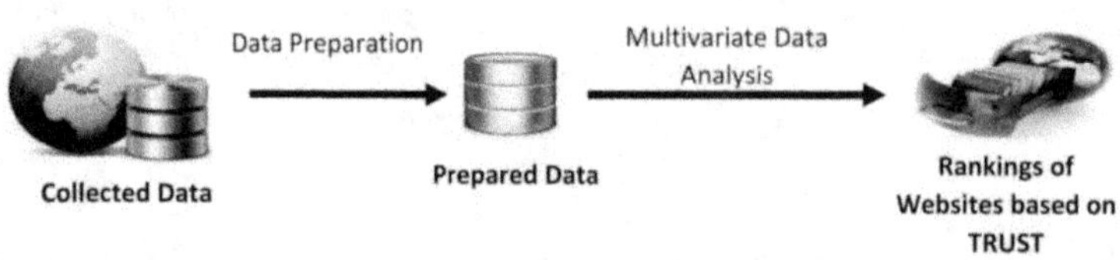

Data Preparation

Every time, when analysis was done, raw data collected from Similarweb.com was cleaned using visual inspection features (summary and histograms) available in R to exclude the outliers. The cleaned data was then transformed using z-score normalization. "It is done on the values for an attribute (say X) using mean and standard deviation of X. Normalized values are computed as:

$$x_i' - \frac{x_i - \overline{X}}{\sigma_x}$$

where, x_i = a value in X and x_i' =new normalized value

It is done to ensure that attributes with larger domains name do not dominate attributes with smaller domains and to avoids the dependence on the choice of measurement units (also referred standardisation of data). It helps in giving all attributes an equal weight" (*Han, J., Kamber, M., & Pei, J. 2012*). Cleaned data was normalised for all the attributes corresponding to web metrics chosen and categorical ranking was labelled using data discretization (or concept hierarchy generation) by a binning method. Three bins were used for categorising as it was found in a direct study in (*Nurse, JRC, Agrafiotis, I., Goldsmith, M., Creese, S., & Lamberts, K. 2014*) that 5 or more levels of trust instead of 3 become "more challenging for individuals to perceive". The same has been supported by (*Idris, NH, Jackson, MJ, & Abrahart RJ 2011*).

Data Analysis

Several multivariate analysis techniques were studied to analyse this data. Multiple Discriminant Analysis (MDA) techniques was used as it comes up with the best suitable situation for the data gathering, since all the web metrics gathered are metric whereas trust is non-metric in nature. In MDA, a variation is formed to create scores from each observation that will maximally differentiate between observation group. Based on the nature of variate, MDA can further be of two types:

1. Linear Discriminant Analysis (LDA)
2. Quadratic Discriminant Analysis (QDA)

Both LDA and QDA were applied on a dataset of all six months individually and on the complete data set of six months as a whole to obtain both linear and quadratic variate as a measure for trust classification of websites. The results obtained through LDA on a dataset of a month of June 2014 can be seen in Figure 6. Since 3 classes for trust are used as discussed in the previous sections, 2 Discriminant functions (LD1 and LD2) are obtained to significantly classify the attributes, as a number of functions obtained is always 1 less than the number of classified groups of the variable (here, trust). LD1 and LD2, as shown in Figure 6 represents Discriminant Loadings for all the four web metrics chosen as antecedents of Trust. "The proportion of trace is the proportion of between class variance that is explained by successive discriminant functions" (*Hair, JF, Black, WC, Babin, BJ, & Anderson, RE 2013*). Classification matrix was obtained by applying these Discriminant functions to test the performance of this technique and misclassification error obtained was 29.33% as depicted in Figure 7. Similarly, QDA was performed

Figure 6. Screenshot for the results obtained through LDA for dataset of June, 2014

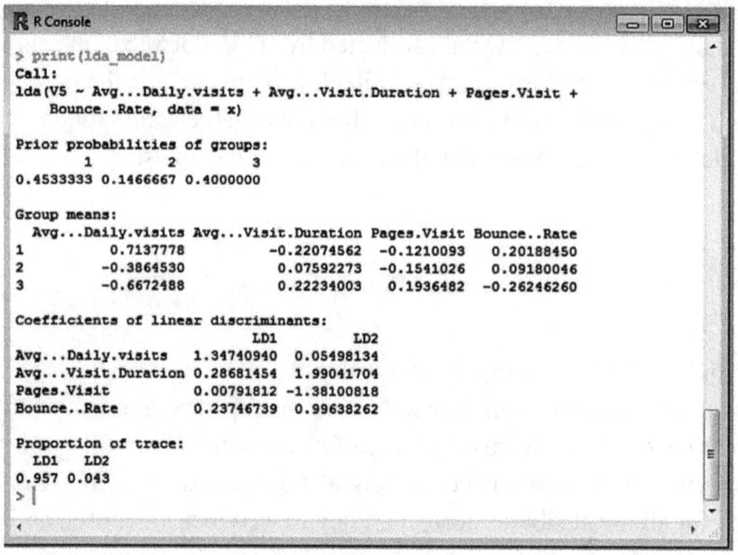

Figure 7. Classification matrix obtained through LDA of dataset of June, 2014

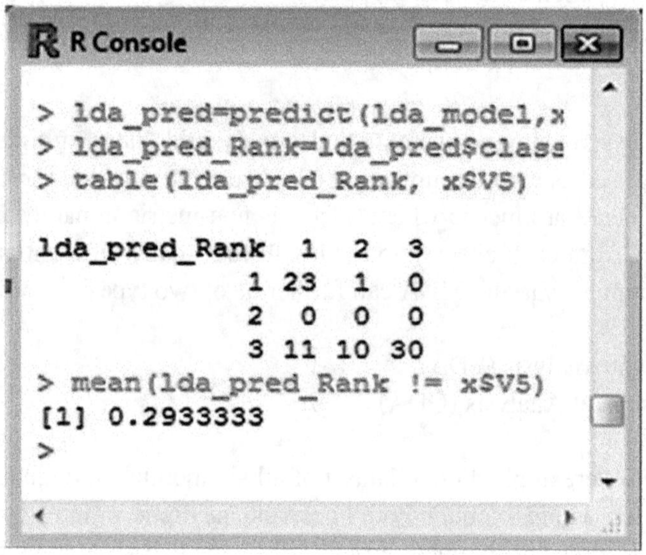

and misclassification error obtained decreased to 21.33% as depicted in Figure 8. In all the figures, 1 represents the most trustworthy and 3 represents a least trustworthy class.

Similarly, LDA and QDA were applied on dataset of July 2014, August 2014, September 2014, October 2014, November 2014 and consolidated data of June 2014 to November 2014. The complete analysis is detailed in next section.

Figure 8. Results of QDA and classification matrix of dataset of June, 2014

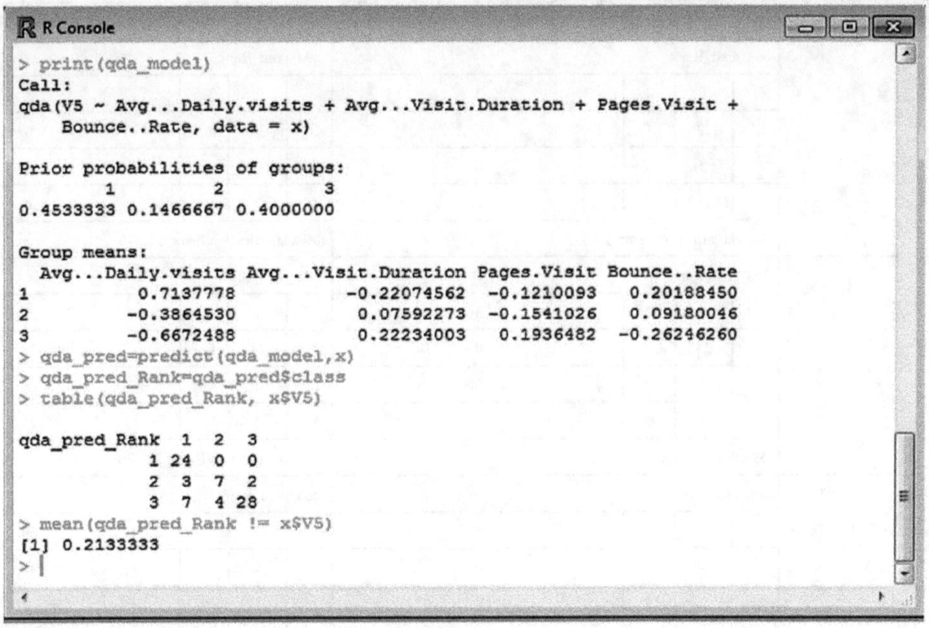

ANALYSIS

Table 2 enlists the classification matrix obtained after applying LDA and QDA. Misclassification errors are also mentioned. Classification matrix can be treated as error matrix. It is a "specific table layout that allows visualisation of the performance of an algorithm and contains information about actual and predicted classifications" (*Confusion Matrix 2015*). Ideally, off-diagonal matrix's element should be zero as diagonal elements depicting the number of correct classifications and off-diagonal elements depict erroneous classifications. Overall Misclassification Error was calculated in each case using R. It represents the percentage of websites which were wrongly classified. Firstly, it was observed that QDA was much better than LDA as their average misclassification errors were 19.23% and 28.65% respectively. Secondly, Misclassification Error of number of 1's (i.e. websites having most trustworthy label) was nearly same in both LDA and QDA. It is known that QDA is costlier to compute than LDA, as former requires (K*p + K*p*p) calculations of parameters (p), whereas LDA requires (K*p + p*p) calculations. Here K is a covariance matrix corresponding to the number of classes (*Discriminant Analysis, 2015*). Since the aim of our study is to provide users with most trustworthy websites (having label 1) at higher positions while searching any information, it can be aptly achieved through both LDA and QDA applied on Web Analytical data, though QDA is preferred if preciseness is to be maintained across all the websites under consideration. A trade-off can be maintained accordingly. Thirdly, Misclassification error of consolidated data of 6 months is much less than individual month's misclassification error (except for the dataset of October 2014). This indicates that with time, if data is consolidate and analysis is done, then better results can be achieved.

These results (Table 2) are in contour with our expected and desired outcome of trust based on human performance behaviour and attitudinal factors. There is no biasing in results as data collected is authentic and without notice of users (through Web Analytics tools) thus foregoing any chance of it being maligned or prejudiced.

Table 2. Classification Matrix and Misclassification error

S. No.	Month of Dataset	Classification Matrix Obtained as Result of LDA				Classification Matrix Obtained as Result of QDA			
1.	June 2014	lda_pred_Rank				qda_pred_Rank			
			1	2	3		1	2	3
		1	23	1	0	1	24	0	0
		2	0	0	0	2	3	7	2
		3	11	10	30	3	7	4	28
		Misclassification Error: 29.33%				Misclassification Error: 21.33%			
2.	July 2014	lda_pred_Rank				qda_pred_Rank			
			1	2	3		1	2	3
		1	24	1	0	1	24	1	0
		2	0	0	0	2	3	7	2
		3	7	13	27	3	4	6	25
		Misclassification Error: 29.16%				Misclassification Error: 22.22%			
3.	August 2014	lda_pred_Rank				qda_pred_Rank			
			1	2	3		1	2	3
		1	24	0	0	1	24	1	0
		2	2	6	4	2	4	10	1
		3	5	10	21	3	3	5	24
		Misclassification Error: 29.16%				Misclassification Error: 19.44%			
4.	September 2014	lda_pred_Rank				qda_pred_Rank			
			1	2	3		1	2	3
		1	21	3	0	1	24	1	0
		2	2	5	2	2	3	10	1
		3	8	6	23	3	4	3	24
		Misclassification Error: 30%				Misclassification Error: 17.14%			
5.	October 2014	lda_pred_Rank				qda_pred_Rank			
			1	2	3		1	2	3
		1	26	1	0	1	28	1	0
		2	1	5	0	2	1	9	1
		3	6	9	24	3	4	5	23
		Misclassification Error: 23.61%				Misclassification Error: 16.66%			
6.	November 2014	lda_pred_Rank				qda_pred_Rank			
			1	2	3		1	2	3
		1	24	2	0	1	28	0	0
		2	4	3	3	2	3	9	3
		3	5	10	23	3	2	6	23
		Misclassification Error: 32.43%				Misclassification Error: 18.91%			
7.	June 2014 to November 2014	lda_pred_Rank				qda_pred_Rank			
			1	2	3		1	2	3
		1	26	1	0	1	28	0	0
		2	2	6	2	2	2	10	2
		3	7	8	22	3	5	5	22
		Missclassification Error: 27.02%				Missclassification Error: 18.91%			

MODEL-2 (THE CREDIBILITY MODEL)

In just two decades or so, the Internet has incorporated itself into our lives as an essential, if not necessary, tool for information and communication. The surplus of information and data available online, coupled with the heavy trust on the Web by information-seekers raises the issue of the quality of information found and credibility of online information. Shortly after the problem of establishing credibility in the online environment was recognized, we tried to resolve the problem statement by our given approach, in which numerous factors are needed to be examined to decide the level of the credibility of the websites.

The data and its source on the web is generally not filtered by experts or professional mechanisms. There are no such universal or globally standards which is accepted worldwide for publishing and posting online and the data which is available through web links can effortlessly copied from a wrong source, or altered or produced namelessly. It not only provides false information to the user but can also mislead the users. Thus, it would be very helpful and useful for users to have a methodology which can compute the credibility score of websites and to some extent not end up using the incredible information.

The factors taken into consideration for the later part of this study related to assessing the credibility of a website portrays the quantitative aspects of web credibility. Taking quantitative factors into consideration would not only help in understanding these factors mathematically but at the same time bring up an image of the proposed model in front of the prospective users comprising of students, teachers and researchers, helping them in assessing the credibility of any website in an unambiguous manner hence making the information they use for their study more credible. Many application programming interfaces (API's) are used for this purpose to get real time data available in databases on the internet. Authentic APIs like Google search API have been used to keep the data authentic, unbiased and intact. Figure 9 depicts the overall architecture and dependencies of "THE CREDIBILITY MODEL".

The user gives in a search term as an input which is passed through Google search API to fetch relevant search URL's related to the search term. These individual URL's are further given as input to other API's for sentiment analysis, user rating and several other relevant factors which count for the credibility of any website. The output result from each API for every URL is assigned a weight based on which the final composite score is assigned to each website. Choice based conjoint analysis technique is used. In this technique pair-wise ranking of all possible factors is done to give dominant attributes more priority based on how logical the pair of those two factors are. This part of research focusing on credibility of websites was implemented in three phases over a period of four months (Figure 10). The whole study is in lines with the study found in (*Aggarwal, S., Van Oostendorp, H., Reddy, Y. R., & Indurkhya, B. 2014*)

PHASE-1

In this phase, identification of various quantitative factors which affect the credibility of any website were identified. Research papers and journals containing previous works related to trust and credibility were studied and four factors were chosen. The factors were:

1. **Domain Type:** Takes into consideration various types of domains to which websites belong. (.gov -Government websites; .com -commercial websites; .edu -educational websites; .in -informational websites; others -other websites).

Figure 9. Overall Architecture and Dependencies

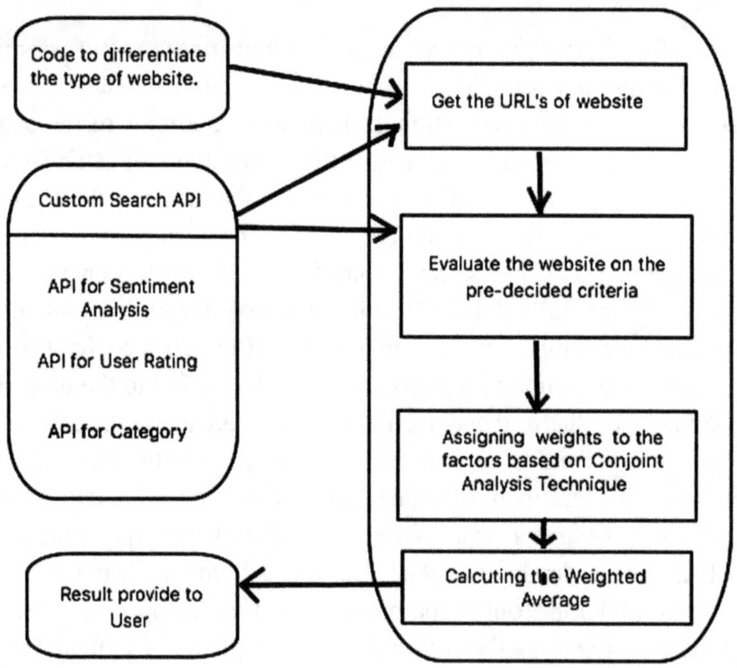

Figure 10. Implementation phases of Credibility model

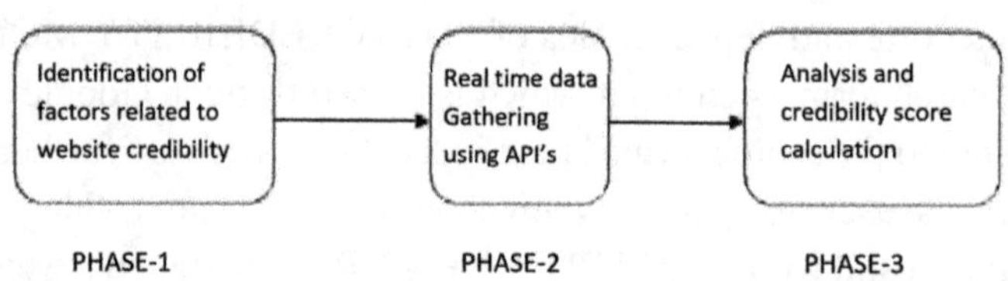

2. **Category of Website:** This factor determines the category to which the content of a website belongs (Negative, questionable, Neutral, Positive).
3. **Reputation of Website**: Reputation of websites are measured for targets in several *components*. For each {target, component} pair that website has, the system computes two values: the estimate reputation of a website and the confidence in reputation. Together, these two components indicate the amount of trust in the target in the given component (website).
4. **Sentiment of Content:** Takes into consideration the sentiment to discover how people actually feel about the content (Positive, negative, Neutral).

PHASE-2

Post successfully identification of factors related to credibility of websites, in the second phase, data gathering was done. For every URL obtained as a search result of a search term, values of each identified factors were obtained for every URL using relevant API's.

- **Google Custom search API:** This API was used to gather links related to a search term entered by the user.
- **WOT (web of trust) API:** This API was used to retrieve data related to category and reputation of content on a given URL.
- **IMB BLUEMIX ALCHEMY API:** Real-time data retrieval of sentiment of content on a given URL (website) was done using this API.

Data gathering was done using above-mentioned API's and Python 2.7.5. Further analysis, based on values of factors obtained took place in the subsequent phase.

PHASE-3

The final phase of the "CREDIBILITY" model aimed at proposing a technique to provide a credibility score to every website after analysing the retrieved data values.

Fundamentally the proposed "CREDIBILITY" model uses conjoint analysis to examine how people values different factors (benefits, function, feature) that makes up an individual product and service. Regarding credibility analysis of websites, conjoint analysis helps in weighing the importance of possible values of every factor and accordingly assigns weights to all possible values. Table 3 represents the final weights assigned to the possible factor values after performing conjoint analysis. For the same, PAPRIKA method was used. The PAPRIKA method involves the decision-making technique where one has to answer a series of questions, which is based on his/her expert knowledge or on his/her judgment. Every question in a questionnaire is based on choosing between two hypothetical alternatives or attributes at a time and involving a trade off while the other criteria/attributes are same. Each time he or she answers a pair-wise-ranking question, PAPRIKA adapts it and based on his/her answers and all preceding answers, it chooses another question. Again, based on his/her answer, another question is created. This process keeps on going. It adaptively means that in some contexts PAPRIKA is familiar as a kind of adaptive conjoint analysis (www.1000minds.com).

Table 3 gives the weights assigned to the factors after performing the conjoint analysis as explained above.

SCORE CALCULATION

Obtaining a credibility score for every website related to the search query is the goal of this proposed model. After successfully assigning weights to all the possible values of factors affecting credibility of website, mean score of the values was obtained for each factor for a given website. It was calculated to obtain a score between 0 to 100.

$$Ci = \left(f1 + f2 + f3 + f4 + \ldots + fn\right)$$

Where:

Table 3. Assigned weights after Conjoint analysis

Factor	Possible Type	Weights
Category	Negative	0
	Questionable	22.02
	Neutral	73.39
	Positive	100
Reputation	Very Poor	0
	Undefined	0
	Poor	24.66
	Unsatisfactory	73.06
	Good	73.97
	Excellent	100
Domain Type	Others	0
	Commercial	3.571
	Informational/Network	18.57
	Educational/Academic	78.57
	Government	100
Sentiment	Negative	0
	Positive	41.89
	Neutral	100

Ci -is the credibility score calculated.

fn -is the weight of nth factor according to Table 3.

n -is the number of factors which affect the credibility of websites.

Score calculation was done using python 2.7.5 and final output contained top 7 to 10 websites (depending on the search term) sorted in descending order of their credibility score with the most credible website on the top along with the values of the factors (Domain type, Sentiment, reputation & Category). Figure 11 shows the final output of "THE CREDIBILITY MODEL" for the search term "Isro Space Launch".

VALIDATING MODEL-2 (THE CREDIBILITY MODEL) WITH RESPECT TO HUMAN JUDGMENT FOR CREDIBILITY

One of the aspects of this study was to exploit the decision-making power of humans with respect to TRUST and CRDIBILITY to understand its correlates, so it is really important to have some degree of correlation between how humans decide with respect to credibility to rank websites, and at the same time how the proposed model ranks the websites based on certain identified factors of credibility.

To carry out this validity test, a survey was conducted in a closed group of around 93 students in computer science department of a college. This validity test took place in three phases. In the first phase five websites were selected randomly based on the result of the search query "Isro space launch" for the validity test. A questionnaire was designed to assess the credibility of websites, in which the participants were asked to prioritize the listed factors namely Information accuracy, Ease of use, Website reputation and User interface, according to what they thought was the most important factor. After prioritizing the factors the participants were asked to visit all the five websites and search information for the term "Isro space launch". On each website, they rated few criteria on a five point Likert scale for every website (Table 4). The search term and websites were kept constant throughout this validity test to bring uniformity in the judging criteria and accordingly finding the correlation.

After successfully conducting the survey, the collected data was cleaned and 74 entries were taken into consideration for further analysis. Data was imported in R. Figure 12 shows the snapshot of entries of first 33 participants. P1, P2, P3, P4 in the first snapshot (data1) are the priorities given by the participants for the above mentioned factors and in the second snapshot (data2), uiw, enw, iaw, wrw represent Likert scale ratings on a scale of five for User-interface, Ease of navigation, Information accuracy and Website reputation respectively.

VALIDITY TEST ANALYSIS OF "THE CREDIBILITY MODEL" USING R

For evaluation of any website based on various factors, it is very important to judge the quality of a website. All the factors involved in the evaluation of the quality of any website may not have equal contributions. Some factors may be more pronounced whereas some may be having less contribution in the quality of that website. Weighing the factors with respect to their contribution is the most suitable

Table 4. Criteria rated for all the five websites on a five point Likert scale by the participants of the survey

FACTORS
User Interface
Ease of navigation
Information accuracy
Website reputation

Figure 11. Top 7 CREDIBLE websites for the search term "Isro space launch"

```
isro.gov.in Excellent Positive Government positive 85.4725
thehindu.com Excellent Positive Commercial neutral 75.89275
economictimes.indiatimes.com Excellent Positive Commercial positive 61.36525
ndtv.com Excellent Positive Commercial positive 61.36525
blogs.wsj.com Excellent Positive Commercial positive 61.36525
firstpost.com Excellent Positive Commercial negative 50.89275
en.wikipedia.org Excellent Positive Organization negative 50
```

Figure 12. Data imported in R

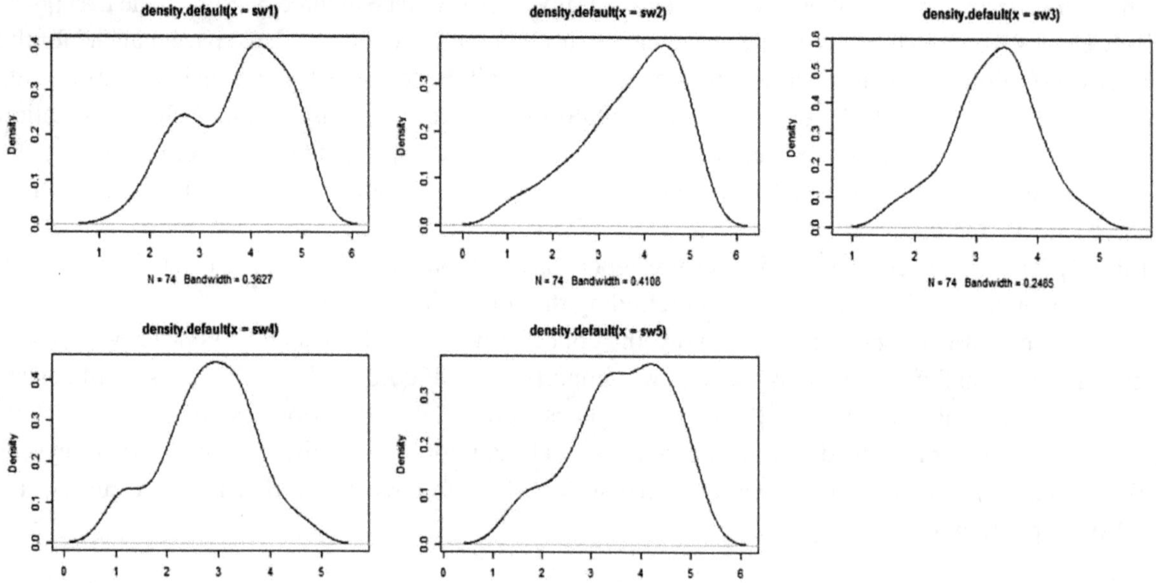


```
> sw1
 [1] 2.4 3.9 2.2 1.9 3.8 3.5 4.8 2.5 4.1 3.7 3.0 5.0 4.7 4.0 4.3 2.2 4.2 3.8 4.9 4.6 1.4 3.7 3.7 4.1 5.0 4.8 4.2 4.5 4.1 2.9 4.3 4.3 4.1 3.3 2.8 4.2 3.6 2.7
[39] 3.9 2.6 4.7 4.7 4.9 4.3 4.7 3.5 2.7 2.1 2.0 5.0 3.0 2.6 4.1 4.0 2.1 3.6 2.6 2.7 2.7 4.9 5.0 4.4 5.0 4.0 3.9 2.6 4.8 4.2 5.0 5.0 3.3 2.8 4.0 3.2
> sw2
 [1] 3.0 4.9 3.2 1.0 3.4 3.2 4.4 5.0 4.4 5.0 4.6 4.4 4.9 5.0 3.5 2.0 3.2 4.4 4.8 3.7 3.8 5.0 2.1 5.0 4.1 4.6 3.0 3.7 4.5 3.5 4.6 4.6 1.3 4.8 3.1 3.8 1.8 4.0
[39] 4.8 2.8 4.2 5.0 4.6 4.2 1.4 4.1 2.5 5.0 1.0 3.9 3.0 1.7 3.6 5.0 2.9 2.7 2.5 2.2 2.2 4.3 4.1 4.5 3.8 3.9 4.3 3.5 3.4 2.3 4.2 2.8 3.4 4.4 4.0 4.6
> sw3
 [1] 2.4 3.0 3.2 3.4 2.4 3.3 4.2 2.7 3.6 2.2 2.0 2.9 3.8 3.1 2.2 2.8 4.7 4.0 3.2 3.6 3.8 2.7 1.6 3.5 4.9 4.2 2.0 4.2 4.0 3.4 3.7 3.7 3.4 3.8 2.3 3.1 3.3 2.8
[39] 3.0 3.0 2.8 2.6 3.0 4.7 3.5 1.6 3.5 3.3 3.3 2.8 3.0 3.3 4.1 3.0 3.7 3.5 3.0 2.7 2.7 3.7 4.1 3.5 3.8 3.3 4.3 3.5 3.6 3.4 4.4 3.8 3.8 1.8 3.0 3.7
> sw4
 [1] 2.2 2.8 2.6 3.3 2.6 2.1 3.6 2.6 3.3 1.4 1.0 3.2 1.0 3.4 3.3 3.6 2.9 2.9 2.0 3.0 1.4 1.2 4.1 3.5 1.0 3.2 1.0 2.7 2.1 2.4 2.2 2.2 2.7 3.4 2.6 1.5 4.2 2.8
[39] 2.0 3.2 1.8 3.6 4.7 3.1 2.7 2.1 2.7 3.6 3.7 2.0 3.0 3.9 3.6 3.0 3.5 4.5 2.7 2.5 2.5 3.3 2.3 2.9 2.9 3.3 4.7 3.5 4.0 2.5 2.8 3.2 1.2 2.3 4.0 3.5
> sw5
 [1] 3.2 4.0 2.5 1.9 1.8 4.8 4.7 4.0 3.3 3.4 4.4 3.7 4.4 3.4 3.4 4.4 4.0 3.3 4.7 5.0 4.6 2.4 3.5 4.1 4.7 3.3 4.8 4.5 3.2 4.4 4.1 4.1 3.5 3.7 3.0 2.4 4.3 2.6
[39] 1.9 3.4 1.5 5.0 4.3 4.0 2.7 2.0 3.0 1.7 5.0 1.3 3.0 4.2 4.1 3.0 3.3 3.3 3.0 2.6 2.6 4.9 4.4 3.2 3.1 3.6 5.0 4.0 5.0 1.5 5.0 4.6 4.3 3.7 4.0 3.9
>|
```

approach to follow. Rank-sum (*RS*) approach has been used to assign weights to the prioritised criteria by the participants of the survey. Every participant had a set of weights assigned to his priority list of criteria with all the weights of a participant's criteria summing up to 1.

After assigning individual set of weights to the prioritised criteria list for all the 74 entries, a final score of all the five websites visited by the participant was calculated by multiplying the assigned weights with the corresponding Likert scale value of the criterion and then adding all the criteria to get a single value between 0 to 5. Likewise, a score was obtained for all the remaining four websites for every participant. Figure 13 shows the list of scores of all the five websites. SW1, SW2, SW3, SW4 and SW5 represents score of the websites 1, 2, 3, 4 and 5 respectively in form of a vector. There are total of 74 entries in every (SW) score vector.

Single score for every website was calculated by finding mean of individual website score vector (SW) and then arranging it in descending order (highest score website on the top). Table 5 shows the individual ranks of the website according to "The CREDIBILITY Model" and Survey conducted respectively. It yielded a Spearman's correlation value of 0.70.

Figure 13. Density distribution graph and scores of all the five websites

> data1

	P1	P2	P3	P4
1	User interface	Information accuracy	Ease of navigation	Website reputation
2	Website reputation	Information accuracy	User interface	Ease of navigation
3	Information accuracy	Website reputation	Ease of navigation	User interface
4	Information accuracy	Ease of navigation	Website reputation	User interface
5	Information accuracy	User interface	Ease of navigation	Website reputation
6	Information accuracy	Website reputation	User interface	Ease of navigation
7	Information accuracy	Ease of navigation	Website reputation	User interface
8	Information accuracy	User interface	Ease of navigation	Website reputation
9	Information accuracy	Website reputation	Ease of navigation	User interface
10	Information accuracy	Ease of navigation	Website reputation	User interface
11	Information accuracy	Ease of navigation	User interface	Website reputation
12	Information accuracy	Website reputation	User interface	Ease of navigation
13	Information accuracy	Ease of navigation	User interface	Website reputation
14	User interface	Ease of navigation	Information accuracy	Website reputation
15	Website reputation	Information accuracy	User interface	Ease of navigation
16	User interface	Ease of navigation	Website reputation	Information accuracy
17	Ease of navigation	Information accuracy	User interface	Website reputation
18	Information accuracy	Ease of navigation	Website reputation	User interface
19	Website reputation	Information accuracy	Ease of navigation	User interface
20	Information accuracy	Website reputation	Ease of navigation	User interface
21	User interface	Ease of navigation	Information accuracy	Website reputation
22	Ease of navigation	Information accuracy	User interface	Website reputation
23	Ease of navigation	User interface	Information accuracy	Website reputation
24	Ease of navigation	Website reputation	User interface	Information accuracy
25	Information accuracy	User interface	Ease of navigation	Website reputation
26	Ease of navigation	Website reputation	User interface	Information accuracy
27	Information accuracy	Ease of navigation	Website reputation	User interface
28	Information accuracy	User interface	Ease of navigation	Website reputation
29	Information accuracy	Website reputation	Ease of navigation	User interface
30	User interface	Ease of navigation	Information accuracy	Website reputation
31	Information accuracy	Website reputation	Ease of navigation	User interface
32	Information accuracy	Website reputation	Ease of navigation	User interface
33	Information accuracy	User interface	Ease of navigation	Website reputation

> data2

	uiw1	uiw2	uiw3	uiw4	uiw5	enw1	enw2	enw3	enw4	enw5	wrw1	wrw2	wrw3	wrw4	wrw5	iaw1	iaw2	iaw3	iaw4	iaw5
1	1	2	3	2	2	5	4	3	2	2	4	2	3	1	5	2	4	1	3	5
2	3	5	3	2	4	2	4	3	3	4	4	5	3	3	4	5	5	3	3	4
3	4	3	5	2	1	2	4	3	3	3	2	3	3	2	2	2	3	3	3	3
4	3	1	2	3	1	2	1	4	4	2	3	1	4	3	2	1	1	3	3	2
5	3	4	3	2	1	4	3	2	3	3	5	4	3	2	1	4	3	2	3	2
6	1	1	2	3	4	2	3	4	4	5	5	5	3	1	5	4	3	4	2	5
7	3	2	4	3	5	5	4	4	3	4	5	5	5	4	5	5	5	4	4	5
8	4	5	2	3	4	2	5	3	3	4	1	5	3	3	4	2	5	3	2	4
9	4	4	4	4	4	4	4	4	4	4	3	4	4	3	3	5	5	3	3	3
10	3	5	2	2	5	4	5	2	2	5	5	5	3	1	3	3	5	2	1	2
11	3	5	2	1	4	3	5	2	1	4	3	5	2	1	4	3	4	2	1	5
12	5	4	5	5	4	5	5	5	4	4	5	5	2	2	3	5	4	2	3	4
13	5	5	4	1	4	4	5	3	1	4	5	4	5	1	4	5	5	4	1	5
14	4	5	3	3	4	4	5	3	4	3	4	5	4	2	3	4	5	3	4	3
15	4	3	2	4	3	3	4	2	3	3	5	4	1	4	4	4	3	4	2	3
16	4	2	1	3	5	1	2	5	4	3	1	2	3	4	5	1	2	3	4	5
17	3	3	4	3	4	4	4	5	3	4	5	4	4	2	4	5	2	5	3	4
18	2	3	4	3	3	2	5	4	4	2	5	5	4	3	4	5	4	4	2	4
19	4	5	4	1	5	5	4	3	2	5	5	5	4	3	5	5	5	2	1	4
20	3	3	4	4	5	4	3	4	5	5	5	4	4	4	5	5	4	3	1	5
21	1	4	4	2	5	1	3	4	1	4	5	5	4	1	4	1	4	3	1	5
22	3	5	1	2	4	4	5	3	1	2	3	5	4	1	2	4	5	3	1	2
23	4	3	1	2	5	4	1	2	5	3	1	2	3	5	4	4	3	1	5	2
24	4	5	3	4	4	4	5	4	3	4	4	5	3	4	4	5	5	4	3	5
25	5	2	5	1	4	5	5	5	1	5	5	5	4	1	5	5	5	5	1	5
26	4	3	5	2	3	5	5	4	2	4	5	5	4	5	3	5	5	4	5	2
27	4	3	2	1	5	4	3	2	1	5	5	3	2	1	4	4	3	2	1	5
28	4	4	4	4	4	4	5	5	4	4	5	3	4	3	5	5	3	4	1	5
29	3	4	4	2	3	3	5	4	2	4	4	5	4	1	3	5	4	4	3	3
30	4	2	3	2	5	2	5	4	3	4	5	2	4	3	4	1	5	3	2	4
31	3	5	4	2	4	4	5	4	1	4	4	5	3	2	3	5	4	4	3	5
32	3	5	4	2	4	4	5	4	1	4	4	5	3	2	3	5	4	4	3	5
33	5	2	3	1	4	2	1	3	4	5	2	1	3	4	5	5	1	4	3	2

Finding correlation between the two sets of ranks obtained helped in determining the similarity between the results obtained by the proposed CREDIBILITY model and actual human judgment results for assessing the credibility of any website.

Table 5. Individual ranks of websites

Websites	Rank According to Model-2 (The CRDIBILITY Model)	Ranks According to the SURVEY
www.Isro.gov.in	1	1
www.thehindu.com	2	3
www.ndtv.com	3	4
www.firstpost.com	4	5
www.wikipedia.in	5	2

correlation= 0.70

The results obtained after the analysis of survey are fairly in strong correlation with the results obtained using THE "CREDIBILITY" MODEL (Model-2) thereby seeking us to the desired goal of our research to exploit and understand human behaviour of making decisions with respect to trust and credibility.

COMPARISON OF "THE CREDIBILITY MODEL" WITH THE EXISTING TOOL

Towards the end of this study, a comparison has been done between the proposed Credibility Model, which is based on credibility and WOT (Web of Trust) which ranks websites based on its TRUSTWORTHINESS. This comparative study in a way brings in light the relationship between trust and credibility and how credibility is followed by trust.

In this phase, we had taken four search terms for better accuracy and had obtained the ranks of websites for every term using the trustworthiness score provided by WOT for every website related to the search query. Search terms were selected on the basis of latest news headlines at the time of conduction of this study.

Search terms were as follows:

1. Isro space launch
2. Kashmir terrorism justified
3. Naxalite terrorism
4. H1B visa policy

On calculating the credibility score using "THE CREDIBILITY MODEL", there were cases where we had same credibility score for more than one website indicating same credibility of the websites. So, two cases were considered, namely:

- Considering websites with common credibility scores.
- Considering websites without common credibility score (Selecting any one of the websites with same credibility score).

Table 6 and Table 7 depicts the cases mentioned above.

Table 6. Comparison including websites with common credibility score "Isro space launch"

Websites	Score From WOT	Rank From WOT	Rank From Model-2	Score From Model-2
isro.gov.in	91	1	3	85.4725
thehindu.com	92	2	1	75.89275
economicstimes.indiatimes.com	86	3	6	61.36525
ndtv.com	89	3	5	61.36525
blog.wsj.com	92	3	1	61.36525
firstpost.com	90	6	4	50.89275
en.wikipedia.org	84	7	7	50

Correlation = 0.5822

Table 7. "Kashmir Terrorism Justified"

Websites	Score From WOT	Rank From WOT	Rank From Model-2	Score From Model-2
e-ir.info	88	7	3	66.115
firstpost.com	90	3	4	61.36525
quora.com	89	4	4	61.36525
time.com	93	1	1	75.89275
indianexpress.com	88	7	4	61.36525
ndtv.com	89	4	7	60.4725
carnegieendowment.org	93	1	2	75
projectcensored.org	89	4	8	60.4725
govinfo.library.unt.edu	76	9	9	58.6075

Correlation = 0.5822

Average correlation value between ranks of the Credibility Model (Model 2) and Survey = 0.70
Average correlation value between ranks of the Model 2 and WOT (without duplicate credibility scores) = 0.71
Average correlation value between ranks of the Model 2 and WOT (with duplicate credibility scores) = 0.89

These high correlation values indicates the success of our study of finding trustworthy and credible information from the huge pool of information provided as websites by search engines through the internet.

CONCLUSION

This study proposed a new credibility model based on its previous study of the trust model by one of the authors and compared it with an existing tool and human judges as well. From every aspect, the study has given the positive results thus giving an impetus in the field of assessing and corroborating the trustworthiness and credibility of the websites.

Table 8. "Naxalite terrorism"

Websites	Score From WOT	Rank From WOT	Rank From Model-2	Score From Model-2
ctc.usma.edu	94	1	1	80.115
news18.com	82	6	4	50.89275
quora.com	89	4		50.89275
dnaindia.com	90	2	3	61.36525
en.wikipedia.org	84	5	6	50
cfr.org	90	2	2	61.4725
satp.org	80	7	7	50

Correlation = 0.8280

Table 9. "H1B Visa Policy"

Websites	Score From WOT	Rank From WOT	Rank From Model-2	Score From Model-2
uscis.gov	94	1	1	85.4725
money.cnn.com	94	1	2	75.89275
firstpost.com	85	8	3	50.89275
nytimes.com	94	1	2	75.89275
usatoday.com	93	4	3	50.89275
livemint.com	88	6	3	50.89275
qz.com	91	5	3	50.89275
newindianexpress.com	88	6	3	50.89275
en.wikipedia.org	84	9	9	50
axios.com	60	10	10	19.38525

Correlation = 0.8102

Table 10.Comparison excluding websites with common credibility score "Isro space launch"

Websites	Score From WOT	Rank From WOT	Rank From Model-2	Score From Model-2
isro.gov.in	91	2	1	85.4725
thehindu.com	92	1	2	75.89275
ndtv.com	89	3	3	61.36525
firstpost.com	90	4	4	50.89275
en.wikipedia.org	84	5	5	50

Correlation=0.90

Table 11. "Kashmir terrorism justified"

Websites	Score From WOT	Rank From WOT	Rank From Model-2	Score From Model-2
e-ir.info	88	5	3	66.115
firstpost.com	90	3	4	61.36525
time.com	93	1	1	75.89275
ndtv.com	89	4	5	60.4725
carnegieendowment.org	93	1	2	75
govinfo.library.unt.edu	76	6	6	58.6075

Correlation = 0.8280

Table 12. "Naxalite terrorism"

Websites	Score From WOT	Rank From WOT	Rank From Model 2	Score From Model 2
ctc.usma.edu	94	1	1	80.115
news18.com	82	5	4	50.89275
dnaindia.com	90	2	3	61.36525
en.wikipedia.org	84	4	5	50
cfr.org	90	2	2	61.4725

Correlation = 0.8660

Table 13. "H1B Visa Policy"

Websites	Score From WOT	Rank From WOT	Rank From Model-2	Score From Model-2
uscis.gov	94	1	1	85.4725
money.cnn.com	94	1	1	75.89275
firstpost.com	85	3	3	50.89275
en.wikipedia.org	84	4	4	50
axios.com	60	5	5	19.38525

Correlation = 0.9727

The concept of credibility assessment can find application in many fields with research and academics fields being at the top. It is very much essential to know the credibility of the information used in any research or for training and teaching purposes. This study demonstrates that it is possible to design a model which can be used to define the credibility of a website.

'Websites are for humans'. So, behaviour of humans should be tracked to ensure decision-making while consuming any kind of information from web. The authors have presented a systematic and pertinent study which has shown acceptable results while ranking the categorical websites according to trust they induce and maintain with their users. The initial part of this study dealing with website trust has been done only in the dominion of health whereas the later part of this study dealing with credibility of websites has been done for content-driven websites.

The identified factors fairly justify their dependencies on the criteria TRUST and CREDIBILITY by exhibiting acceptable correlation. The unaccounted factors can further be identified and added to enhance the proposed model's accuracy. This initiating platform can be further explored for quantifying trust of content-driven websites. Initial trust labels can be obtained from other supervised or unsupervised learning algorithms for further improvisation.

REFERENCES

Aggarwal, S., Van Oostendorp, H., Reddy, Y. R., & Indurkhya, B. (2014, September). Providing Web Credibility Assessment Support. In *Proceedings of the 2014 European Conference on Cognitive Ergonomics* (p. 29). ACM.

Ajzen, I. (1991). The theory of Planned Behaviour. *Organizational Behavior and Human Decision Processes*, *50*(2), 179–211. doi:10.1016/0749-5978(91)90020-T

Alexander, J. E., & Tate, P. (1999). *Web Wisdom: How to evaluate and create information quality on the web.* Lawrence Erlbaum.

Aljazzaf, Z. M., Perry, M., & Capretz, M. A. M. (2011). *Towards a Unified Trust Framework for Trust Establishment and Trust Based Service Selection*. IEEE CCECE. doi:10.1109/CCECE.2011.6030647

AnalysisD. (2015). Retrieved from http://www.stats.ox.ac.uk/~teh/teaching/MS1b/l07a-qda.pdf

Baker, L., Wagner, T. H., Singer, S., & Bundorf, M. K. (2003). Use of Internet and e-mail for health care information: Results from a national survey. *Journal of the American Medical Association*, *289*(18), 2400–2406. doi:10.1001/jama.289.18.2400 PMID:12746364

Belanger, F., Hiller, J. S., & Smith, W. J. (2002). Trustworthiness in electronic commerce: The role of privacy, security, and site attributes. *The Journal of Strategic Information Systems*, *11*(3-4), 245–270. doi:10.1016/S0963-8687(02)00018-5

Bhattacherjee, A. (2002). Individual trust in online firms: Scale development and initial test. *Journal of Management Information Systems*, *19*(1), 211–241. doi:10.1080/07421222.2002.11045715

Calvert, P. J. (2001). Scholarly Misconduct and Misinformation on the World Wide Web. *The Electronic Library*, *19*(4), 232–240. doi:10.1108/EUM0000000005747

Carson, R. C. (1969). *Interaction Concepts of Personality*. Chicago: Aldine.

Chen, S. C., & Dhillon, G. S. (2003). Interpreting dimensions of consumer trust in e-commerce. *Information Technology Management*, *4*(2/3), 304–318. doi:10.1023/A:1022962631249

Cheshire, C., Antin, J., Cook, K. S., & Churchill, E. (2007). General and Familiar Trust in Websites. *Knowledge, Technology & Policy*, *23*(3), 311–331.

Cheskin Research & Studio Archetype/Sapient. (1999). *e-Commerce Trust Study*. Author.

Chopra, K., & Wallace, A. W. (2002). Trust in Electronic Commerce. *Proceedings of the 36th Hawaii International Conference on System Sciences HICCS'03*.

Clifton, B. (2008). *Advanced web metrics with Google Analytics*. Indianapolis, IN: Wiley Publishing, Inc.

Cline, R. J., & Haynes, K. M. (2001). Review consumer health information seeking on the internet: The state of art. *Health Education Research*, *16*(6), 671–692. doi:10.1093/her/16.6.671 PMID:11780707

Dayal, S., Landesberg, H., & Zeisser, M. (1999). How to build trust online. *Marketing Management*, *8*(3), 64–69.

Eastin, M. S., & Guinster, N. M. (2006). Worried and wired: Effects of health anxiety on information seeking and healthcare utilization behaviors. *Cyberpsychology & Behavior*, *9*(4), 494–498. doi:10.1089/cpb.2006.9.494 PMID:16901253

English, C., Terzis, S., & Wagealla, W. (2004). Engineering Trust based collaborations in a global computing environment. *Proceedings of the Second International Conference on Trust Management*, 135-145. doi:10.1007/978-3-540-24747-0_10

Eysenbach, G., & Kohler, C. (2002). How do consumer search for and appraise health information on the World Wide Web? Qualitative study using focus group usability tests and in-depth review. *BMJ (Clinical Research Ed.)*, *324*(7337), 573–577. doi:10.1136/bmj.324.7337.573 PMID:11884321

Fishbein, M., & Ajzen, I. (1975). *Belief, Attitude, Intention and Behaviour: An Introduction to theory and Research*. Addison-Wesley.

Gains, S. O. Jr, Lyde, M. D., Panter, A. T., Steers, W. N., Rusbult, C. E., Cox, C. L., & Wexler, M. O. (1997). Evaluating the circumplexity of interpersonal traits and the manifestation of interpersonal traits in interpersonal trust. *Journal of Personality and Social Psychology*, *73*(3), 610–623. doi:10.1037/0022-3514.73.3.610

Gefen, D., Karahanna, E., & Straub, D. W. (2003). Trust and TAM in online shopping: An integrated model. *Management Information Systems Quarterly*, *27*(1), 51–90.

Gefen, D., Karahanna, E., & Straub, D. W. (2003). Inexperience and experience with online stores: The importance of TAM and trust. *IEEE Transactions on Engineering Management*, *50*(3), 307–321. doi:10.1109/TEM.2003.817277

Gefen, D., & Straub, D. W. (2003). Managing user trust in B2C e-services. *e-Service Journal*, *2*(2), 7–24. doi:10.2979/esj.2003.2.2.7

Hair, J. F., Black, W. C., Babin, B. J., & Anderson, R. E. (2013). *Multivariate Data Analysis: A Global Perspective* (7th ed.). Pearson.

Han, J., Kamber, M., & Pei, J. (2012). Data Mining: Concepts and Techniques (3rd ed.). Morgan Kaufmann. doi:-1-4419-1428-6_3752 doi:10.1007/978

Hasan, L., Morris, A., & Probets, S. (2009). *Using Google Analytics to Evaluate the Usability of E-CommerceSite*. Human Centered Design. doi:-3-642-02806-9_8110.1007/978

Hernon, P. (1955). Disinformation and Misinformation through the Internet: Findings of an exploratory Study. *Government Information Quarterly*, *12*(2), 133–139. doi:10.1016/0740-624X(95)90052-7

Hoffman, D. L., Novak, T. P., & Peralta, M. (1999). Building consumer trust online. *Communications of the ACM*, *42*(4), 80–85. doi:10.1145/299157.299175

Hong, I. (2007). A survey of web site success metrics used by Internet-dependent organizations in Korea. *Internet Research*, *17*(3), 272–290. doi:10.1108/10662240710758920

Hong, S.-M. (2012). An exploratory study of the Users' Behavior on Social Network Site. In *Proceedings of the Ninth International Conference on Information Technology-New Generations*. IEEE. doi:10.1109/ITNG.2012.69

Idris, N. H., Jackson, M. J., & Abrahart, R. J. (2011). Colour coded traffic light labeling: A visual quality indicator to communicate credibility in map mash-up applications. *Proceedings of the International Conference on Humanities Social Sciences, Science & Technology*.

Ivory, M. Y., Sinha, R. R., & Hearst, M. A. (2001). *Empirically validated web page design metrics. SIGCHI conference on Human factors in computing systems*. Seattle, WA: ACM.

Jarvenpaa, J. S., Knoll, K., & Leidner, D. E. (1998). Is anybody out there? Antecedents of trust in global virtual teams. *Journal of Management Information Systems*, *14*(4), 29–64. doi:10.1080/07421222.1998.11518185

Jarvenpaa, S. L., Tractinsky, J., & Vitale, M. (2000). Consumer trust in an internet store. *Information Technology Management*, *1*(1&2), 45–71. doi:10.1023/A:1019104520776

Johnson-George, C. J., & Swap, W. C. (1982). Measurement of specific interpersonal trust: Construction and validation of a scale to assess trust in a specific other. *Journal of Personality and Social Psychology*, *43*(6), 1306–1317. doi:10.1037/0022-3514.43.6.1306

Juvina, I., & Oostendorp, H. (2006). Individual differences and behavioral metrics involved in modeling web navigation. *Universal Access in the Information Society*, *4*(3), 258–269. doi:10.1007/s10209-005-0007-7

Kaushik, A. (2007). *Web Analytics: An hour a Day*. Indianapolis, IN: Wiley Publishing, Inc.

Kim, D., & Benbasat, I. (2003). Trust-related arguments in internet stores: A framework for evaluation. *Journal of Electronic Commerce Research*, *4*(2), 49–64.

Kohli, S., & Kumar, E. (2009). Certainty Factor Based Analysis for Measuring Users Satisfaction with Search Engine. *International Journal of Information processing (IJIP)*, *3*(1).

Kohli, S., & Kumar, E. (2011). *Evolution of user dependent model to predict future usability of a search engine*. Academic Press.

Kohli, S., & Singal, H. (2015). A methodological approach for Quantizing Trust from Human Behavior for Content-Driven Websites. *International Journal of Sensors Wireless Communications and Control*, *5*(1), 32–46. doi:10.2174/2210327905999150521111919

Kohli, S., & Singal, H. (2015). A methodological approach for Quantizing Trust from Human Behaviour for Content-Driven Websites. *International Journal of Sensors, Wireless Communications and Control*, *5*(1), 32-46.

Kong, W., & Hung, Y. T. C. (2006). Modeling initial and repeat online trust in B2C e-commerce. In *Proceedings of HICSS'06*. IEEE.

Lam, Y. H., Zhang, Z., & Ong, K. L. (2005). Trading in Open Marketplace Using Trust and Risk. *Proceedings of the IEEE/WIC/ACM International Conference on Intelligent Agent Technology*.

Lewis, T. (2006). Seeking health information on the internet: Lifestyle choice or bad attack of cyberchondria? *Media Culture & Society*, *28*(4), 521–539. doi:10.1177/0163443706065027

Marchand, D. (1990). Managing information quality. In I. Wormell (Ed.), *Information Quality: Definitions and Dimensions*. London: Taylor Graham.

MatrixC. (2015). Retrieved from http://en.wikipedia.org/wiki/Confusion_matrix

Mayer, R. C., Davis, J. H., & Schoorman, F. D. (1995). An integrative model of organizational trust. *Academy of Management Review*, *20*(3), 709–734.

McKnight, D. H., & Chervany, N. L. (2001). What trust means in e-commerce customer relationships: An interdisciplinary conceptual typology. *International Journal of Electronic Commerce*, *6*(2), 35–59. doi:10.1080/10864415.2001.11044235

McKnight, D. H., Choudhury, V., & Kacmar, C. (2002). Developing and validating trust measures for e-commerce: An integrative typology. *Information Systems Research*, *13*(3), 334–359. doi:10.1287/isre.13.3.334.81

Mu, B., & Yuan, S. (2010). *A method for Evaluating Initial Trust Value of Direct Trust and Recommender Trust.* Academic Press.

Nafi, K. W., Kar, T. S., Hossain, M. A., & Hashem, M. M. A. (2012). An advanced Certain Trust Model Using Fuzzy Logic and Probabilistic Logic Theory. *International Journal of Advanced Computer Science and Applications, 3*(12).

Nurse, J. R. C., Agrafiotis, I., Goldsmith, M., Creese, S., & Lamberts, K. (2014). Two sides of the coin: Measuring and communicating the trustworthiness of online information. *Journal of Trust Management*, *1*(1), 5. doi:10.1186/2196-064X-1-5

Pan, B., Hembrooke, H. A., Gay, G. K., Granka, L. A., Feusner, M. K., & Newman, J. K. (2004). *The Determinants of Web Page Viewing Behavior: An Eye-Tracking Study*. ACM Transactions. doi:10.1145/968363.968391

Paul, D. L. (2000). *Telemedicine: a study of virtual collaboration and trust in hypercompetitive environments* (Dissertation). Department of Management Information Systems, University of Texas at Austin.

Peterson, E. (2004). *Web analytics demystified: A marketer's guide to understanding how your web site affects your business*. Celilo Group Media and CafePress.

Peterson, E. T. (2006). *The Big Book of Key Performance Indicators*. Web Analytics Demystified Series, Book Two. Celilo Group Media and CafePress.

Poole, M. S. (2004). Trust, Trait Theory, and Collaboration in Telemedicine: An Empirical Test. *Proceedings of the 37th Hawaii International Conference on System Sciences*. IEEE. doi:10.1109/HICSS.2004.1265374

R Core Team. (2014). *R: A language and environment for statistical computing.* R Foundation for Statistical Computing. Retrieved from http://www.R-project.org/

Ridings, C. M., Gefen, D., & Arinze, B. (2002). Some antecedents and effects of trust in virtual communities. *The Journal of Strategic Information Systems*, *11*(3&4), 271–295. doi:10.1016/S0963-8687(02)00021-5

Salo, J., & Karjaluoto, H. (2007). A conceptual model of trust in the online environment. *Online Information Review, 31*(5), 604–621. doi:10.1108/14684520710832324

Sentiment and Text Analysis Engine – AlchemyAPI. (2017). Retrieved from http://www.alchemyapi.com/api

Shankar, V., Urban, G. L., & Sultan, F. (2002). Online trust: A stakeholder perspective, concepts, implications, and future directions. *The Journal of Strategic Information Systems, 11*(3-4), 325–344. doi:10.1016/S0963-8687(02)00022-7

Sillence, E., Briggs, P., Fishwick, L., & Harris, P. (2004). *Trust and mistrust of online health sites.* SIGCHI; doi:10.1145/985692.985776

Similarweb. (2015). Retrieved from http://www.similarweb.com/

Singal, H., & Kohli, S. (2014, September). Conceptual model for obfuscated TRUST induced from Web Analytics data for content-driven websites. In *Advances in Computing, Communications and Informatics (ICACCI, 2014 International Conference on* (pp. 2781-2785). IEEE. doi:10.1109/ICACCI.2014.6968622

Singal, H., & Kohli, S. (2015, May). Escalation of TRUST analysis in web. In *Proceedings of the 12th ACM International Conference on Computing Frontiers* (p. 56). ACM.

Singal, H., & Kohli, S. (2016). Mitigating Information Trust: Taking the Edge off Health Websites. *International Journal of Technoethics, 7*(1), 16–33. doi:10.4018/IJT.2016010102

Singal, H., & Kohli, S. (2016). Trust Necessitated through Metrics: Estimating the Trustworthiness of Websites. *Procedia Computer Science, 85*, 133–140. doi:10.1016/j.procs.2016.05.199

Singal, H., & Kohli, S. (2016, March). Intellectualizing TRUST for Medical Websites. In *Proceedings of the Second International Conference on Information and Communication Technology for Competitive Strategies* (p. 83). ACM.

Sutcliffe, A. (2002). Assessing the Reliability of Heuristic Evaluation for Website Attractiveness and Usability. In *Proceedings of the 35th Hawaii International Conference on System Sciences.* IEEE. doi:10.1109/HICSS.2002.994098

The importance of reliable online health information. (2015). *Prescient Digital.* Retrieved from http://www. prescientdigital.com/articles/e-health/the-importance-of-reliable-online-health-information/

Walraven, A., Brand-Gruwel, S., & Boshuizen, H. P. A. (2009) How students evaluate information and sources when searching the World Wide Web for information. *Computers & Education, 52*(1), 234-246.

Wiggins, J. S., Phillip, C. K., & James, N. B. (1982). *Circumplex models of interpersonal behavior in clinical psychology. In Handbook of Research Methods in Clinical Psychology* (pp. 183–221). New York: Wiley-Interscience.

Xin, L., Leyi, S., Yao, W., & Zhaojin, X. (2013). A Dynamic Trust Conference Algorithm for Social Network. *Proceedings of the IEEE Eighth International Conference on P2P, Parallel, Grid, Cloud and Internet Computing.*

Compilation of References

Abbas, F., Rajput, U., & Oh, H. (2016). PRISM: PRivacy-Aware Interest Sharing and Matching in Mobile Social Networks. *IEEE Access: Practical Innovations, Open Solutions*, *4*, 2594–2603. doi:10.1109/ACCESS.2016.2564985

Abbasi, A., Chen, H., Thoms, S., & Fu, T. (2008). Affect Analysis of Web Forums and Blogs Using Correlation Ensembles. *IEEE Transactions on Knowledge and Data Engineering*, *20*(9), 1168–1180. doi:10.1109/TKDE.2008.51

Abbasi, A., France, S., Zhang, Z., & Chen, H. (2011). Selecting Attributes for Sentiment Classification Using Feature Relation Networks. *IEEE Transactions on Knowledge and Data Engineering*, *23*(2), 447–462. doi:10.1109/TKDE.2010.110

Ackermann, M. R., Martens, M., Raupach, C., Swierkot, K., Lammersen, C., & Sohler, C. (2012). StreamKM++: A clustering algorithm for data streams. *ACM Journal of Experimental Algorithmics*, *17*(1), 173–187. doi:10.1145/2133803.2184450

Adewole, K. S., Anuar, N. B., Kamsin, A., & Sangaiah, A. K. (2017). SMSAD: A framework for spam message and spam account detection. *Multimedia Tools and Applications*, 1–36. doi:10.1007/s11042-017-5018-x

Afroz, S., Islam, A. C., Stolerman, A., Greenstadt, R., & McCoy, D. (2014, May). Doppelgänger finder: Taking stylometry to the underground. In *Security and Privacy (SP), 2014 IEEE Symposium on* (pp. 212-226). IEEE.

Aggarwal & Yu. (2007). A Survey of synopsis construction in data streams. Advances in Database Systems, 31, 169-207.

Aggarwal, C. C., Watson, T. J., Ctr, R., Han, J., Wang, J., & Yu, P. S. (2003). A framework for clustering evolving data streams. In *VLDB* (pp. 81–92). Berlin: VLDB Endowment. doi:10.1016/B978-012722442-8/50016-1

Aggarwal, S., Van Oostendorp, H., Reddy, Y. R., & Indurkhya, B. (2014, September). Providing Web Credibility Assessment Support. In *Proceedings of the 2014 European Conference on Cognitive Ergonomics* (p. 29). ACM.

Ahmed, F., & Abulaish, M. (2013). A generic statistical approach for spam detection in online social networks. *Computer Communications*, *36*(10), 1120–1129. doi:10.1016/j.comcom.2013.04.004

Ajzen, I. (1991). The theory of Planned Behaviour. *Organizational Behavior and Human Decision Processes*, *50*(2), 179–211. doi:10.1016/0749-5978(91)90020-T

Akcora, C., Carminati, B., & Ferrari, E. (2011). Network and profile based measures for user similarities on social networks. *IEEE International Conference on Information Reuse and Integration (IRI)*, 292–298.

Akcora, C. G., Carminati, B., & Ferrari, E. (2013). User Similarities on Social Networks. *Social Network Analysis and Mining Journal Springer*, *3*(3), 475–495. doi:10.1007/s13278-012-0090-8

Al Hasan, M., & Zaki, M. J. (2011). A survey of link prediction in social networks. In Social network data analytics (pp. 243-275). Springer US. doi:10.1007/978-1-4419-8462-3_9

Alexander, J. E., & Tate, P. (1999). *Web Wisdom: How to evaluate and create information quality on the web.* Lawrence Erlbaum.

Aljazzaf, Z. M., Perry, M., & Capretz, M. A. M. (2011). *Towards a Unified Trust Framework for Trust Establishment and Trust Based Service Selection.* IEEE CCECE. doi:10.1109/CCECE.2011.6030647

Almishari, M., Kaafar, D., Oguz, E., & Tsudik, G. (2014, November). Stylometric linkability of tweets. In *Proceedings of the 13th Workshop on Privacy in the Electronic Society* (pp. 205-208). ACM.

Al-Moslmi, T., Albared, M., Al-Shabi, A., Omar, N., & Abdullah, S. (n.d.). Arabic senti-lexicon: Constructing publicly available language resources for Arabic sentiment analysis. Journal of Information Science, 1–18.

AnalysisD. (2015). Retrieved from http://www.stats.ox.ac.uk/~teh/teaching/MS1b/l07a-qda.pdf

Anandakumar, H., & Umamaheswari, K. (2017). An Efficient Optimized Handover in Cognitive Radio Networks using Cooperative Spectrum Sensing. *Intelligent Automation & Soft Computing,* 1–8. doi:10.1080/10798587.2017.1364931

Anandakumar. (2014). Energy Efficient Network Selection Using 802.16g Based GSM Technology. *Journal of Computer Science, 10*(5), 745–754. doi:10.3844/jcssp.2014.745.754

Anandakumar, H., & Umamaheswari, K. (2017). Supervised machine learning techniques in cognitive radio networks during cooperative spectrum handovers. *Cluster Computing, 20*(2), 1505–1515. doi:10.1007/s10586-017-0798-3

Andreassen, C. S., Billieux, J., Griffiths, M. D., Kuss, D. J., Demetrovics, Z., Mazzoni, E., & Pallesen, S. (2016). The relationship between addictive use of social media and video games and symptoms of psychiatric disorders: A large-scale cross-sectional study. *Psychology of Addictive Behaviors, 30*(2), 252–262. doi:10.1037/adb0000160 PMID:26999354

Angulakshmi, G., & Chezian, R. (2014). Article. *International Journal of Advanced Research in Computer and Communication Engineering, 3*(7), 5.

Asur, S., & Huberman, B. A. (2010, August). Predicting the future with social media. In *Web Intelligence and Intelligent Agent Technology (WI-IAT), 2010 IEEE/WIC/ACM International Conference on* (Vol. 1, pp. 492-499). IEEE. doi:10.1109/WI-IAT.2010.63

Aydoğan, E., & Akcayol, M. (2016). A comprehensive survey for sentiment analysis tasks using machine learning techniques. In *INnovations in Intelligent SysTems and Applications (INISTA), 2016 International Symposium on.* Sinaia, Romania: IEEE. doi:10.1109/INISTA.2016.7571856

Azarbonyad, H., Dehghani, M., Marx, M., & Kamps, J. (2015, August). Time-aware authorship attribution for short text streams. In *Proceedings of the 38th International ACM SIGIR Conference on Research and Development in Information Retrieval* (pp. 727-730). ACM. doi:10.1145/2766462.2767799

Babcock, B., Datar, M., & Motwani, R. (2003). Load Shedding Techniques for Data Stream Systems. *Proceedings of 2003 Workshop on Management and Processing of Data Streams.*

Babcock, B., Babu, S., Datar, M., Motwani, R., & Widom, J. (2002). Models and issues in data stream systems. *Proceedings of PODS.* doi:10.1145/543613.543615

Baker, L., Wagner, T. H., Singer, S., & Bundorf, M. K. (2003). Use of Internet and e-mail for health care information: Results from a national survey. *Journal of the American Medical Association, 289*(18), 2400–2406. doi:10.1001/jama.289.18.2400 PMID:12746364

Bamman, D., & Smith, N. A. (2015, May). *Contextualized Sarcasm Detection on Twitter.* ICWSM.

Baralis, E., & Garza, P. (2012). I-prune: Item Selection for Associative Classification. *International Journal of Intelligent Systems, 27*(3), 279–299. doi:10.1002/int.21524

Barbieri, F., Saggion, H., & Ronzano, F. (2014). Modelling sarcasm in twitter, a novel approach. *WASSA, ACL, 2014*, 50.

Barbieri, N., Bonchi, F., & Manco, G. (2014, August). Who to follow and why: link prediction with explanations. In *Proceedings of the 20th ACM SIGKDD international conference on Knowledge discovery and data mining* (pp. 1266-1275). ACM. doi:10.1145/2623330.2623733

Barzilay, R., & Lapata, M. (2005). Collective content selection for concept-to-text generation. In *Proceedings of the conference on Human Language Technology and Empirical Methods in Natural Language Processing* (pp. 331-338). Stroudsburg, PA: Association for computational linguistics.

Bastian, M., Heymann, S., & Jacomy, M. (2009). Gephi: An open source software for exploring and manipulating networks. *International AAAI Conference on Weblogs and Social Media.*

Batagelj, V., & Pajek. (n.d.). *Program for Large Network Analysis*. Retrieved from http://vlado.fmf.uni-lj.si/pub/networks/pajek

Bataineh, L., Bataineh, L., Abu-Shanab, E., & Abu-Shanab, E. (2016). How perceptions of E-participation levels influence the intention to use E-government websites. *Transforming Government: People. Process and Policy, 10*(2), 315–334.

Batrinca, B., & Treleaven, P. C. (2015). Social media analytics: A survey of techniques, tools and platforms, *Open access at springer. AI & Society, 30*(1), 89–116. doi:10.1007/s00146-014-0549-4

BBC. (2014). *US Secret Service seeks Twitter sarcasm detector.* Retrieved from http://www.bbc.com/news/technology-27711109

Becker, K., & Tumitan, D. (2013). Introdução à mineração de opiniões: Conceitos, aplicações e desafios. *Lectures of the 28th Brazilian Symposium on Databases.*

Belanger, F., Hiller, J. S., & Smith, W. J. (2002). Trustworthiness in electronic commerce: The role of privacy, security, and site attributes. *The Journal of Strategic Information Systems, 11*(3-4), 245–270. doi:10.1016/S0963-8687(02)00018-5

Benevenuto, F. Ribeiro, F., & Araújo, M. (2015). Métodos Para Análise de Sentimentos em Mídias Sociais. *Brazilian Symposium on Multimedia and the Web (Webmedia).*

Benevenuto, F., Rodrigues, T., Almeida, V., Almeida, J., & Gonçalves, M. (2009). Detecting spammers and content promoters in online video social networks. In *Proceedings of the 32nd International ACM SIGIR Conference on Research and Development in Information Retrieval*. New York: ACM.

Berry, D., & Sazonov, E. (2015, April). Clustering technical documents by stylistic features for authorship analysis. In SoutheastCon 2015 (pp. 1-5). IEEE. doi:10.1109/SECON.2015.7132936

Berry, M., & Kogan, J. (2010). Text Mining: Applications and Theory. Wiley. doi:10.1002/9780470689646

Bhargava, M., Mehndiratta, P., & Asawa, K. (2013, December). Stylometric analysis for authorship attribution on Twitter. In *International Conference on Big Data Analytics* (pp. 37-47). Springer International Publishing. doi:10.1007/978-3-319-03689-2_3

Bhatnagar, S. (2003). *The economic and social impact of e-government.* A background paper for UNDESA publication: E-government the citizens and the state: Debating governance in the information age. World Public Sector Report.

Bhat, S. Y., & Abulaish, M. (2013). Community-based features for identifying spammers in online social networks. In *Proceedings of the International Conference on Advances in Social Networks Analysis and Mining*. IEEE. doi:10.1145/2492517.2492567

Bhattacherjee, A. (2002). Individual trust in online firms: Scale development and initial test. *Journal of Management Information Systems*, *19*(1), 211–241. doi:10.1080/07421222.2002.11045715

Bholane Savita, D., & Gore, D. (2016). Sentiment Analysis on Twitter Data Using Support Vector Machine. *International Journal of Computer Science Trends and Technology*, *4*(3), 365–370.

Bojanowskia, M., & Corten, R. (2014). Measuring segregation in social networks. *Social Networks Journal Elsevier*, *39*, 14–32. doi:10.1016/j.socnet.2014.04.001

Bollen, J., Mao, H., & Zeng, X. (2011). Twitter mood predicts the stock market. *Journal of Computational Science*, *2*(1), 1–8. doi:10.1016/j.jocs.2010.12.007

Bonacich, P., Holdren, A. C., & Johnston, M. (2004). Hyper-edges and multidimensional centrality. *Social Networks Journal Elsevier*, *26*(3), 189–203. doi:10.1016/j.socnet.2004.01.001

Bonato, A., Janssen, J., & Prałat, P. (2010). A Geometric Model for On-line Social Networks. *Proceedings of the International Workshop on Modeling Social Media ACM*. doi:10.1145/1835980.1835984

Borgatti, S. P., Everett, M. G., & Freeman, L. C. (2002). *Ucinet for Windows: Software for Social Network Analysis*. Analytic Technologies.

Braverma, V., Ostrovsky, R., & Zaniolo, C. (2009). Optimal Sampling from sliding windows. *Proceedings of 28th ACM SIGMOD-SIGACT-SIGART symposium on Principles of database systems*, 147-156. doi:10.1145/1559795.1559818

Breiman, L. (2001). Random forests. *Machine Learning*, *45*(1), 5–32. doi:10.1023/A:1010933404324

Brindha, S., Prabha, K., & Sukumaran, S. (2016). A Survey on Classification Techniques for Text Mining. In *Advanced Computing and Communication Systems (ICACCS), 2016 3rd International Conference on*. Coimbatore, India: IEEE. doi:10.1109/ICACCS.2016.7586371

Brown, G., Howe, T., Ihbe, M., Prakash, A., & Borders, K. (2008). Social networks and context-aware spam. In *Proceedings of the ACM conference on Computer Supported Cooperative Work*. ACM.

Buche, A., Chandak, M. B., & Zadgaonkar, A. (2013, June). Opinion mining and Analysis: A survey. *International Journal on Natural Language Computing*, *2*(3).

Burbank, J., Chimento, P., Haberman, B., & Kasch, W. (2006). Key Challenges of Military Tactical Networking and the Elusive Promise of MANET Technology. *IEEE Communications Magazine*, *44*(11), 39–45. doi:10.1109/COMM.2006.248156

Buschmeier, K., Cimiano, P., & Klinger, R. (2014). An impact analysis of features in a classification approach to irony detection in product reviews. *Proceedings of the 5th Workshop on Computational Approaches to Subjectivity, Sentiment and Social Media Analysis*, 42–49. doi:10.3115/v1/W14-2608

Calvert, P. J. (2001). Scholarly Misconduct and Misinformation on the World Wide Web. *The Electronic Library*, *19*(4), 232–240. doi:10.1108/EUM0000000005747

Cambria, E. (n.d.). New avenues in Opinion mining and sentiment analysis. *IEEE Intelligent Systems, 28*(2), 15–21.

Carrillo de Albornoz, J., Plaza, L., Gervás, P., & Díaz, A. (2011). A joint model of feature mining and sentiment analysis for product review rating. In *ECIR'11 Proceedings of the 33rd European conference on Advances in information retrieval* (pp. 55-66). Berlin: Springer. doi:10.1007/978-3-642-20161-5_8

Carson, R. C. (1969). *Interaction Concepts of Personality*. Chicago: Aldine.

Carvalho Filho, J. A. (2014). *Mineração de Textos: Análise de Sentimentos Utilizando o Tweets Referentes a Copa do Mundo* (Dissertação de Mestrado). Universidade Nova de Lisboa, Quixadá.

Chan, P. P., Yang, C., Yeung, D. S., & Ng, W. W. (2015). Spam filtering for short messages in adversarial environment. *Neurocomputing, 155*, 167–176. doi:10.1016/j.neucom.2014.12.034

Cheang, H. S., & Pell, M. D. (2011). Recognizing sarcasm without language: A cross-linguistic study of English and Cantonese. *Pragmatics & Cognition, 19*(2), 203–223. doi:10.1075/pc.19.2.02che

Chen, H., & Zimbra, D. (2010). AI and Opinion Mining. *IEEE Intelligent Systems, 25*(3), 74–80.

Chen, H., Li, X., & Huang, Z. (2005, June). Link prediction approach to collaborative filtering. In *Digital Libraries, 2005. JCDL'05. Proceedings of the 5th ACM/IEEE-CS Joint Conference on* (pp. 141-142). IEEE.

Chen, H., Chung, W., Xu, J. J., Wang, G., Qin, Y., & Chau, M. (2004). Crime data mining: A general framework and some examples. *Computer, 37*(4), 50–56. doi:10.1109/MC.2004.1297301

Chen, S. C., & Dhillon, G. S. (2003). Interpreting dimensions of consumer trust in e-commerce. *Information Technology Management, 4*(2/3), 304–318. doi:10.1023/A:1022962631249

Chen, T., Xu, R., Lu, Q., Liu, B., Xu, J., Yao, L., & He, Z. (2014, April). A sentence vector based over-sampling method for imbalanced emotion classification. In *International Conference on Intelligent Text Processing and Computational Linguistics* (pp. 62-72). Springer. doi:10.1007/978-3-642-54903-8_6

Chen, X., & Wang, L. (2017). A Cloud-Based Trust Management Framework for Vehicular Social Networks. *IEEE Access: Practical Innovations, Open Solutions, 5*, 2967–2980. doi:10.1109/ACCESS.2017.2670024

Chen, Y., Dawes, S. S., & Chen, S. (2017, June). E-government Support for Administrative Reform in China. In *Proceedings of the 18th Annual International Conference on Digital Government Research* (pp. 329-335). ACM. doi:10.1145/3085228.3085269

Cheshire, C., Antin, J., Cook, K. S., & Churchill, E. (2007). General and Familiar Trust in Websites. *Knowledge, Technology & Policy, 23*(3), 311–331.

Cheskin Research & Studio Archetype/Sapient. (1999). *e-Commerce Trust Study*. Author.

Chidananda, H. T., Sagnika, S., & Sahoo, L. (2017, February). Survey on Sentiment Analysis: A Comparative Study. *International Journal of Computers and Applications, 159*(6), 4–7. doi:10.5120/ijca2017912952

Chiluka, N., Andrade, N., & Pouwelse, J. (2011, April). A link prediction approach to recommendations in large-scale user-generated content systems. In *European Conference on Information Retrieval* (pp. 189-200). Springer Berlin Heidelberg. doi:10.1007/978-3-642-20161-5_19

Chopra, K., & Wallace, A. W. (2002). Trust in Electronic Commerce. *Proceedings of the 36th Hawaii International Conference on System Sciences HICCS'03.*

Chu, Z., Widjaja, I., & Wang, H. (2012). Detecting social spam campaigns on twitter. In *Proceedings of International Conference on Applied Cryptography and Network Security*. Singapore: Springer. doi:10.1007/978-3-642-31284-7_27

Clifton, B. (2008). *Advanced web metrics with Google Analytics*. Indianapolis, IN: Wiley Publishing, Inc.

Cline, R. J., & Haynes, K. M. (2001). Review consumer health information seeking on the internet: The state of art. *Health Education Research*, *16*(6), 671–692. doi:10.1093/her/16.6.671 PMID:11780707

Coleman, J. S., Katz, E., & Menzel, H. (1966). Medical Innovation: A Diffusion Study. Bobbs-Merrill.

Conz, J. (2010). IRONIA VERBAL: Teorias e Considerações (Graduação em Letras). Universidade Federal do Rio Grande do Sul, Porto Alegre.

Correa, C. D., & Ma, K. L. (2011). Visualizing social networks. In Social Network Data Analytics. Springer Science+ Business Media. doi:10.1007/978-1-4419-8462-3_11

Cover, T., & Hart, P. (1967). Nearest neighbour pattern classification. *IEEE Transactions on Information Theory*, *13*(1), 21–27. doi:10.1109/TIT.1967.1053964

Cresci, S., Di Pietro, R., Petrocchi, M., Spognardi, A., & Tesconi, M. (2017). The paradigm-shift of social spambots: Evidence, theories, and tools for the arms race. In *Proceedings of the 26th International Conference on World Wide Web Companion*. ACM.

Daks, A., & Clark, A. (2016). Unsupervised Authorial Clustering Based on Syntactic Structure. *ACL*, *2016*, 114.

Dave, K., Lawrence, S., & Pennock, D. M. (2003, May). Mining the peanut gallery: Opinion extraction and semantic classification of product reviews. In *Proceedings of the 12th international conference on World Wide Web* (pp. 519-528). ACM. doi:10.1145/775152.775226

Davidov, D., Tsur, O., & Rappoport, A. (2010, July). Semi-supervised recognition of sarcastic sentences in twitter and Amazon. In *Proceedings of the fourteenth conference on computational natural language learning* (pp. 107-116). Association for Computational Linguistics.

Dayal, S., Landesberg, H., & Zeisser, M. (1999). How to build trust online. *Marketing Management*, *8*(3), 64–69.

DeBarr, D., & Wechsler, H. (2010). Using social network analysis for spam detection. *Advances in Social Computing*, 62–69.

Deng, S., Sinha, A. P., & Zhao, H. (2017, February). Adapting sentiment lexicons to domain-specific social media texts. *Decision Support Systems*, *94*(C), 65–76.

Dobra, A. (2016). *Sketch-Based Multi-Query Processing over Data Streams*. Data Stream Management. Springer Berlin Heidelberg.

Dobra, A., Garofalakis, M., Gehrke, J., & Rastogi, R. (2002). Processing Complex Aggregate Queries Over Data Streams. *Proceedings of SIGMOD*. doi:10.1145/564691.564699

Domingos, P., & Hulten, G. (2000). Mining high-speed data streams. *Proceedings of the 6th ACM SIGKDD international conference on knowledge discovery and data mining*, 71–80.

Dong, Y., Tang, J., Wu, S., Tian, J., Chawla, N. V., Rao, J., & Cao, H. (2012, December). Link prediction and recommendation across heterogeneous social networks. In *Data Mining (ICDM), 2012 IEEE 12th International Conference on* (pp. 181-190). IEEE. doi:10.1109/ICDM.2012.140

Dooms, S., De Pessemier, T., & Martens, L. (2014, April). Mining cross-domain rating datasets from structured data on twitter. In *Proceedings of the 23rd International Conference on World Wide Web* (pp. 621-624). ACM. doi:10.1145/2567948.2579232

Dwyer, C., Hiltz, S. R., & Passerini, K. (2007). Trust and Privacy Concern Within Social Networking Sites: A Comparison of Facebook and MySpace. *Proceedings: Americas Conference on Information System.*

Eastin, M. S., & Guinster, N. M. (2006). Worried and wired: Effects of health anxiety on information seeking and health-care utilization behaviors. *Cyberpsychology & Behavior, 9*(4), 494–498. doi:10.1089/cpb.2006.9.494 PMID:16901253

Educational Research Institute, School Effectiveness Study. (2012). Retrieved from http://eduentuzjasci.pl/en/oprojekcie-2/502-the-project.htmlEgan

Egele, M., Stringhini, G., Kruegel, C., & Vigna, G. (2017). Towards detecting compromised accounts on social networks. *IEEE Transactions on Dependable and Secure Computing, 14*(4), 447–460. doi:10.1109/TDSC.2015.2479616

Ekstrand, M. D., Riedl, J. T., & Konstan, J. A. (2011). Collaborative filtering recommender systems. *Foundations and Trends® in Human–Computer Interaction, 4*(2), 81-173.

El-Alfy, E. S. M., & Al-Hasan, A. A. (2016). Spam filtering framework for multimodal mobile communication based on dendritic cell algorithm. *Future Generation Computer Systems, 64*, 98–107. doi:10.1016/j.future.2016.02.018

Emanuelsson, O., Nielsen, H., Brunak, S., & Von Heijne, G. (2000). Predicting subcellular localization of proteins based on their N-terminal amino acid sequence. *Journal of Molecular Biology, 300*(4), 1005–1016. doi:10.1006/jmbi.2000.3903 PMID:10891285

English, C., Terzis, S., & Wagealla, W. (2004). Engineering Trust based collaborations in a global computing environment. *Proceedings of the Second International Conference on Trust Management*, 135-145. doi:10.1007/978-3-540-24747-0_10

Evans, J. R. (2013). *Business Analytics Methods, Models and Decisions.* Pearson Education, Inc.

Eysenbach, G., & Kohler, C. (2002). How do consumer search for and appraise health information on the World Wide Web? Qualitative study using focus group usability tests and in-depth review. *BMJ (Clinical Research Ed.), 324*(7337), 573–577. doi:10.1136/bmj.324.7337.573 PMID:11884321

Ezpeleta, E., Zurutuza, U., & Hidalg, J. M. G. (2016). A study of the personalization of spam content using facebook public information. *Logic Journal of the IGPL, 25*(1), 30–41. doi:10.1093/jigpal/jzw040

Fang, Z. (2002). E-government in digital era: concept, practice, and development. *International Journal of the Computer, the Internet and Management, 10*(2), 1-22.

Fishbein, M., & Ajzen, I. (1975). *Belief, Attitude, Intention and Behaviour: An Introduction to theory and Research.* Addison-Wesley.

Freeman, L. C. (1978b). Segregation in social networks. *Sociological Methods & Research, 6*(4), 411–429. doi:10.1177/004912417800600401

Freeman, L. C. (1979). Centrality in Social Networks Conceptual Clarification. Social networks Journal. *Elsevier Sequoia S.A., 1*(3), 215–239.

Frey, B. J., & Dueck, D. (2007). Clustering by passing messages between data points. *Science, 315*(5814), 2007. doi:10.1126/science.1136800 PMID:17218491

Fung, G. (2003, October). The disputed Federalist Papers: SVM feature selection via concave minimization. In *Proceedings of the 2003 Conference on Diversity in Computing* (pp. 42-46). ACM. doi:10.1145/948542.948551

Fu, S., Hu, C., Hu, Y., Sun, B., Ying, W., & Shi, P. (2016). Information Diffusion Mechanisms in Online Social Networks. *IEEE First International Conference on Data Science in Cyberspace (DSC)*, 312-317. doi:10.1109/DSC.2016.46

Gaber, M. M., Zaslavsky, A., & Krishnaswamy, S. (2005). Mining data streams: A review. *SIGMOD Record*, *34*(2), 18–26. doi:10.1145/1083784.1083789

Gains, S. O. Jr, Lyde, M. D., Panter, A. T., Steers, W. N., Rusbult, C. E., Cox, C. L., & Wexler, M. O. (1997). Evaluating the circumplexity of interpersonal traits and the manifestation of interpersonal traits in interpersonal trust. *Journal of Personality and Social Psychology*, *73*(3), 610–623. doi:10.1037/0022-3514.73.3.610

Galán-García, P., Puerta, J. G. D. L., Gómez, C. L., Santos, I., & Bringas, P. G. (2016). Supervised machine learning for the detection of troll profiles in twitter social network: Application to a real case of cyberbullying. *Logic Journal of the IGPL*, *24*(1), 42–53.

Gansner, E. R., & North, S. C. (2000). An open graph visualization system and its applications to software engineering. *Software, Practice & Experience*, *30*(11), 1203–1233. doi:10.1002/1097-024X(200009)30:11<1203::AID-SPE338>3.0.CO;2-N

Gao, H., Chen, Y., Lee, K., Palsetia, D., & Choudhary, A. (2012). Towards online spam filtering in social networks. In *Proceedings of the Network & Distributed System Security Symposium (NDSS)*. ACM.

Garofalakis, M., Gehrke, J., & Rastogi, R. (2016). *Data Stream Management: A Brave New World. In Data Stream Management* (pp. 1–9). Springer Berlin Heidelberg. doi:10.1007/978-3-540-28608-0

Ge, Z., Sun, Y., & Smith, M. J. (2016). *Authorship Attribution Using a Neural Network Language Model*. arXiv preprint arXiv:1602.05292

Gefen, D., Karahanna, E., & Straub, D. W. (2003). Inexperience and experience with online stores: The importance of TAM and trust. *IEEE Transactions on Engineering Management*, *50*(3), 307–321. doi:10.1109/TEM.2003.817277

Gefen, D., Karahanna, E., & Straub, D. W. (2003). Trust and TAM in online shopping: An integrated model. *Management Information Systems Quarterly*, *27*(1), 51–90.

Gefen, D., & Straub, D. W. (2003). Managing user trust in B2C e-services. *e-Service Journal*, *2*(2), 7–24. doi:10.2979/esj.2003.2.2.7

Ghosh, A., & Veale, T. (2016). Fracking Sarcasm using Neural Network. In WASSA@ NAACL-HLT (pp. 161-169). Academic Press. doi:10.18653/v1/W16-0425

Gimenes, G. P., Gualdron, H., Raddo, T. R., & Rodrigues, J. F. (2014, March). Supervised-learning link recommendation in the DBLP co-authoring network. In *Pervasive Computing and Communications Workshops (PERCOM Workshops), 2014 IEEE International Conference on* (pp. 563-568). IEEE. doi:10.1109/PerComW.2014.6815268

Gimpel, K., Schneider, N., O'Connor, B., Das, D., Mills, D., Eisenstein, J., & Smith, N. A. (2011, June). Part-of-speech tagging for Twitter: Annotation, features, and experiments. In *Proceedings of the 49th Annual Meeting of the Association for Computational Linguistics: Human Language Technologies: short papers-Volume 2* (pp. 42-47). Association for Computational Linguistics.

Girvan, M., & Newman, M. E. J. (2002). Community structure in social and biological networks. *Proceedings of the National Academy of Sciences of the United States of America*, *99*(12), 7821–7826. doi:10.1073/pnas.122653799 PMID:12060727

Gomez-Rodriguez, M., Leskovec, J., & Krause, A. (2010). Inferring Networks of Diffusion and Influence. *Proceedings of the 16th ACM SIGKDD International Conference on Knowledge Discovery and Data Mining*, 1019-1028. doi:10.1145/1835804.1835933

Gonçalves, M. A. (2010). *Abordagens para Avaliação Automática da Qualidade de Conferências cientificas: um estudo de caso em ciência da computação* (Dissertação de Mestrado). Universidade Federal de Minas Gerais, Belo Horizonte.

Gonçalves, P. (2013a). Comparing and combining sentiment analysis methods. In *Proceedings of the First ACM Conference on Online Social Networks (COSN '13)*. New York, NY: ACM. doi:10.1145/2512938.2512951

Gonçalves, P., Dores, W., & Benevenuto, F. (2012). Panas-t: Uma escala psicométrica para medição de sentimentos no twitter. *Proceedings of the Brazilian Workshop on Social Network Analysis and Mining (BraSNAM)*.

González-Ibánez, R., Muresan, S., & Wacholder, N. (2011, June). Identifying sarcasm in Twitter: a closer look. In *Proceedings of the 49th Annual Meeting of the Association for Computational Linguistics: Human Language Technologies: Short Papers-Volume 2* (pp. 581-586). Association for Computational Linguistics.

Govindarajan, M., & M., R. (2013). A Survey of Classification Methods and Applications for Sentiment Analysis. *International Journal of Engineering Science*, *2*(12), 11–15.

Green, R. M., & Sheppard, J. W. (2013, May). Comparing Frequency-and Style-Based Features for Twitter Author Identification. *FLAIRS Conference*.

Groh, G., & Hauffa, J. (2011, July). *Characterizing Social Relations Via NLP-Based Sentiment Analysis*. ICWSM.

Gruzd, A. (2016). *Netlytic: Software for Automated Text and Social Network Analysis*. Retrieved from http://Netlytic.org

Guha, S., Mishra, N., Motwani, R., & O'Callaghan, L. (2000). Clustering data streams. In *IEEE Symposium on Foundations of Computer Science*. IEEE Computer Society.

Guille, A., Hacid, H., Favre, C., & Zighed, D. A. (2013). Information Diffusion in Online Social Networks: A Survey. *ACM SIGMOD*, *42*(2), 17–28. doi:10.1145/2503792.2503797

Guimaraes, R. G., Rosa, R. L., De Gaetano, D., Rodriguez, D. Z., & Bressan, G. (2017). Age Groups Classification in Social Network Using Deep Learning. *IEEE Access: Practical Innovations, Open Solutions*, *5*, 10805–10816. doi:10.1109/ACCESS.2017.2706674

Guns, R., & Rousseau, R. (2014). Recommending research collaborations using link prediction and random forest classifiers. *Scientometrics*, *101*(2), 1461–1473. doi:10.1007/s11192-013-1228-9

Hackney, R. A., & Tassabehji, R. (2016). *Advancing e-Government in Developing Countries: a quantitative analysis towards citizen-cenric public services within sub-Saharan Africa*. Academic Press.

Hair, J. F., Black, W. C., Babin, B. J., & Anderson, R. E. (2013). *Multivariate Data Analysis: A Global Perspective* (7th ed.). Pearson.

Hammond, S. M., Boettcher, S., Caudy, A. A., Kobayashi, R., & Hannon, G. J. (2001). Argonaute2, a link between genetic and biochemical analyses of RNAi. *Science*, *293*(5532), 1146–1150. doi:10.1126/science.1064023 PMID:11498593

Han, J., Kamber, M., & Pei, J. (2012). Data Mining: Concepts and Techniques (3rd ed.). Morgan Kaufmann. doi:-1-4419-1428-6_3752 doi:10.1007/978

Handrick, D. (n.d.). *Complete History of Social Media: Then and Now*. Retrieved from https://smallbiztrends.com/2013/05/the-complete-history-of-social-media-infographic.html

Hannon, J., Bennett, M., & Smyth, B. (2010, September). Recommending twitter users to follow using content and collaborative filtering approaches. In *Proceedings of the fourth ACM conference on Recommender systems* (pp. 199-206). ACM. doi:10.1145/1864708.1864746

Hastie, T., Tibshirani, R., & Friedman, J. (2008). The elements of statistical learning: data mining, inference and prediction (2nd ed.). Springer.

Hatzivassiloglou, V., & McKeown, K. R. (1997, July). Predicting the semantic orientation of adjectives. In *Proceedings of the eighth conference on European chapter of the Association for Computational Linguistics* (pp. 174-181). Association for Computational Linguistics. doi:10.3115/979617.979640

He, Q., Glas, C. A., Kosinski, M., Stillwell, D. J., & Veldkamp, B. P. (2014). Predicting self-monitoring skills using textual posts on Facebook. *Computers in Human Behavior*, *33*, 69–78. doi:10.1016/j.chb.2013.12.026

Hernon, P. (1955). Disinformation and Misinformation through the Internet: Findings of an exploratory Study. *Government Information Quarterly*, *12*(2), 133–139. doi:10.1016/0740-624X(95)90052-7

Hoffman, D. L., Novak, T. P., & Peralta, M. (1999). Building consumer trust online. *Communications of the ACM*, *42*(4), 80–85. doi:10.1145/299157.299175

Hong, I. (2007). A survey of web site success metrics used by Internet-dependent organizations in Korea. *Internet Research*, *17*(3), 272–290. doi:10.1108/10662240710758920

Hong, S.-M. (2012). An exploratory study of the Users' Behavior on Social Network Site. In *Proceedings of the Ninth International Conference on Information Technology-New Generations*. IEEE. doi:10.1109/ITNG.2012.69

Hu, M., & Liu, B. (2004). Mining and summarizing customer reviews. In *KDD '04 Proceedings of the tenth ACM SIGKDD international conference on Knowledge discovery and data mining* (pp. 168-177). New York, NY: ACM. doi:10.1145/1014052.1014073

Huang, Z., & Lin, D. K. (2009). The time-series link prediction problem with applications in communication surveillance. *INFORMS Journal on Computing*, *21*(2), 286–303. doi:10.1287/ijoc.1080.0292

Hulten, G., Spencer, L., & Domingos, P. (2001). Mining time-changing data streams. *Proceedings of the seventh ACM SIGKDD international conference on knowledge discovery and data mining*, 97–106. doi:10.1145/502512.502529

Hu, M., & Liu, B. (2004). Mining opinion features in customer reviews. In *Proceedings of the 19th National Conference on Artifical Intelligence*. AAAI Press.

Hussein, D. (2016). A survey on sentiment analysis challenges. *Journal Of King Saud University -. Engineering and Science*. doi:10.1016/j.jksues.2016.04.002

Hutto, C. J., & Vader. (2014). A parsimonious rule-based model for sentiment analysis of social media text. *Eighth International AAAI Conference on Weblogs and Social Media.*

Hu, X., Chu, T. H. S., Leung, V. C. M., Ngai, E. C.-H., Kruchten, P., & Chan, H. C. B. (2015). A Survey on Mobile Social Networks: Applications, Platforms, System Architectures, and Future Research Directions. *IEEE Communications Surveys and Tutorials*, *17*(3), 1557–1581. doi:10.1109/COMST.2014.2371813

Idris, N. H., Jackson, M. J., & Abrahart, R. J. (2011). Colour coded traffic light labeling: A visual quality indicator to communicate credibility in map mash-up applications. *Proceedings of the International Conference on Humanities Social Sciences, Science & Technology.*

infoDev. (2002). *The E-government Handbook for developing countries.* A Project of Infodev and The Center for Democracy and Technology.

Ingle, A. (2014). Sentiment analysis: Sarcasm detection of tweets. Nagpur.

Isaksson, C., Dunham, M. H., & Hahsler, M. (2012). SoStream: Self organizing density-based clustering over data stream. In *MLDM* (pp. 264–278). Berlin: Springer Berlin Heidelberg. doi:10.1007/978-3-642-31537-4_21

Ivory, M. Y., Sinha, R. R., & Hearst, M. A. (2001). *Empirically validated web page design metrics. SIGCHI conference on Human factors in computing systems.* Seattle, WA: ACM.

Jadhav, R., & Wakode, M. S. (2017, March). Survey: Sentiment Analysis of Twitter Data for Stock Market Prediction. *International Journal of Advanced Research in Computer and Communication Engineering*, *6*(3), 558–562. doi:10.17148/IJARCCE.2017.63129

Jain, P., Kumaraguru, P., & Joshi, A. (2013). @I Seek 'fb.me': Identifying Users across Multiple Online Social Networks. *Proceedings of the 22nd International Conference on World Wide Web (WWW) 13 Companion*, 1259-1268.

Janssen, J., Hurshman, M., & Kalyaniwalla, N. (2015). Model Selection for Social Networks Using Graphlets. *Internet Mathematics. Taylor & Francis*, *8*(4), 338–363. doi:10.1080/15427951.2012.671149

Jarvenpaa, J. S., Knoll, K., & Leidner, D. E. (1998). Is anybody out there? Antecedents of trust in global virtual teams. *Journal of Management Information Systems*, *14*(4), 29–64. doi:10.1080/07421222.1998.11518185

Jarvenpaa, S. L., Tractinsky, J., & Vitale, M. (2000). Consumer trust in an internet store. *Information Technology Management*, *1*(1&2), 45–71. doi:10.1023/A:1019104520776

Jeong, S., Noh, G., Oh, H., & Kim, C. K. (2016). Follow spam detection based on cascaded social information. *Information Sciences*, *369*, 481–499. doi:10.1016/j.ins.2016.07.033

Jiang, C., Chen, Y., & Liu, K. J. R. (2014). Graphical Evolutionary Game for Information Diffusion Over Social Networks. *IEEE Journal of Selected Topics in Signal Processing*, *8*(4), 524–536. doi:10.1109/JSTSP.2014.2313024

Jin, X., Lin, C., Luo, J., & Han, J. (2011). A data mining-based spam detection system for social media networks. In *Proceedings of the VLDB Endowment*. ACM.

Jo, Y., & Oh, A. (2011). Aspect and sentiment unification model for online review analysis. In *WSDM '11 Proceedings of the fourth ACM international conference on Web search and data mining* (pp. 815-824). New York, NY: ACM. doi:10.1145/1935826.1935932

Johnson-George, C. J., & Swap, W. C. (1982). Measurement of specific interpersonal trust: Construction and validation of a scale to assess trust in a specific other. *Journal of Personality and Social Psychology*, *43*(6), 1306–1317. doi:10.1037/0022-3514.43.6.1306

Joshi, A., Sharma, V., & Bhattacharyya, P. (2015, July). Harnessing Context Incongruity for Sarcasm Detection. ACL, (2), 757-762. doi:10.3115/v1/P15-2124

Joshi, A., Tripathi, V., Patel, K., Bhattacharyya, P., & Carman, M. (2016). *Are Word Embedding-based Features Useful for Sarcasm Detection?* arXiv preprint arXiv:1610.00883

Joshi, M., Das, D., Gimpel, K., & Smith, N. A. (2010, June). Movie reviews and revenues: An experiment in text regression. In *Human Language Technologies: The 2010 Annual Conference of the North American Chapter of the Association for Computational Linguistics* (pp. 293-296). Association for Computational Linguistics.

Juarez, J., Dwivedi, A., Hammons, A., Jones, S., Weerackody, V., & Nichols, R. (2006). Free-Space Optical Communications for Next-generation Military Networks. *IEEE Communications Magazine*, *44*(11), 46–51. doi:10.1109/MCOM.2006.248164

Juola, P. (2008). Authorship attribution. *Foundations and Trends® in Information Retrieval, 1*(3), 233-334.

Juola, P., & Mikros, G. K. (2016). Cross-linguistic stylometric features: A preliminary investigation. *International Conference on Statistical Analysis of Textual Data.*

Juvina, I., & Oostendorp, H. (2006). Individual differences and behavioral metrics involved in modeling web navigation. *Universal Access in the Information Society, 4*(3), 258–269. doi:10.1007/s10209-005-0007-7

Kalaivani, P., & Shunmuganathan, D. (2013). Sentiment classification of movie reviews by supervised machine learning approaches. *Indian Journal of Computer Science and Engineering, 4*(4), 285–292.

Kalamkar, P. N., & Phakatkar, A. G. (2013). Opinion mining in figures of speech in text. *International Journal of Scientific Engineering Research, 4*(10), 1132–1134.

Kamal, A. E. (2006). Algorithms for multicast traffic grooming in WDM mesh networks. *IEEE Communications Magazine, 44*(11), 96–105. doi:10.1109/MCOM.2006.248171

Kaushik, A. (2007). *Web Analytics: An hour a Day*. Indianapolis, IN: Wiley Publishing, Inc.

Kaytoue, M., Pitarch, Y., Plantevit, M., & Robardet, C. (2015). What effects topological changes in dynamic graphs? Elucidating relationships between vertex attributes and the graph structure. *Social network Analysis and Mining Journal Springer, 5*(1), 1-17.

Kempe, D., Kleinberg, J., & Tardos, E. (2003). Maximizing the Spread of Influence through a Social Network. *Proceedings of the 9th ACM SIGKDD International Conference on Knowledge Discovery and Data Mining*, 137-146. doi:10.1145/956750.956769

Keretna, S., Hossny, A., & Creighton, D. (2013, October). Recognising user identity in Twitter social networks via text mining. In *Systems, Man, and Cybernetics (SMC), 2013 IEEE International Conference on* (pp. 3079-3082). IEEE. doi:10.1109/SMC.2013.525

Kešelj, V., Peng, F., Cercone, N., & Thomas, C. (2003, August). N-gram-based author profiles for authorship attribution. In *Proceedings of the conference pacific association for computational linguistics, PACLING* (Vol. 3, pp. 255-264). Academic Press.

Khan, K., Baharudin, B., & Khan, A. (2014). Identifying Product Features from Customer Reviews Using Hybrid Patterns. *The International Arab Journal of Information Technology, 11*(3), 281–286.

Khonji, M., Iraqi, Y., & Jones, A. (2015, May). An evaluation of authorship attribution using random forests. In *Information and Communication Technology Research (ICTRC), 2015 International Conference on* (pp. 68-71). IEEE. doi:10.1109/ICTRC.2015.7156423

Kim, S., & Hovy, E. (2004). Determining the sentiment of opinions. In *COLING '04 Proceedings of the 20th international conference on Computational Linguistics*. Stroudsburg, PA: Association for Computational Linguistics. doi:10.3115/1220355.1220555

Kim, D., & Benbasat, I. (2003). Trust-related arguments in internet stores: A framework for evaluation. *Journal of Electronic Commerce Research, 4*(2), 49–64.

Kimura, M., Saito, K., Nakano, R., & Motoda, H. (2010). Extracting influential nodes on a social network for information diffusion. Data mining Knowledge discovery. *Journal of the Association for Computing Machinery, 20*(1), 70–97.

Klimmt, B., & Yang, Y. (2004). *Introducing the Enron Corpus*. CEAS Conference.

Kohli, S., & Kumar, E. (2009). Certainty Factor Based Analysis for Measuring Users Satisfaction with Search Engine. *International Journal of Information processing (IJIP), 3*(1).

Kohli, S., & Kumar, E. (2011). *Evolution of user dependent model to predict future usability of a search engine*. Academic Press.

Kohli, S., & Singal, H. (2015). A methodological approach for Quantizing Trust from Human Behaviour for Content-Driven Websites. *International Journal of Sensors, Wireless Communications and Control, 5*(1), 32-46.

Kohli, S., & Singal, H. (2015). A methodological approach for Quantizing Trust from Human Behavior for Content-Driven Websites. *International Journal of Sensors Wireless Communications and Control*, *5*(1), 32–46. doi:10.2174/2210327905999150521111919

Kolachalam, S. (2012). An Overview of E-government. *Economia Aziendale Online*, (1), 1-12.

Kong, W., & Hung, Y. T. C. (2006). Modeling initial and repeat online trust in B2C e-commerce. In *Proceedings of HICSS'06*. IEEE.

Koppel, M., Schler, J., & Argamon, S. (2009). Computational methods in authorship attribution. *Journal of the American Society for Information Science and Technology*, *60*(1), 9–26. doi:10.1002/asi.20961

Koppel, M., Schler, J., & Argamon, S. (2011). Authorship attribution in the wild. *Language Resources and Evaluation*, *45*(1), 83–94. doi:10.1007/s10579-009-9111-2

Korkontzelos, I., Nikfarjam, A., Shardlow, M., Sarker, A., Ananiadou, S., & Gonzalez, G. H. (2016, August). Analysis of the effect of sentiment analysis on extracting adverse drug reactions from tweets and forum posts. *Journal of Biomedical Informatics*, *62*(C), 148–158. doi:10.1016/j.jbi.2016.06.007 PMID:27363901

Kranen, P., Günnemann, S., Fries, S., & Seidl, T. (2010). MC-tree: Improving Bayesian anytime classification. Lecture Notes in Computer Science, 6187, 252–269.

Kranen, P., Assent, I., Baldauf, C., & Seidl, T. (2011). The ClusTree: Indexing micro-clusters for anytime stream mining. *Knowledge and Information Systems*, *29*(2), 249–272. doi:10.1007/s10115-010-0342-8

Kreuz, R. J., & Caucci, G. M. (2007). Lexical influences on the perception of sarcasm. In *Proceedings of the Workshop on Computational Approaches to Figurative Language*. Stroudsburg, PA: Association for Computational Linguistics. doi:10.3115/1611528.1611529

Kreuz, R. J., & Glucksberg, S. (1989). How to be sarcastic: The echoic reminder theory of verbal irony. *Journal of Experimental Psychology. General*, *118*(4), 374–386. doi:10.1037/0096-3445.118.4.374

Ku, L., Liang, Y., & Chen, H. (2006). Opinion Extraction, Summarization and Tracking in News and Blog Corpora. *AAAI Spring Symposium: Computational Approaches to Analyzing Weblogs*, 100-107.

Kumar, P., & Sinha, A. (2016). Real-Time Analysis and Visualization of Online Social Media Dynamics. *IEEE International Conference on Next Generation Computing Technologies*, 362-367. doi:10.1109/NGCT.2016.7877442

Kumawat, D., & Jain, V. (2015). POS Tagging Approaches: A Comparison. *International Journal of Computers and Applications*, *118*(6).

Kummer, O., & Savoy, J. (2012). Feature Selection in Sentiment Analysis. In *CORIA 2012 Proceedings of the 9th Conference on Information Retrieval and Applications* (pp. 273-284). Bordeaux.

Lam, Y. H., Zhang, Z., & Ong, K. L. (2005). Trading in Open Marketplace Using Trust and Risk. *Proceedings of the IEEE/WIC/ACM International Conference on Intelligent Agent Technology.*

Last.fm dataset. (n.d.). *The official song tags and song similarity collection for the Million Song Dataset*. Retrieved from http://labrosa.ee.columbia.edu/millionsong/lastfm

Layton, R., Watters, P., & Dazeley, R. (2010, July). Authorship attribution for Twitter in 140 characters or less. In *Cybercrime and Trustworthy Computing Workshop (CTC), 2010 Second* (pp. 1-8). IEEE. doi:10.1109/CTC.2010.17

Lee, G., Yun, U., & Ryu, K. H. (2014). Sliding window based weighted maximal frequent pattern mining over data streams. *Expert Systems with Applications, 41*(2), 694–708. doi:10.1016/j.eswa.2013.07.094

Lee, K., Caverlee, J., & Webb, S. (2010). Uncovering social spammers: social honeypots+ machine learning. In *Proceedings of the 33rd International ACM SIGIR Conference on Research and Development in Information Retrieval*. ACM. doi:10.1145/1835449.1835522

Leite, D., Costa, P., & Gomide, F. (2010). Evolving granular neural network for semi-supervised data stream classification. In *The 2010 international joint conference on neural networks* (pp. 1–8). IEEE. doi:10.1109/IJCNN.2010.5596303

Leskovec, J., & Krevl, A. (2014). *SNAP Datasets: Stanford Large Network Dataset Collection*. Retrieved from http://snap.stanford.edu/data

Leskovec, J., Huttenlocher, D., & Kleinberg, J. (2010). *Signed Networks in Social Media*. CHI. doi:10.1145/1753326.1753532

Leskovec, J., Kleinberg, J., & Faloutsos, C. (2005). Graphs over Time: Densification Laws, *Shrinking Diameters and Possible Explanations. ACM SIGKDD International Conference on Knowledge Discovery and Data Mining (KDD).*

Lewis, T. (2006). Seeking health information on the internet: Lifestyle choice or bad attack of cyberchondria? *Media Culture & Society, 28*(4), 521–539. doi:10.1177/0163443706065027

Li, J. S., Monaco, J. V., Chen, L. C., & Tappert, C. C. (2014, November). Authorship authentication using short messages from social networking sites. In *e-Business Engineering (ICEBE), 2014 IEEE 11th International Conference on* (pp. 314-319). IEEE. doi:10.1109/ICEBE.2014.61

Li, J., & Wang, A.G. (2015). A framework of identity resolution: evaluating identity attributes and matching algorithms. *Security Informatics Journal, 4*(6).

Li, Lee, & Shan. (2004). An efficient algorithm for mining frequent itemsets over the entire history of data streams. *Proceedings of the international workshop on knowledge discovery in data streams.*

Li, Liu & Song. (2011). A new classification algorithm for data streams. *Int. J. Modern Education and Computer Science, 4*, 32–39.

Liben-Nowell, D., & Kleinberg, J. (2007). The link-prediction problem for social networks. *Journal of the Association for Information Science and Technology, 58*(7), 1019-1031.

Liebrecht, C. C., Kunneman, F. A., & Van Den Bosch, A. P. J. (2013). *The perfect solution for detecting sarcasm in tweets# not*. Academic Press.

Li, J., Yan, H., Liu, Z., Chen, X., Huang, X., & Wong, D. S. (2017). Location-Sharing Systems With Enhanced Privacy in Mobile Online Social Networks. *IEEE Systems Journal, 11*(2), 439–448. doi:10.1109/JSYST.2015.2415835

Link, A. J., Robison, K., & Church, G. M. (1997). Comparing the predicted and observed properties of proteins encoded in the genome of Escherichia coli K-12. *Electrophoresis, 18*(8), 1259–1313. doi:10.1002/elps.1150180807 PMID:9298646

Lin, P. C., & Huang, P. M. (2013). A study of effective features for detecting long-surviving twitter spam accounts. In *Proceedings of the 15thInternational Conference on Advanced Communication Technology (ICACT)*. IEEE.

Li, T., Liu, A., & Huang, C. (2016). A Similarity Scenario-Based Recommendation Model With Small Disturbances for Unknown Items in Social Networks. *IEEE Access: Practical Innovations, Open Solutions, 4*, 9251–9272. doi:10.1109/ACCESS.2016.2647236

Liu, K., Hogan, W. R., & Crowleya, R. S. (2011). Natural language processing methods and systems for biomedical ontology learning. *Journal of Biomedical Informatics*, *44*(1), 163–179. Retrieved from http://migre.me/thZEQ

Liu, B. (2010). Sentiment analysis and subjectivity. In N. Indurkhya & F. Damerau (Eds.), *Handbook of Natural Language Processing* (2nd ed., pp. 627–661). CRC Press.

Liu, B. (2010b). Sentiment analysis: Amultifaceted Problem. *IEEE Intelligent Systems*, *25*(3), 76–80.

Liu, B. (2012). *Sentiment analysis and opinion mining*. San Rafael, CA: Morgan & Claypool.

Liu, C., Ling, H., Zou, F., Yan, L., Wang, Y., Feng, H., & Ou, X. (2014). Kernelized Neighborhood Preserving Hashing for Social-Network-Oriented Digital Fingerprints. *IEEE Transactions on Information Forensics and Security*, *9*(12), 2232–2247. doi:10.1109/TIFS.2014.2360583

Liu, C., Liu, J., & Jiang, Z. (2014). A Multiobjective Evolutionary Algorithm Based on Similarity for Community Detection From Signed Social Networks. *IEEE Transactions on Cybernetics*, *44*(12), 2274–2287. doi:10.1109/TCYB.2014.2305974 PMID:25296410

Liu, W., & Lü, L. (2010). Link prediction based on local random walk. *EPL*, *89*(5), 58007. doi:10.1209/0295-5075/89/58007

Liu, Y., Huang, X., An, A., & Yu, X. (2007, July). ARSA: a sentiment-aware model for predicting sales performance using blogs. In *Proceedings of the 30th annual international ACM SIGIR conference on Research and development in information retrieval* (pp. 607-614). ACM. doi:10.1145/1277741.1277845

Li, X., & Chen, H. (2013). Recommendation as link prediction in bipartite graphs: A graph kernel-based machine learning approach. *Decision Support Systems*, *54*(2), 880–890. doi:10.1016/j.dss.2012.09.019

Li, Z., Fang, X., Bai, X., & Sheng, O. R. L. (2016). Utility-based Link Recommendation for Online Social Networks. *Management Science*.

Lo, R. T. W., He, B., & Ounis, L. (2005). Automatically building a stopword list for an information retrieval system. *Journal on Digital Information Management*, *5*, 17-24.

Lukin, S., & Walker, M. (2017). *Really? well. apparently bootstrapping improves the performance of sarcasm and nastiness classifiers for online dialogue.* arXiv preprint arXiv:1708.08572

Lü, L., & Zhou, T. (2011). Link prediction in complex networks: A survey. *Physica A*, *390*(6), 1150–1170. doi:10.1016/j.physa.2010.11.027

Lunando, E., & Purwarianti, A. (2013). Indonesian social media sentiment analysis with sarcasm detection. *Advanced Computer Science and Information Systems (ICACSIS), 2013 International Conference*, 195–198. doi:10.1109/ICACSIS.2013.6761575

Lusseau, K., Schneider, O. J., Boisseau, P., Haase, E., Slooten, E., & Dawson, S. M. (2003). The bottlenose dolphin community of Doubtful Sound features a large proportion of long-lasting associations. *Behavioral Ecology and Sociobiology*, *54*(4), 396–405. doi:10.1007/s00265-003-0651-y

Maas, A. L., Daly, R. E., Pham, P. T., Huang, D., Ng, A. Y., & Potts, C. (2011, June). Learning word vectors for sentiment analysis. In *Proceedings of the 49th Annual Meeting of the Association for Computational Linguistics: Human Language Technologies-Volume 1* (pp. 142-150). Association for Computational Linguistics.

Ma, C., Prendinger, H., & Ishizuka, M. (2005). Emotion estimation and reasoning based on affective textual interaction. In *Affective Computing and Intelligent Interaction* (Vol. 3784, pp. 622–628). Berlin: Springer. doi:10.1007/11573548_80

Malviya, V., & Gupta, G. P. (2015). Performance Evaluation of Similarity Based Link Prediction Schemes for Social Networks. *IEEE International Conference on Next Generation Computing Technologies*, 654-659. doi:10.1109/NGCT.2015.7375202

Manku, G. S., & Motwani, R. (2002). Approximate frequency counts over data streams. In *Proceedings of the 28th international conference on very large data bases*, (pp. 346–357). Academic Press. doi:10.1016/B978-155860869-6/50038-X

Marchand, D. (1990). Managing information quality. In I. Wormell (Ed.), *Information Quality: Definitions and Dimensions*. London: Taylor Graham.

Marcotte, E. M., Pellegrini, M., Thompson, M. J., Yeates, T. O., & Eisenberg, D. (1999). A combined algorithm for genome-wide prediction of protein function. *Nature*, *402*(6757), 83–86. doi:10.1038/47048 PMID:10573421

Martinez-Romo, J., & Araujo, L. (2013). Detecting malicious tweets in trending topics using a statistical analysis of language. *Expert Systems with Applications*, *40*(8), 2992–3000. doi:10.1016/j.eswa.2012.12.015

Masson, A. R., Hayel, Y., & Altman, E. (2017). Posting Behavior Dynamics and Active Filtering for Content Diversity in Social Networks. *IEEE Transactions on Signal and Information Processing over Networks*, *3*(2), 376–387. doi:10.1109/tsipn.2017.2696738

Masud, M. M. (2010). Classification and novel class detection in data streams with active mining. In *Pacific-Asia Conference on Knowledge Discovery and Data Mining*. Springer Berlin Heidelberg. doi:10.1007/978-3-642-13672-6_31

Masud, M. (2009). *Integrating novel class detection with classification for concept-drifting data streams*. Machine Learning and Knowledge Discovery in Databases. doi:10.1007/978-3-642-04174-7_6

Masud, M. M., Chen, Q., Khan, L., Aggarwal, C. C., Gao, J., Han, J., & Oza, N. C. et al. (2013). Classification and adaptive novel class detection of feature-evolving data streams. *IEEE Transactions on Knowledge and Data Engineering*, *25*(7), 1484–1497. doi:10.1109/TKDE.2012.109

Masud, M. M., Gao, J., Khan, L., Han, J., & Thuraisingham, B. (2011, June). Classification and Novel Class Detection in Concept-Drifting Data Streams under Time Constraints. *TKDE*, *23*(6), 859–874.

MatrixC. (2015). Retrieved from http://en.wikipedia.org/wiki/Confusion_matrix

Matsumoto, S., Takamura, H., & Okumura, M. (2005). Sentiment classification using word sub-sequences and dependency sub-trees. In *PAKDD'05 Proceedings of the 9th Pacific-Asia conference on Advances in Knowledge Discovery and Data Mining* (pp. 301-311). Berlin: Springer. doi:10.1007/11430919_37

Mayer, R. C., Davis, J. H., & Schoorman, F. D. (1995). An integrative model of organizational trust. *Academy of Management Review*, *20*(3), 709–734.

Maynard, D., & Greenwood, M. A. (2014). *Who cares about sarcastic tweets? Investigating the impact of sarcasm on sentiment analysis*. LREC.

Maynard, D., & Greenwood, M. A. (2014, May). *Who cares about Sarcastic Tweets? Investigating the Impact of Sarcasm on Sentiment Analysis*. LREC.

Mbogo, G. K., & Visheratin, A. A. (2017). Build hybrid scientific similarity networks using research papers and social networks. Procedia Computer Science, 2507, 211.

McCord, M., & Chuah, M. (2011). Spam detection on twitter using traditional classifiers. In *Proceedings of the International Conference on Autonomic and Trusted Computing*. Springer. doi:10.1007/978-3-642-23496-5_13

McGlohon, M., Glance, N. S., & Reiter, Z. (2010, May). Star Quality: Aggregating Reviews to Rank Products and Merchants. ICWSM.

McKnight, D. H., & Chervany, N. L. (2001). What trust means in e-commerce customer relationships: An interdisciplinary conceptual typology. *International Journal of Electronic Commerce*, *6*(2), 35–59. doi:10.1080/10864415.2001.11044235

McKnight, D. H., Choudhury, V., & Kacmar, C. (2002). Developing and validating trust measures for e-commerce: An integrative typology. *Information Systems Research*, *13*(3), 334–359. doi:10.1287/isre.13.3.334.81

Meesuksabai, W., Kangkachit, T., & Waiyamai, K. (2011). Hue-stream: Evolution-based clustering technique for heterogeneous data streams with uncertainty. *Advanced Data Mining and Applications - 7th International Conference*, 27–40. doi:10.1007/978-3-642-25856-5_3

Meligy, A. M., Ibrahim, H. M., & Torky, M. F. (2015). A framework for detecting cloning attacks in OSN based on a novel social graph topology. *International Journal of Intelligent Systems and Applications*, *7*(3), 13–20. doi:10.5815/ijisa.2015.03.02

Miles, , Huberman, & Lotto. (1986). Qualitative Data Analysis: A Sourcebook of New Methods. *Educational Evaluation and Policy Analysis*, *8* (3), 329-331.

Miller, G. A. (1995). Wordnet: A lexical database for English. *Commun. ACM*, *38*(11), 39–41.

Mishra, A., Kanojia, D., & Bhattacharyya, P. (2016, February). *Predicting Readers' Sarcasm Understandability by Modeling Gaze Behavior*. AAAI.

Mislove, A., Macron, M., Gummadi, K. P., & Druschel, P. (n.d.). Measurement and Analysis of Online Social Networks. *Proceedings of the 7th ACM SIGCOMM conference on Internet measurement*. Doi:10.1145/1298306.1298311

Mitchell, T. (2006). *The discipline of machine learning*. Academic Press.

Mohammad, S. (2012). #emotional tweets. In **SEM 2012: The First Joint Conference on Lexical and Computational Semantics – Volume 1: Proceedings of the main conference and the shared task, and Volume 2: Proceedings of the Sixth International Workshop on Semantic Evaluation (SemEval 2012)*. Montréal, Canada: Association for Computational Linguistics.

Mohammad, S. M., & Turney, P. D. (2013a). Crowdsourcing a word-emotion association lexicon. Academic Press.

Mohammad, S. M., Kiritchenko, S., & Zhu, X. (2013b). *Nrc-canada: Building the state-of-the-art in sentiment analysis of tweets*. Academic Press.

Moody, J., Daniel, A., Farland, M., & Moll, S.B. (2005). Visualizing Network Dynamics. *American Journal of Sociology*. doi:10.1086/421509

Moore, P., Sharma, M., Xhafa, F., & Barolli, L. (2013). Context and the Cloud Situational Awareness in Mobile Systems. *IEEE International Conference on Network-Based Information Systems*, 551-558. doi:10.1109/NBiS.2013.92

Mu, B., & Yuan, S. (2010). *A method for Evaluating Initial Trust Value of Direct Trust and Recommender Trust*. Academic Press.

Myers, S. A., Zhu, C., & Leskovec, J. (2012). Information Diffusion and External Influence in Networks. *Proceedings of the 9th ACM SIGKDD International Conference on Knowledge Discovery and Data Mining*, 33-41. doi:10.1145/2339530.2339540

Nafi, K. W., Kar, T. S., Hossain, M. A., & Hashem, M. M. A. (2012). An advanced Certain Trust Model Using Fuzzy Logic and Probabilistic Logic Theory. *International Journal of Advanced Computer Science and Applications, 3*(12).

Nasukawa, T., & Yi, J. (2003, October). Sentiment analysis: Capturing favorability using natural language processing. In *Proceedings of the 2nd international conference on Knowledge Capture* (pp. 70-77). ACM. doi:10.1145/945645.945658

Nettleton, D. F. (2013). Data mining of social networks represented as graphs. *Computer Science Review Elsevier Journal*, *7*, 1–34. doi:10.1016/j.cosrev.2012.12.001

Newman, M. E. J. (2003). The structure and function of complex networks. *SIAM Review*, *45*(2), 167–256. doi:10.1137/S003614450342480

NielsenS. M. R. (2012). Retrieved from http://blog.nielsen.com/nielsenwire/social/2012/

Nikolaev, A. G., Razib, R., & Kucheriya, A. (2015). On efficient use of entropy centrality for social network analysis and community detection. *Social Networks Journal Elsevier*, *40*, 154–162. doi:10.1016/j.socnet.2014.10.002

Nirkhi, S., Dharaskar, R. V., & Thakare, V. M. (2016). Authorship Verification of Online Messages for Forensic Investigation. *Procedia Computer Science*, *78*, 640–645. doi:10.1016/j.procs.2016.02.111

Niu, Q., Xia, S., & Zhang, L. (2009). Association Classification Based on Compactness of Rules. *2009 Second International Workshop on Knowledge Discovery and Data Mining*. doi:10.1109/WKDD.2009.160

Norris, D. F., & Reddick, C. G. (2013). Local e-government in the United States: Transformation or incremental change? *Public Administration Review*, *73*(1), 165–175. doi:10.1111/j.1540-6210.2012.02647.x

Nurse, J. R. C., Agrafiotis, I., Goldsmith, M., Creese, S., & Lamberts, K. (2014). Two sides of the coin: Measuring and communicating the trustworthiness of online information. *Journal of Trust Management*, *1*(1), 5. doi:10.1186/2196-064X-1-5

O'Keefe, T., & Koprinska, I. (2009, December). Feature selection and weighting methods in sentiment analysis. *Proceedings of the 14th Australasian document computing symposium*, 67-74.

O'Connor, B., Balasubramanyan, R., Routledge, B. R., & Smith, N. A. (2010). From tweets to polls: Linking text sentiment to public opinion time series. *ICWSM*, *11*(122-129), 1-2.

Okuno, S., Asai, H., & Yamana, H. (2014, October). A challenge of authorship identification for ten-thousand-scale microblog users. In *Big Data (Big Data), 2014 IEEE International Conference on* (pp. 52-54). IEEE. doi:10.1109/BigData.2014.7004491

Ortony, A., Clore, G. L., & Foss, M. A. (1987). The referential structure of the affective lexicon. *Cognitive Science*, *11*(3), 341–364. doi:10.1207/s15516709cog1103_4

Owais, S., Nafis, P., & Khanna, S. (2015). An Improved Method for Detection of Satire from User-Generated Content. *(IJCSIT). International Journal of Computer Science and Information Technologies*, *6*(3), 2084–2088.

Oza, N. C. (2005). Online bagging and boosting. IEEE international conference on systems, man and cybernetics, 3, 2340–2345. doi:10.1109/ICSMC.2005.1571498

Pagolu, V., Reddy, K., & Panda, G. (2016). Sentiment analysis of Twitter data for predicting stock market movements. In *International Conference on Signal Processing, Communication, Power and Embedded System (SCOPES)*, 2016 (pp. 1345-1350). Paralakhemundi, India: IEEE. doi:10.1109/SCOPES.2016.7955659

Pallegedara, D., & Pan, L. (2014). Investigating Facebook Groups through a Random Graph Model. *Journal of Multimedia. Finland*, *9*(1), 25–35.

Pan, B., Hembrooke, H. A., Gay, G. K., Granka, L. A., Feusner, M. K., & Newman, J. K. (2004). *The Determinants of Web Page Viewing Behavior: An Eye-Tracking Study*. ACM Transactions. doi:10.1145/968363.968391

Pang, B., & Lee, L. (2008). Opinion mining and sentiment analysis. *Foundations and Trends in Information Retrieval, 2*(1-2), 1-135.

Pang, B., & Lee, L. (2008). Opinion mining and sentiment analysis. *Foundations and Trends® in Information Retrieval, 2*(1–2), 1-135.

Pang, B., Lee, L., & Vaithyanathan, S. (2002). Thumbs up? Sentiment classification using machine learning techniques. *Proceeding of the conference on empirical methods in natural language processing*, 79-86.

Pang, B., & Lee, L. (2004). A sentimental education: Sentiment analysis using subjectivity summarization based on minimum cuts. *Proceedings of the ACL*, 271–278. doi:10.3115/1218955.1218990

Panicker, N. J., & Devadas, L. (2015). Filtering the walls in online social networks. *International Journal of Advanced Research in Computer Science and Software Engineering, 5*(5), 45–52.

Papapetrou, O., Garofalakis, M., & Deligiannakis, A. (2015). Sketching distributed sliding window data streams. *VLDB Journal, 24*(3), 345-368.

Patel, M., & Mistry, M. (2015). A Review: Text Classification on Social Media Data. *IOSR Journal of Computer Engineering, 17*(1), 80-84.

Paul, D. L. (2000). *Telemedicine: a study of virtual collaboration and trust in hypercompetitive environments* (Dissertation). Department of Management Information Systems, University of Texas at Austin.

Peng, J., Choo, R. K. K., & Ashman, H. (2016, August). Astroturfing detection in social media: Using binary n-gram analysis for authorship attribution. In Trustcom/BigDataSE/I SPA, 2016 IEEE (pp. 121-128). IEEE.

Perera, C., Liu, C. H., Jayawardena, S., & Chen, M. (2014). Context-aware Computing in the Internet of Things: A Survey on Internet of Things from Industrial Market Perspective. *IEEE Access: Practical Innovations, Open Solutions, 2*, 1660–1679. doi:10.1109/ACCESS.2015.2389854

Perera, C., Zaslavsky, A., Christen, P., & Georgakopoulos, D. (2014). Context Aware Computing for the Internet of Things: A Survey. *IEEE Communications Surveys and Tutorials, 16*(1), 414–454. doi:10.1109/SURV.2013.042313.00197

Peterson, E. (2004). *Web analytics demystified: A marketer's guide to understanding how your web site affects your business*. Celilo Group Media and CafePress.

Peterson, E. T. (2006). *The Big Book of Key Performance Indicators*. Web Analytics Demystified Series, Book Two. Celilo Group Media and CafePress.

Pokou, Y. J. M., Fournier-Viger, P., & Moghrabi, C. (2016). Authorship Attribution Using Small Sets of Frequent Part-of-Speech Skip-grams. In *FLAIRS Conference* (pp. 86-91). Academic Press.

Poole, M. S. (2004). Trust, Trait Theory, and Collaboration in Telemedicine: An Empirical Test. *Proceedings of the 37th Hawaii International Conference on System Sciences*. IEEE. doi:10.1109/HICSS.2004.1265374

Poria, S. (2016). *A Deeper Look into Sarcastic Tweets Using Deep Convolutional Neural Networks*. Nanyang Technological University.

Pradhan, V. M., Vala, J., & Balani, P. (2016, January). A Survey on Sentiment Analysis Algorithms for Opinion Mining. *International Journal of Computers and Applications, 133*(9), 7–11. doi:10.5120/ijca2016907977

Prasanna & Reddy. (2010). A Survey on Different Trends in Data Streams. *Proceedings of 2010 IEEE International Conference on Networking and Information Technology.*

Prasanna & Reddy. (2015). Efficient mining of Data Streams using Associative Classification Approach. *International Journal of Software Engineering and Knowledge Engineering, 25*(3), 605-631.

Pratanwanich, N., & Lio, P. (2014, December). Who wrote this? Textual modeling with authorship attribution in big data. In *Data Mining Workshop (ICDMW), 2014 IEEE International Conference on* (pp. 645-652). IEEE. doi:10.1109/ICDMW.2014.140

Prieto, M. V., Alvarez, M., & Cacheda, F. (2013). Detecting linkedin spammers and its spam nets. *International Journal of Advanced Computer Science and Applications*, *4*(9), 189–199.

Qian, T., Liu, B., Chen, L., & Peng, Z. (2014, January). Tri-Training for Authorship Attribution with Limited Training Data. ACL, (2), 345-351. doi:10.3115/v1/P14-2057

R Core Team. (2014). *R: A language and environment for statistical computing.* R Foundation for Statistical Computing. Retrieved from http://www.R-project.org/

Raj, K. G., & Yinping, Y. (2017). CrystalNest at SemEval-2017 Task 4: Using sarcasm detection for enhancing sentiment classification and quantification. In *Proceedings of the 11th International Workshop on Semantic Evaluation.* Vancouver, Canada: SemEval '17.

Rajadesingan, A., Zafarani, R., & Liu, H. (2015, February). Sarcasm detection on Twitter: A behavioral modeling approach. In *Proceedings of the Eighth ACM International Conference on Web Search and Data Mining* (pp. 97-106). ACM. doi:10.1145/2684822.2685316

Rajalaxmi, R. R., & Ramesh, A. (2014). Binary bat approach for effective spam classification in online social networks. *Australian Journal of Basic and Applied Sciences*, *8*(18), 383–388.

Rangel, F., & Rosso, P. (2016). On the impact of emotions on author profiling. *Information Processing & Management*, *52*(1), 73–92. doi:10.1016/j.ipm.2015.06.003

Reyes, A., & Rosso, P. (2012). Making objective decisions from subjective data: Detecting irony in customer reviews. *Decision Support Systems*, *53*(4), 754–760. doi:10.1016/j.dss.2012.05.027

Reyes, A., Rosso, P., & Veale, T. (2013). *A multidimensional approach for detecting irony in twitter. In Language Resources and Evaluation* (pp. 1–30). Springer Netherlands.

Richardson, M., Agrawal, R., & Domingos, P. (2003). *Trust Management for the Semantic Web.* ISWC.

Ridings, C. M., Gefen, D., & Arinze, B. (2002). Some antecedents and effects of trust in virtual communities. *The Journal of Strategic Information Systems*, *11*(3&4), 271–295. doi:10.1016/S0963-8687(02)00021-5

Riloff, E. (2013). *Sarcasm as contrast between a positive sentiment and negative situation*. EMNLP.

Riloff, E., Qadir, A., Surve, P., De Silva, L., Gilbert, N., & Huang, R. (2013, October). *Sarcasm as Contrast between a Positive Sentiment and Negative Situation* (Vol. 13). EMNLP.

Rimon, M. (2005). Sentiment classification: Linguistic and non-linguistic issues. *Proceedings of Israel Association for Theoretical Linguistics, 21.*

Robins, G., Pattison, P., & Woolcock, J. (2005). Small and other worlds: Global network structures from local processes. *American Journal of Sociology*, *110*(4), 894–936. doi:10.1086/427322

Rocha, A., Scheirer, W. J., Forstall, C. W., Cavalcante, T., Theophilo, A., Shen, B., & Stamatatos, E. (2017). Authorship attribution for social media forensics. *IEEE Transactions on Information Forensics and Security*, *12*(1), 5–33. doi:10.1109/TIFS.2016.2603960

Rodrigues, R. G., Dores, R. M., & Camilo-Junior, C. G. (2016, January). SentiHealth-Cancer: A sentiment analysis tool to help detecting mood of patients in online social networks. *International Journal of Medical Informatics*, *85*(1), 80–95. doi:10.1016/j.ijmedinf.2015.09.007 PMID:26514078

Rossetti, G., Berlingerio, M., & Giannotti, F. (2011, December). Scalable link prediction on multidimensional networks. In *Data Mining Workshops (ICDMW), 2011 IEEE 11th International Conference on* (pp. 979-986). IEEE. doi:10.1109/ICDMW.2011.150

Rossetti, G., Pappalardo, L., Kikas, R., Pedreschi, D., Giannotti, F., & Dumas, M. (2016). Homophilic network decomposition: A community-centric analysis of online social services. Social Network Analysis and Mining (SNAM). *Journal Springer*, *6*(103), 1–18.

Roy, A., Kucukural, A., & Zhang, Y. (2010). I-TASSER: A unified platform for automated protein structure and function prediction. *Nature Protocols*, *5*(4), 725–738. doi:10.1038/nprot.2010.5 PMID:20360767

Ruhi. (2014). Social Media Analytics as a Business Intelligence Practice: Current Landscape & Future Prospects. *Journal of Internet Social Networking & Virtual Communities.*

Saengthongloun, B. (2013). Ac-stream: Associative classification over data streams using multiple class association rules. *Computer Science and Software Engineering (JCSSE), 2013 10th International Joint Conference on.* doi:10.1109/JCSSE.2013.6567349

Salas-Zárate, M. P., Valencia-García, R., Ruiz-Martínez, A., & Colomo-Palacios, R. (2017, August 1). Feature-based opinion mining in financial news: An ontology-driven approach. *Journal of Information Science*, *43*(4), 458–479. doi:10.1177/0165551516645528

Salo, J., & Karjaluoto, H. (2007). A conceptual model of trust in the online environment. *Online Information Review*, *31*(5), 604–621. doi:10.1108/14684520710832324

Santos, F. (2013). *Mineracão de Opinião em Textos Opinativos Utilizando Algoritmos de Classificação* (Graduação). Universidade de Brasilia, Brasilia.

Sapkota, U., Bethard, S., Montes-y-Gómez, M., & Solorio, T. (2015, May). Not All Character N-grams Are Created Equal: A Study in Authorship Attribution. In HLT-NAACL (pp. 93-102). Academic Press. doi:10.3115/v1/N15-1010

Scellato, S., Noulas, A., & Mascolo, C. (2011, August). Exploiting place features in link prediction on location-based social networks. In *Proceedings of the 17th ACM SIGKDD international conference on Knowledge discovery and data mining* (pp. 1046-1054). ACM. doi:10.1145/2020408.2020575

Schwartz, R., Tsur, O., Rappoport, A., & Koppel, M. (2013). Authorship attribution of micro-messages. In *Proceedings of the 2013 Conference on Empirical Methods in Natural Language Processing* (pp. 1880-1891). Academic Press.

Sebastiani, F. (2002). Machine learning in automated text categorization. *ACM Computing Surveys*, *34*(1), 1–47. doi:10.1145/505282.505283

Seidl, T., Assent, I., Kranen, P., Krieger, R., & Herrmann, J. (2009). Indexing density models for incremental learning and anytime classification on data streams. *Proceedings of the 12th international conference on extending database technology: advances in database technology*, 311–322. doi:10.1145/1516360.1516397

Sentiment Analysis on Movie Reviews. (2015). Retrieved February 09, 2017, from https://www.kaggle.com/c/sentiment-analysis-on-movie-reviews/data

Sentiment and Text Analysis Engine – AlchemyAPI. (2017). Retrieved from http://www.alchemyapi.com/api

Seroussi, Y., Bohnert, F., & Zukerman, I. (2012, July). Authorship attribution with author-aware topic models. In *Proceedings of the 50th Annual Meeting of the Association for Computational Linguistics: Short Papers-Volume 2* (pp. 264-269). Association for Computational Linguistics.

Seroussi, Y., Zukerman, I., & Bohnert, F. (2011, June). Authorship attribution with latent Dirichlet allocation. In *Proceedings of the fifteenth conference on computational natural language learning* (pp. 181-189). Association for Computational Linguistics.

Setubal, J. C., Meidanis, J., & Setubal-Meidanis. (1997). *Introduction to computational molecular biology*. PWS Pub.

Shalev-Shwartz, S., & Ben-David, S. (2014). *Understanding machine learning: From theory to algorithms*. New York: Cambridge University Press. doi:10.1017/CBO9781107298019

Shankar, V., Urban, G. L., & Sultan, F. (2002). Online trust: A stakeholder perspective, concepts, implications, and future directions. *The Journal of Strategic Information Systems*, *11*(3-4), 325–344. doi:10.1016/S0963-8687(02)00022-7

Sharma, V., You, I., Kumar, R., & Kim, P. (2017). Computational Offloading for Efficient Trust Management in Pervasive Online Social Networks Using Osmotic Computing. *IEEE Access: Practical Innovations, Open Solutions*, *5*, 5084–5103. doi:10.1109/ACCESS.2017.2683159

Sheridan, W., & Riley, T. B. (2006). Comparing e-government vs. e-governance. *Commonwealth Center for e-Governance*, 1-5.

Sidorov, G., Velasquez, F., Stamatatos, E., Gelbukh, A., & Chanona-Hernández, L. (2014). Syntactic n-grams as machine learning features for natural language processing. *Expert Systems with Applications*, *41*(3), 853–860. doi:10.1016/j.eswa.2013.08.015

Sillence, E., Briggs, P., Fishwick, L., & Harris, P. (2004). *Trust and mistrust of online health sites*. SIGCHI; doi:10.1145/985692.985776

Silva, R. S., Laboreiro, G., Sarmento, L., Grant, T., Oliveira, E., & Maia, B. (2011, June). 'twazn me!!!('automatic authorship analysis of micro-blogging messages. In *International Conference on Application of Natural Language to Information Systems* (pp. 161-168). Springer Berlin Heidelberg. doi:10.1007/978-3-642-22327-3_16

Similarweb. (2015). Retrieved from http://www.similarweb.com/

Simon, H. A. (1983). Machine learning: An artificial intelligence approach. Springer Berlin Heidelberg.

Singal, H., & Kohli, S. (2014, September). Conceptual model for obfuscated TRUST induced from Web Analytics data for content-driven websites. In *Advances in Computing, Communications and Informatics (ICACCI, 2014 International Conference on* (pp. 2781-2785). IEEE. doi:10.1109/ICACCI.2014.6968622

Singal, H., & Kohli, S. (2015, May). Escalation of TRUST analysis in web. In *Proceedings of the 12th ACM International Conference on Computing Frontiers* (p. 56). ACM.

Singal, H., & Kohli, S. (2016). Mitigating Information Trust: Taking the Edge off Health Websites. *International Journal of Technoethics*, *7*(1), 16–33. doi:10.4018/IJT.2016010102

Singal, H., & Kohli, S. (2016). Trust Necessitated through Metrics: Estimating the Trustworthiness of Websites. *Procedia Computer Science*, *85*, 133–140. doi:10.1016/j.procs.2016.05.199

Singal, H., & Kohli, S. (2016, March). Intellectualizing TRUST for Medical Websites. In *Proceedings of the Second International Conference on Information and Communication Technology for Competitive Strategies* (p. 83). ACM.

Singh, A. P., & Gordon, G. J. (2008, August). Relational learning via collective matrix factorization. In *Proceedings of the 14th ACM SIGKDD international conference on Knowledge discovery and data mining* (pp. 650-658). ACM. doi:10.1145/1401890.1401969

Smed, T. D., Nijs, L., & Daelemans, W. (2014). Creative Web Service with Pattern. Academic Press.

Smith, L. J., Bolin, K. A., Schwalbe, H., MacArthur, M. W., Thornton, J. M., & Dobson, C. M. (1996). Analysis of main chain torsion angles in proteins: Prediction of NMR coupling constants for native and random coil conformations. *Journal of Molecular Biology, 255*(3), 494–506. doi:10.1006/jmbi.1996.0041 PMID:8568893

Sokolova, M., & Lapalme, G. (2009). A systematic analysis of performance measures for classification tasks. *Inf. Process. Manage., 45*(4), 427–437.

Soman, S. J., & Murugappan, S. (2014). A study of spam detection algorithm on social media networks. *Journal of Computational Science, 10*(10), 2135–2140. doi:10.3844/jcssp.2014.2135.2140

Song, J., Lee, S., & Kim, J. (2011). Spam filtering in twitter using sender-receiver relationship. In Recent advances in intrusion detection (pp. 301-317). Springer Berlin/Heidelberg. doi:10.1007/978-3-642-23644-0_16

Song, X., Jiang, S., Yan, X., & Chen, H. (2014). Collaborative Friendship Networks in Online Healthcare Communities: *An Exponential Random Graph Model Analysis. In International Conference on Smart Health. Springer.*

Souza, M. V. S. (2012). *Mineração de Opiniões Aplicada a Mídias Sociais* (Dissertação de Mestrado). Universidade Católica do Rio Grande do Sul, Porto Alegre. Retrieved from http://migre.me/thZxK

Spears, R. (1998). *NTC's American English learner's dictionary: The essential vocabulary of American language and culture.* NTC Pub. Group.

Stamatatos, E. (2009). A survey of modern authorship attribution methods. *Journal of the American Society for Information Science and Technology, 60*(3), 538–556. doi:10.1002/asi.21001

Stamenkovic, I., Amiot, M., Pesando, J. M., & Seed, B. (1989). A lymphocyte molecule implicated in lymph node homing is a member of the cartilage link protein family. *Cell, 56*(6), 1057–1062. doi:10.1016/0092-8674(89)90638-7 PMID:2466575

Stefanie, A., & Claudio, C. (2011). *The Economic and Social Impacts of E-government.* Freiburg University.

Stein, T., Chen, E., & Mangla, K. (2011). Facebook immune system. In *Proceedings of the 4th Workshop on Social Network Systems* (pp. 8). ACM.

Stepan, T., Morawski, J. M., Dick, S., & Miller, J. (2016). Incorporating Spatial, Temporal, and Social Context in Recommendations for Location-Based Social Networks. *IEEE Transactions on Computational Social Systems, 3*(4), 164–175. doi:10.1109/TCSS.2016.2631473

Stringhini, G., Kruegel, C., & Vigna, G. (2010). Detecting spammers on social networks. In *Proceedings of the 26th Annual Computer Security Applications Conference (ACSAC).* Austin, TX: ACM.

Suganya, M., & Anandakumar, H. (2013). Handover based spectrum allocation in cognitive radio networks. *2013 International Conference on Green Computing, Communication and Conservation of Energy (ICGCE).* doi:10.1109/ICGCE.2013.6823431

Sutcliffe, A. (2002). Assessing the Reliability of Heuristic Evaluation for Website Attractiveness and Usability. In *Proceedings of the 35th Hawaii International Conference on System Sciences.* IEEE. doi:10.1109/HICSS.2002.994098

Swami, A. D., & Khade, B. S. (2014). A text based filtering system for OSN user walls. *International Journal of Advanced Research in Computer Science and Software Engineering*, *4*(2).

Taboada, M. (2011). Lexicon-based methods for sentiment analysis. Computational Linguistics, 37(34), 267–307.

Tanbeer, S. K., Ahmed, C. F., Jeong, B.-S., & Lee, Y.-K. (2009). Sliding Window-based frequent pattern mining over data streams. *Elsevier, Information Sciences*, *179*(July), 3843–3865. doi:10.1016/j.ins.2009.07.012

Tang, J., Chang, S., Aggarwal, C., & Liu, H. (2015, February). Negative link prediction in social media. In *Proceedings of the Eighth ACM International Conference on Web Search and Data Mining* (pp. 87-96). ACM. doi:10.1145/2684822.2685295

Tayal, D. K., Jain, A., Arora, S., Agarwal, S., Gupta, T., & Tyagi, N. (2015). Crime detection and criminal identification in India using data mining techniques. *AI & Society*, *30*(1), 117–127. doi:10.1007/s00146-014-0539-6

Tepperman, J., Traum, D., & Narayanan, S. (2006). " Yeah Right": Sarcasm Recognition for Spoken Dialogue Systems. *Ninth International Conference on Spoken Language Processing*.

The importance of reliable online health information. (2015). *Prescient Digital.* Retrieved from http://www. prescient-digital.com/articles/e-health/the-importance-of-reliable-online-health-information/

Thelwall, M. (2013). *Heart and Soul: Sentiment Strength Detection in the Social Web With SentiStrength*. Academic Press.

Thomas, K., Grier, C., Ma, J., Paxson, V., & Song, D. (2011). Design and evaluation of a real-time url spam filtering service. In *Security and Privacy (SP), 2011 IEEE Symposium on*. IEEE. doi:10.1109/SP.2011.25

Torra, V., Shafie, T., & Salas, J. (2016). Data Protection for Online Social Networks and Stability for Graphs. *IEEE Transactions on Emerging Topics in Computing*, *4*(3), 374–381. doi:10.1109/TETC.2015.2433923

Tsai, P. S. M. (2009). Mining frequent itemsets in data streams using the weighted sliding window model. *Elsevier, Expert Systems with Applications*, *36*(March), 11617–11625. doi:10.1016/j.eswa.2009.03.025

Tumasjan, A., Sprenger, T. O., Sandner, P. G., & Welpe, I. M. (2010). Predicting elections with Twitter: What 140 characters reveal about political sentiment. *ICWSM*, *10*(1), 178–185.

Turney, P. (2002). Thumbs up or thumbs down? Semantic orientation applied to unsupervised classification of reviews. In *Proceedings of the 40th annual meeting of the association for computational linguistics* (pp. 417-424). Stroudsburg, PA: Association for Computational Linguistics.

Turney, P. D., & Littman, M. L. (2003). Measuring praise and criticism: Inference of semantic orientation from association. *ACM Transactions on Information Systems*, *21*(4), 315–346. doi:10.1145/944012.944013

Udommanetanakit, K., Rakthanmanon, T., & Waiyamai, K. (2007). E-stream: Evolution-based technique for stream clustering. ADMA, 605–15. doi:10.1007/978-3-540-73871-8_58

United Nations (UN). (2002). *Benchmarking E-government: A Global Perspective*. New York: Stephen A. Ronaghan.

United Nations (UN). (2004). *UN Global E-government Survey*. New York.

United Nations (UN). (2006). *Global E-government Readiness Report 2005*. New York: From E-government to E-inclusion.

United Nations (UN). (2008). UN E-Government Survey 2008, From E-government to connected government. New York: UN.

United Nations (UN). (2010). United Nations E-government Survey 2010, Leveraging e-government at a time of financial and economic crisis. New York: UN.

United Nations (UN). (2012). *United Nations E-government Survey 2012, E-government for people*. UN.

United Nations (UN). (2014). United Nations E-government Survey 2014, E-government for the future we want. New York: UN.

United Nations (UN). (2016). United Nations E-government Survey 2016, E-government in support of sustainable development. New York: UN.

Utsumi, A. (2000). Verbal irony as implicit display of ironic environment: Distinguishing ironic utterances from nonirony. *Journal of Pragmatics*, *32*(12), 1777–1806. doi:10.1016/S0378-2166(99)00116-2

Vapnik, V. N. (1995). *The nature of statistical learning theory*. New York, NY: Springer-Verlag New York, Inc. doi:10.1007/978-1-4757-2440-0

Veale, T., & Hao, Y. (2010). Detecting ironic intent in creative comparisons. *ECAI*, *215*, 765–770.

Viegas, F. B., Wattenberg, M., Ham, F. V., Kriss, J., & McKeon, M. (2007). ManyEyes: A Site for Visualization at Internet Scale. *IEEE Transactions on Visualization and Computer Graphics*, *13*(6), 1121–1128. doi:10.1109/TVCG.2007.70577 PMID:17968055

Wahid, F. (2011). Explaining history of egovernment implementation in developing countries: an analytical framework. Electronic Government, 38-49.

Wallace, B. C., Kertz, L., & Charniak, E. (2014). Humans require context to infer ironic intent (so computers probably do, too). *Proceedings of the 52nd Annual Meeting of the Association for Computational Linguistics*, 2, 512-516. doi:10.3115/v1/P14-2084

Walraven, A., Brand-Gruwel, S., & Boshuizen, H. P. A. (2009) How students evaluate information and sources when searching the World Wide Web for information. *Computers & Education, 52*(1), 234-246.

Wang, H., Lu, Y., & Zhai, C. (2010). Latent aspect rating analysis on review text data: a rating regression approach. In *KDD '10 Proceedings of the 16th ACM SIGKDD international conference on Knowledge discovery and data mining* (pp. 783-792). New York, NY: ACM. doi:10.1145/1835804.1835903

Wang, C., Lai, J., Huang, D., & Zheng, W. (2013). SVStream: A support vector-based algorithm for clustering data streams. *IEEE Transactions on Knowledge and Data Engineering*, *25*(6), 1410–1424. doi:10.1109/TKDE.2011.263

Wang, P., Xu, B., Wu, Y., & Zhou, X. (2015). Link prediction in social networks: The state-of-the-art. *Science China. Information Sciences*, *58*(1), 1–38.

Wang, Z., Wu, Z., Wang, R., & Ren, Y. (2015, November). Twitter sarcasm detection exploiting a context-based model. In *International Conference on Web Information Systems Engineering* (pp. 77-91). Springer. doi:10.1007/978-3-319-26190-4_6

Watson, D., Clark, L. A., & Tellegen, A. (1988). Development and validation of brief measures of positive and negative affect: The panas scales. *Journal of Personality and Social Psychology*, *54*(6), 1063–1070. doi:10.1037/0022-3514.54.6.1063 PMID:3397865

Wiggins, J. S., Phillip, C. K., & James, N. B. (1982). *Circumplex models of interpersonal behavior in clinical psychology. In Handbook of Research Methods in Clinical Psychology* (pp. 183–221). New York: Wiley-Interscience.

Wilensky, U. (1999). *NetLogo: Center for Connected Learning and Computer-Based Modelling*. North Western University. Retrieved from http://ccl.northwestern.edu/netlogo

Wilson, T., Wiebe, J., & Hoffmann, P. (2005). Recognizing contextual polarity in phrase level sentiment analysis. In *Proceedings of the conference on Human Language Technology and Empirical Methods in Natural Language Processing* (pp. 347-354). Stroudsburg, PA: Association for Computational Linguistics. doi:10.3115/1220575.1220619

Xia, F., Jedari, B., Yang, L. T., Ma, J., & Huang, R. (2016). A Signaling Game for Uncertain Data Delivery in Selfish Mobile Social Networks. *IEEE Transactions on Computational Social Systems*, *3*(2), 100–112. doi:10.1109/TCSS.2016.2584103

Xiao, M., Wu, J., Huang, L., Cheng, R., & Wang, Y. (2017). Online Task Assignment for Crowdsensing in Predictable Mobile Social Networks. *IEEE Transactions on Mobile Computing*, *16*(8), 2306–2320. doi:10.1109/TMC.2016.2616473

Xia, W., Cao, M., & Johansson, K. H. (2016). Structural Balance and Opinion Separation in Trust–Mistrust Social Networks. *IEEE Transactions on Control of Network Systems*, *3*(1), 46–56. doi:10.1109/TCNS.2015.2437528

Xin, L., Leyi, S., Yao, W., & Zhaojin, X. (2013). A Dynamic Trust Conference Algorithm for Social Network. *Proceedings of the IEEE Eighth International Conference on P2P, Parallel, Grid, Cloud and Internet Computing.*

Xu, H., Sun, W., & Javaid, A. (2016). Efficient spam detection across online social networks. In *Proceedings of the International Conference on Big Data Analysis (ICBDA)*. IEEE. doi:10.1109/ICBDA.2016.7509829

Yang, C., Harkreader, R., & Gu, G. (2011). Die free or live hard? empirical evaluation and new design for fighting evolving twitter spammers. In Recent Advances in Intrusion Detection (pp. 318-337). Springer Berlin/Heidelberg.

Yang, J., Yang, C., & Wei, Y. (2016). Frequent Pattern Mining Algorithm for Uncertain Data Streams Based on Sliding Window. *Intelligent Human-Machine Systems and Cybernetics, 2016 8th International Conference on, 2*. doi:10.1109/IHMSC.2016.293

Yang, J., & Leskovec, J. (2012). *Defining and Evaluating Network Communities based on Ground-truth*. ICDM.

Yang, J., Yang, L., & Zhang, P. (2015, June). A New Link Prediction Algorithm Based on Local Links. In *International Conference on Web-Age Information Management* (pp. 16-28). Springer International Publishing. doi:10.1007/978-3-319-23531-8_2

Yang, Y., Lichtenwalter, R. N., & Chawla, N. V. (2015). Evaluating link prediction methods. *Knowledge and Information Systems*, *45*(3), 751–782. doi:10.1007/s10115-014-0789-0

Yano, T., & Smith, N. A. (2010, May). What's Worthy of Comment? Content and Comment Volume in Political Blogs. ICWSM.

Yardi, S., Romero, D., Schoenebeck, G., & Boyd, D. (2009). Detecting spam in a twitter network. *First Monday*, *15*(1). doi:10.5210/fm.v15i1.2793

Yoon, J. W., Kim, H., & Huh, J. H. (2010). Hybrid spam filtering for mobile communication. *Computers & Security, 29*(4), 446-459.

Yu, K., Chu, W., Yu, S., Tresp, V., & Xu, Z. (2007). Stochastic relational models for discriminative link prediction. In Advances in neural information processing systems (pp. 1553-1560). Academic Press.

Yu, X., Gu, Q., Zhou, M., & Han, J. (2012, April). Citation prediction in heterogeneous bibliographic networks. In *Proceedings of the 2012 SIAM International Conference on Data Mining* (pp. 1119-1130). Society for Industrial and Applied Mathematics. doi:10.1137/1.9781611972825.96

Yu, X., Ren, X., Sun, Y., Gu, Q., Sturt, B., Khandelwal, U., & Han, J. et al. (2014, February). Personalized entity recommendation: A heterogeneous information network approach. In *Proceedings of the 7th ACM international conference on Web search and data mining* (pp. 283-292). ACM. doi:10.1145/2556195.2556259

Zachary, W. W. (1977). An information flow model for conflict and fission in small groups. *Journal of Anthropological Research, 33*(4), 452–473. doi:10.1086/jar.33.4.3629752

Zhang, H. Y., & Wang, W. (2009). Application of Bayesian method to spam SMS filtering. In *Information Engineering and Computer Science, 2009. ICIECS 2009. International Conference on.* IEEE. doi:10.1109/ICIECS.2009.5365176

Zhang, Mishra, & Thai. (2014). Recent Advances in Information Diffusion and Influence Maximization of Complex Social Networks. In *Opportunistics Mobile Social Networks.* Taylor and Francis Group.

Zhang, S., Zheng, X., & Hu, C. (2015). A Survey of Semantic Similarity and its Application to Social Network Analysis. *Proceedings of IEEE International Conference on Big Data (Big Data)*, 2362-2367.

Zhang, Sun, Zhu, & Fang. (2010). Privacy and Security for Online Social Networks: Challenges and Opportunities. *IEEE Network, 24*(4). DOI: 10.1109/MNET.2010.5510913

Zhang, L., Liu, B., Lim, S. H., & O'Brien-Strain, E. (2010, August). Extracting and ranking product features in opinion documents. In *Proceedings of the 23rd international conference on computational linguistics: Posters* (pp. 1462-1470). Association for Computational Linguistics.

Zhang, M., Yang, P., Tian, C., & Tang, S. (2017). You Can Act Locally With Efficiency: Influential User Identification in Mobile Social Networks. *IEEE Access: Practical Innovations, Open Solutions*, *5*, 136–146. doi:10.1109/ACCESS.2016.2632900

Zhang, T., Ramakrishnan, R., & Livny, M. (1997). BIRCH: A new data clustering algorithm and its applications. *Data Mining and Knowledge Discovery, 1*(2), 141–182. doi:10.1023/A:1009783824328

Zhang, X., Furtlehner, C., & Sebag, M. (2008). Data streaming with affinity propagation. In *ECML/PKDD* (pp. 628–643). Springer Berlin Heidelberg.

Zhang, Y. C., Medo, M., Ren, J., Zhou, T., Li, T., & Yang, F. (2007). Recommendation model based on opinion diffusion. *EPL, 80*(6), 68003. doi:10.1209/0295-5075/80/68003

Zhu, T., Gao, H., Yang, Y., Bu, K., Chen, Y., Downey, D., & Choudhary, A. N. et al. (2016). Beating the artificial chaos: Fighting OSN spam using its own templates. *IEEE/ACM Transactions on Networking*, *24*(6), 3856–3869. doi:10.1109/TNET.2016.2557849

Zudilova, T. V., & Ivanov, S. E. (2017). The clustering methods in graph models of social networks. *Applied Mathematical Sciences*, *11*(21), 1007–1017. doi:10.12988/ams.2017.7389

Zuker, M., Mathews, D. H., & Turner, D. H. (1999). Algorithms and thermodynamics for RNA secondary structure prediction: a practical guide. In *RNA biochemistry and biotechnology* (pp. 11–43). Springer Netherlands. doi:10.1007/978-94-011-4485-8_2

About the Contributors

Himani Bansal has done her Engineering from Rajasthan University in 2006 followed by a corporate experience with a reputed company for about two and a half years. Further, to fulfil her academic interests, she completed her Masters and Doctor of Philosophy from Birla Institute of Technology, Mesra, India. Apart from enhancing her academics, she has served as Assistant Professor in various reputable Engineering Colleges and Universities. Currently, she is working with Jaypee Institute of Information Technology, Noida, India. Over 11 years of accomplished career demonstrates her success with excellent academic record, extensive background of involvement in team building activities, effective communicator with excellent planning, organizational and negotiation strengths as well as the ability to lead, reach consensus, establish goals, and attain results. Many reputed certifications such as SAP-ERP Professional from prestigious company SAP India Pvt. Ltd., UGC National Eligibility Test (NET), IBM Certified Academic Associate DB2 9 Database and Application Fundamentals, Google Analytics Platform Principles by Google Analytics Academy, E-Commerce Analytics by Google Analytics Academy and RSA (Rational Seed Academy) by IBM India are in her kitty. She has penned many research papers for various International Journals and Conferences. She also has books to her credit along with edited chapters in International book series. She is also awarded Eighth Annual Excellence Award in Research Journal Awards for the outstanding article by IGI Global for "Mitigating Information Trust-Taking the edge off health websites". She has served as section editor, guest editor, convener and session chair for various upright Journals and Conferences such as SCPE, NGCT, IndiaCom, CSI Digital Life, IJAIP, JGIM, ICACCI, ICCCA, etc. and has reviewed many research papers. She has also organized, coordinated and attended FDPs, Trainings, Seminars and Workshops. She has also coordinated workshops for IIT Bombay under NMEICT program initiated by Ministry of HRD, India. She serves as Life Member of various professional societies such as CSI, ISTE, CSTA and IAENG.

Gulshan Shrivastava is graduated in Computer Science & Engineering from the Maharishi Dayanand University, India. He also earned his M.Tech. degree in Information Security from GGSIPU Delhi, India and MBA degree in Information Technology & Finance from Punjab Technical University, India and pursuing the Ph.D. degree in Computer Science & Engineering from the National Institute of Technology Patna, India. He has co-editor of more than 3 books, author of more than 6 book chapters, 30 articles in International Journals and Conferences of high repute including IEEE, Elsevier, ACM, Springer, Inderscience, IGI Global, Bentham Science etc. His biography was selected in the Marquis Who's Who in the World, 2017. He is also serving as Associate Editor of Journal Global Information Management (JGIM), IGI Global and Section Editor of Scalable Computing (SCPE). He is also serving many journals as editorial board member and as member, international advisory board of several national and international journals. Moreover, he has also delivered expert talk, guest lecturers in International

Conference and serving as reviewer for Journals of IEEE, Springer, Inderscience, IGI Global etc. He is Publicity Chair in ICACCE-2018, SICBS-2017. He also served as Organizing Chair of Special Session in ICRTCSE in 2017 in Malaysia, in Springer Third IC3T, 10th INDIACom; 3rd IEEE ICCSSGD, ACM 2nd ICICTCS in 2016 in India. He has also served as founder and organizing chair of International Workshop on Recent Trends in Security and Forensic Investigation ICT in conjunction with IEEE 4th International Conference on Advanced in Computing & Communication Engineering (ICACCE-2018), Paris, France in June 2018. He is currently actively working on a project for risk monitoring and android behavior analysis. He has also served as Technical program committee (TPC) member of International conferences worldwide. He is member of IEEE, CSI, ACM, SIGCOMM, and many professional bodies. He was also visiting researcher with Datec Ltd., Papua New Guinea (PNG) in 2010. At present, He is working as research scholar in the Department of Computer Science & Engineering, National Institute of Technology Patna (Institute of National Importance), India. He has an ardent inclination towards field of Analytics. His research interest includes Information security, Android, Data Analytics, Cyber Security & Forensic, Mobile Computing, Intrusion detection and Computer networks.

Nhu Gia Nguyen received the PhD degree in Computer Science from Ha Noi University of Science-VietNam National University, Vietnam. Now, he is Vice Dean of Graduate School- Duy Tan University, Viet Nam. He has a total academic teaching experience of 18 years with more than 50 publications in reputed international conferences, journals and online book chapter contributions (Indexed By: SCI, SCIE, SSCI, Scopus, ACM, DBLP). His area of research includes: Network Communication, Security and Vulnerability, Network Performance Analysis and Simulation, Cloud Computing, Image Processing in Biomedical. Recently, he has been the technique program committee, the technique reviews, the track chair for international conferences: FICTA 2014, ICICT 2015, INDIA 2015, IC3T 2015, INDIA 2016, FICTA 2016, IC3T 2016, IUKM 2016, INDIA 2017, under Springer-ASIC/LNAI Series. Presently he is Associate Editors of the International Journal of Synthetic Emotions (IJSE).

Loredana-Mihaela Stanciu received her PhD in Biomedical Engineering from Politehnica University Timisoara, Romania, in 2008. In 2001, she was hired as Teaching Assistant at the Automation and Applied Informatics Department, Automation and Computer Science Faculty of Politehnica University Timisoara and is currently Associate Professor. She has been interested in areas such as human hand prosthesis, artificial intelligence, neural networks, embedded system and affective computing. He studied psychology, graduating in 2015 Systemic Family Therapy at The Areopagus Center for Christian Studies and Contemporary Culture, Timisoara. She wrote two books, 30 scientific articles, was director or member of seven scientific projects and teaches courses as Object Oriented Programming, Concurrent Programming, Visual Programming and Computer Architecture. (Rimjhim . - Contributing Author) Rimjhim is a research scholar, writer and philosopher. She has authored few papers and written many quotations and blogs. She is currently pursuing her Computer Science and Engineering doctoral from IIT Patna, India. She has completed her masters from NIT Patna, India.Her research interests are Wireless Sensor Network, Data Mining, Machine Learning, Deep Learning, Network Science, etc. She writes blogs, quotations in leisure time and is very much interested in literary works. Additionally, she held various positions as Student Captain, Prefects, Secretary and volunteered many programs and celebrations since her school days.

* * *

Anuja Arora completed PhD in Computer Science and Engineering from Banasthali University, India in 2013.She has 14 years of academia experience and 1.5 years of industry experience. She is Associate Professor at Jaypee Institute of Information Technology, India. Her primary research interest includes web mining techniques, Social network analysis and mining, web testing, Semantic Web, and data mining. She has published several research papers in many reputed international journals and conferences related to above-mentioned research area. She has been actively researching the domain of the Social media and social network analysis and mining, with focus on its contributions to the various research domains and has several years of research experience. She has successfully organized special sessions and workshops.

Ritu Banga is currently teaching in Panipat Institute of Engineering and Technology, Panipat as an Assistant Professor. Her research areas are Privacy and Security in Online Social Media, Cryptography, Digital Forensics, Database System Security and Big Data Analytics. She has attended various workshops, conferences, and seminars. She is a technically sound person and has learning abilities for new technologies. She also possesses comprehensive knowledge of subjects like Database Management, Computer Networking, and Operating System.

Haroldo Barroso is a Professor at University of Sul and Sudeste of Pará, Master in Computer Science.

Manav Dhar is a B-Tech graduate in computer science and his major interest are mainly in competitive programming/coding, science, analytics, statistics and playing chess as hobby. About his early life and childhood Manav Dhar was born on October 16, 1995 and brought up in a middle-class joint family in Noida,UttarPradesh,India and did his schooling higher secondary from Cambridge school Noida.Based upon his earlier performance in higher secondary and JEE- main results he was selected in JIIT for B-tech course, computer science engineering, started from 2013 and completed in 2017.During his B-Tech, he also pursued a course on JAVA & Big data (Hadoop). Manav Dhar also participated in many programming activities during his course conducted by JIIT like cyber Shishti and Knuth cup from time to time.

Reetika Gairola is presently working as a software engineer in a reputed organization. She has done Masters in Computer Science from Jaypee Institute of Information Technology (JIIT), Noida, India in The year 2016. She has done her bachelors from Graphic Era University, Dehradun, India in The Year 2014. Her interest area includes Natural Language Processing, Semantic Web, Data Structures, Data Mining, Machine Learning, Soft Computing, and Big Data Analytics.

Bhawna Gupta completed M.Tech in Computer Science & Engineering from Jaypee Institute of Information Technology, Noida. She has received her B.Tech degree in Computer Science & Engineering from Meerut Institute of Technology. Her research interest includes Social Network Analysis, Databases, Data Mining and Web Technologies. She has published research papers in referred journals in these areas. She has hands-on experience on Angular JS and React technologies and developed various web-apps.

Anandakumar Haldorai, Assistant Professor (SG), Department of Computer Science and Engineering, Akshaya College of Engineering and Technology, Coimbatore, Tamilnadu, India has completed his Master's in Software Engineering from PSG College of Technology, Coimbatore. Currently he is pursuing his PhD in Information and Communication Engineering from PSG College of Technology under, Anna University, Chennai. He has published more than 35 papers in international journals. His research areas include Cognitive Radio Networks, Mobile Communications and Networking Protocols.

Arti Jain is presently working with Jaypee Institute of Information Technology (JIIT), Noida, India as Assistant Professor (Grade-II). She has done masters from Birla Institute of Technology and Science, Pilani and recently pursuing her Ph.D. (CSE) from JIIT in the area of Natural Language Processing. Her area of interest includes Semantic Web, Data Mining, Machine Learning, Soft Computing, and Big Data Analytics. She has published several research papers in reputed journals and conferences.

Shikha Jain is presently working with Jaypee Institute of Information Technology (JIIT), Noida, India as Assistant Professor (Senior Grade). She has received her Ph.D. in computer science from Jaypee Institute of Information Technology, Noida, India, in the area of Affective Computing. Her area of interest includes Machine Learning, Soft Computing, Emotion Modeling, Affective Gaming and Programming Language for Emotion Models. She has published several research papers in reputed journals and conferences.

Somya Jain is currently working as an Assistant Professor at the Department of Computer Science, Jaypee Institute of information technology, Noida, India. She obtained her Bachelor's degree from Kurukshetra University and Master's degree from NSIT, University of Delhi in Computer Science. She is pursuing PhD in the area of social networks. Her area of interest include data mining, machine learning, social networks and computer networks.

Prasanna Kompalli received the Bachelor's Degree in Mechanical Engineering from Osmania University in 2000, Master's Degree in Computer Science and Engineering from Osmania University in 2002 and the PhD degree in Computer Science from Jawaharlal Nehru Technological University, Hyderabad in 2016. She is currently working as Professor & Dean in Department of Information Technology in Gokaraju Rangaraju Institute of Engineering and Technology. Her research interests include data stream mining, machine learning, intrusion detection using data mining and web mining.

Gopal Krishna is working as an Assistant Professor of Computer Science and Engineering in Netaji Subhas Institute of Technology, under Aryabhatt Knowledge University, Patna, Bihar, India. He has done his M.Tech in Information Technology from National Institute of Technology Patna, Patna, Bihar, India and B.Tech in Computer Science and Engineering from Rajasthan Technical University, Rajasthan, India. His area of research are Social Networking, Data Analytics, Machine Learning and Wireless Sensor Networks. He has almost 5 years of experience in academics, industry and research.

Pawan Kumar has completed Master of Technology in Computer Science from Jaypee Institute of Information Technology, Noida, India in 2015. He is presently working as Project Engineer at Central Research Laboratory, Bharat Electronics Limited, Government of India, Ministry of Defence, Ghaziabad, India. He is an aspiring re searcher with a distinctive affinity towards social networking, diffusion modeling, social media analytics, etc. He is vibrant towards opportunities of learning and contributing for social cause.

Vijay Kumar is an educator, philanthropist, manager, and writer. He has been teaching poor children since his college days. As per him, education can help improve the standard of living of a person and so can reduce the incidences of crime, diseases, etc. He has been working in SAIL since 2014 in various roles. He did his graduation in Metallurgical and Materials Engineering from National Institute of Technology, Nagpur and was awarded Bachelor of Technology on 15th September 2013. He lives in Bokaro, Jharkhand, India.

Akanksha Mehndiratta is an Assistant professor of Department of Computer Science at Jaypee Institute of Information Technology, Noida. She has completed Mtech in 2013. she has more than 4 years of experience in teaching. Her area of interests is machine learning, computer networking, database management, and artificial intelligence. She has a rich knowledge of new technologies. She has published research papers in international conferences and also participated in many conferences and workshops.

Suriya Murugan, Assistant Professor, Department of Computer Science and Engineering, Velammal College of Engineering and Technology, Madurai, Tamilnadu, India has completed her Master's in Computer Science and Engineering from Anna University, Coimbatore. She has published more than 15 papers in international journals. His research areas include Cognitive Radio Networks, Mobile Communications and Networking Protocols.

Arpita Narayan is working as an Assistant Professor of Computer Science and Engineering in Netaji Subhas Institute of Technology, under Aryabhatt Knowledge University, Patna, Bihar, India. She has done her M.Tech in CSE from Birla Institute of Technology, Mesra, India. Her research area are social networking, data analytics and information security. She has 3 years of experience in academics and research.

Sheng-Lung Peng is a full Professor of the Department of Computer Science and Information Engineering at National Dong Hwa University, Taiwan. He received the BS degree in Mathematics from National Tsing Hua University, and the MS and PhD degrees in Computer Science and Information Engineering from the National Chung Cheng University and National Tsing Hua University, Taiwan, respectively. His research interests are in designing and analyzing algorithms for Combinatorics, Bioinformatics, and Networks. Dr. Peng has edited several special issues at journals, such as Soft Computing, Journal of Internet Technology, Journal of Computers and MDPI Algorithms. He is also a reviewer for more than 10 journals such as IEEE Transactions on Emerging Topics in Computing, Theoretical Computer Science, Journal of Computer and System Sciences, Journal of Combinatorial Optimization, Journal of Modelling in Management, Soft Computing, Information Processing Letters, Discrete Mathematics, Discrete Applied Mathematics, Discussiones Mathematicae Graph Theory, and so on. He has about 100 international conferences and journal papers. Dr. Peng is now the director of the Library and Information Center of NDHU and an honorary Professor of Beijing Information Science and Technology University of China. He is a secretary general of Institute of Information and Computing Machinery (IICM) in Taiwan. He is also a director of the ACM-ICPC Contest Council for Taiwan. Recently, he is elected as a supervisor of Chinese Information Literacy Association and of Association of Algorithms and Computation Theory (AACT). He has been serving as a secretary general of Taiwan Association of Cloud Computing (TACC) from 2011 to 2015 and of AACT from 2013 to 2016. He was also a convener of the East Region of Service Science Society of Taiwan from 2014 to 2016.

Arulmurugan Ramu received his PhD. degrees in Information and Communication Engineering from Anna University, Chennai, Tamil Nadu, India. He is currently working as Assistant Professor in the Department of Information Technology, Bannari Amman Institute of Technology, Sathyamangalam, Tamil Nadu. His research interests include Digital Image Processing, Biomedical Image Processing Computer vision, pattern recognition, and machine learning.

Bisma Shah is working as a Lecturer at University of Kashmir, Jammu & Kashmir. She has been brought up and is currently living in Srinagar, Jammu & Kashmir. She received her M.Tech in Computer Science Engineering from Jamia Hamdard, New Delhi and holds B.E in Computer Science Engineering from University of Kashmir, Jammu & Kashmir. Her research areas include Sentiment Analysis, Machine Learning, Image Processing, Artificial Intelligence, Data Mining and Cloud Computing. Besides, she has a good hold on Networking, LAMP(Linux, Apache, MySql, Php), MATLAB, etc. She loves reading novels, cooking, and singing.

Prakhar Shukla was born in Lucknow, India, in 1993. He completed his schooling from Lucknow Public School, Lucknow. Then moved to Noida for further studies. Prakhar graduated from Jaypee Institute of Information Technology (JIIT) in 2017 with a Bachelor of Technology (B. TECH) in Computer science. He has always been keenly interested in the field of Analytics and looks forward to pursue a career in this field. While Prakhar was pursuing his Bachelor's degree, in 2016 he completed a summer project in the field of analytics and data modeling from Indian Institute of Management, Lucknow (IIML). Prakhar's hobbies include photography, exploring new places and cooking.

Farheen Siddiqui is working as Assistant Professor at Jamia Hamdard New Delhi.She has over 15 years of teaching experience.Her research area includes software engineering, semantic web, sentiment analysis and cloud computing.

Adwitiya Sinha has completed her doctoral studies from Jawaharlal Nehru University (JNU), New Delhi in 2015. She has obtained M.Tech. in Computer Science and Technology in 2010 from JNU. She has also completed M.C.A. and B.C.A. in 208 and 2006. She is a recepient of Senior Research Fellowship from CSIR, New Delhi & UGC Research Scholarship. Presently, she is working as an Assistant Professor in JIIT, Noida-62. Her application-based research is mainly focussed on performance analysis of energy-efficient wireless communication, sensor networking, data aggregation/prediction techniques and collaboration of sensor-based applications with social networking (social sensing).

Anu Taneja is a Ph.D scholar (CSE) in Jaypee Institute of Information Technology, Noida. She has received her M.Tech degree in Computer Science & Engineering from MDU, Rohtak, in 2012. Now working as an Assistant Professor in Banarsidas Chandiwala Institute of Information Technology affiliated to Guru Gobind Singh Indraprastha University, Delhi since Aug, 2013 to till date. She has qualified UGC-NET (Computer Science), December 2014. Her research interest includes optimization and approximation based algorithms, data mining, and knowledge discovery in databases. She has published papers in referred journals in these areas.

Index

M

N

O

P

R

S

T

U

W

www.ingramcontent.com/pod-product-compliance
Lightning Source LLC
LaVergne TN
LVHW060421300926
849162LV00006B/1493